Charismatic Captivation

Authoritarian Abuse

and

Psychological Enslavement

in

Neo-Pentecostal Churches

How To Recognize & Be Set Free From It!

Dr. Steven Lambert

Charismatic Captivation
ISBN 1-887915-00-1
Library of Congress Catalog Card Number: 95-95271
© Copyright 1995 by
Steve Lambert Ministries, Inc.
P.O. Box 744
Jupiter, FL 33468-0744

Published by
Steve Lambert Ministries, Inc.
P.O. Box 744
Jupiter, FL 33468-0744

Printed in the USA by

Morris Publishing
3212 E. Hwy 30 • Kearney, NE 68847
800-650-7888

CONTENTS

"For there are many rebellious men, empty talkers and deceivers who must be silenced because they are upsetting whole families, teaching things they should not teach, for the sake of sordid gain....for this cause reprove them severely that they may be sound in the faith not paying attention to...myths and commandments of men who turn away from the truth. To the pure all things are pure; but to those who are perverted and unbelieving, nothing is pure, but both their mind and their conscience are perverted. They profess to know God, but by their deeds they deny him, being detestable and disobedient, and worthless for any good deed. But as for you, speak the things which are fitting for sound doctrine."

—THE APOSTLE PAUL (Titus 1:10-2:1)

Chapter One

INTRODUCTION

It was in the year of 1976, nineteen years before the publication of this book, that an extremely unusual and inordinately poignant prophecy came forth in a church service in South Florida. It was a dire warning concerning an impending disaster—a tidal wave driven by a ferocious wind that would strike the state of Florida with raging fury, wreaking unimaginable devastation and destruction to the State. It would form in the Atlantic Ocean, the prophecy predicted, and strike land with full fury on the southeast coast of Florida and traverse the entire breadth of the State, subsequently turning northward, ripping unto the State's northern extremities, and continuing still further northward to impact another nearby southern state, where it would ultimately rest and dissipate.

Extensive decimation and ruin would lie in its wake. Somehow, ultimately, the impact of this killer wind and wave, the prophecy predicted, would be felt across the nation and even the world. Multitudes of lives would be destroyed, it warned, thousands would be left shipwrecked, many of whom would never fully recover but would be lost forever.

The unusual prophetic admonition was sensational, and thus was widely disseminated, generating great debate and controversy. Understandably, the extraordinary and extremely dramatic prophecy produced shock waves wherever it was heard, which was primarily in "charismatic" churches and circles. Soon, frightened groups were hurriedly making plans to leave the State. Others attributing credibility to the prophecy, made preparations to stay in their homes

1

and ride it out. Still others who heard the prophecy rejected it out-of-hand as foolish nonsense.

The very tenor of the prophecy, and the unction with which it came, coupled with the fact that the validity and accuracy of the prophetic gifting of the person who spoke the message had been proven and attested to over and over again, made it next to impossible to immediately dismiss the message as the word of some mystical or occultic crackpot, or even as that of a sincere, but overzealous and misdirected believer.

Reports of the event and transcripts of the prophecy quickly circulated over the length and breadth of the state of Florida, particularly in churches embracing the "charismata" gifts of the Spirit. Within hours, telephone calls were pouring in to scores of church offices across the State from concerned members wanting to know their pastor's reaction and advice with regard to the prophecy.

The gist of that prophecy is indelibly imprinted on the pages my mind. Though no one at the time could have comprehended its full import and significance as time would later reveal, the moment I heard the prophecy I knew unequivocally that its Words had the familiar reverberation of Words that had emanated from the very Throne of God. So powerful was its content that to this day I have never forgotten it.

There were reports coming in from various parts of the State that some who had heard about the prophecy were hurriedly preparing to leave Florida until the storm passed over. Others were storing up provisions and making preparations to ride it out. Reactions by churchgoers who heard of the message, ranged from shear terror and utter panic to complete dismissal and mockery.

For several weeks, debate and controversy continued to swirl, especially within Charismatic and some Pentecostal circles. Could this possibly be a true prophetic warning from God? Or, was it just

2

an outburst of vain babbling, the product of someone's vain imaginations? Could it simply be summarily dismissed out of hand with little consideration? After all, thousands or perhaps millions of lives could be at stake here.

The answer to all those questions would soon be manifest! The saga of what transpired with regard to that prophesied tidal wave is the focus of this book.

Prophecy Validated, Prophetess Vindicated

In the end, Roxanne Brandt's prophetic prediction, to which I have been alluding, proved to be accurate, and she was in this regard vindicated. There indeed did come a violent tidal wave of gigantic proportion that impacted the State of Florida, wreaking immense destruction statewide. Its broad and far-reaching swath of devastation did indeed commence in South Florida, Ft. Lauderdale, to be specific. Indeed, the true assessment of the destruction to individuals, families, groups, and the purposes of God is yet to be fully calculated. But, it is a certainty, I believe, that the effects and the impact of this wind of false doctrine were far greater and far more pervasive than anyone has ever comprehended.

Though she was maligned and ridiculed right up until her death concerning this prognostication by the Spirit, Roxanne Brandt was right. Only that which she foresaw and predicted was not a *natural* tidal wave, but a *spiritual* one. The language of her prophecy was not natural, but spiritual. The words used by the Holy Spirit in the prophecy, of which Roxanne was only a human intermediary, are spiritually appraised, and therefore cannot be properly understood by the carnal mind. It was the same terminology used by the Holy Spirit to speak to us through this God-inspired, canonized text penned by the Apostle Paul:

As a result, we are no longer to be children, tossed here and there by WAVES, and carried about by every WIND OF

DOCTRINE, by the trickery of men, by craftiness in deceitful scheming; but speaking **THE TRUTH**.... *(Eph. 4:14,15)*

What hit the state of Florida wreaking untold damage to the peninsula, and in turn reached far beyond the borders of the southeastern-most corner of this country, was a **SPIRITUAL TIDAL WAVE!** A tidal wave of heresy propelled by a wind of false doctrine, from which the Body of Christ has not yet, in earnest, even begun to recover.

Hurricane Andrew: Coincidence?

No tidal wave or wind of the magnitude and caliber predicted by the prophecy was ever forthcoming in the natural realm, until sixteen years later in August of 1992, when Hurricane Andrew indeed did strike the southeastern coast of Florida in the region of Metro-Miami. The most ferocious Hurricane ever actually measured, Andrew packed sustained winds of over 185 m.p.h. and maximum winds in excess of 200 m.p.h. During its record-speed traversal across the Atlantic from its origination just off the shores of Africa, it maintained an eery and unprecedented straight and undeviating path which did not vary more than two degrees over its entire two-thousand miles trek. Only minutes after it slammed mercilessly into the southeastern coast of Florida at dawn, the largely residential communities of Kendall and Florida City lied in utter ruin and virtual annihilation.

Andrew wreaked the greatest catastrophic financial loss in American history. Large segments of Metro-Miami's financial infrastructure was decimated. Homestead Air Force Base no longer existed. Instantaneous, monstrous, and long-lasting governmental deficits were created. Scores of insurance companies and conglomerates were immediately rendered insolvent and soon were defunct. Financial markets around the world were immediately impacted and still reel in the after-shocks of Andrew.

4

Introduction

Was this the killer wind and tidal wave that was predicted sixteen years earlier? Perhaps. Certainly, the similarities of Andrew and the predicted wind/wave are striking and even startling.

But, beyond the matter of the similarity of the occurrence in the natural and the prophecy is the weightier matter of its spiritual significance. Many prophets and prophetic Bible expositors today postulate that often the events that take place in the natural are an indicator of spiritual occurrences and phenomenon (See, 1 Cor. 15:46, e.g.). Personally, I concur with that postulation. In this volume I will offer what I believe is convincing corroboration that the tidal wave and destructive wind predicted by the prophecy, though it may have had a *natural* fulfillment as well, was primarily a *spiritual* demonically-inspired tidal wave and wind of doctrine, and that wave and wind was the Discipleship/Shepherdship doctrine and movement. Apparently coincidentally, it was three months before Hurricane Andrew struck the state of Florida that I began writing this book.

In the mid-1970's an alliance of five ministers was formed, out of which would be spawned a spiritual wind and wave of destruction and devastation in the spiritual realm of no less ferocity and magnitude as that of Hurricane Andrew in the natural. It originated in Africa, gained strength in the Atlantic Island of Puerto Rico, and eventually entered the U.S. at the southeastern coastal town of Ft. Lauderdale, Florida. It speedily cut its swath of destruction across the breadth and length of the state of Florida, even impacting several other southern states. Ultimately, this spiritual tidal wave and wind of doctrine shook spiritual foundations and institutions around the world. Some two score years later, Christendom (though unnoticed by many) is still reeling and attempting to regain its balance.

In these pages, I chronicle the history of the Discipleship/Shepherdship movement, past and present, and the pervasive impact the Discipleship/Shepherdship/Covenant doctrines had and continue to have within much of Christendom. Generally, the conventional consensus regarding this matter is that it is moot and now has little or no bearing in the Church-At-Large, in that the movement is defunct, purportedly only a smattering of small groups spawned by it remain, and that the associated doctrines have been repudiated. *CHARISMATIC CAPTIVATION* challenges and disproves that assertion, presenting convincing evidence that much to the contrary, the erroneous and errant Discipleship/Shepherdship/Covenant doctrines and the unScriptural authority structures and abusive practices they engender very much remain a viable and integral, albeit latent, part of the very fabric, foundation, and functions of the mainstream of the Pentecostal/Neo-Pentecostal Church.

Over the years, multiplied thousands at the minimum have been caught in the death-grip of this *"snare of the trapper."* Still today multitudes remain bound in the tormenting throes of this vile (albeit, incredibly, to many, innocuous) form of religious captivation, having been indoctrinated to accept the abusive and oppressive domination of their shepherd-taskmasters as being proper, normative, and even beneficial. Families, fraternal relationships, and whole churches, and even worse, the faith and trust of many, have been destroyed through this dastardly and diabolical machination of the devil.

By no means is this mere conjecture on my part, but rather, as a thirty-five year resident of the state of Florida as well as pastor and itinerant minister in the Pentecostal/Charismatic church-realm for nearly twenty years, I have witnessed firsthand the incalculable and pervasive spiritual devastation wrought by this wave and wind of strong delusion, having personally known hundreds and known *of* thousands who have been captivated by this subtle scheme. Yet, my profound personal passion regarding this matter is augmented by an even deeper source, which is that I have lived for nearly twenty years with the agonizing pain of having beloved family members caught in the web of this dastardly, demonic, but cloaked deception. This ever-present and thus far uncured sting I bear related to this matter has made it far more than a mere abstract theological issue to me, but one to which I feel strongly compelled to bring attention, and to make some contribution toward its correction.

Moreover, beyond the personal anguish, the motivation for the writing of this poignant book and to join the battle to right this spiritual wrong, emanates also from a Divine call and mandate to me, which has been validated by a recurring prophetic word of the Lord that I would bear to "Pharaohs" the Divine Demand to "Let My people go!" *CHARISMATIC CAPTIVATION* constitutes partial fulfillment of that Divine charge by perhaps the most effective of all mediums—the published, written word.

I will be forthright and upfront concerning the content of this work. *CHARISMATIC CAPTIVATION* unabashedly and straight-forwardly challenges certain aspects of the conventional, the traditional, the institutional, and the status quo in much of the Church-realm, not for the mere sake of challenging or criticizing the ecclesiastical establishment, but because absolutely essential Divinely-inspired reproof is long overdue, and the lives and even eternal destiny of multitudes of affected, though unaware, believers are at stake. *CHARISMATIC CAPTIVATION* is a medium of advocacy on behalf of untold multitudes of innocent sheep of God's flock being unsuspectingly subjected to exploitative enslavement by self-aggrandizing and unscrupulous leaders for their personal advancement and the expansion of their own private kingdoms.

Admitted Agenda, No Apologies

This is a book written to dispel error. For that I make no apologies, nor have any regrets. Dispelling error, as explained in various places in this book, is an absolutely essential and intrinsic part of God-appointed and anointed ministry. One of the primary motivations behind the writing of the vast majority of New Testament Epistles was the correcting and dispelling of error. The major theme of the Bible is the expression of Truth, which by its very nature debunks myth, and defines, exposes, and corrects error.

The Bible frequently likens the Truth of God's Word and Kingdom to "light." The purpose of the light, whether in the natural or the spiritual sense, is to dispel darkness. In the Creation, the light of God's Word as He spoke it dispelled the darkness that was hovering over the surface of the Earth (Gen. 1:2). It is extremely significant that the first matter God dealt with in the Creation was the darkness. The first Words God spoke in the genesis transaction were, *"Let there be Light!"* which, of course, meant: Let there be Light **on the Earth** because God, we are told, **IS** Light (1 Jn. 1:5), and thus Light has always existed.

Next, God then proceeded forthwith to declare the Light/Truth/ Word to be "good" and to separate the Light from the darkness, bringing into existence on the Earth two diametrically opposed phenomena, one called "day" and the other "night," both of which were governed by the presence or absence of Light. Light is to rule over darkness, and certainly not the other way around. Exposing, dispelling, and ruling over darkness is the intrinsic role of Light.

In the same way, spiritually speaking, exposing darkness is a solemn Divine charge to all believers (Eph. 5:11), who by virtue of having been enlightened by the True Light are now themselves the *"light of the world"* (Mat. 5:14). To us who are the "light of the world," Jesus commanded: *"Let your light shine before men in such a way that they may* **SEE** *your good works and glorify your Father who is in heaven."* As the Light of Jesus shines through us, others are enabled to see and the darkness of evil is exposed and dispelled.

God **IS** Light, we are told (1 Jn. 1:5). We are also told that the Word of God is God (Jn. 1:1), and it is the Word of God, that is to

8

say, the Light, which enlightens every man who receives the Light (Jn. 1:9). Believers are commanded to walk in the Light as God walks in the Light, which means to walk in God's Truth, which is one and the same as God's Word. God's Word is Truth and Light, and all three of these are a part of who God is. In other words, God, God's Word, the True Light, and Truth are all synonymous terms. To walk and abide in each and all of these is to walk and abide in God. To walk and abide in each and all of these is to dispel darkness.

The Heeding of the Call

As I said, I make no apology for engaging in dispelling darkness, that is to say in correcting error, bringing forth reproof, and debunking heresies, for the purpose of establishing and defining the Truth. The one regret I do have, however, is for failing to write this book many years sooner as I was instructed to do by the Lord. I confess I disobeyed a Divine charge for at least thirteen years.

In so stating, I do not at all mean to assert that the contents of this volume, if published sooner, would by any means have been sufficient in itself to have averted the disastrous effect of the Discipleship/Shepherdship heresy. (In fact, what may appear to be an ironic and even enigmatic assertion, especially in this volume, is that it may well be that it was not God's will for the spiritual catastrophe of the Discipleship/Shepherdship Movement to have been averted, for He may permit such demonic doctrinal debacles to be inflicted upon the Body of Christ to compel us to mature to the place wherein we are performing the Divine command that we test all teaching against Scripture.) Rather, I am merely acknowledging that the Lord intended for this book to have come forth long before it has. Perhaps, had it been published earlier, it could have done some good. Perhaps not. But, since, even by the most earnest prayer, I cannot change in any measure that which is past, and since it is at this time that I *have* written this book, all I can now do is entrust its effectuality to the God who redeems the time.

Ironic Benefits of Delay

However, after a number of years of candid reflection, I must say, that if there is any redeeming aspect of my delay in heeding the call, it is that it has served to further highlight to myself my own human frailty and vulnerability to delusion, if in no other form than mere "stinkin' thinkin'." In addition, this further corroborated awareness concerning my own proclivities, I believe, has served as a very useful and perhaps even necessary backdrop against which for me to appropriately address this issue with a greater degree of meekness and compassion. This realization, along with innumerable other dealings of the Lord within my life in the interim since the initial call, have together served to temper the natural temptation lurking within to become censorious, and to make me ever mindful of the necessity to approach the matter of Godly reproof with great mercy and forbearance, remembering that one who is truly *spiritual* as opposed to *religious* will restore one who has been caught in the throes of deception in *"a spirit of gentleness,"* looking to himself and realizing his own intrinsic fallibility and vulnerability to temptation, error, and delusion (Gal. 6:1).

In a way, the elapsed time during the thirteen or so years I put off heeding the call of the Lord regarding the writing of this book has had its benefits, among which are that it has allowed me to become increasingly immersed in the requirement incumbent upon everyone whose task and assignment it is to bring Godly and Biblical reproof, correction, and exhortation, which is, to bring it not only with boldness and without adulteration, but also, in the words of the inveterate Apostle Paul to the younger Timothy, *"with great patience and instruction"* (2 Tim. 4:2). I somehow know, instinctively, that the import of this statement is to convey to every minister, to whom the onus of God-ordained spiritual reproof has been assigned, the requisite to be forbearing and merciful in reproving those who are wandering about as a blind person in the blackness of spiritual error.

Introduction

Healing, Not Hurt

In this regard, I can say with absolute confidence, that in no way is it my intent to be caustic, castigating, or judgmental. Rather, my attitude and approach to the issue at hand is much like that of the physician to whom has fallen the unsavory and unenviable task of informing a long-time patient who is also a beloved friend that a malignant, cancerous tumor has invaded his body, which must, if death is to be averted, be removed straightway by means of surgery. No physician relishes the task of telling the patient the dire and disheartening news, but it must be done. The seasoned physician approaches the matter with a deep sense of compassion and concern, yet with necessary frankness and forthrightness, for it is his deep affection for the patient that requires him to be absolutely candid in his diagnosis, prognosis, and prescribed treatment in order to save his beloved friend's life.

Metaphorically, that is precisely the scenario in this undertaking. The error being addressed in this book, spiritually speaking, is a profoundly cancerous and deadly issue, which requires radical surgery for the spiritual health and welfare of the afflicted. *Someone* must assume the responsibility of the compassionate and caring physician, frankly and forthrightly informing the unwitting patient the devastating news that he is afflicted with something that is potentially fatal, and that the only hope for survival is that he submit himself to the surgeon's scalpel forthwith. For you see, intrusive surgery is the **ONLY** way to remove the cancerous tumor. There are no other options.

Now just as in the case of surgery in the natural in which the scalpel must be ultra-sharp, the sharper the better, so also it is with spiritual surgery, in which case the scalpel is none other than the Word of God, which by its very nature, *"is sharper than a double-edged sword."* The Sword of the Lord is razor-edge sharp by design and necessity, so as to be able to divide asunder with microscopic precision and lightening-speed that which is of the Spirit of God from that which is not.

Such precise and definitive excision is the purpose of the Scalpel of the Spirit. Yes, it is intrusive, and painful, and it seems somewhat violent. Yes, it wounds, but it is a surgical wound of absolute necessity, a wound unto preservation of life and the arrest of imminent and inevitable death. The Sword of the Spirit inflicts a wound that in the end brings joy, healing, restoration, recovery, and Life, not sorrow, or mourning, or spiritual death. No one has ever died from its surgical incision and excision.

There is no just cause for being angry with the surgeon, for neither he nor his scalpel is the adversary or source of adversity. No, the adversary and source of adversity is **the cancer**! Faithful and wholly beneficial are the wounds inflicted by the surgeon. He wounds to preserve and improve life, and to avert death.

As a spiritual physician, long ago I dedicated my life to caring for my patient—the Body of Christ. I love the Body of Christ and my consuming labor is to see her in perfect Divine spiritual health and fully conformed into the Image of Christ. Like various parts of the Body of Christ upon whom the Apostles Paul and John in their day were required to perform spiritual surgery to remove cancerous heretical teaching, so also in some parts of the Body of Christ today "deception-ectomies" are needed, to remove various spiritual cancers which have invaded them. The Scalpel of the Spirit is the **only** way! There is no other way.

However, the trained surgeon, fully cognizant of the gravity of the situation, and that life or death rests in his hands, performs the delicate operation with the *confidence* that comes only by way of seasoning and developed *craft*, but yet with measured *caution*, doing what must be done, wounding to bring healing, not with rancor, but a profound sense of duty, affection, and compassion.

Introduction

The surgeon is friend, not foe. The **cancer** is the foe. And, as the proverb so aptly says, *"Faithful are the wounds of a friend."*

I come as friend and fellow, not foe, Body of Christ, to appeal, to reason, to plead, not to rebuke. Though I do indeed come with the two-edged Scalpel of the Spirit in my hand, the incisions I make are the faithful wounds of a friend to bring healing, health, and Life.

Notwithstanding, though it is with mercy and compassion that I have written this book, at the same time, I admit without regret, that I write also with passion, directness, and a two-fold purpose. First, I write as an admonition to unsuspecting newly Born-Again believers who are totally unaware of the snares of captivity which lie in wait for them in connection with the heretical doctrines and practices addressed herein. Second, I have written in response to a Divine call to trumpet forth a Divine warning that God will no longer tolerate the devious devices of those who twist and pervert Scripture in order to justify the "lording over" of their fellow brethren which they practice purportedly "in the name of the Lord" and under the guise of some demented form of "authority" for their own purely self-aggrandizing purposes of building their own private kingdoms in which they subjugate unto themselves the Sheep of God's Flock!

> *Then the Word of the Lord came to me saying, "Son of man, prophesy **against** the shepherds of Israel. Prophesy and say to those shepherds, 'Thus says the Lord God, "Woe, shepherds of Israel who have been feeding themselves! Should not the shepherds feed the flock? You eat the fat and clothe yourselves with the wool, you slaughter the fat sheep without feeding the flock. Those who are sickly you have not strengthened, the diseased you have not healed, the broken you have not bound up, the scattered you have not brought back, nor have you sought for the lost; BUT WITH FORCE AND SEVERITY YOU HAVE DOMINATED THEM!"'" (Ezk. 34:1-4)*

13

What you hold in your hands, dear reader, truly is a labor of love, bathed in much prayer. I pray with all my heart it will have a sufficiency to set some captives free from the powerful grip of demonic deception and captivation, and to turn others back from the seductive and deceptive allure of illegitimate and unsanctioned religious predomination. My earnest and heartfelt prayer is that everyone who in any way has ever been a participant in the extremely injurious Discipleship/Shepherdship dogmas and practices will read and give heed to the information and overtures proffered in these pages, and that one day we shall meet on the shores of Paradise!

Chapter Two

BACKGROUND

The matter of the Discipleship/Shepherdship controversy and "movement" is virtually unknown to many believers who have come to the Lord since the controversy erupted in the mid-1970s. Additionally, apparently there are many who came to the Lord prior to the development of the Discipleship movement who, nonetheless, have no awareness or only a vague awareness of its existence. Personally, I do not know how such a highly publicized and public controversy could have possibly escaped any believer's notice, nevertheless, that is the claim of many.

Despite that unawareness, however, those who are unaware are not by virtue of that unawareness unaffected by the matter. Quite to the contrary, many of those same people who claim to be totally uninformed concerning the controversy attend churches where the basic tenets of Discipleship are being espoused and practiced, albeit, in most cases, now covertly. It is these uninformed and unsuspecting victims of deception I most hope to reach with the message of this book.

There are a large number of professing believers who are not of this category of the uninformed, who are quite aware of this controversial matter, who have nevertheless, evidently of their own free will, opted to align themselves with these heretical beliefs and practices by attending churches and groups who espouse them. They have apparently made this choice despite the fact that the Discipleship/Shepherdship philosophies, doctrines, and practices

15

have been unequivocally repudiated and proven to be utterly false, and their originators since fallen into disrepute.

My hope is that those who continue to associate themselves with these doctrines and practices will read and seriously weigh the evidence presented in these pages, and that they will, as a result, renounce and repent from these destructive heretical teachings and practices. That is my hope and prayer, as well as my reason for writing this book.

Sadly and unfortunately, however, it has been my experience that many of those who have been heavily indoctrinated by *"doctrines of demons"* such as this, which are inspired by *"deceitful (seducing, KJV) spirits"* and promulgated *"by means of the hypocrisy of liars,"* tend to become *"seared over in their conscience as with a branding iron"* (1 Tim. 4:1,2) by the error. In other words, the false doctrine becomes virtually indelibly imprinted upon the minds of those who have been fully indoctrinated by the devilish error. The deception permeates the entire belief system of those indoctrinated by it. Unless they are willing to yield to supernatural deliverance by the Spirit of God, as the brand seared into the hide of a cow by means of a red-hot branding iron is unremovable, it is virtually impossible to remove this deception from the minds of those who have been infected with it.

There are some who have defected from the Charismatic cults which espouse these doctrines and employ these practices, and been liberated from the throes of the enslavement they engender, fortunately, but there are many more who have not than there are who have. In the case of those who have, their rescue required the supernatural intervention of God—with God all things are possible—to excise the spiritual cancer growing within their soul and to bring recovery. Many of the fully indoctrinated, however, have thus far chosen not to accept the emancipation extended to them by Christ, choosing, for some dark and inexplicable reason, instead to remain forever ensnared in the snare of the trapper.

16

Background

Many of these poor souls, because of the indoctrination they have received, are literally petrified at the thought of departure from the group of which they are a part and the "covering" of its leaders, for fear that they would forfeit rightstanding with God, incur His wrath and curses upon themselves, and be eternally damned.

Notwithstanding, I write, hoping and believing that some will hear within these pages their Emancipation Proclamation emanating from an All-Powerful, All-forgiving God who in the twinkling of an eye can set the captive free, and who desperately wants to do so. It is He who has declared, "**WHOSOEVER** shall call upon the Name of the Lord, *shall be delivered*!"

In order to have a thorough understanding of this whole matter, fully comprehending the effect and impact these hyper-authoritarian doctrines and practices have had upon individual believers and the collective Body of Christ, it is absolutely essential not only to understand the essence of the Discipleship/Shepherdship doctrines and practices themselves and why they were erroneous, but also to have some historical perspective of the so-called "movement" they spawned. It is for this reason and this reason alone, in the face of this apparent lack of awareness by many people concerning the matter, that I present in this chapter a synoptic history of the Discipleship/Shepherdship "movement," its primary principals and more prominent critics, as well as the effects the movement and its teachings has had upon the Church at-large and the Charismatic/Pentecostal segment in particular. By far, however, the main body of this volume is comprised of chapters devoted to examination of these doctrines and practices themselves and their unScripturality, and to the overriding objective of showing those captivated by them how to be liberated.

The Genesis of the Charismatic Movement

Evolving essentially, though unofficially, and to a large extent unintentionally, out of the Pentecostal Movement of the earlier part of this century, the Charismatic Movement had its inception in 1960 with a series of events involving Dennis Bennett, an Episcopalian rector, who along with a significant number of other Episcopalians, received the Baptism in the Holy Spirit. The Movement continued to develop and take shape as a similar but yet distinct and somewhat diverse Movement from its precursor throughout the decade of the 1960's.

In the process of time, various groupings, clusters, and even some "spiritual" cliques, if you will, began to form, comprised of a growing number of believers sharing one thing in common—a new experience called, "the Baptism of the Holy Spirit." These gatherings were primarily a forum for sharing experiences, fellowship, mutual encouragement, and receiving more teaching regarding the Spirit-baptized life and walk. Initially, they were intentionally informal, unstructured, non-directive, and non-authoritarian.

The Charismatic Movement (and this is what made it distinctive from its predecessor, the Pentecostal Movement) at its inception, was not at all sectarian in nature. In general, the clarion call trumpeted forth by the principal proponents and expositors of the Charismatic Movement at the outset was not a call "to come *out* from among them," but an invitation and exhortation "to come *into* a deeper fulness of the Spirit." Clearly, the *Divine* intent for the Charismatic Movement was not to further reinforce denominational walls and divisiveness, nor to create new ecclesiastical organizations, but rather just the opposite—to impact multitudes trapped behind denominational walls who longed for more of God's Power and Essence to be tangibly manifest in their lives.

For the first ten years, in fact, the primary thrust of the Movement stayed within the auspices of Divine purpose. This new Wind of the Spirit billowed across denominational partitions, impacting, to some degree at least, most all of the mainline churches and denominations. Swirling first, as I mentioned, among the Episcopalians, it soon had extended to certain segments of the Lutherans,

Background

Methodists, Catholics, Presbyterians, Mennonites, and even among a large portion of the multiplicity of Baptist factions, not only in the U.S. but also in Canada, South and Central America, and abroad. In addition to impacting the mainline denominations, even individual Pentecostal churches soon began to embrace or at least acquiescently tolerate the somewhat more demonstrative Charismatic style of worship and manifestations in the Gifts of the Spirit, as well as the various teachings indigenous to the Charismatic Movement which gradually evolved.

In retrospect, it is awesome how much was accomplished in the course of only ten years, and all basically under the exclusive inspiration and direction of Jesus, the Head of the Church, and His Divine Representative, the Holy Spirit, virtually void of human assistance. Thousands of existing believers were being introduced to a whole new dimension of the "Abundant Life" Christ came to give, injecting new life and fire into many of the dead or dying churches of which they were apart. Moreover, this fresh fire of fervor was even beginning to attract, like a moth to candlelight, fairly significant numbers of new believers as the promise-filled teaching of *"a new and living way"* was proclaimed.

A host of new ministries emerged, some enjoying meteoric ascent into national and international scope and notoriety. Torrents of Charismatic literature gave rise to new publishing companies and new life to many heretofore floundering publishing houses publishing Christian material. Christian radio and television, though used moderately by a small number of preachers previously, really came of age, even spawning whole new networks and exclusively Christian, independent stations. A small number of unaffiliated, autonomous, non-denominational churches began to emerge, mostly out of necessity, in order to "go on with the Lord" after whole segments of newly Spirit-baptized believers and ministers found themselves being given "the left foot of disfellowship" from their former churches.

The Fab Five

Frankly, things were basically sailing along amazingly well for the first decade of the Charismatic Renewal until a group of four (later expanded to five) men emerged from relative obscurity to stake their claim on the burgeoning Charismatic conglomerate. Apparently, they had concluded that the supernatural administration of Jesus and the Holy Spirit over the Church during the denouement of this new Movement, void of human involvement (or, interference) as it was, simply was not enough. What this Movement needed, they theorized, was some good, old-fashioned human organization, man-centered authoritarianism, and ecclesiastical hierarchy. Moreover, apparently, they were the anointed ones who had been called upon by God to assist Jesus and the Holy Spirit in getting the Charismatic Movement "organized."

The "Fab Five" alliance consisted of Derek Prince, Bob Mumford, Charles Simpson, Don Basham, and Ern Baxter. A less known sixth associate was John Poole. Together these individuals formed the organization that would be "the center of one of the most violent controversies (i.e., the Discipleship/Shepherding controversy) in Protestant charismatic history,"[1] Christian Growth Ministries (CGM), headquartered in Ft. Lauderdale, Florida.

Initially, the ministries of four of the five (Baxter, being the fifth, who joined the others in 1974) converged prior to the formation of CGM under the umbrella of another organization, Holy Spirit Teaching Mission (HTSM), a Charismatic teaching-guild of sorts comprised primarily of denominationally affiliated Charismatic ministers and lay-leaders. The official organ through which the CGM leaders propagated their teachings was *New Wine* magazine, originally begun under the auspices of HSTM. The relationship among the Fab Five was further cemented when they were asked by the HSTM in 1970 to step up their role in the leadership of the organization when "a moral problem and financial difficulties threatened its future."[2] The Fab Five not only accommodated that

Background

request, but eventually took the matter a step further, forming their own organization, CGM, over which they installed themselves as leaders, and took over *New Wine* magazine as well.

The objective of CGM purported by the founders "was to bring Spirit-baptized Christians to maturity and to teach church-building,"[2] which on the surface seemed to be worthy and proper purposes. And, in 1972 the group curtailed their regular teaching sessions in Ft. Lauderdale to begin a campaign to expand their influence and promulgate their private doctrines and practices nationwide by means of regional conferences.

Fab Five Introduce Discipleship Doctrines

However, it soon surfaced that their particular brand of theology of "maturity" and "church-building" included unproven, unscriptural, and excessive concepts regarding authority, submission to established authority, shepherding, and discipleship, all of which, in their proper perspective and within the bounds of Biblical propriety and Divine intent, are bona fide and important precepts in true Christianity. Central also to the theology of the CGM principals was a notion that every believer, laymen and ministers alike, must have a "personal pastor." It was this assertion upon which the shepherdship relationships were predicated, and which, as alluded to earlier, resulted in a "chain-of-command" (a nomenclature which they and their proteges took great pains in avoiding) schematic, of sorts, which the Discipleship/Shepherdship teachers claimed to be the Scriptural paradigm for the concept of authority they espoused.

This vertical, descending, "chain-of-command" was a pyramid-shaped, multi-tiered organizational structure, which had at the top echelon of the pyramid (it just so happened) none other than the Fab Five themselves, who claimed (conveniently) to be in "submission" to each other. This arrangement, they purported, acted as a fail-safe "checks and balance" system to totally preclude

21

them from falling prey to the corruptive properties of absolute power to which, historically, so many others (albeit, less spiritual than they, of course) succumbed.

Descending, then, from the individual members of the "Quintumvirate" were pastors ("shepherds" they were called) of local churches from all over the country who were personally "submitted" to one of these Five as their "personal pastor." Though the "submission" was supposedly "personal," by extension, according to the tenets of the Discipleship/Shepherdship teaching, this meant that, ultimately, so also were the submitters' ministries and churches submitted to these men and, technically, to CGM. In essence, this was the salient point over which controversy eventually erupted. In addition to the local pastors at this authority level, there were also certain itinerant ministers whose ministries were recognized, approved, and even "authorized" (they termed it) by the CGM Quintumvirate, who likewise were "submitted" to one of the Five.

Then, under these local pastors in the flow chart of authority and submission came the associate pastors, church-elders, deacons, and lay-leaders (usually called Fellowship or Cell Group Leaders, or something similar) who were "submitted" to these local pastors within the organizational structure of their local ministries and churches, who were in turn "submitted" ultimately to one of the CGM leaders. (In some cases there were also intermediate "middle management" leaders at the local pastor echelon, consisting of some "recognized" older ministers to whom other younger local pastors were "submitted," in order to provide a type of oversight and a supposed mentor-protege relationship.)

Finally, there were the "sheep" themselves. All of the former comprised the superior class of "Shepherds," while those submitted to their care in their churches were the "sheep." In many cases, this metaphorical moniker attributed to the saints of God was not used in the same affectionate sense as it is used in the Bible and even by

Background

Jesus Himself to describe the very special personal and caring relationship between a shepherd and his sheep that typically exists among nomadic sheep-herders. Rather, many of the Discipleship/ Shepherdship adherents came to maintain a very condescending and demeaned view of believers as "just dumb sheep," as many came to call them, dumb sheep, whose ability to reason was next to non-existent, which prevented them from knowing what was best for them. Therefore, it was the role of the shepherd, under this widely-held concept concerning "underling" believers, to tell the dumb sheep what to do, where to go, and to basically make their decisions for them, because the sheep were just too stupid to be able to do all this for themselves.

The Multi-Level Structure

One thing that has always struck me as being odd about this whole authority structure proposed by these men as the paradigm for the whole Body of Christ that warrants pointing out is its striking resemblance to certain secular, pyramiding, multi-level sales organizations that have come to be so prominent over the last thirty years or so. It is also quite interesting, whether coincidentally or not, that several of these men as well as some of their submitters have been associated with multi-level marketing organizations. Apparently, this is something which escaped the notice of most observers for years.

Funny thing about these multi-level schemes, usually it is only those at the top of the pyramid who realize significant wealth, primarily off the "blood, sweat, and tears" (not to mention financial resources) of wide-eyed and naive "down-liners" who haven't yet figured out that it's basically only the elite few at the top of the pyramid who receive the lion's-share of the benefit and revenue. Because of this inequitable bent, these kinds of multi-level companies are under the constant scrutiny of State-Attorneys who have the duty to protect the public from fraudulent and unfair business schemes.

Perhaps the multi-level schematic of the CGM leaders would have been a little more plausible had it not been they themselves who just happened to be at the top of the pyramid. As the writer of the article which I have been quoting observed:

> They had a national network of followers who formed pyramids of sheep and shepherds. Down through the pyramid went the orders, it was alleged, while up the same pyramid went the tithes."[3]

The overall result of the expanding CGM campaign was that:

> "...large numbers of charismatic pastors began to be shepherded by the CGM leaders, a development that went uncharted but not unnoticed. It was uncharted because these relationships were personal and not institutional, so there were never any published lists of pastors and congregations being shepherded by CGM leaders...."[4]

These comments by the writer hint at one of the aspects of the CGM leaders' operations and agenda that perhaps was the most suspicious and disconcerting, which was that some aspects of same were shrouded in secrecy and concealment. Many meetings of higher echelon leaders were unpublicized and the substance of those meetings by agreement were considered "confidential" by the participants. It seemed that while their was a public aspect of their efforts in which there was a definite, defined, and overt plan to proliferate their teachings and influence at the very minimum nationally if not internationally (and there were numerous international participants as well), there was also a very esoteric aspect of their agenda and operations which was kept in concealment. There has been a sentiment by some ministers over the years that some of this secrecy resulted from a distinct effort by the CGM leaders in collusion with the significant network of pastors and ministers submitted to them to identify and "mark" ministers who opposed the Discipleship doctrines and practices and the CGM agenda, and, in effect, "black-ball" them from Charismatic ministry circles, the main purpose of which tactic was individual and collective self-preservation. Secrecy and esotericism should always be viewed with suspicion, for bona fide operations of God are never *"done in a corner"* (Ac. 26:26).

Now, no explanation has ever been given by the Five as to how it was that they knew that God had chosen and appointed them in particular of all the men of God in the world to this unique status as ecclesiastical prefects over the then burgeoning Charismatic Movement, or as to what it was that made them so uniquely qualified for such a post. Nor, was any enlightenment offered as to the reasons for the supposed Divine election of CGM as *the* "umbrella organization" for all other "authorized" Charismatic ministries, as they implied. Rather, these were things that were just to be recognized and accepted by one and all without question. Moreover, due homage and obeisance (plus your tithe, if you were a minister and wanted to be "recognized" and "approved") were also expected. Anyone who did not merely accept all this and docilely fall in line, or who dared to criticize any aspect of it, was branded a rebellious malcontent and dissident.

In light of the revelations which eventually became public knowledge regarding the whole CGM controversy, it is now fairly apparent that the authority and influence which these five men had was (and in the case of the one who continues to maintain his authority over thousands of believers and hundreds of pastors and their churches, Charles Simpson, *is*) presumed and self-assumed, and they all now appear to be usurpers to "thrones" which never really existed except in their own and their indoctrinated cult-followers' minds. Certainly the stations of authority and ecclesiastical ascendancy these men occupied for a season were never established by God, despite their empirical claims and explanations to the contrary.

All in all, it is now relatively evident that this whole elaborate scheme of the Fab Five was a grandiose, vain-glorious, and humanly-contrived ruse by which they intended, whether with sincere motives or not, to place the entire Charismatic Movement, with its multitudes of new adherents and myriads of ministries and churches under their personal and exclusive dominion and sovereignty. Whether they were naively duped into espousing such an extreme and unrealistic notion, or whether their extensive agenda was motivated by a surrealistic hubris of the highest order, will probably never be known. Nevertheless, what is clear is that this strategy, whether humanly and deliberately contrived, or demonically inspired, amounted to a kind of sophisticated ecclesiastical hegemony, the true end of which could be nothing more than a very unsophisticated and ignoble self-aggrandizement void of any true spiritual essence or virtuous benefit.

Moreover, what is abundantly clear regarding the whole matter is that there was never even the remotest chance that the One, True Sovereign God and True Functional-Head of the Church was ever going to allow these usurpers, or any others, to succeed in any such plan the effect of which is naked subversion of the sovereignty as well as the purposes of God for the true Church in the end-times. Rather, in the end, as He always does when men exceed their callings and purposes, *"exceed(ing) that which is written"* (1 Cor. 4:6), and presumptively intrude into affairs and create agenda which are beyond the bounds of Divine appointment and human propriety, God Himself, though usually not until sufficient time has elapsed to allow for the exhibition of the utter foolishness of the perpetrators, will eventually intervene and bring such vain and empty attempts to an abrupt halt.

The Pot Boils Over

As the Discipleship/Shepherdship tempest swirled, it was not long until a number of other prominent leaders within the Charismatic Movement came forward to announce their opposition to the basic tenets being proliferated by the CGM leaders and their constituency. Finally, in 1975 the Discipleship/Shepherdship boiling pot erupted in public controversy, censorship, and outright denunciation.

Pat Robertson (CBN Founder, President) banned the CGM leaders and erased all tapes that included them. Robertson used CBN to pronounce the shepherding teaching "witchcraft" and said the only difference between the discipleship group and Jonestown was "Kool-Aid." Kathryn Kuhlman refused to appear together with Bob Mumford at the 1975 Conference on the Holy Spirit in Jerusalem. Demos Shakarian and the director of FGBMFI declared the CGM leaders persona non grata. The number of voices swelled as criticism came from Dennis Bennett, Ken Sumrall, Thomas F. Zimmerman (General Superintendent of the Assemblies of God), and David du Plessis. [Parenthesis added by author]

The heat of the controversy can be captured by reading an open letter, dated June 27, 1975, from Pat Robertson to Bob Mumford. Robertson said that in a recent visit to Louisville, Kentucky, he found cultish language like "submission" rather than churches, "shepherds" not pastors, and "relationships" but not Jesus. Robertson traveled to ORU and found a twenty-year-old "shepherd" who drew tithes from fellow students as part of their submission. Robertson, drawing from Juan Carlos Ortiz's *Call to Discipleship*, charged the leaders with placing personal revelations (rhema) on par with Scripture. He quoted a devotee as saying, "If God Almighty spoke to me, and I knew for a certainty that it was God speaking, and if my shepherd told me to do the opposite, I would obey my shepherd."[5]

The litany of known Church-leaders publicly denouncing the Prince-Baxter-Mumford-Simpson-Basham consortium was by no means limited to those cited in the article quoted above, but also included a host of others, e.g.: Kenneth Hagin, Kenneth Copeland, Jerry Sevelle, T.L. Osborn, Ken Sumrall, John Osteen, Judson Cornwall, Ralph Mahoney, Charles Trombley, among others. Several books were written to address the error, and a number of ministers disseminated tape series exposing and repudiating the heresy.

Despite attempts by these and other prominent leaders to reason with the CGM leaders and their subscribers, in general, the Five continued to staunchly defend the basic premise of their teaching and to reassert their claim of its Scriptural congruity. Recognizing the adverse effects of the negative publicity and notoriety of the matter, the CGM leaders did, however, put forward what many perceived to be only an appearance of having been mildly chastened and a purported acceptance of some measure of responsibility for reported "excesses" that transpired under their general auspices. However, essentially, the Fab Five fudged on accepting full responsibility by claiming that most of the "errors" were not due to any preceptual imperfection, but rather the result of "excesses" in application committed by overzealous devotees in a few isolated, anomalistic incidences. Despite the public posturing and feeble claims of moderation, the Discipleship leaders and the majority of their devotees were essentially unrepentant and their fundamental practices and beliefs remained virtually unchanged.

The Movement Goes Underground

However, what has transpired over the course of time is that in order to avoid the adverse effects of controversy, the majority of Discipleship proponents and practitioners have gone "underground," so to speak, employing less overt and less conspicuous methods and means of propagation, cloaking and camouflaging their operations behind more subtle and euphemistic, cryptic language.

For example, the extreme concepts initially referred to as concepts of "pastoring" are now termed "shepherding" principles. To give it a more sophisticated and sanctimonious ring, the obsequious relationship between the subjugated (the sheep) and their subjugator (the shepherd) now is called "covenant relationships."

Background

These "relationships" (if you accept that appellation) in many groups espousing Discipleship/Shepherdship/Covenant doctrines and employing variations of the practices advocated under that teaching are actually codified in the form of a "Covenant Agreement" signed by the subjugated in which the subjugated pledges his eternal oath of allegiance and unquestioned obedience and obeisance, along with his financial support, of course, to his "shepherd." Usually, this "covenant" requirement is a matter which is not addressed openly in the public meetings, but is introduced "in private" to attendees who have been around long enough to have become fully indoctrinated with the group's ways and teachings, and to have become psychologically dependent on the group (more on this and other psychological mechanisms employed by Discipleship groups later).

Allow me to say in passing that to me, oaths such as these bear little dissimilarity to the secret oaths and pledges required of initiates into secret societies such as the Masons, Elks, or for that matter, Ku Klux Klan and the Mafia, which essentially bind the inductee to that group for life, or in other words, "Til death do us part." In fact, it has been my experience in dealing with hundreds of people in deliverance from demonic powers that the pledge taken by inductees into these secret societies is precisely the same, in terms of the spiritual impact it induces, as those taken by members of Discipleship/Shepherdship/Covenant cults (as we shall discuss later, this is precisely what these groups are—cults). A plethora of spirits of bondage, witchcraft, and idolatry saunter right through the door willfully opened by the person who enters into such demonic "covenants" of allegiance to men. Additionally, terribly debilitating and subversive satanic soul-ties are formed with the individuals with whom they have "covenanted."

But, in actuality, the spiritual dynamic that is being instigated in the unseen spiritual realm when a person "covenants" with another human being in this manner, agreeing to subject himself to a mere

29

human rather than unto the Lord Jesus Christ, is a pact of idolatry, because, spiritually speaking, wittingly or unwittingly, the subjectee has in essence pledged to submit his human will to his subjugator. In effect, the subjectee has just become the willing slave of his subjector, for the Spirit says, *"Do you not know that when you present yourselves to someone as slaves for obedience, you are SLAVES of the one whom you obey"* (Rom. 6:16).

The ultimate result of such a "pax idolatrus" is that that person has in actuality made the pact, not with that leader, but with demons, for in reality there is no such a thing as an idol, but the idolatrous homage rendered unto "idols," whether they be human or inanimate is *"sacrifice to demons, and not to God"* (1 Cor. 10:19-22). In other words, anyone who makes a spiritual covenant with anyone other than God, covenants with demons, whether they intend to or not, for *"You cannot drink the cup of* (fellowship with) *the Lord and the cup of* (fellowship with) *demons; you cannot partake of the table of the Lord and the table of demons"* (Ibid, v. 21, parenthesis added by author). If you do so covenant and so partake of fellowship with idols (other gods), or demons, you *"provoke the Lord to jealousy"* (Ibid, v. 22). Thus, in actuality this "covenanting" business and paying homage to human leaders is tantamount to paganistic demon worship. The Bible explicitly constrains us against making such "covenants" with anyone other than the Lord Jesus Christ Himself. It specifically commands, *"Do not become slaves of men"* (1 Cor. 7:23).

Tactical Organizational Restructure

In their effort to go "underground" in the face of growing scrutiny, adverse public sentiment, and controversy, Discipleship proponents, groups, and organizations began a concerted effort toward general obfuscation by means of organizational realignment and restructuring. Some defenders have argued that this development was merely a natural and spontaneous transition rather than a deliberate effort toward obfuscation, and that its proximity to any public disreputation was purely coincidental, however. Whichever is true, what was absolutely clear was that a discernable trend toward reorganization, whatever the reasons may have been, did indeed gradually develop. New affiliations and associations were formed. New sanctioning organizations emerged, as well as "networks" of those organizations, all supposedly offering synergistic benefits to ministers and ministries who affiliated themselves with them.

Essentially, all these reorganizational efforts amounted to little more than a smoke-screen and public-posturing, the overall goal of which was to camouflage their largely unchanged goals and purposes of systematic subjugation of individual believers and ultimately a large segment of the collective Body of Christ. Modifications were primarily only cosmetic, aimed at defusing the controversy and rehabilitating the public image. The players were basically the same, and certainly the fundamental teachings and practices were nothing more than only slightly moderated. When the dust settled, the only thing that had changed was not the plan itself but the method of implementation, which was now even more covert and esoteric than before.

The Big Four Networks

Among the more prominent and influential "networks" of charismatic ministers and their ministries which have formed since the eruption of the Discipleship controversy are the National Leadership Conference (NLC), the International Communion of Charismatic Churches (ICCC), the Network of Christian Ministries (NCM), and Charismatic Bible Ministries (CBM). None of these require exclusive affiliation, which means that a minister can be affiliated with more than one, and indeed most are. In fact, some of their membership, and especially their top leaders, are, it so happens, members of several of these organizations.

Moreover, there is a significant amount of interrelations between these organizations, and some of the more prominent leader/speakers are frequent speakers at conferences sponsored by the different organizations. One of the things all of these ministries share in common is that there is among their memberships significant representation of ministers who essentially are proponents of Discipleship teachings and practices in that they employ some variation of those teachings and practices in their ministries.

The NLC was formed in 1979, largely under the initiative, ironically enough, of one of the staunchest critics of the Discipleship theories, Ken Sumrall of Pensacola, Florida. Yet, clearly the NLC has among its membership today ministers who have been proponents, to varying degrees, of Discipleship beliefs and practices, albeit the original members purported to be opponents.

> NLC brought together leaders whose ministries already served networks of charismatic assemblies, in particular Sumrall of Liberty Church, Pensacola, Florida (now with some 350 to 400 local churches); Gerald Derstine of Bradenton, Florida (who followed Sumrall as president); Bill Ligon of Brunswick, Georgia; Russ Williamson of Hopewell Junction, New York; Ernest Gruen of Kansas City; Bob Heil of Hillsboro, Missouri, and Bob Wright of Davidsonville, Maryland. The director of the NLC is Jim Jackson, of Montreat, North Carolina....NLC is clear that it is not a new denomination, but a fellowship of charismatic leaders with *common convictions and a similarity of vision.* NLC churches are often named "Community Church" or "Covenant Church"....[6]

One of these "networks" which has come to be relatively expansive and influential behind the scenes of Charismatic Christendom is the International Communion of Charismatic Churches (ICCC), "led in the United States by Bishops John Mears of Evangel Temple, Washington, D.C., and Earl Paulk of Chapel Hill Harvester Church, Decatur, Georgia."[7] A development arising out of this conglomeration of ministries was the establishment of an elite and exclusive echelon of leaders at the apex of their hierarchy, a clerical clique called the College of Bishops, composed of a scant few men who apparently decided somewhere along the way, after the manner of the Nicolaitans in the first century of the Church (more on this in a subsequent chapter), that they were of sufficient superiority over their fellows to merit the ecclesiastical status of "Bishops." After thus honoring and installing themselves, the founders over time have hand-selected and inducted into their imperial and exalted ranks certain other individuals with expansive ecclesiastical kingdoms composed of large numbers of subjects, which made them worthy of such a status of ascendancy and preeminence over everyone else of lesser status.

The CBM was founded in 1986 by Oral Roberts, and as of 1988 had a membership in excess of 1,200. Of the three organizations mentioned, the CBM is the loosest and least directive in nature. Yet, its membership is likewise largely constituted, especially at the highest levels, by ministers who are also members and top-echelon leaders of some of these other organizations, ostensibly, seeking fellowship with charismatic leaders of "common convictions and a similarity of vision,"[8] which convictions and vision apparently include some form of Discipleship beliefs and practices.

To me, the most enigmatic of all these "networks" is the Network of Christian Ministries (NCM), founded by Charles Green of New Orleans, Louisiana. According to biographical information published by one of NCM's members, Dr. Bill Hamon (President, Christian International—Network of Prophetic Ministries), the NCM was birthed and established to promote the networking of certain individual ministers and ministries who "are willing to co-labor together" in endeavors of mutual interest. I say the NCM is to me the most enigmatic of all these "networks" because of the paradoxical membership mixture, which besides the founder includes on the one hand Bob Mumford and Charles Simpson, two of the original Fab Five founders of the Discipleship heresy, along with others such as Earl Paulk (Chapel Hill Harvester Church), Larry Tomczak (People of Destiny International), and Bob Weiner (Maranatha Ministries) whose ministries incorporated their own variations of the Discipleship teachings and practices, and on the other hand men such as Kenneth Copeland, Ken Sumrall, and the now late Demos Shakarian, all of whom were staunch opponents of the whole Discipleship matter. Other NCM members (as of 1989) include: Oral Roberts, Jack Hayford, Bill Hamon, John Gimenez, Dick Iverson, Houston Miles, Carl Richardson, Larry Lea, Paul Paino, and Dick Benjamin.

Aside from being a member of the NCM, as mentioned, Charles Simpson, following the CGM debacle, founded in 1987 the Fellow-ship of Covenant Ministers and Conferences (FCMC), based in Mobile, Alabama. "FCMC, with approximately 350 members, represents the sector of the discipling-shepherding ministry of CGM that survived the final dissolution of the old CGM team in 1985."[9] Without question, FCMC member churches are the most overt and ardent subscribers to and practitioners of the Discipleship teachings and practices. Though "Covenant Churches" now claim to have moderated their teachings and practices to some degree, they continue to adhere to the basic principles of the original doctrines. "The FCMC theology of covenant is similar to that of NLC, except that a functional commitment (not regarded as a covenant) is made between the pastoring pastor and the pastored pastor."[10]

Like the NLC churches, most FCMC churches have the term "Covenant" in their names. FCMC churches make little bones about espousing Discipleship doctrines and employing Discipleship practices, and often defend same with an overt stridency, unapproachability, and pugnacity. Though Simpson and the FCMC deny being a denomination, the organization with 350

34

church-members has nonetheless become a protodenomination of significant and on-going influence within Christendom.

The Fab Five Today

Now since I have elaborated in the detail I have on the past history and development of the Discipleship/ Shepherdship/Covenant saga, I think it only fair to also report the developments that have transpired with the movement as well as the original CGM leaders since the debacle began, and offer some commentary on the significance of those developments.

Christian Growth Ministries, per se, no longer exists. Derek Prince was the first to leave the group and to publicly repudiate, to some degree, the teachings he had helped to formulate and proliferate, in particular the assertions regarding the requisite of every believer, including ministers, to have a "personal pastor." In 1986 the remainder of the group disbanded, and Mumford, Prince, Basham, and Baxter released everyone who were submitted to them in "covenant relationships."

Don Basham moved to Cleveland, Ohio, and subsequently passed away in March of 1989.

Ern Baxter eventually quasi-retired from public ministry, and relocated to San Diego, California, where he died of leukemia at the age of 79 on July 9, 1993, approximately one year after I began writing this book.

Bob Mumford relocated to California, where he lived for several years while he attempted to get his ministry back on track, apparently meeting with only moderate success. He has since, moved to North Carolina and teamed up with Jim Jackson in a "Christian" community development project. To his credit, Mumford has been the most forthright in his attempt to make amends for past mistakes. In an article published in *Charisma* magazine in August, 1987, he offered a rather vague and hedging "apology," a feeble and apparently ineffective attempt to reconcile the wrongs that had been committed during the Discipleship Movement. He seemed at the time to still be somewhat reticent about admitting to error and accepting blame for the spiritual atrocities incurred, and was certainly mistaken as it turned out if he had surmised that a cursory "statement of regret" would suffice to appease the anger and resentment that he had engendered against himself over the years as one of the primary principals of the Discipleship heresy.

Then in a subsequent *Charisma & Christian Life* article published in February, 1990, reportedly after having sought the advice and counsel of Jack Hayford and others, according to the article, Mumford spoke more as one who was genuinely chastened, repentant, and willing to deal with the issue in a more direct fashion, accepting full responsibility for his error. According to the article, Mumford read a statement in November of 1989 "to a gathering of pastors at the Christian Believers United meeting in Ridgecrest, North Carolina,"[11] in which he said, "'I repent. I was wrong. I ask for forgiveness,' Mumford said about his involvement in the discipleship movement."

The article went on to say:

> ...Mumford decided that he needed to publicly **'repent'** of his responsibility in setting up a system where so many people were hurt by **misuses of authority.** "Some families were split up and lives turned upside down," says Mumford. "Some of these families are still not back together."

> In his statement, Mumford admitted that he had not heeded earlier warnings about **doctrinal error** from Hayford and two others. "While it was not my intent to be willful," he said, "I ignored their input to my own hurt and the injury of others." ...He admitted that there had been an **"unhealthy submission resulting in perverse and unbiblical obedience to human leaders."** He took personal responsibility for these abuses,

saying that many of them happened under his sphere of leadership.

Thus, the upshot of the whole Discipleship/Shepherdship
controversy after some twenty years since its inception is that at
least three and possibly four of the five[12] original proponents of the
Discipleship "movement" have to varying degrees admitted the
doctrines were flawed, erroneous, and wrong. These public
recantations should, one would think, speak loudly and clearly to
all those who continue to espouse these doctrines and in any way
participate in the practices they engender, but incredibly, that has
not been the case.

At present, of the original Fab Five, apparently only Simpson
continues to stubbornly refuse to renounce and repent from the
heretical Discipleship principles and practices. Simpson's intransigence and refusal to acknowledge the erroneousness of Discipleship teaching is reflected in the aforementioned *Charisma &
Christian Life* article reporting Mumford's recantation:

> Charles Simpson told *Charisma* that he supports Mumford's
> statement as it stands in that it comes from Mumford. **But he
> warns against too much analysis and against dismissing
> discipleship principles as a result of this.** Ern Baxter declined
> to comment about Mumford's statement.
>
> Simpson said individual actions did need to be righted. "I have
> done things that I repent of and I do want forgiveness and I do
> want to see restoration," he said. "I say with Moses, who in
> Numbers 11 said, 'Lord, let me not see my wretchedness.' I
> think I have seen some of mine."
>
> **"My problem is not repenting; my problem is to continue
> leading...."**
>
> **Simpson said he still believes in and teaches covenant
> relationships.** "That's the only qualification," he said. " I put
> no qualifications on the fact that I did things wrong. **But I**

CANNOT RENOUNCE all of the [covenant] relationships I have. I CANNOT DO THAT as a matter of conscience."[13]

"Covenant Relationships" With Demons

The last two sentences of the Simpson quip succinctly captures the essence of the overriding problem with the Discipleship teachings, which is religious captivation. I fully believe Simpson when he states categorically, **"But I CANNOT RENOUNCE all of the [covenant] relationships I have. I CANNOT DO THAT as a matter of conscience."** I believe he literally cannot renounce those covenant relationships because the demonic spirits behind them, to which he has subjected himself over many years, have him bound. In fact, I believe (and it pains me deeply to say this) those words were in actuality the words of those demons uttered through the lips of Mr. Simpson.

Typically, when a person becomes indoctrinated by these doctrines of demons, it is as though it has been seared into his or her conscience as with a branding iron (1 Tim. 4:2), and that person has become psychologically enslaved by the demons behind the religious lie. So much so that it becomes virtually impossible, except through the supernatural intervention of God, for that person to renounce the teaching and the idolatrous covenants he has made. Yet, renunciation of those unBiblical teachings and practices, as well as idolatrous covenantal relationships, is the primary requirement for emancipation from the demonic captivation they engender. (This matter of covenants with demons, however, will be discussed in greater depth later in this book.)

Extending a hand of deliverance and recovery to victims of *Charismatic Captivation* resulting from erroneous doctrines and practices is the sole motivation for the writing of this book. And, that hand is extended to every victim of this demonic perpetration, which, I believe includes Mr. Simpson and the other surviving original propagators of the Discipleship doctrines and practices, those who remain proponents and participants, as well as those who were unwittingly captivated in the throes of deception. Debunking and disproving these heretical doctrines is only a necessary precursor to this overriding objective of ministering to those who need ministry.

People are not the problem. Nor are they the adversary, the devil is (1 Pet. 5:8). Without equivocation or qualm, this book is a spiritual counteroffensive, launched against the satanic powers that have been surreptitiously laboring virtually unimpeded and unknown for years within the Church through the propagation of this doctrine of demons. Every weapon of spiritual warfare is deployed herewith, and precisely trained to score a direct hit against these demonic powers, in order to expose and totally annihilate them. That is the sole objective and mission. In no way, is anything in this volume an attack on any person. That would serve no useful purpose.

Most of what God does, He does through willing members of His Body. Jesus is the Head, but we are His Body. The supernatural intervention of God unto those needing His outstretched hand of ministry, of which I have spoken, will likely be manifest only through someone with the fortitude and willingness to be used by the Lord, whatever the personal cost. Thus, having circumspectly counted the cost, selected five smooth stones from the brook of the Spirit, and looked the adversary dead in the eye, I echo the words of David unto the Philistine champion, Goliath:

> *"You come to me with a sword, a spear, and a javelin, but I come to you in the name of the Lord of hosts, the God of the armies of Israel, whom you have taunted. This day the Lord will deliver you up into my hands and I will strike you down and remove your HEAD from you. And I will give the dead bodies of the army of the Philistines this day to the birds of the sky and the wild beasts of the earth, that all the earth may know that there is a God in Israel, and that all this assembly*

may know that the Lord does not deliver by sword or by spear; for the battle is the Lord's and He will give you into our hands. " (1 Sam. 17:45-47)

---

1 H.D. Hunter, "Shepherding Movement," *DICTIONARY OF PENTECOS-TAL AND CHARISMATIC MOVEMENTS*, p. 784, Zondervan [parenthetical explanation added by author].

2 P.D. Hocken, "Charismatic Movement," *DICTIONARY OF PENTECOS-TAL AND CHARISMATIC MOVEMENTS*, p. 137, Zondervan.

3 H.D. Hunter, loc. cit.

4 P.D. Hocken, loc. cit.

5 H.D. Hunter, loc. cit.

6 P.D. Hocken, op cit., p. 141, [Emphasis added by the author].

7, 8, 9, 10 Ibid.

11 "Mumford Repents of Discipleship Errors," Charisma & Christian Life, pp. 15,16, February, 1990, Strang Communications, Inc.

12 Ern Baxter, though, to the author's knowledge, he never publicly repudiated or renounced the Discipleship Doctrines and practices, however did disassociate himself from CGM leaders and related involvement.

13 "Mumford Repents of Discipleship Errors," Op. cit., p. 16 [emphasis added by author].

Chapter Three

NICOLAITANISM

One of the common denominators of false cults, false religions, and the occult is that their doctrines and practices are predicated upon the "isms" of vain, humanly invented philosophies. The same is true of the heretical Discipleship/Shepherdship doctrines, dogmas, and practices, which fact is further corroboration that they are all of the aforementioned characterization: cultic, false, and occultic. One of the most significant "isms" of the Discipleship heresy is one that is specifically mentioned and condemned in the Bible—Nicolaitanism.

In short, Nicolaitanism was an heretical hierarchical system of church-government devised and promulgated by a corrupt sect of usurpers that surfaced toward the end of the First Century A.D. The malevolent and ignoble objectives of these interlopers are succinctly reflected in the etymology of their name—Nicolaitans—a compound Greek word, comprised of two components. The first component is derived from the word "nikao," which means "to conquer." The derivation of the second compound is the word "laos," which refers to the "laity," a term used in the days of the Early Apostolic Church to allude to congregational believers who are not Five-fold Ministers or a part of the governmental presbytery of a church. Combined, these two components precisely convey the overall primary goal of the Nicolaitans, which was to "conquer the laity."

41

It is not clear whether this appellation was an overtly defiant choice by these tyrannical ecclesiastical usurpers themselves, or whether they were so named by their opponents. What *is* abundantly clear from history, however, is that the diabolical teaching and practices devised and promulgated by this band of corrupt and evil clerics were deadly weeds of false teaching virtually identical to that being touted by the Discipleship proponents of today. It is also clear that, because they were not vigorously opposed and extirpated, but were instead permitted to spread through the Church, eventually these doctrines and deeds led to the hierarchical system of the Roman Catholic Church which took the Church into 1,200 long years of spiritual deterioration and devastation.

The teaching of the Nicolaitans was the genesis of the concept that remains yet today in much of Christendom in which an elite class of professional clergy is set in as an ecclesiastical governmental hierarchy to in effect "lord over" the laity. The Nicolaitans taught and instituted a form of ecclesiastical hegemony (domination by force by one entity over another) based on a pyramiding, multilevel ascendancy structure comprised of priests, bishops, and cardinals, and so on, all of whom were under complete subjection to a singular religious potentate, who was venerated as the human substantiation of Christ Himself—the Pope. The residual of this system today, still alive and well and revered by millions of adherents, is the Papal System of the Catholic Church.

The Nicolaitan heresy was virtually identical in essence, as indicated before, to the Discipleship/Shepherdship doctrines and practices promulgated by proponents today. How much more significant that becomes when it is understood that it was primarily these perverse precepts and their promulgators who were responsible for plunging the Church into the spiritual "black hole" of the Dark Ages, from which the collective Church is still in the process of recovery and restoration.

Nicolaitanism

The Dark Ages (313–1517 A.D.) was the period of the Great Apostasy for the collective Church, an occurrence prophesied by the Apostle Paul when he wrote:

> But the Spirit explicitly says that in later times some will **FALL AWAY FROM THE FAITH** paying attention to deceitful spirits and doctrines of demons, by means of the hypocrisy of liars seared in their own conscience as with a branding iron (1 Tim. 4:1,2).

During this age of spiritual darkness, the Truth was subverted by humanistic ideologies and vain philosophies (Col. 2:8)—the *"doctrines of demons"* of which Paul forewarned. Eventually, nearly every remnant of Divine Truth, the foundational teachings upon which the Church had been originally established, was distorted, perverted, diluted, invalidated, abrogated, and abandoned.

The prominent and preeminent role of the Nicolaitans in this cataclysmic and precipitant descent into comprehensive spiritual apostasy dramatically depicts the catastrophic consequences that can ensue when false teachers and false teaching are not exposed and extirpated with finality. It is for this very reason that the Word of God warns, *"A little leaven leavens the whole lump of dough"* (Gal. 5:9). It's also the reason the Lord mandates: *"Clean out the old leaven* (false teaching), *that you may be a new lump,"* and *"Remove the wicked man from among yourselves,"* in order that we might *"celebrate the feast, not with old leaven, nor with the leaven of malice and wickedness, but with the unleavened bread of sincerity and TRUTH"* (1 Cor. 5:7,13,8)

Jesus' Disdain for the Nicolaitan Deeds and Doctrines

Considering the eventual denouement and consequences of the Nicolaitan heresy, it is little wonder why Jesus issued such a terse but severe warning to the Early Apostolic churches through the Apostle John regarding the Nicolaitans in the apocalyptic vision comprising the book of Revelation. It is in His commendation to the church of Ephesus in which Jesus expresses His utter disdain for the premise of such ecclesiastical domination as that proposed and promulgated by the Nicolaitans: *"Yet this you do have, that you hate the **DEEDS** of the Nicolaitans, WHICH I ALSO HATE"* (Rev. 2:6).

Jesus' commendation of the Ephesians for recognizing the hereticality of the ungodly teaching and practices of the Nicolaitans, and their consequential resistance and rejection of the false doctrine is a tribute to the Apostle Paul who founded the church, to Timothy, who Paul personally tutored and sent to be their pastor, and to all the other Five-fold ministers who contributed toward the spiritual development of the Ephesians. They had been so well taught that they were not deceived by men who came to them claiming falsely to be apostles (Rev. 2:2), and they did not succumb to the diabolical doctrines and deeds of the Nicolaitans.

Here Jesus indicates His hatred for the Nicolaitans' *deeds*, which was an allusion to the practices of unauthorized, oppressive domination that were engendered by the heretical doctrines espoused and promulgated by them. In a moment, however, we shall see Jesus' expression of his disdain for the *doctrine, or* teaching, of the Nicolaitans, *"Thus you also have some who in the same way hold the **teaching** (doctrine) of the Nicolaitans"* (Rev. 2:15).

No Such Office: "Bishop"

These hyper-authoritarian doctrines and deeds of the Nicolaitans, which Jesus said He hated, were perpetrated under the auspices of this unScriptural hierarchical system of Church government comprised of priests, bishops, cardinals and so forth, who were all essentially ecclesiastical prefects, under the supreme authority of the ultimate authority of the Pope. I mention this at this point to allude to a related issue—the matter of the resurgence of the classification of "bishop" in an increasing number of so-called Charismatic "networks" emerging today. These so-called "networks" are comprised of affiliated Charismatic church-groups, all claiming to be "independent" and autonomous. The networks deny being denominations, but nevertheless are, at the very least, protodenominations.

Now I am not concerned here with the use of the term "bishop" by certain Pentecostal denominations as a nomenclature for various administrative positions in their hierarchy. While usage of that term is a definite misnomer, it is relatively innocuous in this case, in that it refers to intrinsically benign administrative positions. The term was probably invoked originally in an attempt to attribute greater credibility to those positions by using Biblical terminology. Thus, the use of the term by these denominations is of little concern.

What *is* of concern is the invocation of the term "bishop," as I said, by many of the Charismatic "networks" emerging today. One of these "networks," the International Communion of Charismatic Churches (ICCC), founded by John and Don Mears, which was mentioned in the preceding chapter, has established what they refer to as "the college of bishops," under the auspices of which they confer the supposed "office of bishop" upon certain ministers who preside over "networks" of churches.

This development appears to be a modern manifestation of the Nicolaitan doctrines and practices, which, as we will discuss in the next chapter, is based on an erroneous concept of "positional authority." When you cut through all the rhetoric and apologetics what you have in all this is the institution of illegitimate and Scripturally-unsanctioned ecclesiastical authority structures. It is difficult to reconcile as pure the motives, mindsets, and purposes behind the establishment of such hierarchies, but they smack instead of self-exaltation, predomination, and self-aggrandizement. While that to some may be arguable, most everyone would have to admit that it is certainly quite ironic (and to me, telling) that the Nicolaitan teachings, which Jesus condemned, also led to the establishment of "bishops" and other offices of ecclesiastical ascendancy.

Beyond that, what makes this matter of so-called "bishops," to whom so many today are avowing homage and obeisance, so ludicrous is that there is no such "position" of "bishop" established in the Word of God. The Greek word which is translated in the King James Version (KJV) as "bishop" is the word "episkopos," which literally means to "oversee." This word, as it is used in the original contexts, bears no thought of an *"office"* or position of authority, or echelon of rank, in the Church. Rather, it speaks only of the *function* of ministry in which **everyone** anointed and appointed by the Lord to Five-fold ministry within the New Testament Church operates. In fact, the terms "elder," "overseer," and "shepherd" are all *synonymous* terms referring to the *same* offices of function, which are the Five-fold Ministry offices. If to some the KJV appears to be referring to an "office" or "position" of "bishop," the reason, it is vital to understand, is that the corp of translators appointed by King James in the Medieval Era to the task of developing an English translation of canonized Scripture, which was finally completed in 1611, were working from the mental backdrop of ecclesiastical concepts founded in the Dark Ages, and ecclesiastical structure in place at the time included such positions.

However, the fact that the intention of the Holy Spirit and the original writers in the usage of the word "overseer" in the original letters was to refer, not to a *position* of authority, but rather to ministry *function*, and the fact that the terms "elder," "overseer," and "shepherd" are all synonymous terms referring to the function of those appointed by the Lord to Five-fold Ministry is abundantly evident in two particular passages of Scripture. The first is in the Twentieth Chapter of the Book of Acts, beginning with verse 17, in which the Apostle Paul has called together *"the ELDERS of the church"* at Ephesus, which he had founded, and over which he had apostolic oversight. To the elders, Paul said, *"Be on your guard for yourselves and for all the flock, among which the Holy Spirit has made you OVERSEERS, to SHEPHERD the church of God..."* (v. 28). Here we see the three terms of "elders," "overseers," and "shepherd" being attributed to the same individuals, the latter two of which spoke explicitly of their function in the capacity as the first.

The second proof text is the first three verses of First Peter, Chapter 5, in which Peter as an apostle (an elder who has oversight over other elders by virtue of esteem) addresses the elders of the various churches with this exhortation: *"Therefore I exhort the ELDERS among you, as your fellow elder...SHEPHERD the flock of God among you, exercising OVERSIGHT...."* Again, the same three terms are mentioned here, attributing the functions of shepherding and oversight to the elders collectively.

Hence, we see from these two passages that what the Holy Spirit is communicating through this usage of the word "episkopos" is that all elders, who, according to a preponderance of Scriptural evidence, are the Five-fold Ministers, have two primary functions: to shepherd the flock of God, and to provide spiritual oversight (look after the spiritual well-being) of the flock allotted to their charge by the Holy Spirit. It is referring to the function of Five-fold Ministers (who, incidentally, are all Shepherds, not just the pastors), rather than establishing an authoritarian position of ascendancy and domination over fellow believers as so commonly but wrongly presumed by so many. In fact, the third verse of the previously mentioned passage, while specifically instructing the elders to *shepherd* the flock of God, exercising spiritual *oversight*, explicitly enjoined them against *"LORDING IT OVER those allotted to your charge, but proving to be examples to the flock."*

Thus, to summarize the point, when someone takes upon himself, or has conferred upon him, this purported office "bishop," as certain groups and denominations do, since it really is not validated or sanctioned by Scripture, it harks of a kind of modern-day Nicolaitanism and coerced ascendancy over fellows that is most unseemly, and which certainly is not reflective of the model of servanthood ministers are called to represent in the stead of the Ultimate Servant, and now Lord, Jesus.

Jesus' Condemnation of the Pergamum Church For Accepting the Nicolaitan Heresy

Though the Ephesians were not taken in by the hypothesizing of the Nicolaitans, unfortunately, this was not the case with another of the seven Asia Minor churches addressed by Jesus in the Revelation communicated through John—the Pergamum church. Jesus sharply condemned the Pergamum church because "some" among them (some of which apparently were among the leadership of the church, else it could not have existed in the church long) had indeed been deceived into accepting and espousing the teaching and practices of the Nicolaitans: *"Thus you also have some who in the same way hold the teaching* (doctrine) *of the Nicolaitans"* (Rev. 2:15).

The Nicolaitan lie was not the only deception by which the Pergamum believers had been bewitched, however. For, Jesus also rebuked them because some of their membership also held to some other type of false teaching introduced to them which led to some form of idolatry and immorality the Lord said was akin to the teaching of the false prophet Balaam:

> *But I have a few things against you, because you have there some who hold the teaching of Balaam, who kept teaching Balak to put a stumbling block before the sons of Israel, to eat things sacrificed to idols, and to commit acts of immorality.* (Rev. 2:14)

Proclivity To Deception

Apparently, the Pergamum church had become especially vulnerable to false teaching. Like many groups today, they seem to have even developed a proclivity toward being duped by false

48

teaching. As it is also today, it seems that once a group has begun to receive false teaching, an invisible door in the spirit realm is opened, making them susceptible to additional false teaching and delusion of many different kinds. I have found this to be true in my experience in dealing with different groups and churches. Usually, where there is *some* false teaching and deception, there are *many* different kinds.

Why is this so, and why do some individuals and groups seem to be especially vulnerable to deception, while others are able to resist it and stay on track doctrinally and directionally?

I believe the Lord has shown me the answer to that question. It is revealed in a portion of Scripture where perhaps we would not expect to find the answer; a passage dealing with five main elements—the Second Coming of Christ, the Rapture, the Day of the Lord, the Last-day Apostasy, and the revelation of the Antichrist:

> ...with regard to **the coming of our Lord Jesus Christ**, and our **gathering together** to Him (the Rapture), *that you may not be quickly shaken from your composure or be disturbed either by a spirit or a message or a letter as if from us, to the effect that* **the day of the Lord** *has come. Let no one in any way deceive you, for it will not come unless* **the apostasy** *comes first, and* **the man of lawlessness** *is revealed, the son of destruction....* *And you know what restrains him now, so that in his time he may be revealed. For* **the mystery of lawlessness** *is already at work; only he who now restrains will do so until he is taken out of the way. And then that* **lawless one** *will be revealed.... that is, the one whose coming is in accord with the activity of Satan, [displayed in all kinds of counterfeit miracles, signs and wonders {NIV}], and with all the deception of wickedness for those who perish, because they did not receive the love of the truth so as to be saved.* **For this reason, GOD WILL SEND UPON THEM A DELUDING INFLUENCE (PRO-CLIVITY TO DECEPTION)** *SO THAT THEY MIGHT*

BELIEVE WHAT IS FALSE [THE LIE {margin}*], in order that they all may be judged who did not believe the truth, but took pleasure in wickedness (lawlessness).* (1 Thes. 2:2-12, parenthetical explanations added by the author)

What the Spirit is revealing in this passage is that there will be a period right before the return of Christ, the Rapture of the Church, and the revelation of the Antichrist, in which many ostensible believers will fall away in their relationship with Christ due to a *"deluding influence"* or "proclivity to deception" which the text explicitly states God Himself (as hard as it may be for some who insist on maintaining a humanistic view of God to believe) *"will send upon them."* This deluding influence will have the effect of causing apostate believers to believe lies, false teaching, deception, and to be duped by counterfeit miracles, signs, and wonders perpetrated by Satan himself during that time through counterfeit messengers (ministers) who will arise in the Church falsely claiming to be apostles:

> *...false apostles, deceitful workers, who disguise themselves as apostles of Christ. And no wonder, for Satan disguises himself as an angel* (Greek words for "angel" and "apostle" are synonymous) *of light. Therefore it is not surprising if his servants* ("ministers," Greek) *also disguise themselves as servants of righteousness; whose end shall be according to their deeds.* (2 Cor. 11:13-15)

This grave consequence will, according to the text, be directly linked to the workings of the *"mystery of lawlessness"* which is *"already at work"* to some degree, though presently restrained from full manifestation by the presence of the Church on the Earth until such time as the Church is taken out of the way (raptured) at the return of Christ. That is to say, those who will become susceptible to deception during this time of apostasy will become so because they have continued to maintain some degree of enamorment and involvement with some forms of *"lawlessness."* Instead of fully receiving and believing the whole Truth, and allowing their lives and attitudes to be fully exposed to the Light of Divine Truth, such marginal believers will continue to revel in the dark shadows of deception.

Love of the Truth Produces True Salvation

Moreover, this text indicates that the true essence of the problem lied in the fact that *"they did not receive THE LOVE of the Truth so as to be SAVED."* Unless and until a person acquires a genuine **LOVE** for the Word of God, which is the expression of Divine Truth, he will never be able to fully receive and believe its content in his heart, and thereby make a complete repentance leading unto salvation (2 Cor. 7:10). Indeed, verse ten of our text indicates that these people never did become fully *"saved"* in their hearts, though they no doubt would vehemently contend otherwise.

Having made such a statement, I need to digress momentarily in order to explain. This word "saved" which appears in this verse, is based on the Greek word "sozo," which means "to make whole," "to restore," "to effect recovery," in addition to also carrying the connotation, "to make holy." Based on this, it becomes clear that through the years since the waning days of the Early Apostolic Church many have espoused a far different connotation of this familiar term "saved," which is so basic to fundamental orthodoxy, than the meaning intended by the Holy Spirit in the no less than 108 occurrences in its various forms in the New Testament.

The fact is, being "saved," in the true Biblical sense, has little if anything to do with "having a home in Heaven" as so many modern expositors have so vociferously, adamantly, and repeatedly purported it does. Being saved, in the sense intended by the Holy Spirit, is a matter of being "sanctified," that is, being made holy; it is being restored to the place of holiness and righteousness possessed by Adam before the fall; it is being made whole—spirit, soul, and body (1 Thes. 5:19)—in accordance with the Image of Christ (Rom. 8:29), the Image according to which Man was originally

51

created (Gen. 1:26,27). Being "sozo-ed" is to be made "wholly holy" as well as "wholly whole."

In reality then, the matter of "having a home in Heaven," or more appropriately and importantly, having rightstanding and fellowship with God, according to true Biblical orthodoxy, is dependent upon our submission to the process of being made holy, that is sanctification, which is precisely what the Spirit has said: *"without holiness, no man will see the Lord"* (Heb. 12:14, KJV). Conversely, being saved is not so much predicated on "walking the aisle," "shaking the preachers hand," or parroting some verbatim confession, as purported by so many, though it may indeed all begin that way. So many people focus on the *beginning* of salvation, that is, being "Born Again" (though, certainly that is essential), instead of the really crucial matter—the *finish*. The winners of a race are determined at the finish, not the start. Aside from the obvious fact that to finish a race, one must start the race, the beginning is not the determining factor in regard to the final outcome of a race. The outcome of a race is not determined by who started it, but by who finishes it. It is not the starting of the race that is most consequential once the determination to enter the race is made, but finishing the race without having been disqualified (1 Cor. 9:24-27).

Similarly, the essential matter of salvation is not the matter of being *born* but the matter of *dying*. The matter of being born, whether in the natural or the spiritual, we had absolutely nothing to do with. In both the natural and the spiritual, our birth was a matter of the workings of God, which transpired totally void of any contribution from ourselves. Contrary to the so-called "testimonies" of some who try to take credit for their salvation, the Bible says we were *"Born Again through...the living and abiding Word of God"* (1 Pet. 1:23), and that it was by grace through faith we were saved, and even that was not of ourselves or of our own works, but was the gift of God, so that no one can boast as to his own salvation (Eph. 2:8,9).

Moreover, as I indicated, true salvation is not based on our *birth*, but on our *dying.* We must *"die daily"* to self and sin, crucifying the evil passions and desires of the sin nature which lurks within us (Gal. 5:24). The paradox of the gospel is that if we die, we live, eternally. For the believer, dying is living. This process of dying is sanctification, the process of being made holy, and *"without holiness, no man will see the Lord"* (Heb. 12:14, KJV).

Apostolic Authority Supplanted by the Nicolaitan Doctrines

Jesus' apocalyptic warning against the doctrine and the deeds of the Nicolaitans is more than just interesting. The truth of the matter is that had the early churches given heed to those Divine warnings, the course of history would have been totally different than what it was, because as mentioned before the demonically inspired teaching and practices of the Nicolaitans resulted ultimately in the Papal system which supplanted the apostolic authority upon which the Church was founded. This, indeed, was not only the most egregious and grievous effect of the Nicolaitan heresy, but no doubt also the very objective of the arch-enemy of the Church, Satan, who personally contrived this diabolical deception.

In His now infamous dissertation to Peter and the other Apostles of the Lamb, Jesus declared the Church to be His very own possession, His consuming passion, and that He Himself was its Chief architect and builder, when He proclaimed, *"I will build My Church; and the gates of Hell shall not prevail against it"* (Mat. 16:18). When contemplating this statement, it is imperative to remember that when Jesus said *He* would build His Church, He meant He would build His Church *through*, foremostly, the foundation ministries of apostles and prophets (Eph. 2:20). Prior to His ascension, Jesus personally selected twelve *"disciples"* who by His appointment and anointment became *"apostles"* (Mat. 10:1,2), and relegated to them the task and function of being the chief surrogate builders of His Church. The apostolic precedent He set and never rescinded, remains in effect throughout the Church Age.

Further evidence that apostles are the surrogate "builders" of the Church is found in the Apostle Paul's statement concerning the nature and function of his ministry as an apostle: *"According to the grace of God which was given to me, as a wise MASTER-BUILDER I laid a foundation, and another is building upon it"* (1 Cor. 3:10). The term *"master-builder"* Paul used is the equivalent of what today is called a "general contractor," which is the most concise yet comprehensive definition of the ministry of the apostle in the Bible.

A general contractor is the person responsible for building the building precisely according to the predetermined design of the architect represented on the blueprints. The general contractor, while he must himself be skilled and knowledgeable in each and every phase of construction and installation, cannot, for the sake of the successful completion of the overall project, hinder his effectiveness by becoming involved in the actual labor of any of the particular phases of the construction process. Rather, the function of the general contractor is that of coordination, administration, and oversight of the building process. He must see the overall "big picture" and oversee its completion. He must concentrate his efforts solely on organizing and overseeing the work of all the subcontractors and laborers in his charge, selecting and efficiently employing just the right person for each phase of the building process, in order that the building be built in precise accordance with the specifications of the architectural design.

Apostles are spiritual general contractors. What makes them apostles is that they are graced with and can at any time as necessary flow in the full range of the Ministry Gifts. Plus, they have also been anointed with the gift of spiritual (not to be confused with, business) administration. The spiritual gift of spiritual administration includes for one thing a supernatural ability to discern by the Spirit the spiritual gifts with which believers have been anointed by God, so as to, on behalf of the Lord, appoint the right people to certain spiritual functions and responsibilities. Apostles also employ the range of Ministry Gifts to train and equip other believers to function in their particular gifts and callings, and to coordinate those efforts in a cohesive and collaborative effort toward the spiritual edification of the Church.

The Church is established *"upon the foundation of the apostles and prophets, Christ Jesus Himself being the Cornerstone"* (Eph. 2:19,20). Truth declares unequivocally that the Church Jesus is building is founded upon and will be built up through apostolic authority. The true Church of Jesus can never be established upon any form of government other than apostolic authority. The Church-Age began with apostolic authority in place, and apostolic authority will be in place at its culmination. Moreover, it will only be when the Church returns to apostolic authority and foundation that genuinely significant spiritual advancements will be made.

The nemesis of that apostolic authority has always been, and will always be humanly-contrived, humanly-appointed, politically-based, hierarchical systems of ecclesiastical government. Supplanting of the apostolic authority and government established by Jesus was a primary factor precipitating the Church's gradual descent into the throes of deception and apostasy that transpired in the Dark Ages. Abrogation of apostolic authority in favor of politico/ecclesio hierarchy led to the virtual debacle of the Church as the instrument for implementation of Divine purpose, reducing it instead to being an agent of demonically-inspired humanistic purposes. No other single element was more causal to the deterioration of the Church than this supplanting of apostolic authority.

Similarity of Nicolaitan and Discipleship Heresies

So much more could be said with regard to the imperativeness of apostolic authority in the Church today, but space here will not permit. The point that is being established here is that the teaching and practices of the Nicolaitans and the modern Discipleship teachings and practices are virtually identical. It is an indisputable fact that the Nicolaitan heresy was the primary force leading to the supplanting of apostolic authority in the Early Church, which in turn ultimately led to the apostasy of the Dark Ages. So also the heretical Discipleship/Shepherdship teachings advocate a counterfeit authority system which in effect supplants apostolic authority. The similarity is just too striking to be merely ironic or coincidental. Rather, it is my confident conviction that the Nicolaitan doctrines were planted by Satan in the Early Church to supplant and effect the abrogation of apostolic authority, and in identical fashion the Discipleship/Shepherdship doctrines were implanted by Satan in the Last Day Church with the express intent to supplant apostolic authority, and impede, or if possible, preclude, the restoration of same. In the case of the latter, however, Satan's efforts, in the end, will not be successful, for apostolic authority will indeed be restored to the Church.

We are told through the writing of Solomon that in reality there is nothing which is truly "new":

> *That which has been is that which will be, and that which has been done is that which will be done. So, there is nothing new under the sun. Is there anything of which one might say, "See this, it is new?" Already it has existed for ages which were before us.* (Ecc. 1:9,10)

And so it also is with the unScriptural hypotheses brought forth in the heretical Discipleship doctrines. They are virtually identical to that which was purported by the Nicolaitans, which, as I have said repeatedly, was the seed from which the Papal hierarchy of the Roman Catholic Church was germinated.

The reason for the similarity lies squarely in the fact that these doctrines were not merely contrived in the minds of men. Rather, they genuinely are *"doctrines of demons"* of the ilk prophesied by the Apostle Paul in his letter to his younger protege Timothy (1 Tim. 4:1ff). He foretold that in the last days there would arise patently demonic, but subtle and impelling doctrines of deception that would actually be promulgated by lying, deceiving spirits through the agency of human teachers. These false teachings would be so subtle and impelling that many genuine and sincere believers will be duped by and give heed to them, with the result that bona fide believers will fall away from a true relationship and rightstanding with God into apostasy and perdition.

Indeed, this egregiously erroneous Discipleship/Shepherdship teaching, I am absolutely persuaded, is a doctrine of this ilk. It is contrived by the devil himself and promulgated by his fallen cohorts, demons, with the objective of craftily leading unsuspecting believers into spiritually idolatrous and adulterous covenants with mere men, and away from effectual relationship and rightstanding with God. As I have been establishing, these doctrines and practices are essentially the same age-old attempts by Satan to captivate and control people through the mythical utopian bliss of religious collectivization: *"promising them freedom while they* (Satan and his cohorts) *are the slaves of corruption"* (2 Pet. 2:19, parenthesis added by the author).

We move on now, in the ensuing chapters, to examine in greater depth and detail the erroneous concepts upon which these doctrines are founded, as well as the improper practices they engender.

Chapter Four

ERRONEOUS CONCEPT #1: AUTHORITY

As I have studied and mused upon the matter of the Discipleship heresy, it has become evident to me that it consists of two fundamental parts. One is the spectrum of motivational factors, that is to say, the factors that cause adherents and practitioners of these heretical and unChrist-like teachings and practices to be lured into such blatant illusion and delusion. This first part we have addressed in the previous two chapters. Without a doubt, this first aspect of this matter, involving what it is that would motivate purporting Christians to espouse such perverse doctrines and to engage in these perverted practices of religious hegemony over fellow believers, is by far the more emotional facet of this issue.

However, as you get beyond the emotional aspect to objective analysis, what becomes evident is that the Discipleship heresy is predicated on conceptual error. The spectrum of conceptual error upon which the Discipleship doctrines are based is what comprises the second part of the heresy. These erroneous concepts result from a combination of ignorance, misconception, misinformation, disinformation, misapplication, distortion, and in some cases outright perversion of Divine Truth. This second part of the Discipleship heresy, that of the conceptual errors upon which it is predicated, is the subject of this and the next three chapters.

There are essentially five conceptual errors upon which the Discipleship heresy is predicated: 1) authority, 2) "spiritual covering," 3) "unity," 4) the role of laity, and 5) the role of Five-fold Ministers. The first of these, the erroneous concepts regarding authority, we examine in this chapter. The other areas of conceptual error will be addressed in the ensuing chapters.

One of the most fundamental flaws in the heretical Discipleship/Shepherdship doctrines and practices is patently false concepts in regard to the essential and far-reaching matter of authority. Specifically and primarily, there are five particular aspects of authority which are distorted and misapplied under the auspices of these erroneous teachings: delegated authority, ministerial authority, church-governmental authority, "positional authority," and submission to leaders. We'll address each of those shortly. Before we do, however, I believe it would be beneficial for us to briefly examine the broader issue of the types of authority which *have* been established by God.

Legitimate Authority vs. Illegitimate Authority

In no way is it being said here that there is no valid or effectual authority operable in the Body of Christ and by believers. There is a valid and effectual authority that has been given by God for government in the Church, but the problem is that people misconstrue, distort, pervert, and misapply the principles of authority established by God, and thereby exceed the intents and purposes of valid authority. No other spiritual matter has been so contorted and misapplied as has this matter of authority. Under the auspices of the Discipleship doctrines, both leaders and laymen alike have been duped into such above delineated contravention of the intents of true God-established authority, and consequently have been part and parcel of the implementation of and participation in various kinds and degrees of perversion of authority, which due to that perversion produce, whether advertently or inadvertently, forms of "illegitimate authority."

Some of the most vital and instructive statements contained in the Word of God with regard to legitimate authority are found in the Thirteenth Chapter of the Book of Romans. The second part of the first verse states: *"...For there is no authority except from God, and those which exist are established by God"* (Rom. 13:1b). Implicit in this one statement is four important instructive declarations regarding authority: 1) that there are legitimate governing authorities and authority structures in existence which have been established by God; 2) that the only **legitimate** authority is the governing bodies and authority structures which have been established by God; 3) that all the **legitimate** authority structures which do exist are those that have been established by God; and, 4) any governing authorities or authority structures which have been appointed solely by man without a mandate or sanction from God are **illegitimate**.

Based on this Scripture, it is important, I believe, to identify the different types and levels of authority which exist. Though I do not at all consider myself an expert on the matter, and certainly do not want to sound as if I am delivering the "definitive word" on the matter, after considerable study and meditation, including of the commentaries of others on the subject, I have concluded that there are essentially twelve types and levels of authority which have either been established by God or which have come to be sanctioned by Him. While I would shun dogmatism about this particular conclusion, especially in regard to the number of types of authority, it is, however, interesting that the number twelve in Scripture is emblematic of government or authority. The following is a list of these twelve types and levels of authority appointed or recognized by God, along with a succinct explanation of each. These levels of authority are ascendingly transcendent, that is to say that they rank in preeminence in ascending order. This means that the higher levels outrank and take precedence over the lower levels. They are listed in the order of their rank of preeminence.

1. Sovereign Authority.

The absolute supremacy and sovereignty of the God-Head over the entire universe; *"the summing up of all things in Christ, things in the heavens and things upon the earth"* (Eph. 1:10); the sovereignty of the Creator over the Creation, inherent in every set and inviolable law and principle in the Creation; e.g., the law of gravity, the law of specie-after-specie procreation, the law of sowing and reaping, the law of reciprocity.

2. Veracious Authority.

The absolute authority of The Truth—The Word of God—codified, contained, canonized, and explicitly expressed in Holy Writ (Scripture) [Jn. 17:17].

3. Volitional Authority.

The human will; the free moral agency of every human; given by God to every human-being, inherent with the sovereign and inviolable right to self-government (the right to rule one's own life), inviolable, that is, as long as the free personal choices of one person do not violate or infringe upon those of another person. God has created every person as an individual, a free moral agent, and given them the right to sovereignty over their own life; i.e., a free will. God Himself will not violate a person's will or volition (right to choose); thus, He certainly has not consigned such a right to any mere mortal human over another, save in the case of lawlessness.

This type of authority could also be called "personal authority." It is the inherent authority of every person to govern himself, especially with regard to one's personal affairs and (lawful) choices according to his own conscience. (It must be understood, however, that in the case of a person who has been Born Again, that person enters into a process of sanctification in which he voluntarily and gradually surrenders His own will unto the Lordship of

Christ over every aspect of his life, subjecting his will and life unto the Will and Life of the Lord. The believer's will is by no means taken away or usurped, but rather, on the contrary, the believer exercises his free will in willingly subjecting himself unto the sovereignty of God and the Lordship of Christ.)

4. Domestic Authority.

Authority within the home; i.e., the husband is the surrogate governmental head under the Headship of Christ over the family. This means the husband is responsible to God for providind spiritual leadership in respect to all familial affairs; he is to provide sprititual leadership unto the wife; and, the parents (husband and wife) together as a unit are responsible for the government (plus, the care and training) of the children.

5. Ecclesiastical Governmental Authority.

Authority delegated by Christ to certain individual believers He has anointed and appointed as Five-fold Ministers, who have the responsibility of providing intermediary government (pilotage, steerage) in local churches and *ad hoc* judicature with regard to matters universally affecting the Church-At-Large.

6. Spiritual Ministerial Authority.

Delegated spiritual authority from Christ to minister His supernat-ural power in His stead and on His behalf. This authority could also be called "surrogate spiritual power." This is God- given authority of believers over Satan and his temptations and devices: sickness, disease, temptation, malevolence, disorder, lawlessness, sin, etc. It is the authority ("exousia") given by God to believers to operate the gifts of the Spirit. It is also the enablement and sanction of God to function in a God-anointed and God-appointed spiritual calling or spiritual function.

This also is the "power" ("dunamis") that Jesus said would inure to the Spirit-baptized believer after that the Holy Ghost came upon him, by which to operate works of power that give witness of a risen and living Savior (Ac. 1:8), the same power that Jesus Himself had demonstrated in works of power during His fleshly ministry, which He said would be delegated to believers: *"he who believes in Me, the works that I do shall he do also; and greater works than these shall he do"* (Jn. 14:12). Having triumphed over sin, death, Hell, and the grave, all power and authority over all things was given unto Jesus; which power, prior to ascending into Heaven and sitting down at the right hand of the Father, He in turn delegated to believers:

"All authority has been given to me in heaven and on earth" (Mat. 28:18);

therefore, *"Go into all the world and preach the gospel to all creation....And these signs will accompany those who have believed: in My name they will cast out demons, they will speak with new tongues; they will cast off* (lit.) *serpents, and if they drink any deadly poison, it shall not hurt them; they will lay hands on the sick, and they will recover"* (Mk. 16: 15-18).

7. Civil Authority.

Civil authorities; i.e., secular governments, to include all laws and agencies of same; e.g.: civil laws, courts, Heads-of-State, government agencies and officials, law enforcement agencies and officers.

8. Stipulative Authority.

Authority established by means of legally binding contracts and agreements into which separate parties have voluntarily entered, wherein they have agreed to abide by certain specific stipulations governing their relationship.

9. Entrepreneurial Authority.

Authority of entrepreneurs (business owners) to govern the affairs of the business of which they are the owner, or in which they have a vested, majoritive interest; also includes the spectrum of employer-employee authority.

10. Delegated Authority.

Authority which has been delegated by one person with legitimate authority to another person with the effect that the latter represents the former. This is a kind of surrogate authority, in which one person in authority invests his authority in a subordinate to authorize the latter to effect (operate) the authority of his superior. This kind of authority is usually parochial, or limited to a certain scope and parameters, and *ad hoc*, in the respect that its jurisdiction is limited to a specified purpose and realm of function. This kind of authority is operable and found in virtually every realm of human endeavor.

11. Functional or Motivational Authority.

Authority inuring to a person by virtue of a particular ability, sphere of function, or talent, whether God-given (Motivation or Function Gifts [Rom. 12:6-8]), or acquired through education or training. At times, this type of authority is impromptu and situational, coming into play to meet an arisen need of the moment (e.g., functional authority of a physician happening upon the scene of an auto accident).

12. Customarial Authority.

Customs; societal traditions; cultural ways, methods, manners, practices. This is the lowest level of authority, and is to be honored when it is not contraventive of dictates of the preeminent levels of authority.

Certainly, one cannot even begin to have a proper understanding of the realm of the Kingdom of God without having an understanding of the matter of authority, which becomes even more apparent when one considers that the very term *"Kingdom of God"* is actually connotive of the **Domain of Rule**, **Authority**, or **Government** of God (cf., Rev. 12:10). Indeed, authority is critical and central to spiritual knowledge and understanding, as well as to the matter at hand, the Discipleship heresy and the unauthorized practices of its adherents. Moreover, all true knowledge and understanding concerning authority begins with the most vital and fundamental Truth that God Himself is Authority, that He is the ultimate authority, and the essence and embodiment of authority, and therefore that all legitimate authority emanates from Him and Him alone. Hence, all authority truly established by God, that is to say, **legitimate authority**, is sanctioned by God, and therefore is to be respected and observed.

However, any supposed or purported authority that does not emanate from and has not been established by God is **illegitimate authority**, and as such has no jurisdiction in regards to bearing the sanctioning of God, is not binding, and bears neither the requirement from God to be observed and honored, nor the punitive sword of retribution for violators. Furthermore, any particular body of even God-appointed authority that specifically contravenes the Law of God, that is, the Word of God, has in so doing exceeded its God-ordained jurisdiction, and has thereby effectively dissanctioned itself and rendered itself **ILLEGITIMATE**, thus forfeiting any authority to compel observance and obedience as well as any right to preservation. Such is the case with proponents and practitioners of the Discipleship/Shepherdship doctrines.

Interestingly, one of the passages of Scripture most cited by the Discipleship proponents as a support text for their assertions and theories with regard to the ilk of authority which they purport to have been delegated to ministers is the very text I quoted from earlier, the Thirteenth Chapter of Romans. For them, this text has become their "Magna Carta" of sorts, which by their interpretation grants them license to dominate and control other believers. But, what they fail to understand (or choose to ignore, whichever may be the case) when they so adamantly and vehemently postulate their hypotheses is that the authority specifically alluded to in this chapter is, without equivocation, the **CIVIL** authorities and governing bodies. While there are certain elements of truth with regard to authority in general reflected in these verses, the realm of authority specifically addressed in the Thirteenth Chapter of Romans is that of **SECULAR** government, **NOT** authority within the Church (ecclesiastical authority). Though this is perhaps not explicit in the initial verses of the King James Version, most all of the modern versions do explicitly indicate that it is the **CIVIL** governing authorities being addressed in this chapter; e.g.:

> *Everyone ought to obey the CIVIL authorities...* (v. 1, PME);

> *Let every person be loyally subject to the governing (CIVIL) authorities...* (v. 1, A.B.);

> *Everyone must obey the STATE authorities...* (TEV).

However, incontrovertible proof that civil authority, not ecclesiastical authority, is being alluded to in this text is found in the sixth verse, which, regardless of what version you read, echos in so many words essentially what the Amplified Bible says: *"For this same reason you pay TAXES, for the [civil authorities] are official servants under God, devoting themselves to attending to this very service."* We pay **"taxes"** to civil governments to remunerate them for their service on our behalf, not to the Church. We pay **"tithes"** to our church for the support of our ministers, not **"taxes."** Thus, we know that it is secular government that is being alluded to in these verses, not any supposed authority of ministers over those "under" them as purported by the Discipleship proponents.

Notwithstanding, as I indicated, there are inherent within this very Roman text crucial truths with regard to "legitimate authority" as well. Foremostly, there is an implied distinction between legitimate and illegitimate authority in this passage. The Phillips Modern English version especially highlights this differentiation made in the passage:

> *Everyone ought to obey the civil authorities, for all LEGITI-MATE authority is derived from God's authority, and the existing authority is appointed under God. To oppose (legitimate) authority then is to oppose God, and such opposition is bound to be punished.* (Rom. 13:1,2; parenthesis added by the author)

Indeed, the overriding issue inherent with the heretical Discipleship teachings and practices is not whether there is authority in the Body of Christ and among believers, for we have already established that there is, but rather the nature and scope of that authority, and the distinguishing of *legitimate* authority from *illegitimate* authority.

Now, as I stated earlier, patently false concepts regarding authority is one of the most fundamental flaws in the heretical Discipleship/Shepherdship doctrines and practices. Specifically, there are five particular aspects of spiritual authority that are greatly misconstrued and misapplied under the auspices of these erroneous teachings: delegated authority, ministerial authority, church-governmental authority, "positional authority," and submission to leaders. So let us now examine these twisted and tangled webs of delusion and illusion under the illuminous rays of Scripture; separating Truth from lie, fact from fiction, and the legitimate from the illegitimate with regard to these matters.

Delegated Authority

One of the most basic elements of the Discipleship teachings that deviates from Biblical Truth is the matter of "delegated authority." Put another way, error regarding the matter of "delegated authority" is one of the most fundamental elements of erroneousness of the Discipleship doctrines. Most assuredly, the principle of the delegated authority of Christ is a valid and vital principle. But, the heart of the issue is: what is the authority which Christ has delegated unto believers? That is to say, what is its nature, composition, scope, and sphere of operation? How is it defined? What is included in this authority, and what is excluded? What are its limitations?

In searching for the answer to these all-important and pivotal questions, the Word of God, of course, must be our primary and preeminent source. In this regard, as any other, what God says must be the final authority, the definitive statement. *"Let God be true, and every man a liar."* Neither tradition, nor history, nor the philosophies of men can be our source or guiding light in this regard, but only the Light of perfect and pristine Divine Knowledge and Wisdom.

This matter of authority, the cardinal issue of the ages, because of its profundity, is admittedly a complex matter, not so much perhaps in terms of composition, but rather in explanation and application. As with elucidation of so many other spiritually appraised concepts, words seem to fail the most glib and articulate expositors as they attempt to expound upon the matter of authority. That seems to be the nature of true revelation knowledge from God: it is so profound that in many cases it is nearly impossible to express and explain in human terms, for it is the task of translating the infinite into and unto the finite. Notwithstanding, I have attempted to express as succinctly as possible the essence of the matter as it relates to the focus of this volume, reserving a more comprehensive and detailed exposition of the broader issue of authority and government for another, forthcoming book devoted specifically to that subject.

The issue at hand here is the matter of the authority which Christ has delegated unto believers, its composition and application. Essentially the delegated authority of Christ, according to all that Scripture tells us regarding it, can be distilled down to two forms: one, Spiritual Ministerial Authority, or Spiritual Power, and, two, Ecclesiastical Governmental Authority. Both of these are forms of authority which have indeed been delegated unto the Body of Christ by Christ. However, it is there that the similarities of the two end and their diversities begin.

Spiritual Ministerial Authority (Spiritual Power)

The primary mission of the Church is to be a conduit of the supernatural power of Jesus. Having purchased our redemption by means of the supernatural plan of God, and having triumphed over all things, and having attained all authority both in the Heavens and on Earth, just prior to ascending into Heaven to sit down upon His throne of Sovereignty at the right hand of the Father (Mk. 16:19), Jesus delegated His **spiritual power**—the same supernatural power of God with which He Himself had been endued when He was baptized by the Spirit as the Spirit descended upon Him in the form of a Dove, and the same supernatural power of God which He had operated during His fleshly ministry—unto every believer who would come to receive the Baptism in the Holy Spirit from then on until the Church Age ends. Jesus Himself declared that the Baptism in the Holy Spirit was *"the promise of the Father"* (Ac. 1:4,5), which the disciples were to receive subsequent to their having been Born Again by the regenerative powers of the Holy Spirit on the night of His resurrection (Jn. 20:19-23).

(The disciples, you see, had been Born Again by the Spirit in the evening of that first Easter when Jesus, after having ascended in the Spirit unto God as the True Spiritual High Priest, returned to Earth in His transformed Body and appeared unto them in the Upper Room, passing right through its locked door. Having made peace between us and God, Jesus greeted the Disciples saying, *"Peace be unto you!"* and forthwith proceeded to breathe upon them, saying, *"Receive the Holy Spirit."* It was at that moment that the disciples first received the **LIFE** of Jesus by means of the infilling and the indwelling of the Holy Spirit and were first Born Again.)

But Jesus indicated there was something additional to the **LIFE** of God that the disciples must yet receive in order for them to be His delegates on the Earth, which was the **POWER** of God. Thus, He further instructed them, *"And behold, I am sending forth* **the promise of the Father** *upon you; but you are to stay in the city until you are clothed with* **POWER** *from on high"* (Lk. 24:49). Then, forty days later, Jesus appeared once again unto the disciples,

> *And gathering them together, He commanded them not to leave Jerusalem, but to wait for what the Father had promised, "Which, He said, "you heard of from Me; for John Baptized with water, but you shall be BAPTIZED IN THE HOLY SPIRIT not many days from now...you shall receive POWER when the Holy Spirit has come upon you....* (Ac. 1:4-8).

The purpose of the infilling of the Holy Spirit on Easter evening was to infuse the disciples with the **LIFE** of God, but Jesus said that the purpose of the Baptism in the Holy Spirit was something different, for He said *"when the Holy Spirit has come upon you, you will receive* **POWER TO TESTIFY** *about Me with great effect"* (Ac. 1:8, L.B.). The Greek word Jesus used in this verse translated "power" is "dunamis," which connotes "supernatural enablement." Thus, the import of Jesus' statement is that with the Baptism of the Holy Spirit believers receive supernatural enablement or power to be effectual witnesses of the resurrected Christ.

This supernatural enablement, or, **spiritual POWER**, we will call it here, comes in the form of the Manifestation or Charismatic Gifts of the Spirit (1 Cor. 12:7-11). It is delegated authority of Christ unto every Spirit-baptized believer to minister the supernatural power of God on behalf of and in the stead of Christ. It is of this power that Jesus was speaking when He said, *"Truly, truly, I say to you, he who believes in Me, the works that I do shall he do also; and greater works than these shall he do; because I go to the Father"* (Jn. 14:12). This spiritual power is one facet of the *"delegated authority of Christ."*

It is concerning this facet of delegated authority of Christ as juxtaposed to **"governmental** authority" that misunderstanding and excess arose during the Charismatic Movement, especially when it was later augmented by the inception and interjection of the Discipleship/Shepherdship doctrines and practices. As a result, what transpired among Charismatics was disorder, chaos and confusion, and even a certain amount of ecclesiastical anarchy as many Charismatic believers, especially those infected with the Discipleship "virus," began to confuse spiritual power with the matter of "governmental authority," which, it is vital to understand, is an altogether different matter.

The powerful Wind of the Spirit that began blowing in the sixties and continued until recently, which became known as the "Charismatic Movement," was without a doubt a foreordained and Divinely-orchestrated *"period of restoration"* (Ac. 3:21) and a desperately needed *"time of refreshing"* emanating from *"the presence of the Lord"* (Ac. 3:19). The primary Divine objective of the Charismatic Movement was to bring forth the "recovery" or "rediscovery" of what some refer to as the "Charismatic Gifts," which more appropriately should be called the "Manifestation Gifts."

That objective was indeed accomplished. Even though not as many believers have as yet availed themselves of these gifts of supernatural power as we who have and the Lord also, I am sure, would desire, nevertheless, during the Charismatic Movement, the clarion call of the Spirit was trumpeted forth far and wide throughout Christendom unto all who had an ear to hear. What the Voice of the Spirit declared was the essential Truth that the Dunamis-

Erroneous Concept #1: Authority

Power of God was not merely relegated to the by-gone era of the Early Church, but that it is still operable today, and that the Manifestations of the Spirit were just as available to each and every believer of the Last-Day Church who is willing to lay aside theological predispositions and religious traditions in order to believe the promise of God and receive of this enduement from on High.

The Charismatic Wind of the Spirit came not only to make believers **aware** of the Baptism in the Holy Spirit and the Manifestation Gifts, but also to take it a step further—to actually **activate** every believer willing to avail himself of the Spirit-baptism in the operation of these manifestations of the supernatural Power of God. Indeed, an additional truth emphasized during the Charismatic Move was that the Manifestations of the Spirit are not just operable through some exclusive group of elite people, or through "ordained" ministers only, but also through "ordinary" believers.

Though, happily, the purposes and objectives of God for the Charismatic Move were fulfilled during its span, at the same time, however, as is typical with such restorational moves, in the case of many believers, knowledge came to be exceeded by zeal (Rom. 10:2). In their exuberance, euphoria, and zeal which came as a result of their initiation into this whole realm of operation of the Power of God and the gifts of the Spirit, many believers unfortunately began to *"exceed what is written"* (1 Cor. 4:6), in that they began to mistakenly equate their newly-acquired spiritual **"power"** with **"authority."** This became a fairly widespread occurrence in Charismatic circles. Potentially deceiving slogans such as "We are **ALL** ministers" began to emerge and to be promulgated widely.

Now in the sense that all Spirit-baptized believers are able to "minister" the supernatural gifts of the Spirit as the Spirit distributes and all believers have a viable function in the Body of Christ, it could be said that all believers are "ministers." However, what

73

must be understood, and what was not understood by many Charismatics, is that in no way does that mean that all believers are *Five-fold* Ministers, which is the segment of believers to whom **governmental** authority within the Church *has* been delegated by Christ. In other words, all Spirit-baptized believers have been endowed with **spiritual POWER**, but certainly not all believers, by virtue of that, have been endowed with **governmental AUTHORITY**.

Two particular New Testament passages make this abundantly clear. One is First Corinthians 12:28-30 which indicates that *"God has appointed in the Church, first apostles, second prophets, third teachers...governments....;"* but then specifies, *"ALL are not apostles....ALL are not prophets....ALL are not teachers...."* The other passage is where the Apostle Paul explains that when Jesus was ascending on High on the Day of Ascension from the Mount of Ascension, He delegated His spiritual gifts of spiritual construction and instruction (i.e., the Five-fold Ministry Gifts) unto **certain** believers of His selection and appointment, to wit:

And He gave SOME (not all, only certain ones) *as apostles, and SOME as prophets, and SOME as evangelists, and SOME as pastors and teachers, for the equipping* (instruction) *of the saints for the work of service, to the building* (construction) *up of the body of Christ* (Eph. 4:11,12, parenthesis added by author).

Unfortunately, there has been and for the most part still is great lack of knowledge by many believers concerning the critical difference between **"power"** and **"authority."** It is imperative that believers understand that **"power"** to be a witness of Christ is an entirely different matter than **"authority"** to govern within the Church. The New Testament language makes a distinct difference between these two specters.

The Greek word for "power" is "dunamis," and it connotes "ability" and by extension "capability." "Dunamis" is the word used in describing acts or works of the supernatural power of God, i.e., miracles. Indeed, in the original language, **"dunamis"** (power) is what Jesus said believers receive as a result of the baptism in the Spirit, not "exousia."

On the other hand, the word used to connote "authority" in the New Testament is the Greek word "exousia," which is derived from the word "exesti," meaning "it is lawful." "Exousia" speaks of sanctioning, authority, lawful permission, power to act, the power of authority, the right to exercise power, the power and authority of government and rule, authority of one whose will and commands must be obeyed by subservients. "Exousia" denotes the right and freedom to act; when used in regards to God's authority, it denotes absolute and unrestricted authority; when used of men it denotes delegated authority (actually, since all legitimate authority emanates from God, all authority on Earth and among men is delegated authority from God.)

Specific uses in the New Testament of the word "exousia" include with regard to: apostolic authority (2 Cor. 10:8; 13:10); judicial authority (Lk. 12:5; Jn. 19:10); domestic authority (Mk. 13:34; 1 Cor. 11:10); spiritual ruling or governing authority, domain or realm of authority (Lk. 4:6; Eph. 3:10, 6:12; Col. 1:16, 2:10,15; 2 Pet. 3:22); secular governmental authority (Rom. 13:1f; Lk. 12:11; Tit. 3:1). *Vines Expository Dictionary of New Testament Words* makes this statement with regard to the distinction between these two words and the concepts they convey: "*Dunamis*, power, is to be distinguished from *exousia*, the right to exercise power" (Note, p. 748).

Many new believers birthed during the Charismatic Move did not (and many still do not) understand the critical difference between these two very different matters of **"power"** verses **"authority,"** and merely because God began to use them as agents, or vessels, of His supernatural power, they became puffed up and began to *"think more highly of themselves than they* *ought"* (Rom. 12:3), adopting an unrealistic and improper, inflated and exaggerated view of themselves. Some even went so far as to espouse a kind of religious egalitarianism by which they wrongly believed they were on par in terms of function and authority with those whom God had appointed to be their spiritual leaders. Others made the even more disastrous mistake of thinking that just because they had been used as conduits of the power of Christ over demons and disease that that equated into their appointment as spiritual leaders, rather than merely understanding that this is what true Spirit-baptized lay-believers are *supposed* to do: proclaim the gospel, cast out demons, prophesy, cast aside the effects of demonic attack, and effect healing through the laying on of hands upon the sick—Mark 16:15-18, paraphrased.

It is vital that believers understand that the Manifestation Gifts of the Spirit, while they are giftings which manifest the supernatural **POWER** of **God** (and I emphasize that the source of that power is God, not the believer), do not in any way imply or translate into **governmental AUTHORITY** within the structural order of the Church. To say it yet another way, spiritual **power** manifested through operation of the Manifestation Gifts of the Spirit in no way equates into **authority** to govern within the Church. The Church is governed, *not* by those through whom the **Manifestation** Gifts of **POWER** operate, but by those through whom the **governmental** gifts of **AUTHORITY** operate, and it is the Five-fold Ministry Officers who have been endowed with those gifts and charged with that responsibility. While it is true that all Spirit-baptized believers are ministers of the power of God and the message of Good News, all believers, however, are **NOT Five-fold** Ministers.

Ecclesiastical Governmental Authority

While it is true that every believer is a viable member of the Body of Christ, having been assigned to a vital and specific function in the Body, and empowered by means of the Baptism in the Holy Spirit with spiritual power by which to minister supernaturally to the needs of others as "surrogate ministers" of Christ, if you will, nevertheless, it is vital to understand that spiritual **power** to *minister* on behalf of Christ is not **authority** to *govern* in the Church. The Church does have a government, and that government is effected through governmental officers to whom Christ Himself, the true functional Head of the Church, has delegated His authority for the express purpose of providing government to the Body.

This government of the True Church which Jesus is building, as it has always been since Christ appointed the Apostles of the Lamb as the chief overseers of the building of His Church, is apostolic authority. It is comprised by a cadre of human surrogate spiritual leaders (Five-fold Ministers) who function in the stead of and on the behalf of Christ Himself. Metaphorically speaking, we could say the Five-fold Ministers function as Field Commanders, overseeing the carrying out of the commands and plans of the Supreme Commander-In-Chief, who is Christ. Christ has delegated His authority for government in the Body of Christ and the responsibility for the spiritual development of the saints unto Five-fold Ministers who in effect are Christ's surrogates, His personal "stand-ins," fulfilling these vital functions on the behalf of Christ.

The Five-fold Ministers are the New Testament Levites. The things of the Old Testament were not the real, but the copy, the types and shadows, of the real. The real is the New Testament. The offices of function which the Levites occupied were not the real, but only the types and shadows, the representation of something that could and would only be fulfilled and become real in the New Testament. The Levites, who comprised the spiritual government of Israel, symbolized the true spiritual government of the Church which is now in effect under the New Covenant and in this present New Testament Era. Jesus fulfilled all that was written in the Law and the Prophets when He appointed the Apostles of the Lamb as His representatives to govern the Church.

The offices of apostles and prophets are still the offices upon which the Church of Jesus, the Church Jesus is building (Mat. 16:18), is founded and established (Eph. 2:20). The foundation of any structure is the government of the structure. Though men were temporarily successful in supplanting and overriding the government Jesus originally established the Church on, substituting theirs for His, it is a certainty that, ultimately, that form of government upon which Jesus established the Church at its inception will be the form of government on which it is established at the culmination of the ages, which is apostolic authority. To Him, the Lord of the Church, the Head of the Church, the One who changes not (Mal. 3:6), the One who is the same yesterday, today, and forever—the government of the Church He is building has never changed, but has always been the same. It's just that the Living Ecclesia that He is building and the religious institution that men have been building over the centuries are two distinctly different and separate entities!

In the True Church, Christ is the True, **Functional**-Head, as He has always been, not a "**figure**-head;" *"and the government shall be upon His SHOULDERS"* (Is. 9:6); and the "shoulders" of the Body of Christ are *"the apostles and prophets, Christ Jesus Himself being the Cornerstone, IN WHOM the whole building, being FITTED TOGETHER is growing into a holy...dwelling of God in the Spirit"* (Eph. 2:20-22).

This is the Truth regarding the government of the True Church of Jesus. However, it is distortions, perversions, and excesses (as it is in the case of most all spiritual error) in regard to the scope and role of delegated authority that make the Discipleship doctrines and practices erroneous and aberrational.

Erroneous Concept #1: Authority

A central and oft-addressed theme by Discipleship proponents, especially during the height of that false movement, was and still is the issue of "headship" within the Body of Christ and the local church. For many years, Charismatics especially were subjected to sermons related to this issue week after week, "ad nauseum." Still today, in fact, heavy-handed preaching attributing "headship" to human leaders remains a common refrain of many, especially Discipleship proponents desperately struggling in these days of God- ordained upheaval and turmoil to establish, maintain, and extend their kingdoms.

Despite all these clamorous assertions and expository posturing, the fact of the matter is that the true position of Headship of the True Church is not vacant, and never has been. God has already installed the True governmental Head of the True Church—His name is **JESUS**! Jesus Christ Himself is the undisputed functional Head of the Church (Eph. 5:23, et al.). He is the only One who is worthy to be the Head of the Church, for He bought and paid for the Church with His own sinless, shed Blood. None other than the One with the nail-prints in His hands and feet is worthy to be the Head of the collective Church and individual believers. God emphatically declares to us all: *"But I want you to understand that* **CHRIST** *is the Head of* **every man**.... " (1 Cor. 11:3)!

Though this is the way it is *supposed* to be—that Jesus is the true functional Head of the Church—as it is in a plethora of other regards, the way it is *supposed* to be is a far cry from how it actually *is* in the vast majority of churches. Jesus is nowhere near being the true functional Head in most churches and religious organizations; but rather, if He is given any deference at all, He is relegated to a position as a *"figure*-head" instead of being venerated as the *Functional*-Head. To most believers and churches, the statement that Jesus is the Head of the Church is merely a nice, poetic metaphor, but certainly not something to be taken literally.

79

How could it be?—why you've got everyone from the pastor to all the "jezebels" in the church to the overseers to the presbyters or bishops to the superintendents to the choir director to the deacons to the pulpit committee to the janitor running everything and being the functional heads—everyone **EXCEPT** Jesus.

Instead of Jesus truly being Lord over all, including the local church and the Church-At-Large, to the contrary, leaders contend and compete, sometimes covertly and sometimes overtly, against one another with varying degrees of verve and viscosity for territorial supremacy and "headship" over their private "kingdoms" and domains; humanly-appointed bureaucratic, potentates who *"have seated themselves in the chair of Moses"* within hierarchies of man-made religious organizations exercise interecclesiastical sovereignty, while making pious-sounding statements about Jesus being the Head of the Church; and, congregations of lay-people appoint for themselves by democratic vote the latest "monarch *pro tem*" to reign over their private religious civic-clubs (churches).

Now as I indicated at the outset, the problem is not that the matter of the delegated authority of Christ is not a valid principle. On the contrary, it is both valid and vital. From the very beginning when God said, *"Let Us make man in Our own image, according to Our likeness; and let them* **RULE** *over...all the earth"* (Gen. 1:26), God has been delegating His authority and power unto human beings.

Similarly, the principle of delegated authority of Christ is in operation within the Church. While Christ Himself is the **Head** of the Body, **WE**, the individual members of the Church, are now the **Body** of Christ, *"Now are* **YOU** *Christ's body, and individually members of it"* (1 Cor. 12:27). The Head is that portion of the body which rules the body, in that it does the thinking and sends out the commands. The body is to implement those commands. This is precisely the way it is to work within the Body of Christ: Jesus, the Head, creates the plans and issues the commands; and we, the believers, the Body of Christ, are the ones to whom Christ has committed His plans for implementation.

After Jesus had completed His Earthly mission of reconciliation and redemption, having purchased the Church for His own sole possession (1 Pet. 2:9; Tit. 2:14) by means of His personal suffering and with the currency of His own shed Blood, and after giving some final instruction to those to whom He had delegated His governmental authority over the Church—the Apostles—then *"He was received up into Heaven, and* **SAT DOWN** *at the right hand of God"* (Mk. 16:19). This explicit statement that Jesus *"sat down"* when He was received into Heaven was intended to emphasize the fact that Jesus Himself had now completed all that He personally was ever going to accomplish on the Earth in His flesh and blood form. All that He would accomplish from then on would have to be accomplished through His surrogates, His representatives on Earth—believers, the Body of Christ.

And, so He does yet today. Delegated authority is what this arrangement between the Head and the Body is called. It's a marvelous arrangement, if only the Body would do what it is supposed to do, no more and no less.

However, unfortunately, this is not what has taken place within the typical Pentecostal/Charismatic church today, but rather there are two opposite extremes at work. On the one hand there are the vast majority of believers who have not even begun to effectually and fully operate the spiritual power and potential that has been given to them by God. At the opposite extreme are lay-believers as well as leaders who have exceeded what is written and what is intended by God in terms of their spiritual role, function, and authority. This latter extreme is especially true in the case of churches adhering to Discipleship doctrines and practices, wherein enslaving ecclesiastical authority structures have been instituted, placing heavy yokes, chains, and bonds of religious slavery unto men onto its duped and victimized members.

Erroneous and Enslaving Ecclesiastical Authority Structures

Lack of understanding and misunderstanding regarding the matter of government and proper order in the local church as well as the Church at-large is one of the most problematic matters in the Church today. I believe it is one of the most critical and pressing issues facing the Church. Notwithstanding, it is little addressed by Bible expositors. In this void of Biblical teaching regarding the matter, erroneous church government is pervasive. Yet, there certainly is no void of opinion, which runs the entire gambit from one extreme to the other. The sad state of affairs is that government in most churches is either *democratic* (i.e., people-ruled, which in actuality often amounts to *gynocratic* [women-ruled] government), *oligarchic* (rule by a few, usually laymen who in effect "purchased" their position of preeminence via substantial financial donations), or *autocratic* (absolute rule by a singular dictator). However, the church government prescribed in God's Word is neither democratic, oligarchic, nor autocratic, but rather *theocratic*, which means God, not people, rules.

Indeed, I believe, the matter of Scriptural church government will be the preeminent and overriding issue facing the Church in the days that remain prior to Christ's return to claim the Church as His Eternal Bride. My sense is that until this matter is addressed definitively, authoritatively, and conclusively, and structural reformation takes place in the Church to implement the correct government, further progress with regard to fulfillment of the yet outstanding purposes and plans of God will be minimal.

At the risk of sounding immodest, allow me to say that though I by no means purport to have all the answers, I believe the Lord has given me certain insights into and prophetic revelation concerning this matter of church government, which will be conveyed in another volume devoted to that subject I intend to write following the completion of this book.

Erroneous Concept #1: Authority

In the aforementioned void of understanding and consensus regarding the matter of Scripturally-prescribed church government pervading the post-Apostolic-Age Church, the Discipleship doctrines emerged, prescribing a totally unscriptural, humanly-invented ecclesiastical hierarchical-structure, which in essence was a "chain-of-command" of sorts, composed of ascending echelons of sub-leaders (mostly laymen) appointed by and linking up to the chief leader of the church or group. As pointed out previously, this command structure paradigm theorized under the Discipleship teaching is a pyramidically shaped, multi-level organizational structure virtually identical to the multi-level structure employed by many modern secular sales enterprises, which configuration, ironically, (or perhaps portentiously), has been deemed to be illegal in many states in the U.S. because of the latent potential for inequitable and unfair advantage such an operation affords those at the top echelons.

On the point of the pyramidic shape of these chain- of-command structures, let me say that personally I do not believe it is merely coincidental that they are pyramidic. The pyramids are icons of ancient Egyptian occultism, i.e., devil-worship. Egypt, in fact, symbolizes the kingdom of Satan in Scripture. Of course, Egypt was the world power under whose domination Israel was subjected for four-hundred thirty years until God led them out through a savior-deliverer who was a foretype of Christ, Moses. It is on the basis of all this that I believe the pyramidic configuration of the hierarchy put forth under the Discipleship doctrines not only bears spiritual significance, but in fact, by some ironical twist, actually is Satan's personal signature and the watermark affirming these teachings to be bona fide "doctrines of demons."

This, I believe, is not coincidence, but corroboration that the governmental structure prescribed by the Discipleship/Shepherding teaching, besides being totally incongruous with God's Word, is patently erroneous. It is a demonic system of enslavement, domination, and misuse of authority that, as it has been proliferated by its proponents over the years, has wreaked untold havoc and harm over the width and breadth of the Body of Christ, which to this day remains largely unabated and unredressed. The chief consequence of this unScriptural and subversive false teaching is that true God-anointed, God-appointed governmental authority has been supplanted and significantly devalued, and thousands have been spiritually duped and injured. My personal belief is that this wave of deception, because of the usurpation and contravention of true authority it promotes, has actually caused the demise of untold numbers of fraternal relationships, marriages, families, and churches. (Indeed, after I had been working on this book for several months, more revelations of abuse and injury in churches practicing Shepherdship teachings began surfacing in books and magazine articles, which to me was further confirmation both of the extensiveness of these effects as well as the need for such a work as this one.) If I am right, unrepentant proponents and participants of these heretical doctrines and practices will, in the day of judgment, be required to give account to a holy and wrathful God for such misuse and abuse of authority.

Notwithstanding, there are multitudes of believers and vast numbers of groups and churches who continue to subscribe (some overtly, some covertly) to the basic tenets of this devilish deception which ascribes free-license to self-aggrandizing, dominion-seeking religious dictators to engage in Biblically-enjoined and -condemned religious hegemony in which they lord themselves over the unaware and unassuming sheep of God's flock. The pervasive results and impact of this horrendous spiritual travesty, which continues to be perpetrated upon so much of the Body of Christ under the direction of Satan through his human cooperatives, is no less outrageous and should engender no less of a sense of outrage by aware believers than the most egregious and offensive societal blights against which Christians today are so wanton to publicly protest and display their outrage.

84

Erroneous Concept #1: Authority

The Discipleship/Shepherdship chain-of-command sche-matic is an enslaving structure, and make no mistake about it—it is deliberately designed to be enslaving. I will never forget the shock and outrage I experienced while attending a so-called "Church Growth Seminar" held in a large church in a central Florida city in either 1977 or 1978 (I cannot recall precisely). The keynote speaker was the prominent and highly-regarded pastor of the world's largest Charismatic church, and the organization he had formed was the primary sponsor of the seminar. Ostensibly, the thrust of these seminars, which were conducted in various venues in the U.S. and other countries as well, was to share with the attending pastors so-called "*secrets* of church growth."

In the seminars, the pastor would expound upon the "chain-of-command" structure he had devised and instituted in his own church (located in an Asian country), plus some of the organizational methods he employed in his church to combat the common and ever-present problem that occurs in many churches, that of people entering through the front door, only to exit through the back door; that is to say: "attrition." These supposedly invaluable administrative and structural "revelations and insights" the pastor was touting, attendees were told, were explained more explicitly in a new book he had written and which, fortunately for us all, had just come off the presses in time for this particular seminar. The title of the book blatantly proclaimed the essence of and attitude behind the structure and methods he was proliferating: *"Caught In A Web."* The premise of the book and the seminar was that attrition would be virtually eliminated, or at the very minimum, drastically reduced, in the church in which these "secrets" for "church growth" were employed, in that once a person had become a member, it would be virtually impossible to thereafter leave the church. In the vein of the metaphor, once the prey was "caught in the web" it could never get out alive. This was the corrupt and perverted mentality being expressed at these "church growth seminars," which, to my astonishment and incredulity was

85

enthusiastically received by the majority of pastors (primarily, independent Charismatic and Pentecostal denominational pastors) who attended that seminar.

Moreover, those seminars continued to be very popular for a decade or so. But the most disturbing thing about the principles purveyed in those seminars and in that book, which essentially were Discipleship/Shepherdship doctrines, in my view, is that they became the paradigm or model for literally hundreds of churches and ecclesiastical organizations around the world. The influence of this pastor and these seminars, I believe, gave global credibility to, and were the greatest single vehicle responsible for the proliferation of, these fallacious and demonic teachings and practices.

How illustrative this all is of the fact of the enslavement upon which the Discipleship/Shepherdship doctrines and methodologies are founded. As the book title intimates, the Discipleship adminis-trative-governmental structure is designed to ensnare members and make it very difficult for them to ever leave. To accomplish this dubious goal, Discipleship proponents employ, wittingly or unwit-tingly, a number of psychological techniques commonly used by cult leaders to accomplish essentially the same goals of proliferation and preservation of their kingdoms by means of domination and control and the virtual elimination of attrition. We will address some of those techniques and how to recognize them in subsequent chapters. Here, however, we want to continue to look at the perverted concepts of authority inherent within these Discipleship doctrines and practices.

Absolute Submission

A fundamental and essential tenet of the Discipleship/ Shepherdship system is a dogma which is best described by the term "absolute submission," in which followers are required to, in effect, surrender their personal will unto the many ascending echelons of leaders in the pyramiding chain-of-command, and to obey explicitly and comprehensively the dictates and whims of those many "leaders." Followers are taught that they cannot simply hear from God themselves, but that they must "submit" virtually every matter of importance in their life requiring a decision unto their "leader." They are taught that God requires them to "be in submission," which extrapolates into total obeisance to the chain of human leaders of their group, and into those leaders making many of their decisions for them.

In these groups, it is quite common for members to be compelled to receive the approval (which is usually spoken of as a "confirmation") of their "leader" with regard to such mundane decisions as major and even minor purchases, going on a trip, visiting with relatives, matters concerning the care and nurturing of children, dating, marriage, relocation, and a host of routine decisions individuals and families must make as a normal course of life. Moreover, it is not uncommon for the member's "shepherd" to take on the role of *de facto* advisor and confidant in legal and fiduciary matters, such as estate wills and financial planning, probate, trusts, capital investments and expenditures, and court litigation, even though the "shepherd" is not a professional and has little or no expertise in those fields. Some "shepherds" have even been given power-of-attorney to act as a legal agent on behalf of an "underling." Not infrequently, so-called "shepherds" have used the color of their authority to wrangle their way into being made a beneficiary of estates and death benefits of members as well as interest-holders in business enterprises in exchange for their "advice."

On this last topic, as somewhat of an aside, allow me to point out that it has become vogue for "megachurches" to recruit salaried "estate/trust planners" whose primary goal is to raise funds for the church, which they accomplish by advising and assisting well-to-do and usually elderly members to invest their money in a host of fiduciary investment vehicles available today which will produce returns on their money, provide tax shelter, and provide on-going funds for the church as a living and death beneficiary or assignee. Though these professionals are typically licensed insurance salesmen and securities brokers who often reap additional compensation from commissions paid by the carriers and firms they represent, these churches have the unmitigated gall and lack of integrity to unashamedly anoint them with the title of "pastor" in a thinly veiled attempt to lend additional credibility and confidence to their schemery by giving the impression that the function of these professional money-makers is spiritual and that their advice has spiritual merit and underpinnings. In my opinion, this is sheer deception and nothing less than a modern-day, more sophisticated version of money-changers in the Temple! What makes it especially deplorable, despicable, deceptive, and outrageous to me is that it is all done under the color of spiritual authority.

Absolute submission is an integral and essential element of the Discipleship/Shepherdship theories and practices. However, it is manifest in varying degrees of covertness and overtness by different groups employing them. At one end of the spectrum are proponents and practitioners of these doctrines who hold to and implement an extreme and dogmatic version of absolute submission to the group's leadership, which is very manifest in the structure and modus operandi of the group, both publicly and behind-the-scenes. At the opposite end of the spectrum, are groups who employ a much more subtle and oblique form of absolute submission, which is deliberately kept out of the public services in order to give the impression of freedom and liberty. It is only manifest in the behind-the-scenes aspects, among those who have completed all the requisite indoctrination, initiation, and "proof of loyalty" "tests" so as to become a part of the "inner circle" of leaders and prominent "insiders."

In any case, however, absolute submission is by no means a benign and inconsequential premise, but is an extremely malevolent and destructive mechanism the sole goal of which is unauthorized and ungodly domination and control. Invariably and inevitably, in the case of those who have accepted the premise of absolute submission as being meritorious, and have integrated it into the structure and operations of their ecclesiastical society, whether it is manifested privately or publicly, it becomes the basis for a demonic and extremely injurious form of "brainwashing" and psychological "conditioning" of the constituency. Multitudes of naive and unsuspecting individuals as well as whole families have been psychologically, emotionally, and spiritually damaged by these very powerful mechanisms of domination- and control-oriented indoctrination. Some have suffered such total spiritual shipwreck and disillusionment that recovery requires the supernatural intervention of God.

Be assured, however, that most Discipleship/Shepherdship groups, from the leaders to the members, will vehemently deny adhering to the premise of "absolute submission" or any of the Discipleship doctrines or practices, for that matter. Moreover, they will adamantly insist that their group does not employ any of the techniques, mechanisms, and methodolo-gies inherent in all such aberrant, cultic and occultic theosophies.

Because of the disrepute and disfavor into which the Discipleship/Shepherdship doctrines and practices as well as their proponents fell in the Seventies, many Discipleship/Shepherdship groups, as mentioned in Chapter Two, simply "went underground" with their methodologies, resorting to a more subtle and obscured, "kinder and gentler" modus operandi, disguising their mechanisms, and implementing alternate, less overt terminology. By and by, most Discipleship/Shepherdship groups became increasingly more esoteric (a practice expounded upon further in Chapter Nine), only implementing their methods and mechanisms of domination and control upon new initiates gradually, incrementally as they progressed through the various stages of development in their relationship and status in the group, while redoubling their efforts to give the appearance of liberty in the public services. Before long, the unsuspecting victims are "caught in the web" of spiritual hegemony, from which, because of the illusive and delusive strands of indoctrination, many will never escape.

Now, though there have been countless truly innocent and unsuspecting victims of this demonically-inspired system of unauthorized domination and control, there are a significant number of participants who, driven by selfish-ambition, were actually attracted to it by the allure of becoming so-called "leaders" within the sphere of a group-society where they could attain some measure of "authority" which would give license and sanctioning to their innate desire to dominate and control other people.

A now infamous truism, the authorship of which has been attributed to Lord Acton, states: "Power corrupts; absolute power corrupts absolutely!" Authority coupled with carnality inevitably produces depravity. Those who crave power and authority over others are operating out of a destructive dementia, which, if not arrested by the Cross of Christ, ends up destroying their own lives and the lives of many others. Authority in the hands of those who crave it is the most destructive force known to mankind. It is an historic fact that those selfishly-ambitious would-be world-rulers who craved power and world-domination, eventually became corrupted and demented by that power, and used it not for good and constructive advancement, but for evil and destruction.

All this is why the Lord consigns legitimate authority only unto those who have surrendered their self-will and who have humbled themselves to comprehensive obedience unto the authority of God. In other words, God grants true authority only unto those who, like the Roman Centurion, are men *"under authority"*—God's! The last person to whom God entrusts authority is the person who craves it. God's Way is to humble the exalted and exalt the humble. He does not entrust authority to those who crave the status of being someone "great" and "first," but those whose genuine desire is to be a "servant" and a "slave" of all, following after the pattern of Jesus who *did not come to be served, but to serve, and to give His life a ransom for many"* (Mk. 10:42-45).

All this is also why these absolute authority structures and the absolute-submission-to-human-leaders dogmas are unequivocally not of God. They contravene totally His Word, His Will, and His Ways! Notwithstanding, proponents of the Discipleship doctrines in general and the "absolute submission" dogma in particular twist and pervert certain passages of Scripture and use them as purported "proof-texts" by which to corroborate their corrupt and excessive claims that such slavish obeisance to mere mortals is what the Word of God prescribes. Such cases of perversion of Scripture are far too numerous to examine each one here, but just three of the more stellar examples will suffice to make the point.

One of the most frequently quoted texts by the Discipleship proponents pertinent to the matter of "absolute submission" is Hebrews 13:17, which, for purposes which will soon become clear, I quote here from both the New American Standard and the King James Versions:

> *"Obey your leaders, and submit to them; for they keep watch over your souls, as those who will give an account. Let them do this with joy and not with grief, for this would be unprofitable for you."* (NASV)

> *"Obey them that have the rule over you, and submit yourselves: for they watch over your souls, as they that must give account, that they may do it with joy, and not with grief: for that is unprofitable for you."* (KJV)

This particular verse is an outstanding example of how the poison of deception is concocted by subtle twists and perversions of otherwise perfectly valid truths by Discipleship/ Shepherdship expositors. When they teach on this subject (and believe me, I have heard and studied the teaching of many of them), invariably they use these verses as a basis to spin an expositorial yarn that leads listeners to believe that God is in this verbiage telling believers that they are to be virtual empty-headed marionettes, walking around like zombies in a catatonic-trance, automatically and immediately responding in hypnotic-like total obeisance to every tug on their strings by their leaders. In the case of the extremist proponents of these doctrines, this is not a figurative assessment, but rather precisely what they seem to want out of their followers. As Pat Robertson quipped, the only difference between some of them and Jim Jones essentially is the Kool-Aid.

It is the assignment of corrupt connotations to the key words and phrases of this text that results in their extreme and erroneous extrapolation. The Greek word translated "obey," for instance, does not connote a slavish, cowering, cringing-in-fear, obeisance and servility, and total subjugation. Rather, it signifies to be "persuadable." The dictionary definition of "persuasion" is the act of causing someone to believe or accept, or to do something by appealing to their sense of reason or understanding; to induce to believe or act; to influence; to convince. Concerning the meaning of this word in this passage, Vine's Expository Dictionary of New Testament Words states: "The obedience suggested is **not by submission to authority**, but resulting from **persuasion**" (p. 806).

Additionally, Vines indicates that this Greek word translated "obey" in many English versions, "peitho," is closely related to the word "pisteuo," which means "to trust," and that the difference in the meanings of the two words is that the "peitho" (persuasion-obedience) is produced by "pisteuo" (trust). In other words, the "obedience" that is being spoken of here in the original language is more of a willing compliance and cooperation based on persuasion resulting from established trust and confidence.

Hence, the import of what God is saying here is that believers should display an attitude of willing compliance, cooperation, persuadableness, and convincibleness, toward their spiritual leaders, based on the trust those leaders have established with regard to their spirituality, integrity, and veraciousness; juxtaposed to the contentious, argumentative, non-compliant, and uncooperative attitudes some purported believers display toward their leaders.

This factor of trust and confidence is a very significant and important factor in this whole equation that is often either inadvertently overlooked or intentionally obscured. Some so-called "leaders" have the mistaken belief that because, by whatever means, they have attained unto a position of leadership over others, that that position itself grants them license to control and dominate and be overbearingly authoritative over other people. Indeed, it is on the basis of this very mistaken supposition that many people crave ecclesiastical positions of "authority." However, that simply is not the way it works in the Kingdom of God. Respect and honor, that is to say, esteem, is not a compulsory entitlement, or something that is due a person, merely by virtue of occupation of some so-called "office" or "position" of perceived "authority." *Au Contraire!* Esteem is earned!

The kind of "authority" being spoken of here in this pass-age as well as throughout the Bible is not some kind of heavy-handed, dictatorial, authoritarian, right-of-rule, in which one maintains ascendancy over others, and controls, dominates, dictates, and manipulates his "subjects" for his own self-aggrandizement. But rather, it is an "esteem"—high regard, respect, honor, trust, confidence—one earns as a result of a consistently virtuous and godly life, integrity, and spiritual veracity and proficiency. Though some self-imposed, dictatorial, imperious, ecclesiastical autocrats may, by religious intrigue and equivocation, dupe a cluster of naive adherents into accepting their arbitrary claims of ascendancy predicated on the fallacious concept of "positional-authority," such coerced and ethereal deference is only an empty and unsatisfying substitute for the earned-esteem which is the true object of their craving.

The next key portion of this passage is the object of the cooperation that is suggested, what the NASV translates as *"your leaders,"* and the KJV renders *"them that have the rule over you."* Again, pundits seeking Biblical corroboration of their fallacious concepts of ecclesiastical authority find in this phraseology some very conducive "raw material" which they can distort and manipulate to make it appear to be saying something that simply is not the spirit and intent of its true author, the Holy Spirit. No doubt one factor contributing to the excessive authoritarian interpretation of this verbiage is the rendering proffered by the Seventeenth Century translators commissioned by King James of England—*"them that hath the rule over you"*—which overtly reflects the existing perception with regard to the ecclesio-politico authority of Church leaders in that era when there was no separation of Church and State. During the Medieval Age, you understand, governmental authority of the State rested with the Church. And so, the King James translators viewed those in a position of spiritual responsibility as authoritarian rulers, bearing also the sanctioned authority of the State. In other words, ecclesiastical authority was also State authority.

However, that by no means was the way it was when the writer of the book of Hebrews penned these Holy Spirit-inspired words. The Greek words which conveyed the spirit and intents of the Holy Spirit bore no such authoritarian connotations. A thorough study of the key word of this phrase, "hegemonai," results in the conclusion that the word does not connote those who have some sort of authoritarian rule or sovereignty over others, but rather refers to those persons among the members of the church-group who have become prominent and preeminent within the group. It alludes to those who have distinguished themselves, who have become highly esteemed and regarded by the others because of their outstanding attributes. In fact, the same word is used in other passages telling us to **"esteem"** such persons *"very highly in love* **because of their work"** (not because of any perceived "positional-authority"). This

94

term alludes to those who have become perceived by the others as chief and influential persons among them, not because they occupy some position of authority, but rather by reason of having displayed an inordinate and exemplary degree of excellence in conduct, character, and performance proficiency. The root word from which this word is derived bears no thought of authority whatsoever, but rather literally means to stand before, to go before as a guide, to bring along, to steer, to direct, to guide.

Those who see in this passage the sanctioning or establishment of ecclesiastical authority of "leaders" to rule over the personal and individual lives of others are very badly mistaken and deceived. In the true Body of Christ, there is no such a thing as ruling authority or any form of ascendancy of one individual over other individuals, but rather some believers over years of exemplary living and spiritual proficiency begin to earn the esteem and respect of their fellow-believers as they become living paragons of Truth and Godliness. Those who do not enter into the fold through the *"Door"* of Jesus by means of Jesus-like conduct and spiritual impartation, but instead *"climb up"* through usurpation, coercion, intrigue, human appointment, self-effort and self-promotion, or by whatever other means, are *"thieves and robbers;"* while those who enter merely through the appointment and anointment of the Door (Jesus) are the true shepherds whose sole motive is to truly shepherd the sheep in earnest (Jn. 10:1,2).

Another favorite verse of Discipleship proponents attempting to corroborate their assertions that Scripture establishes the notion of ecclesiastical authority by certain individuals in the Church over others, is one similar to the first and which appears earlier in the same chapter of Hebrews, namely verse seven. Again the KJV presents a typically authoritarian rendition reflective of the totalitarian union of Church and State which existed at that time: *"Remember them which have the rule over you, who have spoken unto you the word of God; whose faith follow, considering the end of their conversation.*" As in the case of the former example, the key word in this text is the Greek word "hegoumenon," derived from "hegeomai," and which alludes to those who have become chief among you, those you have come to recognize as your leaders, whose leadership you have willingly become cooperative and compliant with and yielded to. In this case, the NAS's translation is more apropos: *"Remember those who led you...."*

Notice also that these leaders came to be recognized as such because it was they who spoke the Word of God to them, that is to say, they were their spiritual teachers, who taught them the Truths revealed in the Word of God. Moreover, that which the people were urged to remember about them was the outcome of their exemplary Godly conduct and their outstanding faith, which they were exhorted to imitate. And, it was these attributes of exemplary conduct and faith which earned these leaders the esteem of the people who looked to them for leadership. Thus, we see again that it was **earned esteem**, not some kind of "positional authority," which established these individuals as leaders.

The last of the three examples of purported proof-texts which, in actuality, are the product of misapplication and distortion of the import of Scripture by Discipleship teaching proponents is Titus 3:1, wherein the Apostle Paul instructs his younger protege: *"Remind them to be subject to **rulers**, to **authorities**, to be obedient...."* (NAS); *or "Put them in mind to be subject to **principalities** and powers, to obey **magistrates**...."* (KJV).

Again, as in the Thirteenth Chapter of Romans, we have in this verse components which allude to willing compliance, obedience, and yieldedness to the **CIVIL** authorities and government officials. The root word translated in the NAS as "rulers" and in the KJV as "principalities" is the Greek word "arche," which refers to "**civil** governmental officials." Also the Greek word translated as "authorities" in the NAS, and "powers" in the KJV is "exousia," which refers to the "**civil** authorities." Neither of these words or any of the components of this passage refer to any supposed "authority" in the Church realm among fellow-believers. Once again, based on the import of this passage, the truth is incontrovertibly reaffirmed: the purported ecclesiastical authority some Discipleship/Shepherd-ship teaching proponents contend is inherent in Scripture, wherein certain elite believers who have attained by whatever means unto certain supposed positions of ascendancy exercise rulership over other fellow believers, simply does not exist.

The authority which *does* exist within the domain of the Kingdom of God is a simple matter. The only authority there is in the Kingdom of God is the veracious authority of God's Word; administrative/governmental authority of Elders (i.e., Five-fold Ministers) in the local church; the volitional authority of every person to govern their own individual life; the sovereignty of Christ as the Head of every unmarried woman and every man; domestic authority, wherein the husband under the authority of Christ is the surrogate head of the wife and their dependent minor children; and spiritual power, which is authority over demonic forces, and supernatural miracle-power. That is it!

As far as any supposed "authority" which sanctions any believer to dominate, control, or rule over another believer, however, that simply does not exist in the Kingdom of God. The only place that such an inane and malignant proposition as that exists is in the carnal, unredeemed, unsanctified mind and warped thinking of those who seek such unauthorized dominion over others. Assuredly, it is not a product of "the mind of Christ."

There are two other key phrases in this passage. One is the word translated in both versions *"to be subject to"* which speaks of a willing subjection or yieldedness implemented by the free volitional choice of the person, but which in no way carries any connotation of compulsion or coerced obeisance. The other is what is rendered in the NAS as: *"to authorities, to be obedient."*

In the original language, this is one compound word: "peitharchein." The derivative components are: first, the word "peitho," which as we discussed earlier, means to be yielded, and willingly compliant; and, second, the word "arche," which as we also mentioned refers explicitly to civil governmental authorities. In this case, perhaps the best rendering of the two versions is the KJV, which translates the word as *"to obey magistrates,"* for that is precisely what it means: to obey government officials. So, here again, we find that this text does not support the notion of interpersonal authority among believers, but rather reaffirms its non-existence.

Beyond all of this, is the overriding point that is being established here, which is that the matter of "absolute authority" vested in an elite cabal of leaders linked together in some humanly-devised ecclesiastical hierarchy simply and indisputably is not prescribed or supported by Scripture. The only "absolute authority" that exists, is the sovereign authority of God Himself. Unredeemed and partially redeemed humans will never be fit to share in that level of Divine Authority.

The Myth of "Positional & Universal Authority" Debunked

The supposition of "positional authority," to which I have alluded several times in this chapter as well as in various other places in this book, is a notion that is rudimentary to not only the Discipleship/Shepherdship doctrines but also a number of unfounded hypotheses and ideologies relative to the specter of authority among saints being bandied about in organized Christendom today. Nevertheless, it is just that—an unproven and purely hypothetical supposition that has no foundation in God's Word.

The gist of the supposition of "positional authority," whether or not that specific term is used to represent the basic idea, is that there are authoritarian "positions" of transcendent rank in Christendom, wherein the individuals occupying those positions are of a superior status, stature, and standing than those paltry souls of an inferior status and rank. Theoretically, these positions of privilege and prestige, though entirely abstract and void of defined requisites for attainment, consign to their elite occupants automatic and universal ascendancy and authority over everyone of lesser status.

Many ministers who subscribe to this notion of "positional authority" have gone so far in their lunacy as to view the sphere of their authority which they believe has inured to them merely by virtue of their position as being *universal*, meaning they believe their "authority" is effectual and valid over all other believers, even outside of their local ministry, who are of what they consider to be an inferior "position." A term becoming popular in some circles of late to describe this concept of universal authority is "translocal authority " What all this essentially means is that those who are "bishops" (a purported "office" or "position" proven to be unscriptural elsewhere in this book but nevertheless invoked by some groups as a title for someone who oversees apostles), for example, have universal authority over all other Five-fold Ministers in that the offices of apostle, prophet, evangelist, pastor, and teacher are all of an inferior ranking as that of bishop (despite the fact that there really is no such office). Likewise, an apostle would have authority over all prophets, evangelists, pastors, and teachers everywhere in the world by virtue of the supposed transcendency of that office over the others. And, so on.

However, as we will discuss in greater detail in Chapter Eight, all of these concepts are foreign to all that God reveals in His Word concerning authority. Suffice it to say now for our purposes here that the Word of God prescribes that governmental authority by its very nature is totally parochial. That is to say, governmental authority has only limited and specified scope, which is that it is limited to the sphere of the local church. The extent of any minister's governmental authority is restricted to the local church that he oversees as the under-shepherd to that group of believers. The only exception to that is a bona fide apostolic ministry, in which case the apostle provides general and indirect oversight to local churches via a personal "mentorial" relationship with the senior shepherds of those local churches, who have been appointed by the Holy Spirit, and not any agency or authority of men, to shepherd that local flock.

Many of those who subscribe to and propagate this unfounded idea of ecclesiastical "positional authority" do so because they have found in its tenets instantaneous license, sanctioning, and justification for their carnal passions and proclivities for ascendancy and predominance over others. Indeed, that is the primary reason some people are in the ministry at all. It is a million times easier to gain authority over others through the agency of this purported "positional authority" than through the much more arduous and demanding means of "earned esteem," which, as I have already explained, is the premise for true ecclesiastical leadership prescribed by the Word of God. Many a new church has been started by individuals seeking to satisfy an inward obsession for ascendancy and predominance over others via the formation of a self-made, self-owned ecclesiastical kingdom in which they are the absolute, albeit self-conferred, monarch, having been unable to attain the status of superiority they crave through the legitimate means of earned and merited esteem.

What this ludicrous but nevertheless virtually universally accepted idea of "positional authority" has led to is the institution of a de facto ecclesiastical aristocracy, wherein there is predominance by a relative and minorative few belonging to a privileged class of elite "ministerial nobility." It differs only in degree of sophistication to the pecking order of the animal kingdom, and essentially amounts to a Christian caste system. Notwithstanding, this ecclesiastical aristocracy does indeed exist, it is real, functional, and effectual in the real, fleshly realm of mundane Christianity, despite the fact that it is the absolute antithesis of every tenet of the true Gospel of Christ. It is a time-honored traditional mindset that is deeply entrenched in the collective psyche of organized Christendom. Indeed, it is elemental to the exact same demonically-inspired religious sophistry which produced the papal system that emerged in the Medieval Church and precipitated its descent into apostasy.

Nevertheless, no matter how time-honored and how deeply entrenched, the whole notion of "positional authority" still has no basis whatsoever in God's Word, and thus is not valid. Scripture is so abundantly clear concerning the parity and coequality of the Brotherhood that it is hardly necessary to belabor the point with the citing of the superabundance of proof-passages. Just one will be sufficient to persuade the persuadable who are not contending against God. The one I cite is to me the weightiest passage of all—the admonition Jesus Himself spoke to His disciples, in His discourse of public censure and condemnation of the ultra-religious Pharisees for holding the very kind of ungodly religious attitudes of ascendancy over their fellows have been referring to: *"...all of you are on the SAME LEVEL, as brothers!"* (Mat. 23:8, Living Bible). Those who would argue that this verbiage is simply flawed and liberal paraphrasing of the original will be thoroughly saddened to know that it is quite consistent with the import of the original context.

As it is with every other segment of man's religious sophistry compared to the true Wisdom of God, so also is it in this regard: as high as the Heavens are above the Earth, so are God's Thoughts above our thoughts, and His Ways above our ways. God's Thinking and Ways regarding spiritual leadership is that it is a role of grave responsibility and stringent accountability to be carried out in an attitude of humble servitude. Eternally and irreconcilably juxtaposed against that is the thinking and way of human religious reasoning which prescribes ascendancy and predominance effectualized through "positional authority." On the one hand, God

101

portrays spiritual leadership as a *burden* of **responsibility** bearing *"a stricter judgment"* (Jas. 2:1), while on the other, religious men perceive it as a *benefactor* of **nobility** bearing greater privilege.

Conclusion

As we bring this Chapter to a close, it is my hope that reasonable, reasoning, impartial, and open-minded readers have found within this discussion ample justification for concurrence with the conclusion that the Discipleship/Shepherdship concept of authority is a conglomeration of error, excess, distortion of Truth, and outright deception, and that any similarity of that concept of authority to the concept inherent in Scripture is negligible.

Chapter Five

ERRONEOUS CONCEPT #2: "SPIRITUAL COVERING"

The second primary conceptual error on which the Discipleship/Shepherdship doctrines are established is the matter of "spiritual covering." This matter is a centerpiece of these heretical teachings, and will be the focus of this chapter.

Let me speak plainly and directly: "spiritual covering" as theorized by the Discipleship theosophy is an absolute myth. No semblance of the Discipleship teaching version of "spiritual covering" exists anywhere within the pages of Holy Writ. "Spiritual covering," in the vein that it is presented by Discipleship proponents, is an outright, unmitigated lie! It is a complete fabrication concocted by the originators of these fallacious doctrines by which to facilitate and perpetuate their purely self-aggrandizing objectives of subjugation, domination and control.

Indeed, what the Discipleship proponents refer to as "spiritual *covering*" is really "spiritual *control*." However, even the use of the word "spiritual" in this connection requires some qualification, because the only thing "spiritual" about this unauthorized control is that it is inspired by demon-*spirits* of deception and error. As we shall discuss later in Chapter Nine, what the Discipleship version of "spiritual covering" really is, is nothing less than **witchcraft** and **sorcery**. When the myth has been thoroughly debunked, as it will be within these pages, it will be clear that this doctrine of "spiritual covering," like all the other aspects of the Shepherdship heresy, is a patently false "doctrine of demons" being manifested in these last days precisely in accordance with Holy Prophecy of Scripture which foretells of deception such as this being promulgated by demons in the last days, leading to many falling away from the Lord into apostasy:

> *But the Spirit explicitly says that in later times some will fall away from the faith, paying attention to deceitful spirits and doctrines of demons, by means of the hypocrisy of LIARS seared in their own conscience as with a branding iron. (1 Tim. 4:1,2)*

Proofing the Proof-text

Discipleship proponents point to a particular Pauline dissertation found in the Eleventh Chapter of First Corinthians as the primary purported proof-text for their concept of "spiritual covering." It will soon be evident, however, that, as is typical of the other aspects of Discipleship errors, the assertions made on the basis of these verses are the product of blatant and overt perversion, distortion, misrepresentation, and misapplication of the true import and intent of the passage. The unfortunate effect of this corruption of Canon is essentially the same as that which inured unto the Galatians, which was that they became guilty of "deserting" Christ for a different "christ" and a different gospel:

> *I am amazed that you are so quickly deserting Him who called you by the grace of Christ; for a different gospel; which is really not another; only there are some who are disturbing you, and who want to DISTORT the gospel of Christ. (Gal. 1:6)*

The following is the passage from which the concept of "spiritual covering," as well as several other assertions made by Discipleship proponents, is interpolated. It will be a basis for much of what we discuss in this chapter, thus I have set it in verse-format for easier reference. Also, I have added some explanations appearing in italics and parentheses which will assist in understanding the true import of what is being said in these verses.

Erroneous Concept #2: "Spiritual Covering"

1 CORINTHIANS 11:2-16:

*2 Now I praise you because you remember me in everything, and hold firmly to **the traditions**, just as I delivered them to you.*

*3 But I want you to understand that Christ is the **Head** of every man, and the man* (husband) *is the **head** of a* (singular) *woman* (wife), *and God is the **Head** of Christ.*

4 Every MAN who has something on his Head (Christ) *while praying or prophesying, disgraces his Head* (Christ).

*5 But every woman who has her **head** uncovered* (not under the authority of her husband) *while praying or prophesying, disgraces her **head** (her husband); for she is one and the same with **her whose head is shaved*** (woman taken captive from vanquished enemies and forced against her will to become an Israelite's wife).

*6 For if a woman does not **cover her head*** (allow the authority of her husband to cover and protect her from the spiritual deception of the fallen angels), *let her also have her hair cut off; but if it is disgraceful for a woman to have her hair cut off or her head shaved, **let her cover her head**.*

*7 For a **man** ought **NOT** to have his head covered, since he is the image and glory of God; but the woman* (wife) *is the glory of man* (husband).

*8 For man does **not** originate from woman, but **woman from man**;*

9 for indeed man was not created for the woman's sake, but woman for the man's sake.

*10 Therefore the woman **ought to have authority on her head**, because of the* (fallen) *angels.*

11 However, in the Lord, neither is woman independent of man, nor is man independent of woman.

12 For as the woman originates from the man, so also the man has his birth through the woman; and all things originate from God.

*13 Judge for yourselves: is it proper for a woman to pray to God with **head uncovered**?*

*14 Does not even nature itself teach you that if a **man** has **long hair*** (type for "covering"), *it is a **dishonor** to him,*

*15 but if a **woman** has **long hair**, it is a **glory** to her? **For her hair is given to her for A COVERING** (a protection).*

*16 But if one is inclined to be **contentious**, we have **no other practice**, nor have the churches of God.*

Now I don't want to be crass or unkind, but in my opinion a person must have a doctorate in stupidity or be totally brainwashed to read this text and in all sincerity and earnestness conclude that it says what Discipleship proponents and adherents assert that it says. Indeed, this text has been used as a premise for a number of pretty silly and bizarre notions, ranging from the role of women in the church all the way to the assertion that God is saying here that women are supposed to wear little doilies on their heads when they attend church. So let's examine this passage, and see what it really says and what it does *not* say.

Pertinent Peculiarities of the Language

First of all, an extremely vital fact to keep in mind in all Bible study and interpretation, and one which I must take a moment to point out here at the very outset of our scrutiny of this text, is that the Greek language, in which most of the New Testament was written originally, did not have a specific word for "husband" and "wife" as in the English language. Instead, the word for husband is the word for "man," and the word for "wife" is the word for "woman." The only way to determine whether the reference is to the *male gender-class* or to the *office of husband*, or likewise to the *female gender-class* or the *office of wife*, is by deciphering the intent of the context. This fact is absolutely critical to the particular passage we are examining here and to properly evaluating and understanding its import.

So, with this in mind, careful scrutiny of the context of these verses on the backdrop of the whole of Scripture, leads to the unequivocal and incontrovertible conclusion that the words used here which are translated in many English versions as *"man"* and *"woman"* really should be *"husband"* and *"wife."* Validation of that is inherent in the fact that the principles evoked in this passage are limited in application to the husband and wife relationship. They are **NOT** applicable in the context of general interrelations between men and women, but rather only apply in the sphere of the husband and wife relationship.

Identifying the Subject and Scope

Once these peculiarities of the language are understood, the next matter of utmost importance is identifying the subject and scope of the passage we are examining. For reasons that shall become evident, it is vital to understand that the clear and unmistakable subject of this passage is the matter of *Domestic* Divine Order, that is to say, the order of authority existing among husbands and wives and their children, or to say it yet another way, the government operable within the structure of the **FAMILY** unit. "*Domestic* Authority" is the exclusive focus as well as the limits of the scope of this passage. The aspects and applications of the authority addressed in these verses are limited to the purview of that particular ilk of authority, and cannot be universally applied to any other type of authority.

Recognizing the true focus and scope of this text is crucial to comprehending its import. Not recognizing these parameters, or blatant disregard of them, whichever may be the case, has been a primary factor resulting in the formulation of the fallacious assertions adamantly proclaimed and staunchly defended by Discipleship proponents supposedly based on this passage. To be specific, the matter of "spiritual covering" is the heart of the issue. And, indeed, there is a type of spiritual covering that is addressed in these verses. However, what is critical is that, as stated already, the spiritual covering that is discussed in this context is **NOT** *Ecclesiastical* Authority, that is to say, Governmental Authority within the Church. Rather, *Domestic* Authority is the clear and unequivocal focus of Paul's dissertation here, which the Apostle makes evident in verse three by specifically identifying the topic of this portion of his letter and by expressing explicitly what it is he wants the readers to understand: *"But I want you to understand that **CHRIST** is the*

107

Head of every man, and the MAN (**HUSBAND**) *is the head of a WOMAN* (his **WIFE**), *and GOD is the Head of Christ.*"

Another way to characterize the focus of this passage, which the enbolded portions of this verse bring out, is: "spiritual headship." However, the propensity of some to *"exceed that which is written"* has resulted in the misconstruction and misapplication of this perfectly valid truth and the manufacturing of a kind of so-called "headship" based purely in human imagination without any Scriptural foundation whatsoever. In point of fact, the **only** valid ilk of "spiritual headship" or "spiritual covering" there is, and the only one which is supported by the Word of God, is that which is being addressed here, which is the "spiritual headship" and "spiritual covering" the **husband** provides for his own wife as the God-appointed representative of Christ within the family unit. In no way, however, does this passage contain any evidence or corroboration of the sort of "spiritual covering" Discipleship proponents allege is provided by a **shepherd** to his followers. To extrapolate from this passage a pretext for some sort of "headship" interposable by "spiritual leaders" over subordinate believers is an act of gross distortion, convolution, and misrepresentation of the Word of God, as well as an act of blatant and extreme irresponsibility.

CHRIST—the Only Spiritual Covering for Every Man

Now as I stated initially, Ecclesiastical Authority is decidedly *not* the focus of this passage. Indeed, the only mention of the matter of Ecclesiastical Authority occurs in oblique references in verses four and seven, which actually state the very opposite of what the Discipleship/Shepherdship proponents purport the verses say and the very opposite of the assertions they cite the verses as a proof-text for:

4 Every MAN who has something on his Head (Christ) while praying or prophesying, disgraces his Head (Christ).

Erroneous Concept #2: "Spiritual Covering"

7 For a man ought NOT to have his head covered, since he is the image and glory of God; but the woman (wife) *is* the glory of man (husband).

In verse four, Paul specifically states that, juxtaposed to the married *woman*, who must have a covering of spiritual authority, i.e., a spiritual "head," which role is fulfilled by her husband, any *man* who covers his Head with a "spiritual covering"—a human, surrogate, intermediary "head"—is bringing reproach, dishonor, and disgrace to his Head, because, as Paul indicates repeatedly in this text, the man's Head is Christ Himself. Thus, to characterize the import of the text in another, forthright fashion: in this passage, the Spirit is expressly prohibiting human, surrogate, intermediary spiritual "headship" in the case of **MEN**, in that Christ Himself is the Head, or "spiritual covering" *"of every man"* who is truly Born Again and has truly submitted to the Lordship of Christ over his life.

Notice also the phrase *"while praying or prophesying."* Praying and prophesying are the *spiritual* activities and functions in which believers are to engage. This phrase gives qualification to this statement, making its import to be that it is in the realm of **spiritual** activities and endeavors *in particular* that a *man* is **NOT** to have another human-being as his "head," or as a "covering," for that role and function is to be fulfilled by the Lord Jesus alone. Christ alone is qualified and capable of fulfilling that crucial role and function.

This is vital to the matter of the Discipleship error, because this has been one of the areas of greatest excess and abuse, in that many so-called "spiritual leaders" (especially laymen) in these in-house "chains of command" became extremely caught up in their newly acquired (albeit, illegitimate) authority, for which they were not properly grounded or adequately developed or sufficiently mature spiritually to properly handle, but which they nonetheless began to wield and intrusively interpose into the lives of their "subordinates," including their most private, personal, and even intimate choices and decisions. The outlandish and totally false hypothesis was that each of the multi-levels of "spiritual leaders" over the peonic, subjugated, and supposedly inferior believer were his "spiritual heads" and "spiritual coverings," and whatever communication or correction God desired to relate to the believer, He would relay through one of these surrogate "heads," and so-called "confirmation" of the validity and veracity of the communication would manifest in the form of unanimous "agreement" among all these "heads." Theoretically, if just one of the "heads" in the chain of "heads" did not have "a witness" for the matter, that meant the communication was not from or of God.

This "no witness" poppycock became a primary mechanism of control, manipulation, domination, and other more nefarious activities, in an array of circumstances ranging from preventing members leaving the church or group, to sexually-oriented abuse under the color of spiritual authority. The gravely damaging effect of this absurd and wholly false theosophy and system of religious enslavement is well captured in the quoted impassioned complaint of a former member of the Discipleship Movement responding to Bob Mumford's attempted conciliation with disjoined former followers:

> "Saying I'm sorry wasn't enough....**We had been taught that the men who led us somehow heard from God better than we did.** Even after we left the movement there was that hidden fear that they might be right and we were somehow less of a Christian and had failed God by not being **totally obedient** to them." (*Mumford Repents of Discipleship Errors*, Charisma & Life, February 1990, pp. 15,16)

Though we are certainly to avail ourselves of the ministry God disseminates through Five-fold ministers, and though we are to maintain a compliant and cooperative attitude toward them, and treat them with due honor and respect, no mere human is ever the "head" or "spiritual covering" of **any** other man, especially; **or woman**, for that matter, because "spiritual covering" exists and is effectual **only** in the relationship of the husband to **his own**

WIFE—no other woman. In other words, even a Five-fold minister—apostle, prophet, evangelist, pastor, teacher—is the spiritual "head" of **only ONE** *woman* on this planet—**his own WIFE** (if he is married)! That, my friend, is it! **FURTHER-MORE,** a Five-fold minister is the spiritual "head" of **absolutely** *NO MAN*! I cannot state it any more succinctly or directly than that.

Spiritual Mediators

The premise of absolute submission is predicated on the hypothesis that the spiritual leaders are in effect (though most Discipleship teaching adherents would emphatically deny the attribution) "spiritual mediators" between God and their followers, who assume the role of hearing from God on the behalf of their followers. According to the premise, the followers are spiritually deficient and inferior to the leaders, and thus basically incapable of seeking and hearing from God for themselves and cultivating on-going communion and fellowship with God, so they need a "mediator," someone who supposedly has a more elite status with God, to be a priestly "go-between" between them and God. The hypothesis is that the leaders are much more spiritual than the people, and therefore more capable of receiving from God what is best for their followers. By the way, if that premise sounds familiar to you, you are right, because in essence it is virtually identical to the theories upon which the surrogate priesthood and papal system of Catholicism were based, which, totally supplanted and negated the personal priesthood of believers in the Medieval Church.

This whole matter of "spiritual mediators" is so totally ludicrous and such a complete affront to the truth of the personal priesthood of believers that every knowledgeable believer should be thoroughly disgusted and totally outraged at such an idiotic, outlandish, and even blasphemous notion. The Bible explicitly says: *"There is one God, and ONE mediator also between God and men, the man*

Christ Jesus, who gave Himself as a ransom for all...." (1 Tim. 2:5). There is never, ever to be any "spiritual mediators" between God and men, except the Christ—Jesus Himself. The Man with the nail-prints in His hands is the only true spiritual mediator between God and Man. All the rest are pretentious impostors! Jesus is the only Man who ever lived a perfectly sinless life, which was the requisite enabling Him to become the Spotless Lamb of God, the propitiatory sacrifice, typified by the oblational sacrificial lambs, which the Jewish high priests offered up for the sins of the people century after century.

So also was Jesus the true Spiritual High Priest, who those centuries of natural high priests who offered up the sacrificial lambs year after year represented. Those which came before Him were the types and the shadows, the mere "eikons" (reflections) of the real. Jesus was the real, the source of the reflection. He **was** the Image that the types and shadows reflected. He was the true Sacrificial Lamb who took away the sins of the world. And, He was the true Spiritual High Priest (Heb. 3:1), who offered up the true Sacrificial Lamb—His own sinless life—as a ransom for all, once and for all.

> *And the former priests, on the one hand, existed in greater numbers, because they were prevented by death from continuing, but He, on the other hand, because He abides forever, holds His priesthood permanently. Hence, also, He is able to save completely those who draw near to God through Him, since He always lives to make intercession for them. For it was fitting that we should have such a **High Priest**, holy, innocent, undefiled, separated from sinners and exalted above the heavens; who does not need daily, like those high priests, to offer up sacrifices, first for his own sins, and then for the sins of the people, because this He did ONCE FOR ALL when He offered HIMSELF. (Heb. 7:23-28)*
>
> *...we have such a **High Priest**, who has taken His seat at the right hand of the throne of the Majesty in the heavens, a Minister in*

the sanctuary, and in the true tabernacle, which the Lord pitched, not man. (Heb. 8:1,2)

> *But when **CHRIST** appeared as a **High Priest** of the good things to come, He entered through the greater and more perfect tabernacle, not made with hands, that is to say, not of this creation; and not through the blood of goats and calves, but through His own blood, He entered the holy place once for all, having obtained eternal redemption. (Heb. 9:11,12)*

The point is that the true High Priest has now entered into the true Holy of Holies into the actual presence of God as the ultimate and only effectual Mediator on our behalf (Heb. 9:23,24). He lives evermore in the presence of God as our Intercessor (Heb. 7:25), having appeased His righteous wrath, having taken upon Himself the punishment due us, and having cancelled out our debt of transgressions which separated and disfellowshipped us from God. Hence, since Christ Jesus has accomplished the ultimate on our behalf before God, and perpetually lives in the presence of God as our spiritual High Priest and Intercessor, and since He has made peace for us between ourselves and God forevermore (Rom. 5:1), we hardly need human mediators between us and God.

His once-and-for-all sacrifice and entrance into the true Holy of Holies has granted us all equal access, free access, bold and confident access (Eph. 3:12), not only into the Holy Place, but also even behind the veil into the Holy of Holies, for each of us, even unto the very Throne of Grace itself, that is to say, the very Throne of *"the God of all Grace"* (1 Pet. 5:10). Of this access we are invited to avail ourselves freely, not coweringly but boldly, *"Let us therefore come **boldly** unto the throne of grace that we may obtain mercy, and find grace to help in time of need"* (Heb. 4:16, KJV).

To suggest that any human could do this for us as a mediator between us and God is not only preposterous and absurd, but also an affront to Jesus Himself. It is blasphemy! Those who pose and interpose themselves as mediators between believers and God are

113

fortunate that God has not struck them down dead! Indeed, I believe this very thing will happen in the days ahead. God is now issuing fair warning! If Uzza, the loyal friend and servant of David was struck dead by God for merely touching the religious icon of God's presence, and if Ananias and Sapphira were struck down dead by God for having lied to the Holy Spirit, how much severer punishment would one deserve who is so blatantly blasphemous as to purport to be the spiritual mediator between God and men?

I plead with all those who are engaging in such antichrist blasphemy against the Son of God to repent, **NOW**, while God's grace and mercy are still extended to you! Do not mock this warning! I prophesy that in the coming days, many who continue to spurn and disregard God's warnings in this regard will suddenly fall dead in judgment from God, leaving behind a legacy of unfulfilled aspirations, consternation, mourning, and woe!

A Traditional Precept

It is evident from the initial verse of this dissertation, that the Apostle Paul was not presenting any new concepts therein, but rather was only reaffirming *"the traditions"* (v. 2) which he had already delivered unto the Corinthian church as well as to all the other churches to which he had ministered. Indeed, he commended the Corinthian believers for *"hold(ing) firmly to the traditions, just as* **(HE)** *delivered them to (them)."*

During the span of his ministry, Paul was the premier apostle, the primary spokesman on behalf of God, to the Gentile Church. In that capacity, he reaffirmed and reestablished in the New Testament churches those elements of the Jewish traditional teachings which were appropriate and applicable in the New Testament Age. Some of the practices which had come to be part of the Jewish religious traditions were purely the concoctions of men, and never the explicit or even implicit intents of the Lord. (Someone once observed that though God gave only *ten* commandments through

Moses, by the time Jesus came, the various sects of priests required observance of some *ten-thousand* ceremonial and ritualistic *"commandments of men"* [Mk. 7:6-8].)

However, in the case of the spiritual government, protection, and leadership that the husband was responsible to provide for his wife and family, and the role of government and leadership men were to fulfill in Jewish society, as well as the proper role of women in these respects, this was one portion of Jewish tradition which indeed was congruous with Divine intent, and had not been denigrated or abrogated over the centuries. And, in this portion of his lengthy letter of instruction and reproof to the Corinthians, the Apostle Paul was reaffirming and reminding them that he had delivered this precept as one that was valid under the New Covenant and was to be practiced in the New Testament Church, which he explicitly expresses in the sixteenth verse: *"...we have no other practice, nor have the churches of God."*

Jewish tradition always rightly held that the husband was the human spiritual *head*, or *government*, or *covering*, over his wife. This time-honored traditional precept was predicated on the order of Domestic Authority God had established within the first family unit of the Holy Race (Adam and Eve) subsequent to and as the consequence of their fall into apostasy, which was the direct result of the spiritual beguilement of the woman by the arch-fallen-angel, Satan.

The Weakness of the Woman

You see, despite the preponderance of boisterous protestations and brazen professions being flaunted far and wide by the feminists and homosexuals bent on establishing a gynocentric society and deifying the female gender, and despite the pseudo-Christian, Jezebel-spirited feminists within the Church lobbying for gender-egalitarianism as a precursor to obtaining more and more authority and dominion, God did **NOT** create the genders with natural equality (albeit, He did create them with parity in terms of their status and standing with Him). Rather, the fact of the matter is that God created the female gender of human-being "**WEAKER**" than the male gender (1 Pet. 3:7). (No amount of protestations or professions to the contrary will ever change that! So, rage on, dear hearts!) Not only was the female gender created *"weaker"* than the male *physically*, but also *psychologically* (a scientifically proven physiological fact on both counts). Not only that, but, despite the fact that there is a higher rate of involvement among women in religion than men, in succumbing to the seductions and deception of Satan in the Garden of Eden, becoming *"quite deceived"* (1 Tim. 2:14), Eve openly demonstrated that the woman also was the "weaker" gender *spiritually*.

On this last statement, I can almost hear the uproarious and resounding retort of unrepentant, worldly-minded feminists charading as Christians: "But, the Bible says that in Christ Jesus there is neither male nor female!"

Of course the Bible says that—I know, because I have read it a few hundred times! And, believe me, it means precisely what it says: that **IN CHRIST JESUS**—that is, in the glorified **Spiritual** state that awaits us beyond this present estate of natural humanness, wherein we have received our **FULL** redemption (Rom. 8:23), which is the redemption of our bodies (when the sin nature has been expurgated from our being), in that estate—there is no gender differentiations.

But, we have not yet attained unto that perfected spiritual estate. Though our human spirits are Born Again (Jn. 3:6) by virtue of being filled with the Holy Spirit, we still live out our lives in the natural realm, as *natural* beings. We have not yet been transformed into *spiritual* beings. Our souls and bodies have not yet been fully sanctified and permeated with the Holy Spirit. That will transpire when we are changed in the *"day of redemption"* (Eph. 4:30). Now, in this age, we have been given the Holy Spirit to reside *in* our spirits, charging our spirits with the *Life* of God, and *upon* us, granting us a minor measure of the *Power* of God as a "down-payment," an "earnest pledge," which serves as a "security deposit," of what we *shall* receive when the Spirit fully pervades the part of our being which presently is not fully sanctified (2 Cor. 1:22, 5:5; Eph. 1:14; 1 Thes. 5:23,24). When that happens, we shall truly come into that estate in which we are *"in Christ"* (2 Cor. 5:17); and, we will have been literally *"transformed"* (1 Cor. 15:50-53) into a *"new"* and different *"creature"* in which truly **ALL** *"the old things are passed away"* and *"new things have come"* (2 Cor. 5:17). Then, we shall have been *"transfigured"* into *"a different form"* as was Jesus on the Mount of Transfiguration (Mat. 17:1,2). Moreover, we shall have then entered permanently into that resurrected estate Jesus had entered when He appeared unto the two disciples on the Road to Emmaeus (Mk. 16:12), unto the one hundred and twenty in the upperroom, and unto *"more than five hundred at one time"* (1 Cor. 15:6) after His resurrection.

This state of perfection in Christ—the state to which the Apostle Paul referred when he said: *"when THE PERFECT comes"* (1 Cor. 13:10)—has not yet come. That is why, as Paul explained, we only *"prophesy in part"* and *"know in part"* now, in this current dispensation (1 Cor. 13:9,12)—for we have not yet received the fullness of the Spirit and the accompanying *"powers of the age to come"* (Heb. 6:5) in their fullness and perfection.

Until this state of perfection— *"the perfect"*—does come, we are living in a condition called, "Born Again believer," or "Son-ship." We have been adopted into the Family of God, we are Sons of God, God is our Father, but we have not yet received our *full* inheritance; only a portion of it. Collectively, we are God's "Be-trothed," we are "engaged" to Him, but we have not yet been married to Him. That will take place at the Marriage Supper of the Lamb, which shall transpire at the end of this age when Jesus returns to claim His betrothed Church to be His Eternal Bride. This engagement period we are now in is a "waiting period" of sorts, a proving time, in which we are given the opportunity to prove that we are truly committed to eternal union with our Fianceé'-Husband, if we are truly willing to become His wife, to become subservient to Him, to become His faithful and dedicated "helpmate," to be totally submissive and obedient to His authority—"*the authority of Christ*" (Rev. 12:10)—as our Head.

Until "*the perfect*" comes, and we are transformed out of this estate we are now in, in which we are "*IN the world, but not OF the world,*" in which we *are* saved (our Spirit *only* [Jn. 3:6]), are *being* saved (our soul [Jas. 1:21]), and *will be* saved (our body [Rom. 8:23]), this state in which we have been Born Again spiritually but still live in the natural realm, until then, we still abide in this human estate in which God created huMANs—"*male and female*" (Gen. 1:27). When we are transformed out of this human form, and the mortal puts on immortality, and the perishable puts on imperishability (1 Cor. 15:53), at the last trumpet of God—then shall we be fully "*in Christ Jesus,*" and then shall we have come to be as the angels, who neither marry nor are given in marriage (Lk. 20:34-36), for they are genderless.

Until then, while we yet abide in the human state, as the more astute observers will recognize—there *are* men, there *are* women, the gender-classes *are* extant, and there *are* differences in those genders. The woman is still the "weaker" gender, physically (body), psychologically (soul; i.e., mind, will, emotions), and spiritually (spirit), whether **in** Christ (i.e., saved) or **out** of Christ (i.e., unsaved). This natural estate God has created is a fixed and immutable condition in this dispensation—"*until the perfect comes.*" No matter how "saved" and "sanctified" and "spiritual" a woman becomes, no woman will ever "spiritualize" her way out of the female gender-class God created her in, nor override the God-created attributes of that gender, as so many "super-spiritual" women seem to think they can or have. Until we are all "*changed*"

Erroneous Concept #2: "Spiritual Covering"

(1 Cor. 15:52) at the last trumpet of God, even the most "spiritual" of believers will continue to abide in the human-state and particular gender-class of our natural nativity in which God created us.

Until then, the woman, because God created her the "weaker" of the two genders, will continue to need the spiritual covering, protection, and leadership (government) of her husband, who is of the male gender, which gender, our text states, was created to be *"the Image"* (Greek, *"eikon"* = "reflection") **and** *"the glory"* (Greek, *"doxa"* = visible **man**ifestation in the natural realm) of God; whereas the woman was *not* created to be the glory of **God**, but to be the glory of her **husband** (1 Cor.10:7, literal meaning).

The Purpose of the Covering

Subsequent to and as a result of the fall, which was the result of Eve being *"quite deceived"* spiritually and falling into transgression (1 Tim. 2:14), God placed an intense desire in the woman, to be covered and protected and led by her husband, saying: *"...your desire shall be for your husband, and he shall rule over you"* (Gen. 3:16). The word translated *"rule"* here means to govern. As a protection from spiritual attack, deception, and further transgression, God assigned the husband the role of providing government (covering) to his wife, to be her intermediate and human governor, or *"head,"* under Christ.

Verse ten explains that the woman's need for this protection is: *"because of the ANGELS."* Now although some expositors have confounded the import of this verse, it is really very simple. It is referring to the spiritual assailment perpetrated by the fallen angels (demons), especially in the form of spiritual deception, to which the "weaker" female gender has an inherent vulnerability and proclivity, as Eve vividly demonstrated with her verboten conversation she engaged in with the arch-fallen-angel, Satan, which resulted ultimately in the most dire consequence of her spiritual beguilement—the apostatization of the Holy Race.

Though many people fail to assimilate it, the plain fact is that it was **SPIRITUALLY** that Eve was deceived. She was deceived by a **SPIRIT**—the devil, who seduced her into rebellion by means of a conversation in which she should not have engaged in the first place. Moreover, it was not with regard to some benign, unessential non-spiritual matter that Eve was deceived, but rather she was deceived with regard to the two most fundamental spiritual issues of all: 1) the choice between Eternal Life of God (Tree of Life) versus Eternal Death of Satan (Tree of the Knowledge of Good and Evil); and, 2) the veracity, integrity, and authority of God and His Word; i.e., is God God, and is His Word the ultimate, sovereign authority?

Thus, because it was *spiritually* that the woman was deceived, it is the *spiritual* realm in particular in which the woman needs protection. Hence, it is preeminently to protect the woman from *spiritual* attack and *spiritual* deception that God established the husband as the "*spiritual* covering" or "*spiritual* governor" over the woman, under the ultimate Headship of Christ. And, God has placed within the psyche (soul) of the woman an inherent intense desire—what the Amplified Bible goes so far as to call a *"craving"*—for this government and leadership and protection by her husband.

Paraphrased, the true thrust of what God was saying to Eve as the progenitor of the female gender of the Holy Race and to every woman who would descend from her in perpetuam in this regard in Genesis 3:16 was: "Eve, because of the vulnerability to the spiritual attack of the fallen angels which you demonstrated (in this exchange you just had with Satan) is inherent to your gender, in order to protect you and your genus-posterity from further deception and attack from the fallen angels—from this day forward....I have placed within your psychological make-up an intense yearning for your God-appointed husband and for his government, leadership, and protection over you, and a consuming desire to wholly dedicate

120

yourself and your life to serving him as his select and suitable helpmate."

I believe God did indeed somehow imprint this consuming desire upon the tablet of the woman's psyche, or psychological constitution, and every woman realizes her greatest peace, joy, contentment, and satisfaction when this dedication to her husband is her pursuit. Conversely, it is when women rebel against this God-ordained innate foundational *"desire"* that they become discontented, malcontented, and miserable, and enter into various types and degrees of diversive and dissatisfying pursuits and deviant and demeaning behavior. But, when a woman becomes truly saved, and wholly surrendered to the lordship of Christ, as well as to the intermediate lordship of her husband under Christ, it is therein that she discovers and realizes optimum ecstasy and satiation.

What so many women, today especially, need to be reminded of is the foundational Truth delineated in verses eight and nine of our text: *"man does not originate from woman, but woman from man; for indeed man was not created for the woman's sake, but woman for the man's sake."* God created the man **FIRST**, and fashioned the woman out of the riven side of the man to make her a *"help-mate suitable"* (Gen. 2:20) unto the man. This gynocentric (woman-centered) society that these ungodly, perverse, lesbian-spirited, demon-possessed, authority-craving feminists are hell-bent on forcing upon the world, is the ultimate inversion and perversion of the entire order that God created for humanity. Like it or not, the world is **NOT** supposed to revolve around the woman, as it does today, the evidence of which is conspicuously manifest in the themes and images ubiquitously emblazoned across our television screens and pages of the deluge of print media inundating us at every turn, in which the female gender is exalted to the status of goddess and the female form is worshipped and glorified as divine. On the contrary, women were created by God to be *"helpmates suitable"* to their husbands—dedicated companions and collaborators, committed to co-laboring with their mate toward the accomplishment of their God-given task and assignment: to subdue the earth and rule over it and everything on it (Gen. 1:26-28).

Women (and men) who truly and earnestly desire to be fully aligned—in thought, word, and deed—with God and His Word, Will, and Way, must, in this gynocentric age in which gender-independence is promoted and gender-enmity prevails, see to it that they give special attention and heed to what God said through this First Century apostle and prophet who scribed our text, which remains every bit as true, valid, and apropos today as it did then—that: *"IN THE LORD, neither is woman independent of man, nor is man independent of woman."* God did not create the two genders of male and female of which the human race consists to be contentious rivals and mortal enemies of one another. In a time when racial hatred, or what I call *"ethnic-enmity,"* is pervading and threatening to consume humanity, we need also to recognize the *"gender-enmity"* that has been expanding as a consequence of the feminist movement, originally, and which now is being further fueled by the homosexual movement. It is conceivable that *gender*-enmity could ultimately produce an equally adverse end-result as *ethnic*-enmity. My personal conviction is that Satan sees wholesale gender-enmity and homosexuality as his ultimate weapon in his age-long warfare against God which he continues to wage on the battlefield of human procreation. His intent in further expanding both of these demonic behaviors, along with continuance of the vile atrocity of abortion en masse, is to inhibit and cause as much cessation of human procreation as possible.

Now before we go on, let me make one final comment concerning all that has been said here with regard to women, not to in any way mitigate, ameliorate, or appease, but to simply clarify. These are not the words of a woman-hater, nor the condescending words of a chauvinist, but rather they are echoes of the Words of the Creator. All this was **His** idea, not mine. I'm merely God's reporter, reporting what He has said in His Word. If this rubs the cat the wrong way, as surely it will many, the cat needs to turn around! Which is another way of saying, repent—from all your worldly thinking, casting down vain imaginations and mere speculations and lofty human sophistry raised up against the knowledge of God, and subjugating every thought unto the obedience of Christ (2 Cor. 10:5)! When you do, the grinding, odious, discordant, and resonating, sounds of these words will suddenly become sweet, harmonious, melodious music to your ears.

Basis for Authoritarian Abuse and Licentiousness

Again, I must emphasize that the subject of this passage clearly is **NOT** *Governmental* Authority in the Church. The dissertation is directed specifically to the matter of *Domestic* authority; that is, authority in the family unit. That is made evident in verse three, where the Apostle says: *"But I want you to understand that Christ is **the Head** of every man, and the man is **the head** of a woman, and God is **the Head** of Christ."* As I have already pointed out, another way to characterize the subject of this passage, which the highlighted portions bring out, is: *spiritual* "headship." However, the spiritual headship that is being discussed here, contrary to the assertions made by many, is **not** some sort of "universal" ascendancy, in practice and attitude, of men over women; nor does it speak to any ilk of governmental Authority within the "ranks" of the Church. Rather, the exclusive focus of this passage is "*Domestic* Authority," which is the order of authority within the **FAMILY** structure, in human households. And in the household, within the structure of the family unit, there is only **one** head—the husband; not some "spiritual" leader; not *any* other person. The husband is the unequivocal head in *his* **OWN** house, and not in any other.

Moreover, the misinterpretation and misapplication of the import of this passage to the specter of general interrelations between men and women itself is the basis for one aspect of error inherent in the Discipleship doctrines that is of no small consequence. Specifically, the more radical Discipleship proponents have interpolated these verses to mean that *all* women, married or unmarried, are supposed to be "submitted" and subservient to *all* men, and especially to the "spiritual leaders" of their church or group. Furthermore, they contend Scripture prescribes that the purview of authority of the spiritual leaders of a church extends also into the home, and takes precedence over the authority of the husband in the family unit. It is this totally false assertion that is a common basis for much authoritarian abuse that is taking place right now in the Ninety's in many more church-groups than what most people would ever imagine—most of it, at the time of this writing, yet to be exposed to the light of public knowledge.

For many years, I have known by the revelation of the Spirit that there are at least *scores* of cases in which these doctrines of demons are being used as a pretext and license for authoritarian abuse involving just about every kind of illicit and immoral sexual involvement by compulsion and seduction under the color of clerical authority possible. I predict that very soon God is going to see to it that the unwitting and confused victims of these heinous atrocities are liberated from their captivity, and that the perverted perpetrators of these despicable crimes and irresponsible violations of trust are publicly exposed, expelled from the ministry, prosecuted, and duly punished for their deliberate debauchery and violation against the lives and consciences of their exploited victims. Jesus said that it would be better for such perverted heretics who misuse the trust of their clerical office for such immoral exploitation that a millstone be tied around their neck and they be cast into the sea to drown, than undergo the Divine punishment that awaits them for having caused one of His little ones who had believed in Him to be so violated by such authoritarian abuse.

In the past few months as I have been writing these words, a tempest of this ilk is brewing in what had been a mega-church in

Erroneous Concept #2: "Spiritual Covering"

Atlanta, Georgia, involving a number of the top leaders of that church. When I first heard the accounts, I was not at all surprised, because some five years earlier, at a minister's conference I attended, the senior leader of this church was the keynote speaker. While he was speaking, I discerned a spirit of perversion upon him, that was manifesting in numerous areas of his life and ministry. Immediately I recognized his teachings and beliefs were perverted. But, it was the authoritarian abuse involving sexual immorality I saw clearly by the Spirit that shocked me the most. And I simply knew within my spirit that, though at the time this man was highly regarded by some ministers and was experiencing extensive "success" in building a "network" of affiliated churches who considered him their "bishop," within a relatively short period of time he was going to be exposed and would "fall from grace." What I saw in the Spirit upon him was recently confirmed in a Christian magazine article (February, 1993) in which it was revealed that back in 1960, this man was defrocked and expelled from his denomination based on charges of immorality. The article was reporting about a public scandal that had erupted in which several female staffers had charged this man and his brother, an associate pastor, with authoritarian abuse involving sexual immorality. It is unfortunate that over the course of thirty-three years since the original exposure of his problem, this man apparently never received the deliverance he needed from the evil spirits of perversion vexing him.

Of course, there have been numerous other cases of well-known television evangelists of late being exposed for having been involved in immorality and various abuses and misuses. It is all so very sad, and does indeed cast a long and ominous shadow of reproach upon the vocation of the ministry itself, in a day when more than ever before multitudes desperately need the real help that only Jesus can give and which is being offered through his true and faithful ministers. But, the most unfortunate thing is that there are still more of these kinds of revelations and scandals yet to come.

Moreover, in the process of time, it is going to become very apparent that the specter of authoritarian abuse and licentiousness perpetrated by wayward spiritual leaders is far more prevalent than what has ever been recognized before. Likewise, it will become just as manifest that the subject matter of this book—the heretical Discipleship doctrines, which are concerned primarily with false and fallacious concepts of spiritual authority—has been a primary underlying premise for much of the authoritarian abuse that has taken place among Charismatic/Discipleship churches and groups especially.

The root-cause of the Discipleship heresy is the *"spirit of error"* (1 Jn. 4:6), which is a spirit of perversion, and the "spirit of error," unchecked, will eventually lead to a multiplicity of perversions in virtually every facet of the person's life in which this demon and its cohorts are manifest. In the process of time this spirit will manifest perversion, corruption, and convolution in the inhabitee's spirituality and every aspect and attitude indigenous to their natural life: their morality, marriage, ministry, message, methods, motives, and monetary matters.

In respect to this type of authoritarian abuse, one thing that needs to be pointed out, however, is that it is not just individuals who have been victimized by this spiritually lethal perverse spirit, but so also has the collective Body of Christ, in that Satan has been sowing these weeds of heresy and tares of heretics in God's Field, thereby polluting and severely denigrating its produce, which was precisely his objective.

Erroneous Concept #2: "Spiritual Covering"

Personal Shepherdship

The adulterated concept of "spiritual covering" itself is problematic enough. Yet, its negative effect is increased by the fact that it is the predicate for several other, related elements of error comprising the heretical Discipleship/Shepherdship doctrines and practices, one of which is the matter of "personal shepherdship." Indeed, this element has been the basis for at least as much excess, errancy, and authoritarian abuse as the others already discussed. To those who employ these practices for sordid purposes or with less than pure motives, the perverted concept of "spiritual covering" is sanction for a most insidious kind of unauthorized personal domination and control of their subjects under the auspices of this very delusive and destructive version of "personal shepherding."

As with most other elements of error with these and other false doctrines, this particular component is the result of perversion and adulterization of a valid Truth. The essence of the erroneous concept of "personal shepherding" is that because the spiritual leader, along with the entire chain of leaders emanating from him, provides and in effect *is* the "spiritual covering" for his followers (which we have already shown to be a false hypothesis), the leader has not only the right, but also the duty to interlope into the private and personal affairs of the lives of the members of the group. In essence, the leader becomes the equivalent of tribal chief to the group, whose final approval members of the tribe must have for most every important transaction and decision in their lives, with some variability depending on the particular group and leader. In many cases, members must receive authorization from the leadership for the most mundane matters in their lives, including financial matters and purchasing decisions, matters of career and employment, housing, family, friends, social and educational matters, and just about every segment of the members' lives.

Now, of course there is a very valid role of shepherdship that Five-fold Shepherds (and all Five-fold ministers are under-shep-

127

herds, not just pastors) are indeed ordained by the Lord to fulfill on behalf of the Chief Shepherd (1 Pet. 5:4), Jesus. Indeed, Chapter Eight is wholly devoted to delineating the rightful role of Five-fold ministers as elucidated by the Word of God to the extent that it relates to the errors of the Discipleship teachings. The meaning of the word "shepherd" is to feed and care for, to lead and to guide, and that is the crux of what Five-fold shepherds are to provide on behalf of Christ unto the sheep of God's Fold.

As I have repeatedly indicated in various ways, what is involved in the case of the Discipleship/Shepherdship teaching and practices, unfortunately, is a bastardization of the shepherding principle. And, the core of that corruption is that adherents of this teaching *"exceed what is written"* by trying to impose their leadership authority and responsibility in the *natural* realm rather than limiting it to the *spiritual* realm.

It is absolutely vital for every minister to understand that the context and sphere of his shepherding is limited primarily to the spiritual. While Five-fold ministers may occasionally be able to proffer some inspired or experiential counsel and advice even regarding natural matters, their foremost calling and enablement is to feed, care for, lead, and guide the sheep of God's Flock spiritually and in relation to spiritual matters, not so much natural affairs. We are charged by God with the responsibility to feed His sheep spiritual food, to care for them with the spiritual wherewithal of the Holy Spirit, to lead them unto the one and only true Rock of their Salvation and Provider, Jesus, and after the pattern given us by the Chief Shepherd (Ps. 23) we are to guide them *"in the paths of righteousness,"* which is, the Way, Truth, and Life of Jesus.

When a minister routinely goes beyond the God-set, albeit, invisible, boundaries of his calling and purview of authority, which is the limitation of the *spiritual* realm primarily, and habitually interlopes into the *natural, physical* realm, interposing his own will in the ordinary private matters of his followers' lives, he is engaging in unsanctioned usurpation and illegitimate authority. In the process, he also leaves behind his legitimate duties, responsibilities, and sanctioning from God as an under-shepherd, as well as his effectuality. To take it a step further, a minister who engages in this sort of imposition and usurpation has essentially taken on the role, totally illegitimately, of the husband/father/head of those households and families over which he has imposed his authority; for, as the Scripture delineating true "spiritual covering" (1 Cor. 11:3-16) indicates, the role of headship (i.e., government or leadership) of a household or family in the natural, has been assigned by God to the husband/father of that house.

Another term for this illegitimate interloping and usurpation into another man's domain of authority is—"spiritual adultery."

Spiritual Adultery

Now to some this attribution will seem to be overkill and a bit melodramatic. Yet, in light of Scripture, it is neither. This is precisely what leaders who engage in these practices are engaging in—spiritual adultery. Allow me to explain.

God said the head of **every** woman is her husband, and every woman, at least every *Born Again* woman, has a husband, even those who are widowed, divorced, or never-married. Born Again women who for whatever reason do not have a physical husband with whom they are living are joined to and one with the Ultimate Husband—Jesus Himself (1 Cor. 6:17), the effectuality and efficacy of which fact is determined by the degree of each unmarried woman's receptivity and faith in that fact. When a person other than the legitimate husband/head of a house invades the sanctity of that household by illegitimately interposing his own will and authority upon the woman of that house, that constitutes spiritual adultery. No person, man or woman, including ministers, is authorized to intrude into a household in this fashion.

129

It is with regard to this very sort of illegitimate authoritarian "home-invasion" that one particular New Testament passage alludes and admonishes with especial attribution to the "last days" in which we are now living:

> But realize this, that *in the last days* there will set in perilous times of great stress and trouble—hard to deal with and hard to bear. For people will be *lovers of self and [utterly] self- centered*, lovers of money and aroused by an inordinate (greedy) desire for wealth, proud and arrogant and contemptuous boasters. They will be *abusive* (blasphemous, scoffers), disobedient to parents, ungrateful, unholy and profane. [They will be] treacherous (betrayers), rash [and] *inflated with self-conceit*. *[They will be] lovers of sensual pleasures and vain amusements more than and rather than lovers of God.* For [although] they hold a form of piety (true religion), they deny and reject and are strangers to the power of it—their conduct belies the genuineness of their profession. *AVOID [ALL] SUCH PEOPLE— TURN AWAY FROM THEM. FOR AMONG THEM ARE THOSE WHO <u>WORM THEIR WAY INTO HOMES</u> AND CAPTIVATE SILLY AND WEAK-NATURED AND SPIRITU- ALLY DWARFED WOMEN, LOADED DOWN WITH [THE BURDEN OF THEIR] SINS, [AND EASILY] SWAYED AND LED AWAY BY VARIOUS EVIL DESIRES AND SEDUCTIVE IMPULSES.* [These weak women will listen to anybody who will teach them]; they are forever inquiring and getting information, but are never able to arrive at a recognition and knowledge of the Truth. Now just as Jannes and Jambres were hostile to and resisted Moses, so *THESE MEN ALSO ARE HOSTILE TO AND OPPOSE THE TRUTH. THEY HAVE DEPRAVED AND DISTORTED MINDS, AND ARE REPROBATE AND COUNTERFEIT AND TO BE REJECTED AS FAR AS THE FAITH IS CONCERNED....BUT THEY WILL NOT GET VERY FAR, FOR THEIR RASH FOLLY WILL BECOME OBVIOUS TO EVERYBODY,* as was that of those [magicians mentioned]. (2 Tim. 3:1-9, A.B.)

Erroneous Concept #2: "Spiritual Covering"

I have alluded already to the fact that these false concepts of "spiritual covering" mixed with the "absolute submission" concept makes for an extremely poisonous and potentially lethal rue, which almost invariable eventuates into various forms of authoritarian abuse that frequently entails some kind of illicit sexual exploitation. This, of course, by Bible-definition, is physical fornication and *sexual* adultery, which obviously is utterly sinful and damning, not to mention the horrendous natural and spiritual consequences such abominable abuse and exploitation engender. Nevertheless, though it may be hard to imagine, the fact is that in these situations where leaders illegitimately interlope into the private affairs of their followers, usurping the role of the husband, even in those cases in which no physical fornication and *sexual* adultery have yet occurred, the "*spiritual* adultery" that has been committed is even more heinous and abominable and will produce even graver consequences, both spiritually and in the natural. The reason spiritual adultery of this nature is such a grievous offense to God is that it is **His** authority, albeit, intermediated in the case of the married woman by a human husband, that is being usurped. The true spiritual Husband is Christ, and it is His betrothed that is being assailed when one of His sheep is abused and exploited. Thus, spiritual adultery carries with it an even greater judgment than sexual adultery.

Spiritual Idolatry

Abhorrent as it is, that these Discipleship/Shepherdship doctrines and practices constitute spiritual adultery, there is yet another offense they abet which in terms of gravity may even surpass spiritual adultery. In addition to spiritual adultery, adherents and practitioners of this false theosophy are also fostering and participating in "spiritual *idolatry*" as well.

These doctrines are idolatrous for two related reasons. One, because they lead people away from the objective of whole and complete trust in God alone as the ultimate Source of supply of all things. And, two, because in addition to leading people away from trust in God, they also lead people to put their faith, hope, and trust in mere flesh and bone human leaders for the things God insists we look to Him for, many of the particulars of which I have already addressed.

To merely call idolatry "sin," though it certainly is, somehow seems an extreme understatement, for it is the ultimate affront unto God. Yet, arguably, it is the most pervasive sin of all today among professing believers. Contributing to the prevalence of idolatry within Christendom, no doubt, is the common perception by many that idolatry is something that occurs only in underdeveloped, far-away, foreign lands, or that it is something relegated mostly to ancient civilizations of past ages, while nothing could be further from the truth.

In Galatians 5:20, the Apostle Paul by inspiration of the Holy Spirit listed "idolatry" as one of the fundamental elements of evil comprising the carnal nature, or sin nature, which actually is the nature of the devil himself, and which is also alluded to as the "spirit of disobedience"—the *spirit that is now working in the sons of disobedience"* (Eph. 2:2). So, in other words, because the carnal nature is common to every human, idolatry, then, is a basic tendency of every person ever born.

In simplistic terms, idolatry is making something or someone that to which we look to bring happiness, peace, fulfillment, contentment, and all the things only God is supposed to provide us, which in essence is the definition of a false god.

To put it another way, idolatry is fashioning and forming false gods, or idols, out of one's own vain imaginations. Indeed, idols are really always imaginary, existing solely in the human mind and thoughts. Again by inspiration of the Spirit, in another place, Paul states categorically that those possessing true Spiritual knowledge and understanding *"know that there is no such thing as an idol* (false god), *and that there is no God but one"* (1 Cor. 8:4). False gods are false because they really do not exist, except in the mind of the idolater.

Idolatry in actuality then is merely the product of human thinking, manufactured in the factory of the human mind. It is the act of creating an abstract god within the deep, dark void of human reasoning. At bottom, all idolatry is "mind-idolatry," for it is primarily in the mind that all idolatry exists. In a nutshell, the basis of idolatry is what I refer to as "stinkin' thinkin'."

Moreover, the ilk of idolatry which bona fide believers are most guilty of committing even routinely, though unwittingly, is the idolatry of holding to false and contrived ideas about God that in fact are wholly incongruous with what He Himself has revealed in His Word concerning His Divine Nature, Will, and Ways. When it is all distilled down, idolatry is the ultimate form of arrogance and self-righteousness, for it supplants God and His Word, Will, and Way, and puts in His place a false, humanly formed and fashioned god, one made in our own image and after our own likeness, to affirm and hallow our own humanly contrived ideas and concepts. Thus, idolatry, in my view, is the ultimate offense that the human heart can commit against a Holy and Sovereign God.

A.W. Tozier (1897-1963), who was the pastor of the Christian and Missionary Alliance Church in Toronto and Chicago, for a number of years was also editor of the CMA's official organ, *Alliance Weekly*, as well as a prolific author of books. His spiritual acumen was so highly regarded by his colleagues that many esteemed him a twentieth-century prophet. Despite all his prodigious achievements, he was perhaps best known for his personal intimacy with God, and his book, *The Knowledge of the Holy* (Harper & Row), was a collection of some of his most outstanding messages related to knowing God in personal intimacy. So profound and insightful are his comments regarding the subject of idolatry, as well as exquisitely and eloquently articulated, that they could scarcely be improved upon, making direct quotation the only fitting means of conveyance. The following are excerpts of his commentary, the chronology of which I have taken the liberty of rearranging in order to better serve our purposes here:

> "Let us beware lest we in our pride accept the erroneous notion that idolatry consists only in kneeling before visible objects of adoration, and that civilized peoples are therefore free from it.

> "The essence of idolatry is the entertainment of thoughts about God that are unworthy of Him. It begins in the mind and may be present where no overt act of worship has taken place. 'When they knew God,' wrote Paul, 'they glorified him not as God, neither were thankful; but became vain in their imaginations, and their foolish heart was darkened.'"

> "Among the sins to which the human heart is prone, hardly any other is more hateful to God than idolatry, for idolatry is at bottom a libel on His character. The idolatrous heart assumes that God is other than He is—in itself a monstrous sin—and substitutes for the true God one made after its own likeness."

> "A god begotten in the shadows of a fallen heart will quite naturally be no true likeness of the true God."

> "Wrong ideas about God are not only the fountain from which the polluted waters of idolatry flow; they are themselves idolatrous. The idolater simply imagines things about God and acts as if they were true."

> "Perverted notions about God soon rot the religion in which they appear. The long career of Israel demonstrates this clearly enough, and the history of the Church confirms it."

All false doctrine is, in essence, an assemblage of "wrong ideas about God" and "perverted notions about God," as Tozier put it. How profound and Scriptural is his statement: "**Wrong ideas** about God are not only the fountain from which **the polluted waters** of idolatry flow; they are themselves idolatrous," for "polluted waters" is a metaphor evoked in Scripture to represent false teaching.

Indeed, false teaching is by no means, as some seem to believe, a harmless or inconsequential phenomenon, but rather polluted waters can be lethal, both in the natural and the spiritual. False teaching, which in essence is substituting human ideas and sophistry for the absolute Truth of God's Mind, in fact IS idolatry. *Idolatry* and *false teaching* are synonymous terms. Idolatry always has associated with it some form of false teaching, and false teaching is always an ilk of idolatry. As Tozier so brilliantly articulated it: "The idolater simply imagines things about God and acts as if they were true." In other words, the person engaging in idolatry simply contrives his own doctrine concerning spiritual matters and the composition of "truth," and conducts his life based on those determinations even though they are not congruous with the real Truth which emanates from and is defined by God as Truth in His Word.

Zeal Without Knowledge

A rather ironic and curious characteristic of the idolatry of false teaching is that essentially it is *"zeal without knowledge."* It is quite common for those caught in the throes of deception and false doctrine to be quite zealous and ardent in their spiritual pursuits. Where false teaching is being promulgated—the perpetrators and the adherents commonly are fervently dedicated to their church-group and its purposes, beliefs, and goals. In fact, it is this zealous-ness by participants in aberrant and cult-like religious groups that makes it extremely difficult for caring bystanders to: one, fully recognize and realize the existence of error and errancy; two, to take serious the potential for spiritual and psychological injury and ruin; and, three, to recognize the need for and actually effect appropriate remedial action.

Certainly, this is the case with those who are being duped by these fallacious Discipleship/Shepherdship doctrines. They are often very zealous and even marginally fanatical in their spiritual pursuits. And, in a day when there is far too little fervency for the things of God, most any of us are understandably reluctant to do anything that might douse the fire of someone who *is* on fire ostensibly for God.

The Apostle Paul, speaking of his fellow countrymen, the Jews, said, *"For I bear them witness that **they have a ZEAL FOR GOD**..."* (Rom. 10:2). He was saying that the Jews' zeal for God was genuine and sincere, and certainly no people had more religious zeal than the Jews until then. Nevertheless, their zeal, he went on to say, was *"not in accordance with knowledge."* They had "zeal without knowledge." Their zeal, though extremely fervent, genuine, and unquestionably sincere, nonetheless, was not founded upon Truth. Continuing, the former Hebrew of Hebrews and Pharisee of Pharisees said,

> For not knowing about God's righteousness, and seeking to establish **THEIR OWN**, they did not subject themselves to the righteousness of God. For Christ is the end of the law for righteousness to everyone who believes. (vv. 3,4)

How profound and profoundly apropos the issue Paul addresses here is to the matter of idolatrous false teaching in that he specifically juxtaposes *"zeal for God"* against *"the righteousness of God,"* which actually is referring to "rightstanding with God," or in other words how one obtains rightstanding with God.

When Jesus of Nazareth at the age of thirty was revealed as and took on the role of the Christ, He truly became *"**THE** (only) Way* [to God], ***THE** (only) Truth* [all spiritual truth, wisdom, and understanding), *and **THE** (only) [Eternal] Life* [in communion and fellowship with God]*"* (Jn. 14:6). From the moment Jesus was revealed as the Christ, the Messiah, the Door into fellowship with the Father, from that very moment, Judaism and the Old Covenant (not to be confused with the Old Testament books of the Bible) was made obsolete. That is to say that from the moment the Christ was manifested, faith in Christ was the **ONLY** way to rightstanding with God. The absolution of our sins through Jesus' shed blood became the **NEW** Covenant, the *"new and living way"* (Heb. 10:20) by which those who believed in Him were granted free and equal access unto and communion with God.

From then on, the Old Covenant, wherein rightstanding with God was attained by strict adherence to the ordinances of the Mosaic Law, was no longer in effect. Thus, the statement: *"Christ is the end of the law for righteousness to everyone who believes"* (Rom. 10:4). Christ's manifestation meant the end of the law in regard to obtaining righteousness, or rightstanding, with God through it. Now, *"everyone who BELIEVES"* has rightstanding with God, *"by grace... through faith"* (Eph. 2:8).

The obsolescence of the Old Covenant and its replacement by the New Covenant does not mean, however, as some ignorantly surmise, that the Truth God revealed in the writings comprising the books of the Old Testament section of the Bible are now null and void. It was not God or His Truth that changed between the Old Covenant era and the New Covenant era, but rather only the **WAY** we get to God, that is, the way of attaining unto rightstanding with God.

I always find it fascinating and more than a little ironic that in the very last Old Testament Book, Malachi, God reverberantly declares: *"For I am the Lord, I change not!"* (Mal. 3:6, KJV). I think the Lord strategically planted that statement in that Book for the very purpose of debunking all the religious theorists' claims that somehow He changed between the Old and New Covenants. He did not. As the verse implies, He cannot change, because He is the Sovereign and Perfectly Holy **Lord**. If God were to change His Nature, which is what He is, which is in turn His Word, He could not be God, for mutability signifies prior imperfection. Yet, He is perfectly perfect, and He is the same yesterday, today, and forever, without any *"shadow of turning."*

Because of the perfection and immutability of the Divine Nature, what God said in the Old Testament writings is just as true and trustworthy now in the New Testament age. *"Not one word of ALL his good promises have ever failed"*—whether they are in New or Old Testament writings, and regardless of what era He said it in. I unabashedly repeat that the only thing that has changed between the Old Testament and the New is the **WAY** by which we attain rightstanding with God. Otherwise, what He said and established in the Old Testament is still true in the New Testament dispensation.

If *anything* God said or established in the Old Testament were to have changed, He surely would have told us. Generally speaking, however, God is not given to superfluity. Redundancy is not a requirement in the realm of God, which is to say that it is not mandatory that God reiterate in the New Testament writings something He said in the Old Testament writings in order for it to be effectual in the New Testament Age. Anything He has ever said is **forever** settled in Heaven; it is immutable Divine Law, unless He changes it, and when He changes something He publishes that change brazenly and unmistakably. And, the implications and applications of this irrefutable assertion are great in a number of important areas of doctrine under debate and in dispute today in which mere human opinion and religious bias and tradition are being exalted by some above the revealed knowledge of God.

Getting back to the main point inherent in the Apostle Paul's allusion to the Jews' *"zeal without knowledge,"* he said, *"not knowing about GOD'S righteousness,"* that is to say, the way God had established for the attaining of rightstanding with Him, which is through faith in Jesus the Messiah, not knowing about that, the Jews sought *"to establish THEIR OWN,"* and *"they did not subject themselves to the righteousness of God."* Now this is the ultimate problem with the idolatry of false teaching and indeed every kind of idolatry—it replaces God's method for gaining rightstanding with Him, which method is clearly revealed in His Word, with a contrived and incongruous doctrine which has been fashioned and formed in someone's own human mind. Not knowing about God's righteousness, and not wanting to subject themselves to the specific requisites of God's righteousness, they seek to establish their own. That is precisely what all idolatry is, substituting a false gospel for the true, a false *religion* for God's method for *righteousness*, a false god for the One and Only True God, making a god out of one's own religious thoughts and contrived religious methodologies. It is genuine zeal for wanting to attain unto God-likeness, but on one's own terms, without whole surrender and submission unto God Himself and the Way He has established for attainment of that very status.

It is, I understand, difficult to think of zeal as being anything other than a most commendable and desirable trait. But, not always! In fact, there are case stories in the Bible that illustrate very vividly that misplaced zeal can be quite deadly! A prime example is that of King David who with great zealousness for God in attempting to accomplish the extremely noble and virtuous goal of retrieving the Ark of the Covenant and returning it to its proper place of veneration caused one of his most loyal and beloved servants, Uzza, to be struck down dead by God Himself in an outburst of holy wrath, all because David violated certain particulars of God's established ordinance regarding the method for transportation of the Ark. (David was full of zeal, and his zeal was not for some worldly or self-aggrandizing achievement, but for **THE THINGS OF GOD**! Nevertheless, his misdirected zeal got a beloved friend killed and invoked the wrath of God, despite all the pageantry, and pomp and circumstance, as David along with all of Israel were praising and *"celebrating before God with all their might, even with songs and with lyres, harps, tambourines, cymbals, and with trumpets"* (1 Chron. 13:8).

God tells us that the real life incidences that occurred in Old Testament days *"happened to them as an example and they were written for our instruction, upon whom the ends of the ages have come"* (1 Cor. 10:11). The poignant moral of this story to all of us living at *"the ends of the ages"* is that as needful and desirable as the fervency of zeal is, zeal, no matter how fervent and fiery, cannot and will not ever supersede the necessity of obedience to God's already established Word, Will, and Ways, that is, His ordinances. Even all that we do for and as an offering unto God, must be done or offered up according to the ordinances, according to His Word, Will, and Way. We cannot do it our own way, and have rightstanding with God. Neither can we seek and serve Him according to our own doctrines for seeking and serving Him, and have rightstanding with Him. When the fleeting vapor of our natural life is over, and we stand before the Righteous Judge to be judged on the basis of our deeds (Rom. 2:6, et al.), faithfulness and obedience to Him will be the standard, not how emotional, fervent, or zealous we were. Zeal never overrides or negates the necessity for obedience of the specific requisites of God's ordinances. It's either **HIS** Way, or **NO** way!

Ultimate Accountability

You see, when taken to their fullest extent, what these false teachings culminate in, is an infringement upon the Biblical fact of ultimate accountability to God, which is to say that in the end everyone is accountable to God, and to God alone, for his conduct and for the substance of the life he or she lived. Ultimately, it is to an Almighty and All-Knowing God, that we must give account for the totality of our lives. Ultimately each believer is accountable only to the authority of God, and not to any supposed authority of men.

This Truth and its veracity is unequivocally and wholly supported by the preponderance of Scripture, and proof-texts corroborating this absolute fact are so numerous that to quote them all would require a separate volume of its own. But, there is one passage that states it about as directly and succinctly as it can be stated, which is, Romans 14:12: *("So then EACH OF US shall GIVE ACCOUNT of HIMSELF to GOD.")*

Moreover, the verses that precede this particular passage are also extremely enlightening and germane to this point regarding ultimate accountability unto God. In verse four, Paul poses the consummate question to which every believer would be well-advised to take careful heed: *"Who are you to judge the servant of another?"*

To judge someone else, it is imperative to understand, by its very nature, means that the person who is sitting in the seat of the judge is of a greater status, standing, authority, and behavioral stature, than the one who is being judged. Yet, clearly an overwhelming preponderance of Scripture teaches that as Jesus stated, *"You (all believers) are all on the same level as brothers"* (Mat. 23:8, L.B., parenthesis added by author). As established repeatedly throughout this book, in the Kingdom of God there is absolute parity among believers. *(There is no such a thing as "big me, little you" in the Kingdom of God.)* Oh, to be sure, in real life, demonstration of carnal attitudes of ascendency and arrogance over fellows is just as common among purporting believers as it is in the world. But, that is not the way it really is in the Kingdom of God and from God's perspective. Such fleshly attitudes are of the category of the *"evil passions and desires"* which every believer must crucify if he is going to show forth evidence or fruit that he has been genuinely Born Again and been made a bona fide partaker of the attributes of the Divine Nature (Gal. 5:24; 2 Pet. 2:4).

Notice also in the verse cited (Rom. 14:4) the phrase *"servant of another."* This makes it abundantly clear that every believer is a servant of God, not of any man. Even when of our own volition we lay down our lives to serve others, we do so because the Person we are serving ultimately in so doing is God, not even the people we are serving, though they are the ostensible recipients of our service. The verse continues by saying: *"To HIS OWN MASTER he stands or falls; and stand he will, for THE LORD is able to make him stand."* In saying, *"THE LORD is able to make him stand,"* the passage identifies the *"master"* of the believer as being the Lord Jesus Himself, and not any human.

Verses seven through nine of the same chapter in Romans go on to clearly indicate that every believer "belongs" ultimately to the Lord, and thus is not the subject of any human being in terms of ultimate accountability for his or her life:

For not one of us lives for himself, and not one dies for himself; for if we live, we live FOR THE LORD, or if we die, we die FOR THE LORD; therefore whether we live or die, WE ARE THE LORD'S. For to this end Christ died and lived, that HE might be LORD both of the dead and of the living.

But, the next verse, verse ten, really puts it all into proper perspective by reminding us that none of us have the right to take unto ourselves the status of judge over our fellows with regard to the final analysis, assessment, and adjudication of their lives, as well as the fact that none of us have attained unto the transcendent or elite status required to grant us the right to regard a fellow believer with contempt or condescension, or regard any fellow believer, who is also a joint-heir, that is, equal-heir, with Christ, as in any way inferior or "subjectable" to us so as to be their judges, because we are not the *judges*; rather, we all are the *"judgees,"* being judged ourselves by *"the righteous Judge"* (2 Tim. 4:8):

But you, why do you judge your brother? Or you again, why do you regard your brother with contempt? FOR WE SHALL ALL STAND BEFORE THE JUDGMENT SEAT OF GOD. (Rom. 14:10)

Hebrews 12:23 refers to *"THE Judge of ALL,"* which is none other than God Himself. Hebrews 10:30 plainly tells us: *"THE*

LORD will judge His people," which means that ultimate account-ing and the final adjudication of our lives is relegated to the Lord alone. The reason for this is simple: perfect and perfectly righteous and just judgment requires omniscience and infinite knowledge and wisdom, which we, in our human estate of extremely finite knowl-edge, do not possess. Only God is capable of judging *"the thoughts and intentions of the heart"* with perfect knowledge, wisdom, and understanding, for it is to His eyes, the manifold eyes of the Spirit, **alone** that all that we are is *"open and laid bare"* (Heb. 4:12,13). Only He who knows us most can judge us best. No one knows us, who we really are, the totality of our constitu-tion and the reasons behind it, like God knows us.

Thus, we see the incontrovertible and unequivocal truth that ultimately every believer is accountable to God and not to any mere mortal. As I have said elsewhere in this volume, only the one with the nail prints in His hands is the one who has been found worthy to be our Lord, Master, and Savior. This is precisely the import of James' statement wherein speaking of Jesus He says: *("There is ONLY ONE Lawgiver and Judge, THE ONE WHO IS ABLE TO SAVE and to destroy, but who are you to judge your neighbor?"* (Jas. 4:12).)

So, dear saint of God, the next time someone tries to "pull rank" on you, intimidate, or subjugate you with some humanly contrived, unsanctioned, ineffectual, and non-existent, brand of pseudo-authority, ask that person to stretch forth his or her hands, and look to see if there are nail-holes in those hands. If not, just have a little chuckle within yourself, turn, and walk away, and forget it! Because that person ain't **YOUR** Lord or **YOUR** Master! He's just another pretender and imposter motivated by an antichrist spirit! **PRAISE JESUS, THE ONE WHO IS ABLE TO SAVE AND DESTROY TO THE UTTERMOST, FOR-EVER! HE ALONE IS LORD!**

The Chief Shepherd

What all of this speaks to us and what all ministers need to be reminded of from time to time is that for as much power and authority (along with abundant responsibility) Jesus has vested in us as His "stand-ins," His under-shepherds, to minister unto the Flock of God on His behalf, notwithstanding, and without any equivocation—it is Jesus Christ **Himself**, the King of Kings, and Lord of Lords, who is the **TRUE** and **SUPREME SHEPHERD**. All of the rest of us are not even worthy, compared to Him, to be called after His name or to bear in any degree the title of which He alone has proved Himself so inimitably worthy—*"Good Shepherd."* Those mere under-shepherds on Earth who are so overtly impressed by themselves and their own "accomplishments" would certainly do well to take a cue in humility from the Twenty-Four Chief Elders who, when face to face with *"the One who was sitting on the Throne,"* did *"**cast down their crowns before the Throne**, saying, 'Worthy art **THOU, O LORD**, to receive glory and honor and power.'"*

Compared to the glory of the **SUPREME SHEPHERD**, we are poor and miserable substitutes, mere mortals of flesh and bone, with no worthiness of our own, nothing with which to commend us to God, or in reality even to our own fellows. It is only as we reflect His Image, His glory, His Light, which we do only ever so sporadically and imperfectly, that there is anything comely or of worth within us. We merely reflect, with varying and variable degrees of illumination, unto a lost, broken, downcast, hurting, spiritually bankrupt, and dying world of undone sinners the Image of a glorious and risen Savior who suffered immeasurable shame, disgrace, sorrow, and pain, far beyond anything we could even imagine much less ourselves experience, in order to set the captives free from their bondage and eternal damnation.

Erroneous Concept #2: "Spiritual Covering"

It is these sentiments and understanding the Apostle Peter, who over a period of three and one-half years had walked and talked and eaten and lived with this **GREAT SHEPHERD OF OUR SOULS**, was trying desperately to convey when he wrote:

> *Therefore, I exhort the elders (Five-fold Ministers) among you, as your <u>fellow elder</u> and witness of the sufferings of Christ, and a partaker also of the glory that is to be revealed, shepherd the flock of God among you, <u>exercising oversight not under compulsion, but voluntarily, according to the will of God; not for sordid gain, but with eagerness;</u> nor yet as lording it over those allotted to your charge, but <u>proving to be examples to the flock</u>. And when the **Chief Shepherd** appears, <u>you will receive the unfading crown of glory</u>. (1 Pet. 5:1-4, parenthesis added by author)*

The Amplified Bible's version of this passage conveys in even more graphic terms the sense of what the Apostle was communicating in these words:

> *I warn and counsel the elders among you—the pastors and spiritual guides of the church—as a fellow elder and as an eyewitness [called to testify] of the sufferings of Christ, as well as a sharer in the glory (the honor and splendor) that is to be revealed (disclosed, unfolded): Tend—**nurture, guard, guide and fold**—the flock of God that is [your responsibility], not by **coercion** or constraint but **willingly**; not **dishonorably motivated** by the **advantages and profits** [belonging to the office] but eagerly and cheerfully. Not (as **arrogant, dictatorial and overbearing** persons) **domineering** over those in your charge, but being **examples—patterns and models of Christian living**— to the flock (the congregation). And [then] when the **CHIEF SHEPHERD** is revealed you will win the conqueror's crown of glory.*

To me personally there are few things as repulsive and infuriating as a "spiritual" (or, more appropriately, "religious") leader who is all the very things the above text warns us not to be: arrogant, dictatorial, overbearing, and domineering, over the meek and

145

innocent sheep of God's Flock under his charge. This, to me, is about as despicable as it gets—to take advantage of and exploit the need people have for a human pattern and model of Jesus they can see, and use that need as a pretext to dominate and subjugate those needy people for sordid and self-aggrandizing personal gain. I know that it is also a stench in the nostrils of God! And, if it is so utterly offensive and repulsive to me, one who is of the same fleshly nature as they, it must only be the expansive and encompassing mercy and forbearance of God that keeps Him from wiping such vile vermin completely off the face of the Earth and taking them instantly to their final and just reward.

Whose Flock Is It? Whose Sheep Are They?

I mean, it appears to me that when those in leadership positions engage in such sordid attitudes and activity they have forgotten one very vital and important factor in the scenario, which is that the sheep don't belong to any man. The true sheep of God, which is every truly Born Again believer, are all the sheep of **GOD'S FLOCK**. The true sheep, it will come as a shock to many "leaders," are **GOD'S** sheep, and Jesus is the true Shepherd of God's Fold. They are not the personal possession of human pastors, despite the fact that the attitudes of many pastors seem to reflect that they think they are. Human shepherds, it must never be forgotten, are merely custodial under-shepherds.

The Apostle Peter made all this abundantly clear in the passage we just examined, where, in verse two, he exhorted the presbytery of the local church to *"shepherd THE FLOCK OF GOD."* Moreover, it is on this foundational fact that he bases his further exhortations to under-shepherds not to lord over the flock, but to rather prove themselves examples, visible models, live representations of the Good Shepherd which the sheep can actually behold with their physical eyes.

Another passage which specifically alludes to the fact that it is to **GOD'S FLOCK** that the sheep belong is found in the Apostle Paul's exhortation unto the eldership (Five-fold Ministers) of the church at Ephesus, whom he had called together for a final word of exhortation and admonition prior to his departure to Rome. To these *"episkopos"* (elders, overseers, shepherds) he said:

(*Be on guard for yourselves (and for all* **THE FLOCK**, *among which the Holy Spirit has made you* **overseers**, *to* **shepherd** *the church* **OF GOD** *which he purchased with his own blood. (Ac. 20:28)*

In this passage we see *"the flock"* equated with *"the church of God."* *"The church of God"* is the *"Ecclesia,"* the assemblage of the "called out" saints Jesus referred to when He said, *"I will build My church; and the gates* (lit., powers) *of Hades shall not overpower it."* In this Truth-replete statement, Jesus was succinctly indicating four major points about this *"Ecclesia"* He was personally engaged in building: one, it was His own personal possession, and no other person or group of persons; two, this particular group of called out, consecrated, and set apart believers, the Holy Race, is the only one He Himself is engaged in establishing; three, those "churches" or collections of peoples being led and built by mere men apart from His personal engagement are imposters and bogus counterfeits, false imitations, of the true Church that He Himself is building; and four, that the identifying and distinguishing mark of the true Church that Jesus Himself is building is that the individuals of this Ecclesia, and thus its collective whole as well, are not being overpowered and vanquished in terms of constitution, character, and conduct, by the powers and assailment of the devil's kingdom, Hades.

Relating all this with what Paul said to the elders of the church at Ephesus: the bona fide, Born Again, called out, set apart from the world, sanctified, consecrated believers who comprise this Ecclesia which Jesus is building, are the exclusive possession of

147

Christ Himself; they are the sheep of the Good Shepherd, Jesus; they are the sheep of God's Flock, and not that of any mere human. The true sheep, the sheep of this Ecclesia, are those who *"belong to Christ,"* meaning they are His possession, and are those who *"have crucified the flesh with its* (carnal and worldly and devilish) *passions and desires"* (Gal. 5:24, parenthesis added by author), which speaks of their having been sanctified and set apart in deed, not merely metaphorically.

AntiChrist Wolves

Now the portion of the Apostle Paul's poignant and impassioned exhortation to the Ephesian elders just quoted began with an admonition to *"Be on guard for yourselves and for all the flock...."* The subsequent verses specify what it was that the Apostle told them it was their responsibility from God as shepherds and overseers of God's flock to guard against—the intrusion and infusion of *"savage wolves."* He indicated this was an inevitable occurrence following his departure unto Rome (where he would be put to death), inevitable, presumably, that is, if preclusive action was not taken. Though Paul himself was speaking entirely of the churches of that day to whom he had ministerial responsibility, his Spirit-inspired admonition, especially since it is now part of canonized Scripture, is also a dire and rousing exhortation to the Ecclesia of Christ of every era, including the present one. Here is the entire text:

Be on guard for yourselves and for all the flock, among which the Holy Spirit has made you overseers, to shepherd the church of God which he purchased with his own blood. I know that after my departure SAVAGE WOLVES will come in among you, not sparing the flock; and from among your own selves men will arise, speaking perverse things, to draw away the disciples after them. Therefore be on the alert, remembering that night and day for a period of three years I did not cease to admonish each one with tears. (Ac. 20:28)

Erroneous Concept #2: "Spiritual Covering"

Paul was warning these Five-fold ministers who were charged with edificational and governmental responsibility that there would be persons purporting to be anointed and appointed leaders infiltrating their ranks who were false, self-imposed interlopers motivated by self-aggrandizement, who would exploit the sheep for their own personal sordid gain. Paul seemed to be indicating that some of these *"ravenous wolves in sheep's clothing,"* as Jesus called them, would emerge even out of this very group of current elders who were assembled before him. He said these imposters would teach perverted, erroneous, and unproven doctrines in order to draw away the disciples after *themselves*, in effect causing those disciples to fall away from *Jesus* as their Shepherd in order to follow after and adhere to these errant and bogus ministers.

Now in so deceiving and leading astray those sheep, these seducers would prove they are "antiChrist wolves," possessed and driven by an evil antiChrist spirit of the devil, because they are actually engaged in seducing the sheep to abandon Christ and the Truth in order to follow after these false shepherds and false saviors and their fallacious doctrines and indoctrinations.

This is precisely what is transpiring in the case of the perverted and invalid Discipleship/Shepherdship doctrines and those who propagate them. Nothing could be a more exact fulfillment of what the Apostle Paul predicted would transpire than the overt abuses and excesses in terms of human shepherdship taking place today in groups and churches under the auspices of these fallacious doctrines. Those teaching and operating in accordance with these deviant doctrines are indeed *"drawing away disciples after themselves"* and away from Jesus as their true Shepherd and Savior, abrogating Him in those offices, and substituting themselves instead. Discipleship shepherds via the tenets of these errant doctrines pose and interpose themselves as the de facto shepherd and savior of their followers, even though they may evoke the name of Jesus with superfluity in all the discourse of their public ministry.

149

By *"speaking perverse things,"* these *"savage wolves,"* motivated by sordid and demonic passions and desires for ascendency, adulation, and personal aggrandizement, have set themselves in the place of veneration Christ alone is worthy to occupy. Such usurpation is overtly and quintessentially antiChrist.

Completeness In Christ

As I bring to a close this already full chapter in which we have focused on the folly of the notion of "spiritual covering" provided by mere human shepherds, please allow me to make one final, but no less important, point related to the subject of this chapter that further establishes the complete absurdity of this notion. It has to do with the individual believer's *completeness in Christ.*

In his letter to the believers at Colossae, the Apostle Paul capsulized his ministry and calling in this statement:

> And we *proclaim* Him (Christ), *admonishing every man and teaching every man with all wisdom, that we may present every man COMPLETE IN CHRIST.* (Col. 1:28)

Though his intent was to summarize his own ministry and calling, his statement has afforded us a succinct synopsis of what the ministry per se is about. All of the elements of valid ministry are represented in the verbiage of this verse. The primary function of all ministry is to: *proclaim* (preach) **Christ** as Lord, Master, and Savior of all, juxtaposed to human lords, masters, and saviors; *admonish* (warn) **every human being** of the perils and consequences of disregard and disobedience of God and His Master Plan; *teaching* **every human being** of the principles of the Kingdom of God (i.e., the authority of Christ [Rev. 12:10]); and, to *present* **every human being** (who will give heed to what we minister to them) back to God **COMPLETE IN CHRIST**.

The ultimate goal of all ministry is to make every person who has submitted themselves to the gospel of the authority of Christ over their lives totally **COMPLETE IN CHRIST**; which is to say, spiritually **WHOLE**; which is to say, **HOLY**. This is the ultimate mission of all true ministry and every true minister, to make everyone to whom they minister spiritually complete in **CHRIST**.

Conversely, whether those who subscribe to and engage in them realize it or not, and I am sure there are some who genuinely do not realize it, Discipleship/Shepherdship doctrines and practices by their very nature do not promote the complete dependence on Christ that produces spiritual completion in Christ. Rather, as already discussed, the disposition of these doctrines are decidedly antiChrist in that they teach adherents to place their faith, hope, trust, confidence, and essentially their destiny in the spiritual efficacy of their human leaders, who, the heresy purports, are their effectual mediators unto God. Simply put, Shepherdship followers are taught to place all of their faith in their leaders, rather than looking through them to see Christ Himself as Lord and Savior.

As we shall discuss in the next chapter, those who have been genuinely anointed and appointed by Jesus to Five-fold Ministry offices certainly have a very valid and important role with regard to the spiritual edification of individual believers as well as the collective Church. However, Five-fold Ministers are like the moon to the sun, they have no glory or light of their own, but merely reflect *"the True Light which, coming into the world, enlightens every man"* who believes in the Light (Jn. 1:9). As John the Baptist, Five-fold Ministers are not themselves the light, but rather merely *"bear witness of the Light, that all might believe* [in the True Light] *through (them)"* (v. 7). Ministers are not the source of the Light, they merely reflect and impart unto others the Light and Life of Christ through the *proclaiming* aspect of their ministry, that is, the revelation of Christ via preaching and teaching, coupled with the *portraying* aspect of their ministry, which is the revelation of Christ via their own exemplary conduct after the pattern of Christ.

CHARISMATIC CAPTIVATION

It is by the True Light, Christ Himself, shining on us and in us that the darkness of sin is dispelled and vanquished by the Light of God's Nature. Only Christ, the True Light Itself, the source of the Light, can do that. And, it is this, and this alone that makes us *"complete."* Thus, our spiritual completeness can only be *"in Christ."* But, in Christ, we are indeed complete. And, so absolute and perfect is this condition of *"complete"* that it is intrinsically impossible to improve upon it. Complete is complete. You cannot be more complete than complete.

Hence, when it is all said and done the only role that any human being has played in that completion that is attained "in Christ" is that of merely being a reflector of the glory of the Light, and even that is at best sporadic and imperfect, hindered as it is by the voids of darkness remaining yet within us all.

No, make no mistake about it: all the glory belongs exclusively to the Light, and not the imperfect reflectors.

Let us all therefore resolve to ascribe all glory to the One to whom it belongs, claiming none for ourselves, thereby sparing ourselves the eternal embarrassment and shame that will otherwise be ours when finally we stand before the Throne of the Light and witness firsthand the blinding brilliance of His Glory, which shall reveal our utter inanity, insanity, and hubris of having supposed that we ourselves were anything other than a mere reflector of the Light.

Chapter Six
Erroneous Concept #3: "Unity"

The third erroneous concept at the core of the Discipleship doctrines is the issue of "unity." The subject of unity is a constant theme of leaders of Discipleship/Shepherdship churches. Heavy-handed, brow-beating diatribe hammering home the necessity of promoting and preserving unity within their organization is incessant. Something concerning it is interlaced or underlying within nearly every message coming from the pulpit. However, the problem is that the "unity" that is promoted under the auspices of the Discipleship/Shepherdship doctrines is a false and counterfeit unity on a number of counts.

Discipleship "Unity" is One-directional

Essentially, the Shepherdship proponents' and practicioners' concept of "unity" amounts to absolute submission (which subject is amply addressed elsewhere in this book) by the members to every dictate and whim of the leadership. The leadership rules by fiat, and every member must continually abide in a state of perfect compliance with its every dictum. This so-called "unity" is nothing more than forced subjugation and religious hegemony.

The "unity" they promote and insist upon being operable within their group-society is one-directional, and by no means mutual, in that the "body" (the followers) is required to be at all times in explicit and absolute submission to the "head" (leadership), while relationally the "head" is detached and "set apart" from the "body."

153

The entire onus for "preserving the unity of the Spirit," as they like to refer to it, using Scriptural terminology to legitimize it, lies entirely with the "body." The body must "lay down its life" in order to be submitted to the "head" (despite the fact that the precedent set by the true Head of the Church was precisely the opposite). The body, though composed of the genetic sons of God, is very lightly esteemed by the elitist leadership, and typically regarded as nothing more than "dumb sheep," incapable of sound decision-making and knowing what is best for them, who therefore (for their own good, of course) must be told everything to do.

However, true unity within the Body of Christ does not operate that way. True unity of the Spirit flows out of a mutuality, a oneness in purpose and intent, between the Head (Christ) and the Body (believers). True unity of the Spirit is predicated on and operates by means of interdependency in which both the Head and the Body have equal importance. True unity of the Spirit is a fulfillment of Philippians 2:1-4, in which both the Head and the Body are of the same mind, maintaining mutual love, united in the Spirit, intent on the same solitary purpose (God's), doing nothing from selfish contentiousness or empty conceit, but with humility of mind each regards the other as more important than itself, not merely looking out for its own personal interests, but more concerned about the interests of the other. First of all, it is vital to understand when considering this matter that, as mentioned a number of times throughout this book, the real, true, functional Head of the Body of *Christ* is the *Christ* Himself. Headship over the Body of Christ is comprised entirely by a solitary Person, the Lord Jesus Christ alone:

> But I want you to understand that **Christ is THE Head** of every man. (1 Cor. 11:3)

> And He put all things in subjection under His feet, and gave **Him** as **Head** over all things to the church, (Eph. 1:22)

> ...**Him** who is **THE Head**, even Christ, (Eph. 4:15)

> *For the husband is the head of the wife, as Christ also is **THE Head** of the church, He Himself being the Savior of the body. (Eph 5:23)*

> *...His Beloved Son.... He also is **THE Head** of the body.... (Col 1:13-18)*

> *...and He (Christ) is **THE Head** over all rule and authority; (Col. 2:10)*

Nowhere does Scripture support the absurd though widely-held supposition that certain believers, namely leaders, comprise in whole or part the office of Headship in the Body of Christ. Rather, what the Bible does teach is that **ALL** believers, laymen and leadership alike, are members of the **BODY** of Christ.

> *Now you are Christ's **BODY** and individually **members of IT**. (1 Cor. 12:27)*

The Body of Christ is comprised of a multiplicity of members, every true, Born Again believer being one: *"For the body is not one member, but many"* (1 Cor. 12:14). Together all of those members comprise one, singular, Body of Christ; not one body of believers and another of leaders, but rather one Body:

> *For just as we have many members in **one** body and all the members do not have the same function, so we, who are many, are **one** body in Christ, and individually members **one** of another. (Rom. 12:4,5)*

Is not the cup of blessing which we bless a sharing in the blood of Christ? Is not the bread which we break a sharing in the body of Christ? Since there is **one** bread, we who are many are **one** body; for we all partake of the **one** bread. (1 Cor. 10:16,17)

For even as the body is **one** and yet has many members, and all the members of the body, though they are many, are **one** body, so also is Christ. For by **one** Spirit we were all baptized into **one** body, whether Jews or Greeks, whether slaves or free, and we were all made to drink of **one** Spirit. (1 Cor. 12:12,13)

*But now there are many members, but **one** body. (1 Cor. 12:20)*

Now you are Christ's body, and individually members of it. (1 Cor. 12:27)

Thus, unity among believers comprising the Body is to exist simply because all believers are on the same level as brothers. Moreover, unity between the Body of believers and the Head is to exist because *"the one who joins himself to the Lord is one spirit with Him"* (1 Cor. 6:16).

Based on a False "Peace"

Another reason the "unity" proposed and imposed by the proponents of these unScriptural teachings is invalid is because it is predicated on a false "peace." The matter of "peace" is the second most discussed matter in these excessively authoritative groups. Again, one of their favorite passages in this regard is Ephesians 4:3: *"being diligent to preserve the unity of the Spirit in the bond of peace."* "Peace! Peace! Peace!" they chant incessantly, ad nauseum. And, on the surface, their plea seems to have the ring of something good and desirable. Who in his right mind would be opposed to a prospect of greater peace in *any* segment of human relations than what currently exists?

However, as in the case of the unity itself, so also it is in the case of its supposed means of achievement, which they purport is through their concept of "peace." The so-called "peace" promulgated under the auspices of the Discipleship doctrines and demanded by their practitioners, though, is a false, humanistic peace, incongruous to that of which Scripture speaks. It really is not true "peace," which is founded in unanimity, but rather a "truce," which is an agreement to cease all conflict, usually necessitated because one party has been "over-powered" by another. At the most, what is effected is a "peace *treaty,*" wherein the vanquished (subjugatees) agree to the terms of surrender and subsequent governance dictated by the victors (subjugators).

Proponents and practitioners of these authoritarian doctrines view "peace" as the complete absence of conflict—and that is precisely what they demand. Under the conditions of this "peace," all semblances of critical analysis with regard to any element of the objectives or operations of their organization is totally disallowed and impermissible. Any such critical analysis, they purport, is always indicative of "a rebellious spirit."

They contend that the chief leader is the exclusive "visionary" and "vision-carrier" of and for the group. Thus, God speaks to the leadership alone, imparting exclusively to them in its entirety the "vision" for the ministry. The leadership, you see, has a direct line to Heaven and are omniscient and wholly infallible in hearing from God and receiving direction for the ministry. Their perception of "the vision" is complete and perfect; they see all there is to see of "the vision."

The "dumb sheep," you understand, just aren't "in the loop" of communication from God in these matters at all. They simply aren't qualified or spiritual enough to be able to hear anything from God or to have any substantive input concerning "the vision." Moreover, any "input" anyone not part of the human headship believes they may have to supplement, compliment, or implement "the vision" cannot possibly be valid, and by its very nature can only amount to "di-vision" as well as the fostering thereof. The mere suggestion by a "dumb sheep" that "the vision" could be incomplete, imperfect, or in any way improper, or that the headship could be anything less than omniscient and infallible in the discernment and implementation of it, obviously, can only be inspired by "rebellion to authority."

How adamantly and vociferously Discipleship proponents proclaim and defend silly theorems such as this, yet they are effortlessly debunked and disproved by but the most infinitesimal burst of super-atomic Truth from the Word of God! In this case, the notion that the human headship is the exclusive and complete vision-receiver and vision-holder is totally shattered by a solitary, terse verse: *"But WE have the mind of Christ"* (1 Cor. 2:16). The truth revealed in this verse is that no one member of the Body of Christ can possibly possess within himself the totality of "the mind of Christ." Rather, it is the collective "we" who have the mind of Christ. The omniscience of God is distributed incrementally to the collective members of the Body of Christ. Only in the collective whole of the Body of Christ, is the entire mind of Christ complete and manifest. No one member of the Body shares in the infinite wisdom of God and knows all there is to know.

God has purposely so designed the Body of Christ to insure interdependence among the members. There is a mutuality within the human body as well as the Body of Christ which cannot be evaded, avoided, or circumvented. No one member or portion of the body can perform all or even any of the functions of the body performed by the other members; it can only perform the function *it* is designed to provide. If the ears are dysfunctional, the eye cannot do the hearing for the body; rather, there will be no hearing. Each member is dependent upon the other members of the Body to provide to it the function it is designed to provide. Each member has its function it provides to the Body, but the body is not fully functional, or healthy, unless all of the members are functioning as they should. Moreover, if certain members cease to function properly, the body cannot sustain life, but will die.

It is because of all this that no "one" member or portion of the Body can say to another, "I have no need of thee." No one member is superior to another because each has its own unique function only it can provide. Indeed, the more unseemly and unseen members, such as the liver and kidneys, for example, are the very members whose function is the most vital to our livelihood, while other members, upon which we often bestow the most regard, the elements associated with outward, physical beauty, are not vital to life. For instance, a woman adorns her eyes with eye-makeup and coiffures her hair to enhance her beauty; yet, she would live if she were to by some terrible calamity lose her eyes and hair, though blind and perhaps less beautiful; but she could not live if her heart were to fail.

All of this is the essence of the Apostle Paul's dissertation in First Corinthians Twelve, in which he delineates and discusses the various and diverse functions of the members of the Body of Christ. He explains that though the Body is one, a single entity, yet it is composed of *individual* members, each bearing a unique and specialized function, and it is through the proper functioning of each individual member that the Body is able to successfully perform its collective function (cf., Eph. 4:16).

Man-centered Rather Than Christ-centered Peace

The primary reason that the peace which the Shepherding participants promulgate is a counterfeit peace is that it is man-centered, rather than Christ-centered. You see, true peace emanates only from Christ Jesus Himself, *"For HE HIMSELF is our peace"* ✳ (Eph. 2:14), the Spirit testifies in the Word of God. It is *"the peace OF CHRIST,"* the peace that emanates from Christ Jesus, that we are to let *"rule* [hold sway, act as an arbiter] *in (our) hearts, to which (we) are called in one body"* (Col. 3:15). It is Christ Jesus who is the Child who would be born unto us and the Son who would be given unto us, who is the *"PRINCE of peace"* (Is. 9:6). It is Christ Jesus who Melchizedek, the king of Salem, which translated means the *"KING of peace"* (Heb. 7:2), typified. It is Jesus who is the *"LORD of peace"* who alone, because He is Lord over all, can *"continually grant you peace in every circumstance"* (2 Thes. 3:16).

Jesus Christ is Himself Peace, because true peace is a part of and emanates from God, which is corroborated, for one thing, by the fact that the salutation of twelve of the thirteen Pauline Epistles includes the benediction *"peace FROM GOD"* (the exception, First Thessalonians, he simply invokes "peace" to them without explicit reference to its emanation from God). It is the *"peace OF GOD,"* the peace Jesus gives unto us, which is unlike the "peace" the world gives (Jn. 14:27), *"which surpasses all comprehension, (and which) shall guard your hearts and your minds IN CHRIST JESUS"* (Plp. 4:7). Paul informs us, *"GOD is not a God of confusion (disorder) but OF PEACE"* (1 Cor. 14:33). His valedictory to the Romans included the blessing *"Now may the GOD OF PEACE be with you all. Amen."* (Rom. 15:33), plus the assurance that *"the GOD OF PEACE will soon crush Satan under your feet"* (16:20). The Apostle promised the Philippians that if they practiced *"The things you have learned and received and heard and seen in me,"* then *"the GOD OF PEACE shall be with you"* (Plp. 4:9). He also revealed it is, thank God, *"the GOD OF PEACE"* who sanctifies us (1 Thes. 5:23); (thank God it is as the God of **peace** rather than the God of **wrath**, which He is as well, that He makes us holy). We are told in Hebrews it is *"the GOD OF PEACE, who brought up from the dead the great Shepherd of the sheep in the blood of the eternal covenant, even Jesus our Lord"* who equips us *"in every good thing to do His will, working in us that which is pleasing in His sight, through Jesus Christ"* (Heb. 13:20,21).

True peace, then, is a fruit of the Spirit (Gal. 5:22), the Divine Nature, and emanates from same. Therefore, it is manifest in and through only one breed of person on planet Earth—those who have been regenerated and infused with the Divine Nature, which is the Holy Spirit. It cannot be manufactured or merely simulated. Nor can it be legislated. True peace is a matter of the heart, which is the reason that until the Kingdom Rule of Christ is effected upon the Earth among people, races, and nations, peace will not exist in the world.

Indeed, the thing that seems to be so difficult for the majority of Christians to comprehend and accept even if they do comprehend it is the unequivocal fact that **Jesus did not come in His first visitation upon the Earth to bring peace to the Earth.** Perhaps, the thing that has contributed as much as anything else to the notion that Christ came to bring peace upon the Earth is the melodious and highly inspirational Christmas carols charged with lyrical jubilation concerning "peace on Earth" which are sung ad infinitum during every Christmas Season all over the world. Just a few examples are:

Hark! the herald angels sing,
"Glory to the new-born King;
Peace on earth, and mercy mild,
God and sinners reconciled. (Hark! The Herald Angels Sing)

O morning stars together
Proclaim the holy birth,
And praises sing to God the King,
And **peace to men on earth.** (O Little Town Of Bethlehem)

It came upon the midnight clear,
That glorious song of old,
From angels bending near the earth,
To touch their harps of gold.
"Peace on earth, good will to men,
From heaven's all-gracious King
The world in solemn stillness lay
To hear the angels sing." (It Came Upon The Midnight Clear)

Of course, these lyrics are taken from the King James Version of Luke 2:14, which renders the doxology of the angel of the Lord thusly: *"Glory to God in the highest, and on earth, peace, good will toward men."* However, that is not the correct translation of the text, which fact is noted by most every English translation published since the KJV. The correct translation is as Marshall's Literal English Translation of the Nestle's Greek Text [The Zondervan Parallel New Testament in Greek and English, 1982] renders it: *"Glory in* (the) *highest places to God and on earth peace among men of goodwill."* The New American Standard Version as well

161

captures the true import of the text: *"Glory to God in the highest, and on earth peace among men with whom He is pleased."*

Thus, we see where the mistranslation of a passage has resulted in a "doctrine of men" that is in truth antithetical to Scripture. For you see, the testimony of the angel of the Lord was not that with the birth of the Christ-Child peace would prevail upon the Earth and Divine goodwill would inure to all men. Rather, the angel was proclaiming that people with whom God was pleased and whose hearts had been infused with goodwill from God—that is, *"as many as received Him"* (Jn. 1:12), the Christ who had been born—to these persons living upon the Earth would peace with God inure, not universally to all of mankind on the Earth. Neither was this peace, peace between men and nations, but rather peace between *believing* men and God. With the birth of the Christ, reconciliation with God had come for all men.

Nowhere does the Word of God teach that Jesus in His first visitation came to bring peace upon the Earth. In fact, the exact opposite is true. Jesus explicitly and unequivocally declared, *"Do not think that I came to bring PEACE ON THE EARTH; I did not come to bring peace, but a sword* [a symbol of conflict, war]*!"* (Mat. 10:34). Jesus tells us not to even think that the reason for His coming in His first visitation was to bring peace on the Earth.) Yet, that is the very thing that the majority of professing Christians think. Indeed, it is this very seemingly unfulfilled promise of peace on Earth among men that is prime fodder for the naysaying mockers and critics of the Gospel, for it is quite obvious that to this day wars and all manner of conflict among men have not only not ceased, but rather have increased. Never since the birth of Christ has there been a time when wars were not on-going among nations. There has never been total peace on the Earth, and there never will be until after the **Second** Coming of Christ! Jesus did not come to bring peace to unregenerate, evil-willed men in this corrupted cosmos, but war and more war, until it is irrefutably established that true peace will only come when the Kingdom of the Prince of Peace is manifest on the Earth and in the hearts of men. He is the Christ, the Savior of all mankind, and there is none other!

After telling us not to think that He came to bring peace on the Earth, Jesus categorically stated, *"I did not come to bring peace, but a sword."* Luke's version of Jesus' statement is: *"Do you suppose that I came to grant peace on the earth? I tell you, no, but rather DIVISION"* (Luke 12:51). Not only do professing Christians suppose, against Jesus' explicit admonition not to, that an inherent purpose of His first coming was to bring peace upon the Earth between peoples and nations, but they also presume, quite falsely, that Jesus' coming should bring automatic peace to all forms and levels of interpersonal relationships, especially familial relationships, and are quite bewildered if that does not take place. However, such an assumption not only is false and foundationless, but it is also humanistic, meaning founded in humanism. The rest of Jesus' statement makes it clear that Jesus will also be the "rock of offense," that is to say, source of division, among relatives as well:

> *Do not think that I came to bring peace on the earth; I did not come to bring peace, but a sword. For I came to set a man against his father, and a daughter against her mother, and a daughter-in-law against her mother-in-law; and a man's enemies will be the members of his household. He who loves father or mother more than Me is not worthy of Me; and he who loves son or daughter more than Me is not worthy of Me. And he who does not take his cross and follow after Me is not worthy of Me. He who has found his life shall lose it, and he who has lost his life for My sake shall find it. (Mat. 10:34)*

We live in an age of humanism. A popular song of the sixties promulgating New Age astrological doctrine calls it "the Age of Aquarius." Anti-Scriptural humanistic doctrines are pandemic in our world. Mankind gropes and longs, almost pathetically now, for an ever-elusive, grandeuristic, universal, utopian "peace" and utter tranquility, in which evil is no more and all semblance of conflict is non-existent.

A prominent drug-toking lyrical bard and "pied piper" of the hedonistic sixties, John Lennon, whose mega-famous group, the Beatles, publicly purported to have eclipsed the popularity of Jesus Christ, transfixed millions of immature-thinking, world-disillusioned, anarchistic listeners with the prospect of an imaginary, grandueristic, utopian, hedonistic, communistic, one-world, Eastern-religion-based, world, in which there were *"no countries"* and not *"anything to fight for"* (no national sovereignty or allegiance), and the world was *"as one"* (one-world government); *"no possessions"* (communism, where all property is communal and state-owned and none privately-owned); *"no religion"* (except false New Age humanism; he really means no Christianity, vis-a-vis, Christ, but rather a hedonism-approving antichrist); *"no heaven"* (he really means no Almighty God); *"no hell"* (don't he wish; hedonism—no right, no wrong, no morality, everything goes, no Divine answerability and retribution) and everyone *"living for today"* (no day of Divine reckoning). *"Imagine"* such a utopia, Lennon cajoled listeners in the song so entitled, which is precisely what one would have to do because such a place is strictly a figment of the imagination and the surrealistic realm of drug-induced hallucination, for such a place does not now and never will exist.

A major element of this antiChrist false religion of humanism that is now so globally pervasive is families and the specter of familial relationships. Simultaneously the family entity as designed by God is being gradually decimated by universal no-fault divorce on-demand, prolific familial abandonment, pandemic unwed sexual romanceships, and homosexuality, on the one hand, and altruistic veneration of family/children to the point of quasi-deification, on the other hand. Children are regarded and even worshiped as gods today by those indoctrinated by the psychology-based philosophy of secular humanism. It is a child's world. Children reign supreme and are treated as royalty. They are arrayed in the trendiest apparel and transported in bedazzling BMW baby-buggies. They are pampered, mollycoddled, fed only the dantiest, dietetically-correct culinary delicacies, their every whim and desire is indulged, and they are inundated with all the latest toys, thingamajigs, and material objects money can buy.

Everywhere you go in public, be it a restaurant or mall or (God-forbid!) an "entertainment attraction" (to which, with all the little unrestrained hellions running loose, there is no attraction for the sane and normal), you are overcome with the sheer pandemonium of shrieking, screaming, fit-throwing, totally undisciplined, "sweet little angels" running wildly around, while their "super-moms and su-per-dads" sit around with adoring, approving, amused smiles on their faces, totally transfixed by the animalistic antics of their "Jetsons"-like "super-kids." The *pedestals* upon which today's ultra-modern-istic, humanism-steeped "yuppies" have set their idolized "guppies" (children) bear more and more striking resemblance to *thrones*. And, God forbid, if you should even consider corporeally disciplining your child, lest a police swat-team, the HRS, and all the judicial powers of the U.S. government be brought down upon you with full fury and force.

True Unity of the Holy Spirit, not the Human Spirit

True peace is a peace which comes from God and is resident within the regenerate heart of the redeemed. It transcends all comprehension and circumstances, and is contingent upon neither. God Himself is the God of Peace. True peace emanates from Him. True peace among humans is the result of having peace *with* God. The peace *of* God emanates to humans who have peace *with* God.

Without the peace *of* God, there will be no real unity. Being *"united with Him"* is the basis for true unity among **humans**. It is the peace of God that is *"the perfect bond"* between brethren and the perfect unity preservative. It is the unity *"of the SPIRIT"* which we are exhorted to preserve (Eph. 4:3) —the unity which is of and emanates from the Spirit, or Life, or Nature, of God—not humanistic unity. True unity is not a product of the **human** spirit, but the **Holy** Spirit. True unity of the Spirit is the by-product of being unified with Christ by virtue of the New Birth and walking in union and unity with the indwelling Spirit of God. True unity is not the product of "a meeting of the minds" or unanimity of men, but the natural by-product of unanimity with the mind of Christ. The groundwork for unity is not "reaching an understanding," but renewing our minds with an understanding of the Word of God, and *standing under* its veracious authority.

True unity is manifest not by men seeking "common ground," but the "higher ground" of the Spirit realm. True unity is not based on men's compromising and reconciliation of differences, but rather conviction and reconciliation of men's sin. True unity is not the result of *talking*, but *walking*, walking in the Spirit, for when we walk in the Spirit, bearing the fruit of the Spirit—love, joy, peace, patience, kindness, goodness, faithfulness, gentleness, and self-discipline—we avoid carrying out the deeds of the flesh that separate fellows, and instead automatically abide in unity with others so abiding. True unity automatically abides among people truly abiding in Christ. In short, true unity is not man-centered, but truly is Christ-centered!

UnScriptural Over-emphasis on Unity Among Believers

Indeed, Christ Himself is the very essence of true unity and peace. Any so-called unity and peace not established upon the foundation-rock of Christ is a Godless, humanistic, and totally counterfeit unity and peace. When men take steps in the natural, fleshly realm to bring about unity and peace among men merely for purposes of self-interest, all they will ever have is a bogus, synthetic, worthless *truce*, rather than true unity and peace.

Erroneous Concept #3: "Unity"

✳ Unity among believers is vital, but it is secondary to unity with God. A significant corroboration of that is represented in the typology of Moses' Tabernacle, in that the Table of Showbread, typifying the Communion Table, one aspect of which is fellowship among fellow believers, was located not in The Most Holy Place of God's presence, but its anteroom, The Holy Place.

Moreover, while the matter of unity among believers is vital when it comes to the Body of Christ accomplishing the purposes of God, on the other hand, one need only to look at the *number* (not to even mention the *meaning*) of passages in Scripture in which the word "unity" is evoked to see that Discipleship/Shepherdship groups have a preoccupation with the matter which far exceeds the emphasis God Himself attributes to it in His Word. There are only a total of **five** passages expressly dealing with the matter of unity among brethren in the entire Bible. Here they are:

*Behold, how good and how pleasant it is for brothers to dwell together in **unity**! (Ps. 133:1)*

*I in them, and Thou in Me, that they may be perfected in **unity**, that the world may know that Thou didst send Me, and didst love them, even as Thou didst love Me. (Jn. 17:23)*

*being diligent to preserve the **unity** of the Spirit in the bond of peace. (Eph. 4:3)*

*until we all attain to the **unity** of the faith, and of the knowledge of the Son of God, to a mature man, to the measure of the stature which belongs to the fulness of Christ. (Eph. 4:13)*

*And beyond all these things put on love, which is the perfect bond of **unity**. (Col. 3:14)*

(To be forthcoming, there are additional passages of Scripture dealing with the general matter of unity which do not specifically use the word "unity;" nevertheless the point is still valid.)

167

Aside from the small quantity of unity passages, an unbiased study of their meaning makes clear there is a distinct difference between the unity of the Spirit God speaks about in His Word and the notion of "unity" taught and demanded by hyper-authority groups and their leaders, even though that is somewhat obfuscated by their constant evoking of these very passages as proof-texts for their perverted perspective. Their spin on these passages is fraught with subtle twisting and adulteration of the Spirit-intended, -inspired import. The net-result of their misconstruing, misapplication, and over-emphasis of the matter of unity is error.

Over-emphasis is over-balance, over-balance is imbalance, and imbalance is error, and "*A false balance* [imbalance] *is an abomination to God*" (Pro. 11:1). Truth consists of counterbalancing components. To avert imbalance, each component of Truth must be counterbalanced by the rest of "*the whole counsel of God*" (Acts 20:27, RSV). The unfortunate dynamic of over-balance is that once it occurs, everything, even that which is good and right, slides toward the imbalance or error and becomes tainted by it. So that, once a person or a group loses spiritual equilibrium, a downward spiral into apostasy is begun. Only the sudden application of a counterbalancing weight equal to the imbalance can halt the descent, rectify the imbalance, and regain the equilibrium.

Excessive Collectivism Produces Erroneous Ecumenicism

Indeed, the over-emphasis of unity among believers that occurred during the Charismatic, Word, and Faith Movements produced error, and tilted even what was good and right about those Movements toward error. Now what is required in order to regain the spiritual equilibrium is forceful application of counterbalancing weights of equal weight from the opposite end of the spectrum.

We must now be made exceedingly aware that there is a danger in over-emphasis of human unity and peace! That danger is this: excessive collectivism produces erroneous ecumenicism! As I discussed in Chapter Two, the devil is literally "hell-bent" on pervading this planet with a Godless, false unity and peace which is patently antiChrist in nature. This counterfeit "peace and safety," to use a Scriptural term, is entirely centered on him and is aimed at establishing his kingdom-reign upon the Earth (foolish imp that he is!), supplanting Christ Jesus and His Kingdom Rule.

The one-world ideology that now pervades global-society is the perverted and seditious schemery of none other than the maniac of maniacs, Satan himself. He is behind it all. He is crazed by the craving to gain everlasting and sovereign rulership of the cosmos. To accomplish that diabolical yet already doomed end, he must gain control of both the secular and the ecclesiastical realms.

Moreover, the primary human weakness upon which his plan hinges is fear, i.e., insecurity. (Fear) was the first and foremost consequence of Adam and Eve's sin and subsequent fall into perdition. It was the first time humanity experienced this powerful emotion. Some experts on the original Mosaic text say that when God came down in the cool of the day to commune with Adam and Eve after their disobedience and fall, upon hearing His voice, they took off running and ran for sixteen miles trying to run away from God because they were so terrified of Him and His voice. Unredeemed mankind has been possessed by this fear ever since. *Roget's International Thesaurus, Fifth Edition (1992)*, lists over two-hundred different phobias known to have been experienced by humans. The undeniable fact is that humanity is filled with fear. The reason for that is that the human essence was permeated with the nature of the devil with the original sin, and Satan is terrified by his knowledge of the final wrathful judgment that awaits him. Thus, that same terror is in every human because every human is infused with the nature of Satan.

It is this insecurity innate to the unredeemed human spirit that leads to the human proclivity to collectivism. Again as I indicated in Chapter Two, collectivism in its various forms is one of the big lies through which Satan promises utopian and universal peace, prosperity, and security. This totally false hypothesis and false hope is one of Satan's primary devices of deception. It will be by means of this very empty expectation evoked through a man he himself will possess that Satan will in the end dupe the entire unsaved world. But, this global collectivism will be powerless to deliver the unsaved from the sudden destruction that will come upon them during the very era when the one-world government led by the AntiChrist will be making its most adamant, audacious, and arrogant pledges of universal *"peace and safety"*: *"While they are saying, 'Peace and Safety!' then destruction will come upon them suddenly like birth pangs upon a woman; and they shall not escape"* (1 Thes. 5:3)!

Satan realizes he must control massive blocks of humanity in both the secular and ecclesiastical realms if he is to succeed in gaining control of the world, and one of the primary devices of deception he employs in both realms toward that end is the false hypothesis and false hope of collectivism. Moreover, it is hardly necessary to elaborate on the well-known fact that there is a global ecclesiastical ecumenicism fast occurring around the world in which the plethora of non-Christian, false religions of the world are uniting to formulate a one-world, "universal church." As end-time enthusiasts know, this is the end-time one-world church predicted by Scripture which will work in tandem with the end-time one-world government. These two entities will comprise a symbiotic "marriage"—the husband and head being the one-world government, and the wife and helpmate being the one-world church.

The primary ecumenical power-source bringing about the so-called "unification" of these false religions to formulate this "universal church" will be the "laying aside" of doctrines and dogmas deemed to be "divisive," accord based on commonalities, and a "spirit of tolerance and acceptance" of diversity in beliefs and practices. The Harlot-Church will include and welcome all the false religions of the world—only true Christianity will be excluded and unwelcome. This one-world church will be "universal" not only in the sense that it will be global, but also because its fundamental theosophy will be a composite of the commonalities of all the various religions, and each sect will be free to practice the beliefs and liturgies indigenous to their own religion.

While knowledgeable true Christians understand and agree this is a totally false ecumenicism, and would consciously resist having anything to do with any segment of the end-time Babylonian system, nevertheless, we must also be aware of the subtleties of excessive collectivism and the false hope of security it extends. An excessive emphasis on collectivism will eventually end in erroneous ecumenicism.

Erroneous ecumenicism requires a "collective mentality" of each adherent in which "the collective good of the group" and allegiance to the group or organization itself becomes the overriding consideration and highest priority. Members are indoctrinated with teaching convincing them of their need to have "a sacrificial spirit" which will lead them to yield every aspect of their lives to the collective mission and vision of the group. There are excessive and improprietous references to the group as members' "family," and familial-type allegiance is expected and demanded. Personal aspirations or callings must be suppressed or totally abandoned in order to expend one's energies in the "higher call" of accomplishment of the mission of the group or organization. Individualism, as will be discussed later, is totally discouraged and disallowed in favor of the common goal.

No matter how meritorious it may sound, "Unity at any cost" must never be an objective. Whenever unity among believers is the objective, a false unity, or erroneous ecumenicism, will inevitably ensue. Unity among believers is the result of unity with God, not the result of pursuing unity itself. When *"we walk in the light as He Himself is in the light, we have fellowship* (i.e., unity) *with one another"* (1 Jn. 1:7).

Moreover, unity as an objective is very dangerous, because it leads to compromise and doctrinal degeneration. That is precisely what has happened with the erroneous ecumenicism being pursued by the forming "universal church." Bona fide Christendom must be careful not to follow the same crooked and corrupt course.

Doctrinal Deviation, Demeanment, and Degeneration

As I have mentioned before, one of the common slogans heard during the Charismatic Movement was: "We must agree to disagree without being disagreeable." In itself, the import of that pun has some merit. Even among the most sincere cohorts, perfect and perpetual agreement is an impossible expectation. Honest and sincere men do sometimes have honest and sincere disagreements. Disagreement is inevitable, but disagreement need not be fraught with divisiveness or produce disharmony. Certainly accord is desirable over discord, harmony over disharmony. It is better that disagreements be dealt with in an amicable rather than antagonistic atmosphere. Nevertheless, we must never yield to the temptation to deviate from established essential doctrines or compromise proper principles in order to "keep the peace." Yet, that is precisely what some have taken this slogan to mean.

Doctrinal deviation is an extremely perilous path to travel. It is an undeniable and unavoidable law of physics that the most infinitesimal degree of deviation from a straight line results in a wider and wider angle of deviation as it extends forth. While it is so very true that the Church is guilty of "majoring on the minors, and minoring on the majors," yet established foundational Truth, i.e., sound doctrine, cannot be violated or deviated.

It is always astonishing, bewildering, and even benumbing to me when I witness the reckless disregard and flippant attitude so many believers, including many preachers, of all camps, demonstrate with regard to the matter of sound doctrine. I am often left aghast and incredulous by the cavalier and frankly ignorant statements of professing believers and preachers in which they demean the importance and necessity of sound doctrine. With my own ears I have heard preachers make such absurd remarks from their pulpits as, "Doctrine ain't important; people are more important than doctrine."

Imparting the essence of God into the lives of people in order to bring renewal and restoration is what the ministry is, and that is absolutely impossible without correct teaching, which is the meaning of "sound doctrine." Literally, the Greek word translated doctrine means "*the* teaching." When its verb form is used, it literally means "the teaching of the teaching." The form of the word which is translated "teacher," or "one who teaches," literally means "teacher of the teaching" or "doctor of the doctrine," and refers to one who is an expert at elucidating, explaining, elaborating, and expounding upon the Truth of God.

The *"living and abiding Word* [rhema] *of God"* (1 Pet. 1:23), which is the Eternal Life of God (Jn. 1:1-14; 1 Jn. 1:1,2) as distinguished from the written Scriptures [logos], which itself is inanimate, dead, lifeless, and unable to impart Life (Jn. 5:39), is the foundation-rock and touchstone of sound doctrine. It is not the opinions of men, but the Word and Wisdom of God. It is not the thoughts of man, but the thoughts of God. Sound doctrine, or correct teaching, is not the reasonings of men, but the Rhema (living Word) of God. It is not the product of human cogitation, but the Person of Christ. Our calling is neither to *analyze* it or *assay* its veracity, but only to *accept*, or believe, it. We need not even *understand* it for it to be effectual in our lives, but only to *stand under* its authority and obey it.

The Greek word translated "sound" literally means "healthy," or "health-, or wholeness-producing." Thus, "sound doctrine" is spiritual-health/wholeness-producing teaching of the Word of God. Sound doctrine, or correct teaching, imparts the Life of God into those who receive, accept, believe, and obey it, and thereby restores a person to the condition of proper spiritual-health and spiritual-wholeness in which Adam and Eve were originally created and abided prior to their fall into perdition.

Maintaining, teaching, and living in accordance with sound doctrine is absolutely vital and imperative. We cannot simply make up our own doctrine, rather it must be predicated entirely on the Word of God. The Word of God *IS* sound doctrine...the *only* sound doctrine. Any teaching or doctrine that does not agree with the whole Word of God is neither correct nor healthy, but rather a lie and will eventually destroy the person who accepts it and patterns his life after it. Neither can we merely deviate from sound doctrine or demean its importance and imperativeness. Doing either results in doctrinal degradation.

God Himself testifies in His Word through the writing of His surrogate spokesman, the Apostle John: *"I have no greater joy than this, to hear of my children walking in the Truth"* (1 Jn. 3:4). Truth is a Person, the Lord Jesus Christ. Jesus is the Personification of the Truth, which is the Word of God. Jesus is the Word of God....the word made flesh (Jn. 1:14; 1 Jn. 1,2). Jesus **IS** "the Teaching." He is the "foundation-rock" upon which the Church is built (Mat. 16:13-18; 1 Cor. 3:11). To denigrate, demean, or devalue the Truth, the Teaching (doctrine), or the Word, is to denigrate, demean, and devalue Jesus Himself, and therefore also the very spiritual foundation upon which every spiritual house (an individual believer's life or a church) is founded. To in any way so *"corrupt the Word of God"* (2 Cor. 2:17), as the Apostle Paul said many do, is utter blasphemy against Jesus and the Holy Spirit, who inspired the writing of the written Word, and who reveals Christ to us through the Word.

Jesus proclaimed that whoever annuls, that is to say, negates or sets aside, any of even the *"least"* of the precepts concerning the Kingdom of God and so teaches others shall himself be called *"least"* in the Kingdom of Heaven, but whoever himself keeps (practices) and teaches them to others shall be called *"great"* in the Kingdom of Heaven (Mat. 5:19,20).

Erroneous Concept #3: "Unity"

The Apostle Paul urged believers to grow up (mature) in every aspect of the Life of Christ and that *"we henceforth be no more children, tossed to and fro, and carried about with every wind of* **doctrine**, *by the sleight of men, and cunning craftiness, whereby they lie in wait to deceive"* (Eph. 4:14, KJV). This speaks of deliberate deception through the means of doctrinal degradation for selfish gain.

The New Testament is replete with warnings that such corruption of the Word of God would take place especially in the last days in which we now live. One of the foremost such passages is the Apostles Paul's admonition in his letter to his young protege, Timothy: *"But the Spirit explicitly says that in the later times some will fall away from the faith, paying attention to deceitful spirits and* **doctrines** *of demons, by means of the hypocrisy of liars, seared in their own consciences as with a branding iron...."* (1 Tim. 4:1,2). The irony within this text is that it indicates bona fide believers will fall into apostasy because they are **paying attention** to deceiving evil spirits and false doctrines concocted and promulgated by demons in this day in which degradation and devaluation of doctrine is rampant.

The Apostle Paul even urged his "son" in the Lord, whom he had personally mentored, Timothy, to remain on in Ephesus following his own departure for Macedonia, specifically, *"in order that (he) may instruct certain men not to teach* **strange doctrines**, *nor pay attention to myths* [non-Biblical teachings]...," because

> *some men, straying from these things, have turned aside to fruitless discussions, wanting to be teachers of the Law, even though they do not understand either what they are saying or the matters about which they make confident assertions. (1 Tim. 1:3-7).*

The writer of Hebrews trumpets forth a similar admonition against being caught up in and enticed by unBiblical teachings, or *"strange doctrines"*: *"do not be carried away by VARIED AND STRANGE TEACHINGS* [doctrines]*"* (Heb. 13:9).

Just as Paul urged Timothy to stay in Ephesus for the expressed purpose of instructing *"certain men not to teach strange doctrine nor pay attention to"* Scripturally unfounded teaching, so also did the apostle charge Titus to remain on the isle of Crete to *"set in order"* what remained by in every Cretan city in which a work had begun appointing as overseeing elders men who were *"holding fast the faithful word which is in accordance with THE TEACHING* [doctrine]*, that he may be able both to exhort in SOUND DOC- TRINE and to REFUTE THOSE WHO CONTRADICT* (the sound doctrine, that is).*"* Indeed, the full text of Paul's charge to Titus is rich with reference to the imperativeness that ministering elders establish believers in sound doctrine both by teaching correct doctrine and by correcting contradictory doctrines as well:

> *For this reason I left you in Crete, that you might **set in order what remains, and appoint ELDERS** in every city as I directed you, namely, if any man be...**holding fast the faithful word which is in accordance with THE TEACHING, that he may be able both to exhort in SOUND DOCTRINE and to refute those who contradict.** For there are many rebellious men, empty talkers and deceivers, especially those of the circumcision, who must be silenced because they are upsetting whole families, **TEACHING things they should not TEACH, for the sake of sordid gain....For this cause REPROVE** [correct] **THEM severely that they may be SOUND in the faith, not paying attention to Jewish myths and commandments of men who turn away from the truth.** To the pure, all things are pure; but to those who are defiled and unbelieving, nothing is pure, but both their mind and their conscience are defiled. They profess to know God, but by their deeds they deny Him, being detestable and disobedient, and worthless for any good deed. **But as for you** [Titus, and by extension, all ministers]**, speak the things which are fitting for SOUND DOCTRINE.** (Titus 1:5-14)

176

Indeed, the appearance in Scripture of these instructions to these two younger ministers has much more significance and purpose than to merely provide the historical record. It also conveys the solemn charge by God unto every Five-fold minister and elder in the Church to *"study to show thyself approved unto God, a workman that needeth not to be ashamed,* [a workman who is] *rightly dividing the word of truth"* (2 Tim. 2:15, KJV), as well as the necessity to counter *"**strange** doctrine,"* or *"myths,"* by teaching **sound** doctrine:

> *I solemnly charge you in the presence of God, and of Christ Jesus, who is to judge the living and the dead, and by His appearing and His kingdom: **preach the word; be ready in season and out of season; reprove, rebuke, exhort, with great patience and instruction** (detailed teaching). For the time will come when they will not endure SOUND DOCTRINE; but wanting to have their ears tickled, they will accumulate for themselves teachers in accordance to their own desires; and will turn their ears from the truth, and will turn aside to MYTHS. But you, be sober in all things, endure hardship, do the work of an evangelist, **fulfill your ministry.** (2 Tim. 4:1-5)*

Indeed, virtually every epistle in the New Testament was written at least partly in order to counter and correct false teaching (doctrine) that was being taught and espoused in the churches to whom the letters were sent. The Apostle Peter indicated it was inevitable that false teachers, sent by the enemy and motivated by selfish ambition and personal gain, would come and infiltrate the churches, *"secretly"* (subtly) introducing damnable occultic (hidden) heresies, or false teachings, that are a product of corruption, i.e., perversion or mutilation, of Scripture, by which they would entice many followers, but whose final end would be spiritual destruction and eternal damnation:

> *But **false prophets** also arose among the people, just as **there WILL** also be **false teachers** among you, who will **secretly introduce destructive {damnable} heresies,** even denying the*

Master who bought them, bringing swift destruction upon themselves. And many will follow their sensuality {pernicious [i.e., deadly, destructive ways]}, and because of them the way of the truth will be maligned; and in their greed {covetousness} they will exploit you with false words; their judgment from long ago is not idle, and their destruction {damnation} is not asleep.... But these, like unreasoning animals, born as creatures of instinct to be captured and killed {destroyed}, reviling where they have no knowledge, will in the destruction of those creatures also be destroyed, suffering wrong as the wages of doing wrong. They count it a pleasure to revel in the daytime. They are stains and blemishes, reveling in their deceptions, as they carouse with you, having eyes full of adultery and that never {cannot} cease from sin, enticing unstable souls, having a heart trained in greed {an heart they have exercised with covetous practices}, accursed children; forsaking the right way they have gone astray, having followed the way of Balaam....These are springs without water, and mists driven by a storm, for whom the black darkness has been reserved. For speaking out arrogant words of vanity they entice by fleshly desires, by sensuality, those who barely escape from the ones who live in error, promising them freedom while they themselves are slaves of corruption; for by what a man is overcome, by this he is enslaved {brought in bondage}. (2 Pet. 2:1-19 {bracketed italicized portions from the KJV}).

The Apostle Paul chided the Galatian church, who he said had been *"bewitched,"* for *"deserting"* Christ *"for a different Gospel,"* which he said was *"really not another"* gospel but rather a distortion or perversion of the Gospel of Christ, and told them that anyone who preached such *"a gospel contrary,"* or counterfeit gospel, was *"anathema,"* or *"accursed"*:

*I am amazed that you are so quickly deserting Him who called you by the grace of Christ; for a **different gospel**; which is really not another; only there are some who are disturbing you, and want to **distort {pervert}** the **GOSPEL OF CHRIST**. But even* *though we, or an angel from heaven, should preach to you **a gospel contrary** to that which you have received, let him be **accursed.** As we have said before, so I say again now, if any man is preaching to you **a gospel contrary** to that which you received, let him be accursed. (Gal. 1:6-9, {bracketed portion from KJV})*

In his letter to the Romans, concerning those who promulgate teachings contrary to *"**THE** teaching,"* the Apostle Paul admonished to *"avoid them"*:

*Now I beseech you, brethren, **mark them which cause divisions and offences CONTRARY TO THE <u>DOCTRINE</u>** which ye have learned; and avoid them. For they that are such serve not our Lord Jesus Christ, but their own belly; and by **good words** [skillful oratory] **and fair speeches** [flattery] DECEIVE the hearts of the simple [untaught]. (Rom. 16:17,18, KJV)*

In his closing remarks in his letter to Timothy, Paul enjoined: *"Teach and preach these principles"*—the principles he delineated within the letter. He followed that charge with these revealing comments concerning those who *"advocate a different doctrine,"* that is, teaching contrary to the teaching he taught in this and his other letters, as well as in all the other aspects of his ministry:

*If anyone advocates a different **doctrine,** and does not agree with **sound words,** those of our Lord Jesus Christ, and with the **doctrine** conforming to godliness, **he is conceited and understands nothing;** but he has a morbid interest in controversial questions and disputes about words, out of which arise envy, strife, abusive language, evil suspicions, and constant friction between **men of depraved mind and deprived of the truth,** who suppose that godliness is a means of gain. (1 Tim. 6:2-5)*

The apostle is saying here that people who corrupt the Truth of the Word of God and concoct contrary teachings, or who, in other words, denigrate doctrine, do so because their minds are void of the Truth and have become corrupted, or depraved, by perverse thoughts of self-gratification and selfish gain.

In his letter to Titus, the Apostle Paul was a little more terse and direct concerning the ulterior motivation of *"an heretick,"* as it reads in the King James Version, and how such a person is to be dealt with: *"Reject a factious man {an heretick} after a first and second warning; knowing that such a man is perverted and is sinning, being self-condemned"* (Tit. 3:10, {bracketed portion from KJV}). The Greek word translated *"an heretick"* in the King James Version, and *"a factious man"* in the New American Standard, literally means "a self-opinionated man," meaning a person who lives by and constantly asserts his own self-willed opinions, rather than living and advocating the will and thoughts of God as revealed by the Word of God. We are straightforwardly told to *"reject"* such a person, *"KNOWING,"* not merely speculating, suspecting, or improperly judging, but *"KNOWING"* that such a person is *"perverted and is sinning,"* and knowing also that it is not we who are condemning him, but rather that he is *"self-condemned,"* condemning himself by his own stubborn, self-willed perversion of the Word of God and outright sinful actions and attitudes against others.

Now a word of caution in this regard. One must be very careful not to condemn or categorize as "a heretic" a person who adamantly and unrepentantly advocates the Truth of the Word of God. Adamantcy and intransigence when it comes to standing on and speaking the Truth is not only not wrong, but it should be the unrelenting and dogged pursuit of every believer. Yet, it is quite common for less developed, less mature, less knowledgeable, and less zealous, professing believers to disparage and label "radical" those who are more arduous in their walk, more Scripturally-knowledgeable, more Spirit-trained, and, frankly, more mature than they. A person who is attempting to fashion his every thought and deed after the Word of God is certainly anything but a heretic, or **self**-opinionated, rather he is **God**-opinionated.

In fact, Jesus indicated that being **self**-willed or **God**-willed is the litmus test of the veracity of the teaching a person advocates. Read carefully the following passage recounting an occasion on which the Jewish religious leaders were questioning Jesus qualifications, and by extension the validity of His teaching:

> *But when it was now the midst of the feast Jesus went up into the temple, and began to **TEACH**. The Jews therefore were marveling, saying, "How has this man become **learned**, having never been **educated**?" Jesus therefore answered them, and said, "My teaching is not Mine, but His who sent Me. If any man is willing to do His will, he shall know of the teaching, whether it is of God, or whether I speak from Myself. **He who speaks from himself seeks his own glory**; but He who is seeking the glory of the one who sent Him, He is true, and there is no unrighteousness in Him." (Jn. 7:14-18)*

Now as a quick aside, in a scant few words, Jesus settles, at least for me, unequivocally, the long-debated question regarding the requisite method of a minister's training, whether or not it must be formal and academic, or if God also employs other means of equipping those whom He appoints. There is little doubt that the persons speaking were "ordained" rabbis who had been trained in the traditional and authorized rabbinical schools, which tradition continues yet today for the training of Jewish rabbis. These rabbis categorically stated that Jesus, though regarded as a "teacher" or "rabbi" by the people, had not been *"educated"* in their rabbinical schools. Yet, after having listened with a critical ear to His teaching, these very erudite academicians unabashedly admitted, though doubtless reticently, that Jesus was indeed *"learned." That* they could not deny, but rather it was concerning the "how," or method, by which He had become so learned which they queried incredulously. Those yet today who adamantly insist that a minister must be "educated" by means of formal and academic curriculum in their seminaries under the tutelage of sophisticated professional theologians are similarly bewildered by the undeniable "learnedness" of those who have been trained not by mere men in the abstractness of removed ivory-tower classrooms, but by God Almighty in real, remote desert dens. The truth of the matter is made clear in this passage: one does not need to be *"educated"* by men in order to be certifiably *"learned"* in *"the things of the Spirit of God"* (1 Cor. 2:12) which are *"taught by the Spirit"* (v. 13). Of such things, the ultimate Teacher is the Spirit of God (1 Jn. 2:27). Of these things, *"they shall all be taught of God"* (Jn. 6:45).

But beyond the matter of the method by which Jesus obtained His knowledge and wisdom, lay the deeper issue which was really the heart of these religious leaders' question: the **veracity or legitimacy** of the teaching. Resisting the temptation to defend and verify Himself by responding to the method matter, Jesus cut instead to the ulterior, ultimate issue. He indicated essentially that the litmus test of the veracity or legitimacy of a person's teaching is inherent in its *origination* and its *objective*. As to origination: whether it originated from God, making it **God**-authored, or from one's own reasonings, making it **self**-authored. As to objective: whether it is **God**-glorifying or **self**-glorifying, for Jesus said: *"He who speaks from himself SEEKS HIS OWN GLORY; but He who is SEEKING THE GLORY OF THE ONE WHO SENT HIM, HE IS TRUE, and there is no unrighteousness in Him."* Jesus' response regarding the teaching He taught was that it originated with God: *"My teaching is not MINE, but HIS who sent Me,"* and that any person who *"is willing to do HIS will"* will know with certainty that it originated with and was authored by God.

Thus, we see in all this that "doctrine" is far from being the optional and odious thing some people make it out to be. Much to the contrary, it is absolutely vital that every believer ensure beyond any doubt that his life is squarely and solidly built upon the foundationstone of sound doctrine, or correct teaching. Every believer and especially ministers are exhorted to *"in all things show yourselves to be an example in good deeds, with PURITY IN DOCTRINE"* (Tit. 2:7). The marginal reading for the word "purity" in this verse is "soundness", and the literal meaning, which is used in the KJV, is "uncorruptedness." The message of the passage is clear: all believers should ensure they are exemplary in both good deeds and sound doctrine, or uncorrupted teaching.

To attain unto this objective we must give heed unto another exhortation from Jesus transmitted through the Apostle Paul:

> *Until I come, **give attention to** the public reading of Scripture, to exhortation, and to **teaching {doctrine}.... Take pains with these things; be absorbed in them,** so that your progress may be evident to all. **Pay close attention to** yourself and to **your teaching {doctrine}, persevere in these things;** for as you do this you will insure salvation both for yourself and for those who hear you (1 Tim. 4:13-16).*

Now as we move on, it is important to understand that this section was not merely a time-consuming tangent. Rather, the vital point being established here is that true unity can never be attained by means of doctrinal deviation, denigration, and demeanment. To put it another way, traveling the crooked path of doctrinal denigration will never transport you to the destination of real unity. On the contrary, sound doctrine, which is the Word of God, is the only path to true peace and unity, for Christ Jesus Himself, the Word made flesh, is our peace.

Strong Delusion

Trifling with the Truth is a grave and even dangerous thing. Personally, I am always wary of individuals who in any way devalue the importance of pursuing the Truth and being established in sound doctrine. And, again, I re-emphasize that when I speak of "sound doctrine," I am not referring to academic, abstract, intellectual theological superfluities, but rather foundational, pragmatic teaching from the Word of God by which one patterns his thinking and conduct in practical God-centered living. Believers not only should not be demeaning or denigrating the Truth, but to the contrary, we should have a genuine love for the Truth, a love that compels us to have a reverent respect for and desire to pursue and preserve the Truth.

There is a very true axiom that those things which we properly respect and cherish have a way of gravitating *toward* us, and those things which we do not, seem invariably to gravitate *away* from us. The matter of Truth is no exception. It has been my studied observation over the years that those who are the most established in the Word of Truth are those who have an intense love, respect, and desire for the Truth. As I have mentioned elsewhere, Truth is a Person—His name is Jesus! The more we draw near to Him by earnestly loving, honoring, and desiring Him, the more He draws near to us (see Jas. 4:8).

We have today in many Pentecostal and Neo-Pentecostal circles and churches a tendency to not properly regard Truth in favor of "the things of the Spirit" (as if the Truth is not a thing of the Spirit). This attitude is a tremendous mistake which carries the potential for major problems. In our quest to operate in the fullest potential available to us of the "power" of God, and to have unhindered "demonstrations of the power of God," there are those, both now and in prior moves, who contend that some groups are so excessively concerned about doing things Biblically and according to proper order that they have "ordered" the Spirit of God right out of their churches.

Of course it is regrettably true that many of our churches which have a heritage rich in operating in the Spirit and power of God have now regressed into dead formalism and religious ritualism. Nevertheless, it is pure folly to attribute that to some sort of "excess" with regard to Biblical doctrine. In fact, precisely the opposite is true. Biblical teaching promotes demonstration of the Spirit and power of God in our midst. When the Truth is being taught, the Holy Spirit desires to corroborate that Truth with signs and wonders following.

Sound *doctrine* never impedes or in any way inhibits *demonstration* of the Spirit. It is not the Truth that kills, but "the letter," or religion. The Truth liberates and gives Life rather than restricting and killing it. Dead churches became dead as a result of having digressed from abiding in the Truth and having egressed into dead religious works.

Jesus said God was seeking a Church of **true** worshipers and that **true** worship was worship *"in Spirit and Truth"* (Jn. 4:23,24). In other words, true worship is worship in which the Spirit and Truth are at perfect equilibrium. The English word "worship" is a contraction of "worth" and "ship," and deals with quantity and quality of honor, devotion, deference, reverence, veneration. "Worship" of God is at bottom the act of expressing to God the quality and quantity of the "worth" we attribute to Him in our heart. True worshipers worship God "in the Spirit" and "in the Truth," simultaneously, with proper and equal quality and quantity attributed to each. When there is an imbalance, or "false balance," of these two components, it is, as we discussed earlier, an abomination to God, and the result is error and errancy.

The Spirit and the Truth are the two primary equilibrant and counterbalancing forces of the Kingdom of God. Manifested in their proper weight, they perfectly counterbalance one another, achieving perfect equilibrium. The "equi-union" (union in equal measure) of these two Spiritual forces produces the ultimate super-atomic Spiritual power. Thus, in this case, instead of incurring the curse of God, as with the abomination of a false balance, you incur the exact opposite—His approval and resultant free-flow of His unrestrained blessings.

Unfortunately, however, there has yet to be a movement in which the Church has successfully achieved such an equi-union of these two forces in which the Spirit and the Truth were at equilibrium, but rather the Church itself invariably brought about the eventual cessation of each former move by imposing an imbalance of either one element or the other—either majoring on manifesting spiritual power while neglecting some portion and measure of the Truth, or vice-versa. However, the final climactic move of God on the planet, which will incorporate the most awesome and unprecedented display of supernatural power in the history of the world and culminate in the "catching up" of the Bride by the Bridegroom, will be precipitated by the first-ever achievement of this equi-union. In this master-movement, the Spirit and the Truth shall converge together in precisely equal weight and balance, perfect counterbalance, achieving exact equilibrium. Then—when Jesus is truly the central figure and focus of the Church, and is flanked by Moses (the prophet of the unchangeable Law and Word of God; i.e., the **Truth**) and Elijah (the prophet of power; i.e., the **Spirit**), each in their proper place, one on the right and the other on the left hand of Jesus, the center-piece of the Kingdom of God—the transfiguration of the Church into the Kingdom and Spirit realm finally can and will transpire (Lk. 9:27- 36; Zech. 4; Rev. 11:4,6).

One of the biggest problems with devaluing doctrine and trifling with the Truth, as some people feel is necessary in order to avoid becoming what they regard to be "too intellectual" or "unspiritual" is—where do you draw the line? I mean, is there really such a thing as too much Truth? or too much teaching of the Truth? Personally, I cannot conceive of how that could be possible, but if it was, how do we know what is "too much?" One thing I do know: I'd rather have too much than too little.

As I said at the outset of this section, trifling with the Truth is a grave and even dangerous thing, and I am always wary of individuals who devalue and demean the importance of pursuing

186

and living by sound teaching or doctrine. This is far from being merely a personal opinion or judgmental attitude, rather it is predicated on the opinion and attitude of God as expressed in His Word, wherein He testifies that He Himself sends *"strong delusion"* upon those who demonstrate a persistent lack of *"love of the Truth"* which will cause them to *"believe what is false"*:

> *And then that lawless one [the Antichrist] will be revealed...; that is, the one whose coming is in accord with the activity of Satan, with all power and signs and false wonders, and with all the deception of wickedness for those who perish, **because they did not receive the love of the truth** so as to be saved. **And for this reason GOD will send upon them A DELUDING INFLU-ENCE {STRONG DELUSION (KJV)} so that they might believe what is false,** in order that they all may be judged **who did not believe THE TRUTH,** but took pleasure in wickedness. (2 Thes. 2:8-12)*

This passage reveals a number of things. One, it indicates in no uncertain terms that without proper respect and regard for the truth, what is termed here as *"the love of the Truth,"* a person simply cannot be "saved" (remember, the root Greek word for "saved" is "sozo," which means saved, sanctified, i.e., made holy, made whole, restored, etc.). A person who denigrates and de-means doctrine just cannot be wholly "saved" or "sanctified," spirit, soul, and body (see 1 Thes. 5:23)—something has to be unrenewed in one of those parts of his being; if he is genuinely "saved" in his spirit, then the sanctification of his soul (mind, will, and emotions) definitely has to be incomplete.

The second thing we see in unmistakable terms in this passage is that denigrating or degrading the Truth will eventually end in delusion, for God Himself will send *"a deluding influence"* or *"strong delusion"* upon those who trifle with the Truth. This will not be the work of the devil, but rather, this passage clearly says that it will be God Himself who will send the deceiving or deluding influence.

It almost sounds evil and cruel that God would do such a thing, but we know that God has no part in evil (Jas. 1:13). It is the same in this case as it is with all judgment that comes to people—it is not God who has brought it on them, but rather they bring it on themselves by violating His order and ordinances. If a person jumps off the top of a building, it is not God's fault if he hurts or kills himself; he brought the result on himself.

God will not strive with people forever. There will come a time when God will send upon people a superabundance of the very thing they have been ceaselessly dealing in—in this case it is deception. If you do not eventually *"receive the love of the Truth"* so as to be sanctified by it, spirit, soul, and body, God will send upon you a deluding influence that will cause you to be hopelessly and helplessly seared over in deception *"in (your) own conscience as with a branding iron"* (1 Tim. 4:2). You will wholeheartedly believe you are pursuing and believing the Truth, but it is in actuality the lies of the devil, *"doctrines of devils"* propagated by *"deceitful spirits"* (ibid, v. 1) that you are so earnestly and adamantly believing.

Sadly, though this passage speaks of the final great apostasy that will occur during the Great Tribulation when the antichrist has been revealed, I am convinced this is not something that will happen only then, but that God has already given some people over to *"reveling in their deceptions"* (1 Pet. 2:13). I have personally seen many people, both in the church and out, to whom this has happened. Certainly, the veracity of this should not be a question to us since, Paul, Peter, and Jude all spoke in their writings of such people to whom this had already occurred back in their day in the Early Church history.

Erroneous Concept #3: "Unity"

As I've often said, the problem with deception, or delusion, is that the person who is deceived is deceived about being deceived. His deception prevents him from knowing he is deceived. Such will be the case with this deluding influence that God will send— once it has come upon people, they will be forever deceived. Their relentless disfinity for the Truth of God will be regarded and rewarded as an affinity for the lies of the devil. They will finally receive their just desserts.

Indeed, the very hypothesis that the power of God can some-how be stifled by sound doctrine is itself ludicrous delusion of the highest order. Scripture declares the **Word** of God **IS** the **power** of God: *"For the WORD* (rhema) *of the Cross...is the POWER* (dunamis) *of God"* (1 Cor. 1:18; cf., Rom. 1:16).

The same import is expressed in Hebrews 1:3, which invokes the phrase *"the Word* (rhema) *of His power* (dunamis)." Now it is important to note two things about this phrase. First, the term translated "Word" is "rhema," which is God's alive/spoken Word, as opposed to the "logos," the written/non-verbal Word, which in itself, in that form, is inanimate and has no effectuality, or power. The Word must be spoken, i.e., verbalized, in order for its power to be effectual, which is the reason, for example, people can have a huge Family Bible displayed prominently on their living room table, yet have none of its power effectual in their lives. The second important thing about this passage is that it does not say "the power of His Word," though that would be a truism as well, for God's Word certainly does have power. Rather, the actual phrasing is evoking an even stronger import—that all of God's power is inherent in His Rhema-Word, that is, His active/living/verbalized Word. How true and consistent that is with the rest of Scripture. In the Creation, we see that God literally **SPOKE** the world into existence. God's creative dunamis-power was unleashed and activated when He vocalized His Word; it did not return unto Him void, but accomplished His desire, the purpose for which it was

189

sent (Is. 55:11). After the creation of Man, over and over again throughout Scripture we see God putting His Word/Will into the mouths of human surrogate spokesmen and compelling them to vocalize it in order to effect His purposes. God always **speaks** whatever He desires (wills) to transpire.

The Word of God and the power of God certainly are not counterposing or contradictory forces. Anything that is a true operation of the Spirit and power of God will always be in complete agreement and harmony with the Word of God. Thus, the unequivocal fact that all of God's dunamis-power is contained in and effectualized through His spoken-Word, and that these two forces concur and work together in tandem, renders absurd and impossible the notion that the Word of Truth, or rightly dividing it to formulate and prove sound doctrine, could somehow hinder or negate the effectuality or operation of the power or Spirit of God. If anything, the obverse of this notion is true: the more congruous with the **Word** of God we are living and operating, the more of the **power** of God will be available for us to operate (cf., Rev. 3:8).

Dunamis-power is effectualized and activated by means of the Rhema, alive/spoken Word of God. The true Gospel does not come *"in word* (logos) *only, but also in power* (dunamis) *and in the Holy Spirit and with full conviction"* (1 Thes. 1:5). The true Gospel is a "full Gospel," a Gospel full of the Spirit and power of God, because *"the kingdom of God does not consist in words* (logos) *only, but in power* (dunamis). *"*

Over-emphasis on Unity with Human Shepherds

Another reason the unity espoused and enforced in these hyper-authoritarian groups is false is that the emphasis is almost entirely on the unity of the "sheep" with their human "shepherds" rather than their unity with Jesus, the Great and Chief Shepherd (Heb. 13:20; 1 Pet. 5:4). (I will not elaborate on this matter extensively, not because it is not vital, but only because its essence is also covered in other places in this book.)

Our being *"united with Him in the likeness of His death"* in order that we might be united with Him in the likeness of His resurrection (Rom. 6:5) is far more important and spiritually imperative than is perfect unity with fellow believers, whether laymen or leadership. In fact, when you get right down to it, the metaphor of sheep and shepherds used to depict the relationship of lay-believers and leader-believers in the Body of Christ certainly has its limitations and really cannot be taken literally, because Jesus actually declared that His sheep *"shall become ONE flock with ONE Shepherd* (obviously referring to Himself)*"* (Jn. 10:16). This passage delineates the dynamic producing the only perfect unity the Body of Christ will experience in this dispensation, which is a unity in the Spirit realm, not the natural realm. Jesus is our True, literal, Shepherd. Leaders in the Body of Christ are only "shepherds" figuratively speaking, making them only surrogate-shepherds. The term is really only attributed to leaders metaphorically in Scripture to depict their role in caring for the sheep of *"the flock of GOD"* (1 Pet. 5:2) on behalf of God, and the attitude and demeanor in which they are to carry out that role, which should be in the way a real-life shepherd tenderly, caringly, and affectionately cares for his sheep.

Church leaders must be extremely vigilant that they do not cross the line and take on the role of being their followers' literal shepherd, for when that occurs, both the leader and his followers are engaging in spiritual idolatry and adultery, which God cannot forever overlook and indulge, but which He must eventually redress first with chastisement and eventually judgment for the unrepentant. It is foremostly the responsibility of the leader to insure and insist that his followers not regard him as their literal shepherd, or spiritual guru. Every church leader must be constantly reminding those to whom he ministers that he is not the "transubstantiation," or bodily manifestation, of Christ, but only a mere human (albeit God-appointed and -anointed) **intermediary**—an envoy, or surrogate spokesman, on behalf of Christ—and that Jesus Himself is the only true spiritual **mediator** between God and men (1 Tim. 2:5).

I firmly believe that judgment will be harsher for the leader who knowingly allows or induces undue and improper adoration or exaltation of himself than it will be for the followers who do it. Now there will always be some people among us, especially the *"silly women laden with sins, led away with divers lusts"* (2 Tim. 3:6, KJV) who will continue to idolize and "star-ize" leaders regardless of how much they are admonished against and even rebuked for it—leaders can do little about that, other than to be sure to avoid such people. Nevertheless, leaders must deplore and discourage every sort and degree of idolization and improper exaltation.

"Covenant Relationships"

One thing that is important to understand about abuse and impropriety associated with and resulting from the deadly weeds of false and fallacious Discipleship/Shepherdship teaching within groups in which they have been implemented is that it is by no means perpetrated exclusively at the level of the leadership. Significant interrelational impropriety and abusive activity also occurs among the "sheep" within these groups, who often act more like "goats," butting and contending with their fellows for dominion and ascendancy, than they do docile "sheep." Often, there is as much strife and predomination transpiring between the sheep as there is by shepherds toward the sheep. In the same chapter in which God pledges to judge self-aggrandizing pastors, He also pledges to judge such striving and dominating "goats":

> *And as for you, My flock, thus says the Lord God, Behold, I will judge between one sheep and another, between the rams and the male **goats**....Therefore, thus says the Lord God to them, "Behold, I, even I, will judge between the fat sheep and the lean*

sheep. Because you push with side and with shoulder, and thrust at all the weak with your horns, until you have scattered them abroad, therefore, I will deliver My flock, and they will no longer be prey; and I will judge between one sheep and another....And I will make a covenant of peace with them and eliminate harmful beasts from the land, so that they may live securely....   (Ezk. 34:17-25)

The vast majority of this sometimes vicious in-fighting and contentious competitiveness among the members of these groups is directly attributable to what, because of its excessive application is another element of error part and parcel to the Discipleship/ Shepherdship doctrines and practices—what is commonly referred to by proponents and expositors of the teaching as "covenant relationships."

In a nutshell, the premise is that since we have come into a covenantal relationship with God through Christ and His shed blood, and consequently have been "adopted" into the Divine Family (all of which, of course, is most true), then therefore we have also automatically entered into a permanent, binding covenant with every other believer who has likewise become a partaker of the same transactions, hence the term "covenant relationships." The primary emphasis of the Discipleship teaching in this regard is the interdependence and "koinonia" (i.e., commonality) among believers which it predicates on the fact that we are now "blood-brothers/sisters" by virtue of our having been adopted into the Family of God.   Typically, there is heavy reliance upon Luke's account in the Book of Acts concerning what took place in the Early Church in the days immediately following the original Pentecostal outpouring of the Holy Spirit:

*And they were continually devoting themselves to the apostles' teaching and to fellowship, to the breaking of bread and to prayer. And everyone kept feeling a sense of awe; and many wonders and signs were taking place through the apostles. And all those who had believed were together, and **had all things in*** *common* [Greek, "koina"; hence, "koinonia"]; *and they began selling their property and possessions, and were sharing them with all, as anyone might have need. And day by day continuing with one mind in the temple, and breaking bread from house to house, they were taking their meals together with gladness and sincerity of heart, praising God, and having favor with all the people. And the Lord was adding to their number day by day those who were being saved. (Acts 2:42-47)*

Lest I be misunderstood, let me hasten to say I wholeheartedly believe the principle of interdependence and commonality among believers is a valid principle, that is, within its Biblical bounds and framework. Of course it is true that all genuinely Born Again believers have been "adopted" into the Family of God, and as a result have become spiritual brothers and sisters in the Lord. So also, the New Testament especially is replete with passages reminding us of our especial responsibility toward "the Brethren." Thus, in no way am I demeaning or diminishing the validity of the special familial-type relationship in which the Brethren all share, or the special responsibility incumbent upon each of us with regard to our brothers and sisters in the Lord. A study of the "one anothers" in the books of the New Testament will bring to light the privilege and responsibility really entailed in Jesus' command to *"love one another."* Moreover, I would wholly concur that this privileged responsibility inherent with our special fraternal relationship has very real and pragmatic application in the natural realm and by no means is to be construed merely as spiritual rhetoric.

Nevertheless, while the principle of interdependence and commonality among believers certainly is a valid principle, as with the other facets of these heretical Discipleship/Shepherdship doctrines, this principle has been distorted and perverted by *"exceed(ing) that which is written,"* and extending its parameters and application beyond the import and intents delineated in Scripture. A common denominator of all heretical teaching is the "super-spiritualization" of perfectly valid principles presented in the

Word of God which are intended to have a fairly natural, pragmatic application, and on the other hand, "naturalization," or codifying in the natural realm, those things which essentially are spiritual metaphors and not intended to have an absolute literal application. The term that describes such super-spiritualization is: "mysticism." Unfortunately mysticism is something which is quite prevalent among Pentecostal and Neo-Pentecostal groups.

It is this deadly rue of Truth mixed with mysticism that has resulted in the Discipleship/Shepherdship version of "covenant relationships." Under the auspices of the fallacious and errant teachings, the application of this Scripturally-valid principle of interdependency and fraternal responsibility among believers is extended far beyond its import and intent, and conveniently transformed into very unScriptural chains of spiritual bondage and captivation. While believers are to value and validate fraternal relationships, as well as demonstrate a certain measure of undeter-able and "unconditional" commitment to one another, those relationships in terms of their application in the natural realm in the here and now are not sacrosanct or inviolable, and they most definitely do have limits.

No one in his right mind would be so foolish as to hold that this interdependence or "koinonia" amongst the Brotherhood does not have limits and boundaries. If you do, I have some bills I would be happy to send you to pay, since absolute interdependence would mean **my** bills are **your** bills. Oh, and there is a new car I am going to order and send you the bill to pay.

Likewise, thank God that the concept of interdependence among believers does not infer an obligation to live under one roof, commune-style, with everyone else who claims to be a Christian. If it did, I'd go looney in a hurry, because I don't know if you've ever noticed, but as my former pastor used to say, "God has some strange kids!" I'm sorry, no one will ever convince me that communal living as a paradigm for believers today is the import of the Acts account of the Early Church as some people contend. As far as I'm concerned there's no roof big enough for more than one family unit. Thank God, while calling us to a certain kind and degree of spiritual *inter*dependence, at the same time, He has mandated a certain kind and degree of *in*dependence as well. Just because we are all part of the "Family of God"—we don't all have to live together under one roof, nor in some sort of a Christian kibbutz.

It is no different than how God has designed it in the natural. We are all members of the human race, but we are not married to everyone, but only to one spouse, and we have our own family with whom we are intimate and to whom we are wholly committed. Moreover, we have our own home we "go home" to each night—otherwise, it would be perfectly okay for a complete stranger to come sashaying into your house in the evening saying, "Hi, folks, I'm home! What's for supper?" We all have blood-relatives, but thank God we don't have to all live together under one roof as one family unit. If we did the insane-asylums and prisons would be far more populated. It's just not humanly possible to be committed to everyone in the same way and degree as we are to our own immediate families, nor is that what God intended. Contrary to the idiotic, New Age, one-world, humanistic philosophies, the human race is not "just one big cosmic-family."

In the same vein but another area of interrelationship, neither, thank God, does interdependence, "koinonia," and "unity" mean that we all have to worship together as members of the same church. Contrary to the absurd humanistic, ecumenical philosophies espoused by some people, independence and autonomy with regard to separate and diverse churches is ordained of God. It is a real shock to some people to learn that the principle of ecclesiastical amalgamation, on the basis of which their denomination or protodenomination was formulated, is not authorized, per se, in Scripture. Besides, I am human and honest enough to admit that while I am doing my level best to try to **love** everyone, and espe-cially *"the household of God,"* I have not yet become so spiritual that I **like** everyone in the house. Some of the dear-hearts in God's house have some pretty strange ideas and very peculiar ways about them. I mean, the Word unabashedly declares we are *"a peculiar people"*—some more peculiar than others, I often add—but thank God, because we have diverse personalities and preferences, we all do not have to worship in the same way, or in the same church, "network," or denomination.

Additionally, no church or group is so sacrosanct that once you have become a member of it you cannot ever leave it without incurring the wrath and punishment of God, as some groups purport. Without question God sets believers into individual bodies, or "spiritual families," if you prefer that metaphor. But, the metaphorical comparison to earthly human families is not to be taken as literally as do the Discipleship/Shepherdship proponents. Many of them adamantly contend that once you have been set into a particular spiritual family, it is the same as being born into a blood-family—you may not like everyone in that family or every-thing about that family, but you are stuck with them nonethe-less—thus, you can never leave that church-group. However, that simply is not true, and you will not find that premise in God's Word. In the case of the our blood-family, we are born into it, and have no choice in the matter as to what family we are going to be born into. But, in the case of our spiritual family, God gives us the volitional latitude to make our own choices in that regard, within the boundaries of the requisite that their doctrine and practices are Scripturally-sound.

In finding a church-group with which we can identify and relate, God allows believers far more latitude than many preachers and layman alike want to allow. It is absolutely imperative in finding such a church-family with whom to be related that we all find one that is congruous with our own particular personality, needs, preferences, and spiritual emphasis. If there is not some measure of a match of these elements, a person will always feel like a proverbial fish out of water attending a church for which he is ill-suited, which is good for neither the church nor that person. The inevitable result, if he does not do the wise thing, which is to leave that church, will be an incurably discontented member who will eventually become something worse—a malcontent.

Many earnest and sincere believers have had the unwanted experience of finding themselves in the very unpleasant position of being very much discontented with the church they attend. That happens sometimes, and it doesn't mean there is any malice involved. In fact, in many cases it is part of the incremental spiritual education plan of God for developing believers to have to move on to another spiritual school of "higher learning" as they progress through the various stages of spiritual growth and development.

One cannot rear a child in the birthing-ward, which is what some churches are and all they will ever be. Thus, soon after the birthing process, the time comes to depart the natal-ward to go "home" where the rearing process takes place. In turn, the properly developing child will eventually outgrow the nursery and kindergarten. Elementary-school ensues, but is only a stepping-stone to middle-school, and middle-school to high-school, which in turn leads ultimately to college and post-graduate programs. No child stays in the same school for his entire educational curriculum, because every school has a different specialty, capabilities, and emphasis. No school is everything to everybody.

So also, there is going to be some "movement" that is of God on the part of believers as they progress through the spiritual development process, because the typical church is much the same as the typical school, having a parochial specialty and emphasis, as well as capabilities. Only the church that has every type of Biblically-prescribed and -ordained ministry functioning can afford

198

believers maximal and comprehensive spiritual development. And, the only church meeting those requisites is the church that has all of the Five-fold Ministry functioning in it, which church, unfortunately, as of this writing, I have yet to personally see. Thus, for those churches which do not have Five-fold ministry functioning within them, as members advance through the various stages of spiritual development, some attrition and turbulence among the membership is inevitable and unavoidable, and will remain so until Five-fold ministry is functioning in earnest in those churches, providing its members with comprehensive spiritual education and edification.

Moreover, I personally believe some of what have been labeled as "church splits" by the disgruntled pastors of the "split" churches, actually were the consequence of this problem. I mean, what is one to do when he finds himself in the position of being committed to a church that steadfastly refuses to mature spiritually, incorporating validated "present-Truth" as it is revealed by God, to continue advancing and taking new territory instead of merely maintaining the status-quo, and to periodically make warranted changes? And, what especially is a person to do if he himself has a valid and validated calling to the ministry? This kind of intransigence and unmalleableness is the real cause of many a so-called "church split" attributed to malcontent members or selfishly ambitious leaders.

Coerced Conformity

To take it a step further, the problem with the Discipleship/Shepherdship concept of "covenant relationships" is that the application of the very valid principle of interdependency and fraternal responsibility among believers is extended beyond its import and intent to virtually nullify and eliminate any semblance of personal autonomy and individuality. Contrary to the prevailing "wisdom" within much of Christendom, "autonomy," "individuality," and the much-maligned "independence" are not "four-letter words." In their proper application and context, these concepts are not incongruous with the Divine Nature and the Christ-likeness. Ezekiel's vision of a wheel within a wheel portrays the precept of "*inter*dependence with *in*dependence" inherent in the Kingdom of God and which is to exist in the administration of the Church of God.

As discussed in some detail in Chapter Four, God has created every human-being with a will, or volition, and endowed us all with the inviolable right to self-rule. So inviolable is that prerogative that not even God will violate or impinge upon it. Even when we choose to subject and subordinate our will unto God's as Jesus Himself did in the Garden of Gethsemane, that in itself is a voluntary exercising of our own free-will. We *choose* to submit and subject our will and purposes unto God and His will and purposes, but He never *coerces* us to do so.

It may come as a surprise to some, but being Born Again does not mean that we forfeit our free-will and right to self-rule in order to become some sort of mindless spiritual robot or zombie. Even after the Holy Spirit inhabits our being, we are still free moral agents, and are given the prerogative and privilege of operating in accordance with God's revealed will, allowing the Holy Spirit to lead and guide us by His inner promptings and urgings, submitting to His desires, and thereby allowing Him to live His Life through us. Being a *willing* participant in this cooperative coexistence is the great joy and privilege of it all. We are not compelled and coerced, but entreated and permitted.

Even when we are indeed Born Again, inhabited by the Spirit of God, and have become doers of His Word—active cooperatives for God on this planet—we still are not merely a contingent of identical "clones." Even then, we still have a certain amount of individuality, we still have the right of self-governance, or autonomy, and we are even given a certain kind and degree of latitude and independence within the bounds of righteousness. Independence is not intrinsically evil. While there is a certain amount of *inter*dependence inherent in our relationships as members of the Body of Christ, nonetheless, God made us *in*dependent as well. Though those two concepts may sound contradictory, in fact they are not, but rather are quite harmonious.

Unity Is Not Uniformity

The point of all this within the context of this chapter is that true unity is not uniformity; nor does it require uniformity. Too often, however, that is how people perceive unity. In fact, it is quite a common thing among humans to view diversity as opposition and even as a threat. People are commonly suspicious, distrusting, and unaccepting of anyone who is significantly different than they. Sadly, that is too frequently the case among believers also, both individually as well as the groups they comprise. But true *"unity of the Spirit"* engenders a oneness and fellowship with members of the Body of Christ actuated in the natural, physical realm, however, based purely on "likenesses" in, of, and by the Holy Spirit. True unity can never be attained on the basis of our fickle carnal personal likes and dislikes. Rather, *"the unity of the Spirit"* is a unanimity in, of, and by the Spirit, produced by the confluence of diversity to create a complimentary and harmonious concinnity (working together) of *"the body for the building up of itself in love"* (Eph. 4:16).

Good and Pleasant Unity

Separating the holy from the profane, we can see from the very first of the unity passages cited, Psalm 133:1, that the unity being described by the Spirit, in that it speaks about *"brothers,"* is a unity that is mutual among all the brotherhood, not just certain ones. Indeed, the pivotal word in this passage is *"brothers."* Despite the claims of those espousing these hyper-authority doctrines, all believers, laymen and leaders alike, are coequal brothers and part of the Brotherhood of Christ.

As it is explained and emphasized throughout this book, regardless of our God-assigned function and responsibilities, status or station in life, all believers are on par as brothers. Jesus explicitly stated that in Matthew 23:8: *"all of you are on the same level, as BROTHERS"* (L.B.). Spiritually, all believers, male and female, leader and layman, are coequal brothers. In a word, we are "peers." Indeed, the overriding point this passage expresses is that unless believers relate and interact with one another as coequal "brothers," there will be no true unity, and their relationships and interactivity, rather than *"good and pleasant,"* will be malevolent and unpleasant, yea miserable.

Having become genetic sons of God through the New Birth, believers are even (cherish the unfathomable thought!) on the same level with Jesus in terms of our heritage and inheritance. Jesus is even our Elder Brother! *"the FIRST-BORN of many BRETH-REN"* (Rom. 8:29). Because *"both He who sanctifies (Jesus) and those who are sanctified (believers) are all from one Father, He is not ashamed to call them BRETHREN, saying, 'I will proclaim Thy name to My BRETHREN'"* (Heb. 2:11,12).

Merely by virtue of the New Birth, every believer is baptized into the family of God, the Brotherhood of Christ (also known as the "Church"). Moreover, God has Himself elevated the entire entity of the Brotherhood of Christ to as sublime a height as possible short of infringement on the God-Head itself! Truly, if we ever fathomed the profound depths of this glorious Truth, all perceived need for preeminence and predominance among the Brethren would be instantaneously and eternally eradicated! Would to God it would be!

The second thing that is clear from just this first passage, Psalm 133:1, is that the unity that is being spoken of here not only is mutually beneficial and produces *"good"* results, but it also is *"pleasant."* However, there is nothing whatsoever pleasant about predomination. In groups where it exists, in which the leadership is employing witchcraft to dominate, control, and subjugate the followers, there is a distinctive foul, foreboding, fiendish sense of demonic captivation tangibly present and readily discernible to those not bewitched by its spell. But, where the Spirit of the Lord truly is present and truly is Lord rather than humans, there is always discernible liberty, liberality, and liberation from the influences of demons (2 Cor. 3:17). So then, if the interrelations among the members of a group is not a *"good and pleasant"* experience, chances are the "unity" being espoused is not a bona fide unity of the Spirit of the Lord, but rather a bogus man-centered unity.

Summary

Summarily then, while unity among believers certainly is vital and desirable, and more can be more readily accomplished for the advancement of the Kingdom of God in an atmosphere in which it prevails, it cannot, however, be correctly argued that God is totally prohibited to accomplish His will and purposes unless perfect unity is in sway. Contention, amiable disagreement on finer, peripheral points, and even a certain amount of personal disaffinity and "personality clashes" between certain individuals will always exist whenever there are multiple persons involved, believers or not; that is only human nature. Utopian unity void of all conflict simply is not going to occur *"until the perfect comes,"* and it is impractical to expect it to. God certainly knows that, and thus He does not require utopian unity to exist in order to perform His Word and Will. Hence, while we should seek and pursue pragmatic unity, or at least harmony, in all human relations as much as is realistically possible, on the other hand, unity with Jesus, true unity of the Spirit, is far more important than person-to-person unity. In fact, if everyone walked in unity of the Spirit and conformity with Christ, unity among humanity would be automatic and universal.

Chapter Seven

ERRONEOUS CONCEPT #4: ROLE OF THE LAITY

As we have already discussed, the governmental structure prescribed by the Discipleship teachings is illegitimate and diametrically opposed to the Biblical pattern and prerequisites for Divine Order and church-government. One of the most blatant and spiritually damaging, common, yet almost totally overlooked, conceptual errors contained in these false teachings concerns the role of laity, and more specifically, the appointment of lay-believers into functions and positions of ministry to which they have not been appointed or anointed to function in by the Lord.

Improper and unscriptural deployment of laity is a problem prevalent throughout the Church, and which was unfortunately further increased as a result of erroneous teaching during the Charismatic Movement. But nowhere is this problem more manifest than in churches where the multi-level Discipleship/Shepherdship authority structure is instituted, which, as explained in some detail previously, is a pyramid-shaped "chain-of-command" consisting of various echelons of so-called "leaders" who almost without exception are lay-believers, that is to say, those not in Five-fold Ministry. These individuals, referred to by various nomenclatures in different groups such as "fellowship group leaders," or "cell group leaders," or simply "leaders," or in some groups even "elders," are regarded within the group to be the spiritual leaders who actually "shepherd" and "disciple" those believers assigned to their cluster-group. Each of these "leaders" is one link in the "chain-of-command" of those local churches, who are "related" (they call it) to an up-line intermediate "supervisor" of sorts (if the church is large enough to warrant this intermediate echelon), who in turn are "related" up the line ultimately to the chief leader of the church, who is usually referred to as the Senior Pastor, or Senior Shepherd, or some similar appellation.

Typically, each of these "leaders" has a covey of members over which they are overseers, which group is often known as cell-groups, fellowship-groups, or something similar. These different echelons of lay-leaders function in essence as spiritual intermediaries between the Senior Shepherd and "the sheep" (the congregants). They are selected and appointed either by the senior leader himself or at least with his final approval.

Of course, those churches which institute this hierarchical structure, claim it is beneficial to the people in that each sheep has a "personal shepherd" to whom to "relate," and that it allows for more "personalized ministry" as the members of the church assemble in smaller groups for what they consider "fellowship" and "personal ministry." Despite the purported benefits, convenience, and various forms of utility such a proposition and structure may appear on the surface to offer, it is, nonetheless, in several very important ways, completely contraventive of and contradictory to the explicit Word, Will, and Way of the Lord with regard to ministry and government within the Church. Moreover, as I have mentioned earlier, this structure is virtually identical to the Nicolaitan system that emerged in the First Century and eventually evolved into the Catholic Papal/cleric system, which system the Lord explicitly condemned in Scripture.

Erroneous Concept #4: Role of the Laity

God Alone Appoints and Anoints

First of all, it contravenes and contradicts God's revealed Word, Will, and Way with regard to appointment of men into ministry offices and functions in the Church. Mortal humans do not possess the perfect omniscience and understanding required to be able to select others for such crucial posts of spiritual leadership. God is the only one who is qualified, by virtue of His infinite Wisdom juxtaposed to finite human reasoning, to properly select and appoint men unto positions of leadership in both *spiritual* and *secular* governments.

All throughout the Bible, it was God who appointed men into leadership positions. And, invariably, those whom God chose, the people rejected, and refused to recognize—from Moses to David to the prophets to Jesus. The same is true yet today: those whom God **ordains**, men **disdain**. On this you can rely: if you are truly **ordained** by God, you will be **disdained** by the vast majority of people, including the very ones to whom God has sent you.

Jesus was the Chief Apostle, the Supreme Sent One, which is what the word "apostle" means: "sent one." Yet, He was the very Stone, the Chief Cornerstone, which the builders rejected. And, Jesus assured every truly called, anointed, appointed, and sent minister that if they rejected Him, the Chief Apostle, the maximally Anointed One, then certainly they will also reject every other anointed one of lesser measure and status. Yet, Jesus explicitly explained that it is not us personally they are rejecting, but the Christ, the Anointed One, in us—The Word of God **MAN**ifested in the flesh: *"...he who rejects you rejects Me, and he who rejects Me rejects He who sent Me"* (Lk. 10:16).

Simply put, the **appointments** of God are evident by the **anointing** with which He endows those He appoints. Those He **appoints**, He **anoints**. No anointing, no appointment. It's just that simple! It is not difficult to recognize the choices God has made for leadership—those He has **appointed** He has **anointed**, with inordinate supernatural enablement and authority to function in certain spiritual capacities with overtly obvious and undeniable supernatural ability and capability.

Moreover, the appointments of God are made purely on the basis of and in the realm of spirituality, not natural, fleshly qualities. Many of those things which men consider to be *disqualifying*, God considers to be *qualifying* in redeemed vessels through whom He has chosen to make His Glory known. In the natural realm, the responsibility of believers is to merely recognize those whom God has anointed, appointed, and sent as surrogate leaders to lead on His behalf, in His stead, and as His personal envoys. In those situations where men are required to "appoint" other men to leadership functions, it is incumbent upon them to recognize those whom the Lord has chosen for appointment to those posts of responsibility by recognizing the anointing and supernatural enablements, or "unctions for function" as we have called them elsewhere, with which the Lord has anointed His selectees.

Hence, in reality, it is only in a semantic sense that men "appoint" men to spiritual functions, for in the truest sense it is God only who makes such selections and appointments. In the final analysis, all that men can do is to recognize what God is doing and has done, remembering that in all these matters the identifying and distinguishing mark from God is the anointing.

Contravention of Divine Order

Another way in which this matter of the appointment of laymen unto leadership positions contradicts the explicit Word, Will, and Ways of the Lord, which therefore renders it invalid, is that it contravenes Divine Order. Everything God does He does properly and in accordance with Divine Order. His entire Kingdom is predicated on Divine Order. None of God's doings are random, haphazard, indiscriminate, or disorderly. Anything that is truly

"Spiritual," that is to say, "Spirit-born," will be completely congruous with Divine Order; it will be orderly. Likewise, everything in the Church, and all spiritual functions, are to be *"done decently and in order"* (1 Cor. 14:40), which means in accordance with Divine Order.

This is especially true in regards to appointment of men into leaderships positions. When it comes to that, not just anybody—any ole Christian—will do. There is Divine Order which God has prescribed for the Church and every matter involved in it, which **MUST** be observed and followed explicitly. However, disregard for the Divine Order of God in this regard especially is rampant throughout organized Christendom. Indeed, this matter of lay-persons occupying positions of function to which they have not been called, anointed, or appointed by God is one of the most detrimental and widespread problems in the Church. Incalculable spiritual damage has been perpetrated upon much of the Body of Christ as a result.

Intrusion and Usurpation by Laymen

Culpability regarding error and excess during the Charismatic Movement was by no means limited to leaders. Certainly, excesses and patented error involving governmental authority were perpetrated by ecclesiastical *leaders* under the auspices of the Discipleship/Shepherdship doctrines and practices. However, many *lay-saints* as well were proactive participants in overt error and contravention of Divine Order, whether wittingly or unwittingly, in that they usurpingly intruded, either through self-appointment or acceptance of appointment by their up-line leaders, into positions of leadership to which they had not been called, appointed, or anointed by *God*. The unfortunate infusion of the erroneous Discipleship teachings during the Charismatic Movement further enhanced the proliferation of the "Charismaniacal" error on which I elaborated in Chapter Four, in which many Charismatics misconstrued spiritual (ministerial) *power* for governmental *authority*. It was on the basis of these misconceptions that many groups and churches espousing Discipleship doctrines and practices appointed lay-saints unto ministerial leadership positions reserved by God for Five-fold Ministers, positions to which those lay-saints had no calling, anointing, or appointment from God.

Such appointments were often predicated, not on spiritual acumen, but on financial, professional, or social, status. Usually, it was those who contributed the most money and were the most socially "prominent" and "prestigious" members of the church who were appointed as down-line leaders. The long and the short of it was that typically those appointed to those leadership positions in the spiritual chain were so appointed not on the basis of their *spirituality* but their *"sociality,"* that is, their social status.

This is not to infer, mind you, that such blatant partiality, personal favoritism, and preferential treatment toward the "rich and famous" is in any way a new phenomenon in ecclesiastical circles, or that it is limited to Discipleship groups. Far from it. Rather, this has been a common occurrence for millennia. Indeed, this "sin of partiality" was a problem already in the First Century churches, as the Elder James' epistle indicates, wherein he not only characterized such practices and the attitudes behind them as outright **SIN**, but also equated them to spiritual **MURDER**, and identified those who engage in such partiality as **TRANSGRESSORS** of the Laws of God:

> *My brethren, do not hold your faith in our glorious Lord Jesus Christ with an attitude of PERSONAL FAVORITISM. For if a man comes into your assembly with a gold ring and dressed in fine clothes, and there also comes in a poor man in dirty clothes, and you pay special attention to the one who is wearing the fine clothes, and say, 'You sit here in a good place,' and you say to the poor man, 'You stand over there, or sit down by my footstool,' have you not made distinctions among yourselves, and become judges with evil motives? Listen, my beloved brethren:*

*did not God choose the poor of this world to be rich in faith and heirs of the kingdom which He promised to those who love Him? But you have dishonored the poor man. Is it not the rich who oppress you and personally drag you into court? Do they not blaspheme the fair name by which you have been called? If, however, you are fulfilling the royal law, according to the Scripture, 'You shall love your neighbor as yourself,' you are doing well. But if you show **PARTIALITY**, you are committing **SIN** and are convicted by the law as **TRANSGRESSORS**. For whoever keeps the whole law and yet stumbles in one point, he has become guilty of all. For He who said 'Do not commit adultery,' also said, 'Do not commit **MURDER.**' Now if you do not commit adultery, but do commit murder, you have become a **TRANSGRESSOR** of the law. (Jas. 2:1-11)*

The many negative effects produced by this particular aspect of patented error—appointment of laymen into leadership functions—was another tragic consequence resulting from incursion of the Discipleship teachings into the Charismatic Movement. In a nutshell, the overall consequence was that much devastation, both spiritual and natural, was wrought in the lives of untold thousands of unwitting victims as a result of the incompetent, unsanctioned, and unsanctified "ministry" perpetrated upon them through these humanly-appointed laymen under the auspices of these unBiblical "doctrines of demons."

David and the Ark: Bringing Back the Glory of God

There is an outstanding story recounted in the Thirteenth and Fifteenth Chapters of Chronicles, which poignantly illustrates God's aversion to such usurpation by laity, and the judgment it can evoke. It also illustrates what must take place in the End-times Church in order to bring back into the Church the Glory of God—the tangible manifestation of God's Presence. It is the story of King David's noble but catastrophic attempt to retrieve and restore to its proper place of veneration in Israel the Ark of the

Covenant, the icon of God's Presence and habitation among the Hebrews.

For twenty years during the reign of Saul, the Ark of the Covenant, the most sacred religious icon of Judaism, had remained in the house of Abinadab in Kiriath-Jearim, ever since it was returned by the Philistines, who had seized it and then sent it back when they were subjected to terrible curses from God while it was in their possession. Yet, even after the Philistines had sent it back, all during the days of Saul's reign and Israel's apostasy from the Lord, the Israelites did not seek the Ark of God's Presence or even have a desire to return it to its proper place of veneration within the heart of the nation. So it remained in the house of Abinadab the Levite in Kiriath-Jearim until finally, sometime after becoming king over all of Israel following the death of Saul, David, himself having a heart after God, set out to bring back the Ark of the Covenant to the capital city of his new kingdom, Jerusalem.

> *Then David consulted with the captains of the thousands and the hundreds, even with every leader. And David said to all the assembly of Israel, 'If it seems good to you, and if it is from the Lord our God, let us send everywhere to our kinsmen who remain in all the land of Israel, also to the priests and Levites who are with them in their cities with pasture lands, that they may meet with us; and let us bring back the ark of our God to us, for we did not seek it in the days of Saul.' Then all the assembly said that they would do so, for the thing was right in the eyes of all the people. (1 Chron. 13:1-4)*

We see in these verses that after consulting with the leaders of the people and the military commanders, David had somehow garnered the unanimous consent and support of the entire nation for his very noble and right idea of bringing back the Ark of the Covenant, for *"the thing was **right** in the eyes of ALL the people"* (a miracle in itself for any religious congregation, this apparent unanimity). In the next few verses we are told that David assembled all of Israel together in a huge processional replete with pomp and circumstance, and set out toward Kireath-Jearim.

After retrieving the Ark from the house of Abinadab the Levite, the massive human procession slowly made its way toward Jerusalem, with the Ark of God being carried on a brand new, specially constructed, wooden, ox-drawn cart, driven by two of David's closest servants, Uzza and Ahio. All along the sojourn, *"David and all of Israel,"* we are told, *"were celebrating before God with all their might, even with songs and with lyres, harps, tambourines, cymbals, and with trumpets."*

What an awe-inspiring sight it surely was—all of Israel worshipping the Lord with all their might, with musicians playing anointedly, and all the people singing and exulting the Lord with maximum jubilance and exuberance!

It all seemed to be such a right, pious, and noble idea! Who could fault it? How could any of this possibly be wrong, especially since it was all being bathed in high-spirited, celebrative worship and praise? Yet, as is soon apparent, *something* is indeed **drastically** wrong, and *someone* does indeed find fault with the proceedings—God Himself, the very One who was the supposed object of their exultation.

Suddenly, without warning, tragedy strikes. The oxen stumble, the cart teeters and the Ark is nearly thrown off. In a natural reflex reaction, Uzza reaches out to steady the Ark and prevent it from being desecrated by falling to the ground. What a seemingly noble and even heroic act by this dedicated servant of David, whose very name, Uzza, means "strength" or "strong one!" But, astonishingly, the anger of the Lord burns against Uzza, and He strikes him dead!

David is stunned and incredulous. Why on earth would God do this—kill one of his most loyal and dedicated workers, whose heroic deed seemed worthy of reward, not punishment? What cause would God have to be so angered with these proceedings?

Despite his total incredulity, David personally assumed complete responsibility in the matter, and began fervently seeking God for answers to these tormenting questions. Anyone who has had a sincere and earnest desire to accomplish something on behalf of God and His Kingdom, but after a great deal of expended effort and energy encounters only seeming defeat, disappointment, and discouragement, is no doubt well familiar with the position David found himself in—humiliated, but not bowed.

Great men like David become so *not* because their every endeavor is successful and because they never experience failure. On the contrary, every great man in history was well acquainted with failure, and became great because of their dogged tenacity in the face of setbacks and temporary failures. Thomas Edison, for instance, failed more than 10,000 times before finally succeeding at making the incandescent light bulb.

Abraham Lincoln, probably the most strategically placed President in American history, first failed at virtually everything he ever attempted. He *failed* in his life more than most people have *tried* in theirs. He failed in business twice, suffered a nervous breakdown once, was defeated in his first bid for the Legislature, defeated for Speaker of the Legislature, defeated for State-Elector, defeated for Congress twice, defeated for the Senate twice, and defeated for Vice President. Finally, "Honest Abe" failed himself right into the highest office in this land when he was elected as the Sixteenth President of the *United* States of America, which surely would not have remained *united* had it not been for the unflagging resolve of this one man to preserve the Union against all odds, a multitude of Union defeats, and an abundance of seemingly insurmountable obstacles. Lincoln's dubious portfolio of failures and setbacks only served to produce in this truly "great" man more character, perseverance, and resolve.

James tells us that the testing of our faith through fiery trials produces in us perseverance, which in the end will result in our being *"perfect"* (mature), *"complete"* (in Christ), and *"lacking in nothing"* (Jas. 1:1-4). Ultimately, that is precisely what all of Abraham Lincoln's so-called "failures" produced in him—a never-say-quit, dogged determination seen in few in the annals of human history. His so-called "failures" made him the one, solitary man of the vast sea of humanity alive at the time who in the Omniscience of God was "qualified" to bear to the end without fainting the immense burdens of the presidency over "a nation conceived in liberty and dedicated to the proposition that all men are created equal," but whose continued existence hung precariously in the balance while noble and heroic men dutifully sacrificed their lives to defend and uphold that ideal.

Indeed, truly great men invariably become great not because they have never experienced failure, but because they refuse to allow failures and frustrations to be final. Great men refuse to allow failure to *break* them, but rather allow it to *make* them. Setbacks do not cause great men to quit and get *bitter*, but rather to move them to increase their resolve and get *better*. Failure, to great men, is their greatest teacher. Success teaches precious little, and frequently is only the precursor to imminent and inevitable failure.

Failure drives godly men back to God, to seek His face, to hear His voice, to search His Word, to comprehend His Will, and to discover His Ways. Godly men who have come to know their God in personal intimacy know that frustration is not final, delays are not denials, and detours are not dead-ends. Especially in these last days in which Satan is employing every last weapon of his arsenal against the saints of God, it is such godly men, who *"know their God"*—that is, those who have an accurate revelation of God's Nature, which they have received in virtually continuous intimacy and fellowship in His Presence, *"praying without ceasing"*—who will **RISE UP** out of seeming defeat, the strong pull of despair, and the death-grip of discouragement, and despite all opposition **"DO**

GREAT EXPLOITS" on behalf of God and the unstoppable advance of His Kingdom (see Dan. 11:32).

David was truly a "great man." No one who has ever lived more deserved that attribution than he. Not because he never failed. Much to the contrary, he experienced many failures and temporary defeats. But, David was great because his failures always drove him **TO** God and not **AWAY** from God. The end-result of all his failures and defeats was that he became closer to God and closer to being like God, *"a man after the heart of God."*

Everyone who has experienced temporary failure in his or her attempted exploits on behalf of God and His Kingdom is well familiar with the process of circumspection David was now going through—prayer....intensified Scripture-study....more prayer....self-examination....repentance....more prayer....contemplation....more prayer. As he sought God regarding this matter, he could not find cause to summarily abandon the original premise—surely God too wanted the emblem of His presence to be returned to Jerusalem and to the proper place of veneration in the collective heart of His people. No, the idea of recovering and restoring the Ark was not the problem, it need not be abandoned, it was right, David concluded. But, for months he agonized over what cause God would have for such righteous indignation so as to strike Uzza dead.

Finally David discovered in the Mosaic ordinances where he had missed it, which he discloses was that: *"No one is to carry the ark of God but THE LEVITES; for the Lord chose them to carry the ark of God, and to minister to Him forever"* (1 Chron. 15:2). The reason that the Lord struck Uzza dead was that God had commanded that the Ark of God's Glory was to be handled and carried only by the **LEVITES**, and it was the **LEVITES** who had been set apart by God to perform the sacred duties of oblation and to tend to the tabernacle and all its furnishings; **no LAYMAN** was

216

even to *"TOUCH IT, lest they die"* (Num. 1:50,51). This was the set ordinance of God. Only the **LEVITES** could carry the Ark of God, and it had to be carried on two poles on the **shoulders** of the **LEVITES** (1 Chron. 15:15; Num. 7:9). This was God's Divine *Order* as well as His set and inviolable Divine *Ordinance*.

This was where David missed it, though he had consulted with the people and the leaders of the people, and even obtained their unanimous consent, he had not consulted with the **LEVITES** concerning this matter. But after he had sought God and searched the Scriptures to see how he had erred, he called together the chiefs of the Levites and said to them:

> *...consecrate yourselves both you and your relatives, that you may bring up the ark of the Lord God of Israel, to the place that I have prepared for it. Because you did not carry it at the first, the Lord our God made an outburst on us, **for we did not seek Him according to the ORDINANCE.***

"...we did not seek Him according to the ordinance." This story conveys in very poignant fashion some vital Truths to us who comprise the Church today regarding the matter of Divine Order. It is not enough to have right ideas and even zealous worship, but we must also seek God according to His ordinances, i.e. His principles of Order. David, you see, had the right **idea** but the wrong **order**. The moral of this story is that *right* ideas, no matter how right, proper, and noble, cannot override *wrong* order. Human *ideas*, regardless of their goodness, must never be given precedence over God's *ideals*. Human *ideas* that violate God's *ideals* are, in the final analysis doomed to failure. In all that we do on behalf of God, it is not enough that our *premise* is right, but we must also observe right *principles*, the principles of the Kingdom of God.

It is astounding to me that there are so many churches which are ignorant of and oblivious to the matter of the Order of God, and who believe that operating according to God's Order is not important as long as you just "love the Lord" and are *zealous* in worshipping Him. But, such "zeal without knowledge," the death of Uzza illustrates so poignantly, can be deadly! Jesus said that *"true worshipers"* are those who worship *"in Spirit AND TRUTH"* (Jn. 4:23), and that, *"If you love Me, you will keep My COMMANDMENTS* (ordinances)*"* [Jn. 14:15].

Prophetic Prefigurement of Structural Reformation

This story also proffers a prophetic prefigurement to the Church today, which is that in the coming days God is going to bring structural reformation within the true Body of Christ in order to set the correct government into the Church. *"The government shall be upon His* (Jesus') *shoulders"* (Is. 9:6). As the Levites were to carry the Ark bearing God's manifest Presence by two poles on their shoulders, so the government of the Last-Day Church shall rest upon the shoulders of Christ, the Apostles and Prophets, and the Five-fold Ministers. Only those churches which have chosen to institute the paradigm of His government will bear His seal, which is the Anointing and the manifested Glory of God.

This restructuring must take place in order to bring the Glory of God back into the Church. The Ark of God's presence, the Glory of God, is going to be manifest only within the camp of those who are willing to allow the government of the Church to truly be borne upon the shoulders of Jesus. Layman-ruled churches, as well as those ruled by monarchial autocrats, shall become as dead, lifeless and listless, spiritually, as Uzza. The last great restorational move of God shall be a move in which the End-time Church will be established in proper Divine Order in accordance with the ordinance of God.

Erroneous Concept #4: Role of the Laity

Jeroboam Judgment

While God in His abundant grace and mercy has until now been staying His hand of judgment against churches for such blatant contravention of His ordinances and ordained Order, it would be a dire and costly mistake to presume that this temporary indulgence will continue forever. As God, during the remaining *"periods of restoration"* (Ac. 3:21), reveals His explicit Will in regard to Divine Order and government within the Church, it will not come in the form of *suggestions*, but rather *commandments*. The structural changes that He will then require will not be *optional*, but rather *mandatory*.

The Lord has told me that in fact He has already made His Will regarding these matters known by the Spirit to some leaders. These, He has told me, really already know the Way which He has ordained for them to walk in, for they have heard His voice behind them clearly whispering into their ear, "This is the Way, walk ye in it!" But, the majority of these have so far refused His leadings and promptings, not wanting to be among the first to begin to implement the wholesale changes obedience would require, nor to endure the vehement opposition from the people and the upheaval that would surely ensue if they were to set out to reverse the traditional and accepted course of "layocracy" they have been following, and to revamp the existing hierarchical structure within their church.

However, God will not endure this blatant non-compliance with His revealed Will interminably. Indeed, there will soon come the time when disobedience of God's explicit, revealed Will and stubborn intransigence in this regard will bring temporal judgment from the hand of God.

In order to corroborate this assertion from Scripture, it is once again from the types and shadows of the Old Testament, which,— *"happened as an examples for US," and "were written for OUR instruction, upon whom the ends of the ages have come"* (1 Cor. 10:6,11)—that we draw another case in point that so poignantly illustrates God's aversion to the appointment of lay-persons to positions of spiritual leadership, as well as the fact that He will eventually bring judgment upon churches that practice such overt contravention of the explicit ordinances of God. This illustration is portrayed in the story of Jeroboam, the first king of Israel following the separation of the tribe of Judah from Israel. The whole saga of Jeroboam with all the pertinent events and circumstances surrounding it is found in the Eleventh through the Fourteenth Chapters of First Kings; for the more studious readers, a somewhat sketchier version appears in the Thirteenth Chapter of Second Chronicles.

The sum of the story is this. In the later years of his life, Solomon, son of David and king of Israel, was seduced by his harem of 300 concubines and 700 foreign wives (who he had married in contravention of God's explicit command to the Israelites not to take wives from the Gentile nations) into falling away from God, and into worship of the false, foreign gods of their nations instead. Not only did Solomon become a practitioner of these false religions, but he even used the nation's public funds to build "high places," shrines and temples of worship dedicated to these idols.

Needless to say, Solomon's headlong descent into depravity and spiritual perdition incurred the wrath and anger of God, which becomes even more understandable and justified when one realizes that the worship rites and rituals to these false gods involved such perverted and grisly practices as child molestation and sacrifice, rape, incest, homosexuality, bestiality, prostitution, live dismemberment, cannibalism, and other inhuman and deviate sexual practices.

As a part of Divine retribution for his apostasy and debauchery, God vowed to wrest the kingship over Israel from the house, or lineage, of Solomon, and to give it to another family. Jeroboam, who had been a personal appointee of Solomon within his administration as a "warden" of sorts over the forced laborers, was the man to whom God gave the kingship over Israel.

To accomplish all of this which He vowed, God caused a political "split" to occur within the confederation of the tribes of Israel. The result of this split was that Judah was disenfranchised from the other remaining ten tribes of Israel, becoming, in essence, a separate nation. Now Scripture explicitly indicates that it was God who caused this split: *"for it was a turn of events from the Lord, that He might establish His word"* (1 Kgs. 12:15). (As an aside, this is proof-positive that it is God Himself who is behind some of the church-splits occurring today with increased frequency, concerning which many have become extremely paranoid and distrustful these days, spawning what I call "split-phobia."). God brought about this segregation of the tribe of Judah in order to preserve the perpetual lineage of kings from the house of David, from which the ultimate King—the Messiah—would descend, as He had promised David He would.

So Rehoboam, son of Solomon and grandson of David, remained king over the now detached tribe of Judah. As a result of this split, we are informed, a split-consciousness developed in the minds of Jews, an innate and universal aversion, if you will, by Jews to the Royalty and Reign of the House of David: *"So Israel has been in rebellion against the house of David to this day"* [v. 19], which aversion ultimately results in the rejection of their Messiah, Jesus Christ.

Jeroboam, however, did not comprehend the plan God had set into motion, and in the passage of time, after ascending to the throne, gradually grew paranoid at the prospect that Israel might one day return to God in their hearts, which would entail also a return to veneration of the house of David, resulting in the enthronement of Rehoboam as king over a reunited Israel, and the dethronement of Jeroboam. Thus, he contrived a plan by which to seduce the Israelites to follow after false gods rather than Jehovah.

Essentially what he did was invent a false and counterfeit religion. He built two golden calves, and decreed them the official gods of Israel, declaring to the nation: *"Behold your gods, O Israel, that brought you up from the land of Egypt."* And, he set up one golden calf as a religious shrine in the city of Bethel, and the other in the city of Dan, in order to divert the Jews away from even entering the city of Jerusalem, which had long been venerated by the Jews as the City of God, and for which there had been a centuries-long, innate, God-placed, affection within the collective Jewish heart. Otherwise, Jeroboam feared, the Jews may one day be wooed back to the City of God and to worship of Jehovah, which would mean the reinstatement of the reign of the house of David and the termination of his own rule.

> *Now this thing (what Jeroboam did) became a sin, for the people went to worship before the one* (i.e., the golden calf) *as far as Dan. (v. 30, parenthesis added by author)*

So we see in the above verse that all this which Jeroboam did was sinful and utterly wicked in the sight of God. Yet, it was what Jeroboam did in addition to all of that which was even more egregious, and is what is pertinent to our discussion here, which is described this way in the Biblical account:

> *"And he made houses (shrines and temples; or, churches) on high places, and made priests FROM AMONG ALL THE PEOPLE WHO WERE <u>NOT OF THE SONS OF LEVI</u>."*
> *(1 Kgs. 12:31, parenthesis added by author)*

As mentioned before in previous chapters, God had set apart the tribe of Levi, the Levites, to minister unto Him, and to serve as ministers and priests on His behalf unto the people. Laymen, that is to say, non-Levites, were strictly prohibited from being priests and from performing any of the duties and functions relegated by God to the Levites. As we saw with Uzza, any layman who merely touched the holy furnishings of the tabernacle which the Levites alone were authorized by God to handle, would be struck dead by

God. Laymen simply could not be priests or perform the functions of the Levitical priests.

But, Jeroboam violated this sacrosanct ordinance, and made non-Levites priests. In a public rebuke, Abijah, king of Judah, when he came up against Jeroboam and his army in battle, severely denounced Jeroboam for this blasphemous profanation, delineating in his denunciation the primary, self-aggrandizing requisite set by Jeroboam for anyone desiring to be ordained as a priest:

> *"So now you intend to resist the kingdom of the Lord in the hands (under the rule) of the sons of David, being a great multitude and having with you the golden calves which Jeroboam made for gods for you.* **Have you not driven out the priests of the Lord, the sons of Aaron and the Levites, and made for yourselves priests like the peoples of other lands? Whoever comes to consecrate himself with a young bull and seven rams, even he may become a priest of what are no gods.** *But as for us, the Lord is our God, and we have not forsaken Him; and the sons of Aaron are ministering to the Lord as priests, and the Levites attend to their work. And every morning and evening they burn to the Lord burnt offerings and fragrant incense, and the showbread is set on the clean table, and the golden lampstand with its lamp is ready to light every evening; for we keep the charge of the Lord our God, but you have forsaken Him.* **Now behold, God is with us at our head and His priests** *with the signal trumpets to sound the alarm against you. O sons of Israel, do not fight against the Lord God of your fathers, for you will not succeed." (2 Chron. 13:8-12, parenthesis added by author)*

Notice what Abijah pointed out to be the dire consequence of Jeroboam's ordination of laymen as priests, which was that in so doing: ***"Have you not driven out the priests of the Lord, the sons of Aaron and the Levites...?"*** This speaks to another of the major problems caused by the appointment of laymen to spiritual ministry functions in the Church intended by God to be performed by the

"Levites," whom the Lord has chosen, anointed, and appointed as priests unto the people, which today are Five-fold Ministers. The ultimate effect is that the Five-fold Ministry Offices are circumvented, and thus, in essence, abrogated and annulled, and the New Testament Levitical priests of the Lord are driven out and displaced. As a result, today, myriads of God's chosen, anointed, and appointed ministers have been precluded from functioning as God has intended, in the capacities and places he has intended, because they have been displaced from their designated functions by laymen.

One of Satan's greatest accomplishments during the spiritual eclipse of the Dark Ages was the abrogation and nullification of the anointed gifts which Jesus gave to the Church for the building up of the Church—the Five-fold Ministry Offices (Eph. 4:7-16). He knows that as long as he can keep these anointed gifts non-functional, he can preclude the building up of the Body of Christ unto the full stature of Christ, thus delaying the eradication of his own kingdom of darkness on the Earth. Satan knows that when the Church truly matures into the Image of Christ, he and his kingdom-reign on this Earth will be brought to an abrupt end in short order, and he along with all his cohorts will finally meet with their destiny and just desserts in the Lake of Fire. Thus, his greatest fear, and the thing he fights the most, is the restoration of the remaining Five-fold Ministry Offices yet to be restored to full function and fruition in the Body of Christ—the foundation ministries of the Church to whom the Cornerstone is attached—the Apostles and Prophets (Eph. 2:20).

So it was that when the Charismatic Movement was gathering momentum and having sweeping effect worldwide, in order to derail the Movement, Satan planted tares and deadly weeds of error and excess in the Garden of God (the Church), in the form of the heretical Discipleship/Shepherdship doctrines of demons, in which was inherent an effective weapon against the restoration of the

Five-fold Ministries—displacement—effectuated via the unautho-rized appointment of laymen into those relegated capacities of leadership. The consequence of Satan's successful implantation of these deadly weeds of false teaching and tares of false leaders has been one of the greatest tragedies and losses in the Church during this Century—the displacement of God's Levites, i.e., Apostles, Prophets, Evangelists, Pastors, and Teachers.

We may never know until *"the perfect* (knowledge) *comes"* how many of these anointed Ambassadors of Christ, due to the necessity common to all of having to make a living and to support their families, have been forced by lack of receptivity and support by the Church, and by displacement by laymen, to abandon in part or whole the ministry to which they were called. My sense in the Spirit is that the number is thousands or possibly even tens of thousands. Indeed, my personal conviction is that over the years of this century alone, when God has been desiring to reestablish all of the Five-fold ministry offices back into their full and proper function in the Church, a significant number of ministries have been essentially "murdered," so to speak, as were the prophets God sent Israel, out of wholesale ignorance and stiff-necked rejection of God's plan, in effect making many of these men of God mod-ern-day martyrs of sorts.

In regard to financial giving, unfortunately, the masses of purporting Christians today, because of their carnality and spiritual insensitivity, ineptness, and ignorance, have an immense propensity for supporting with God's tithes and offerings everything except what God has truly anointed, appointed, and ordained. Most of God's tithes and offerings are going to support humanly contrived organizations and programs which bear no Divine approbation or sanction whatsoever. For instance, Christians are so eager to financially support that ilk of travelling gypsy-minstrel who euphe-mistically refer to themselves as "Evangelists" or "music ministers," many of whom are really nothing more than *"wandering stars"*

(Jude 13) in search of stardom in Christendom, having been unable, in some cases by reason of the mediocrity of their "talent," to attain such a status in the world. How willing, also, are the majority of professing Christians to support professional clerics who perceive the ministry as an attractive occupation inured with certain accouterments of honor and respect (a goodly percentage of those in the ministry), rather than a true vocation, i.e., a "calling" by God to servitude.

The impact of this impropriety and ineptness on the part of the vast majority of Christians in the matter of who they support with their tithes and offerings has been immeasurable in various respects. The loss to those true ministers with a valid ministry appointment from God who should have been receiving their rightful *"share in the altar"* (1 Cor. 9:13), enabling them to fulfill their calling, but whose share was unjustly preempted by unworthy usurpers, has been of enormous consequence over the years. Yet, by far the greatest losses in this terrible tragedy has been not to those men of God, but rather the people of God, believers, the Church at-large, for they have been precluded from receiving the great spiritual edification and impartation of which they could have partaken had these anointed and appointed agents of God not been displaced and prevented from functioning. Satan, the thief, came to steal, kill, and destroy, and God's people have indeed been robbed. It was precisely this consequence Jesus was warning against in His impassioned admonition that whoever receives a prophet, in particular, "as a prophet"—that is to say, assists and allows him to function in the office and anointing of a prophet—shall receive the prophet's "reward," which means: the benefit of the prophet's ministry (Mat. 10:41).

Returning to the story of Jeroboam....Jeroboam's apostate actions angered God. Consequently, God sent intense adversity against Jeroboam by raising up two vicious arch-rivals. The purpose of the adversity was to bring Jeroboam to the place where he would repent from his wickedness against God. But, he refused:

> "...Jeroboam did not return from his evil way, but again he made priests of the high places from among all the people; any who would be ordained, to be priests of the high places. And this event became sin to the house of Jeroboam, even to BLOT IT OUT AND DESTROY IT FROM OFF THE FACE OF THE EARTH." (1 Kgs. 13:33,34)

Indeed, this is precisely what God set out to do immediately: i.e., bring judgment upon the house of Jeroboam, "even to blot it out and destroy it from the off the face of the earth." And, the very next verse says: "At that time Abijah the son of Jeroboam became sick" (1 Kgs. 14:1).

Now when his son became sick unto death, all of a sudden Jeroboam became desperate to hear from the one and only true God, Jehovah, knowing full well that the gods he had compelled Israel to worship were completely bogus and non-existent idols of his own invention. Thus, he devised a surreptitious ruse by which he hoped to bamboozle the now aged prophet Ahijah, who was the messenger of the Lord who had prophesied Jeroboam's kingship, into favoring him with a word from Jehovah God as to the fate of the boy. To carry out his scheme, he made his wife disguise herself, thinking he could hoodwink the old prophet who he surmised to be senile, and sent her to the man of God in secret so that Israel would not know that their king was seeking a word from Jehovah instead of the false gods he had instituted. No doubt Jeroboam rationalized that in view of all the evil he had committed against Jehovah God, there was no way the prophet would be willing to give him a word from God. Hence, the foolish ruse.

But, of course, God was not hoodwinked by the ruse, and He told Ahijah in advance by the Spirit precisely what would be transpiring with regard to the conspiracy of Jeroboam and his wife. Imagine the shock, surprise, and trepidation of Jeroboam's wife when she arrived, supposedly unannounced and secretly, at the house of the aged and now blind prophet, who when he heard the sound of her feet at the door greeted her by saying, *"Come in wife of Jeroboam, why do you pretend to be another woman? For I am sent to you with a harsh message"* (1 Kgs. 14:6).

Then the man of God told the king's wife that this was the message from God which she was to convey to Jeroboam:

> *Thus says the Lord God of Israel, "Because I exalted you from among the people and made you leader over My people Israel, and tore the kingdom away from the house of David and gave it to you—yet you have not been like My servant David, who kept My commandments and who followed Me with all his heart, to do only that which was right in My sight; you also have done more evil than all who were before you, and have gone and made for yourself other gods and molten images to provoke Me to anger, and have cast Me behind your back—therefore behold, I am bringing calamity on the house of Jeroboam, and will cut off from Jeroboam every male person, both bond and free in Israel, and I will make a clean sweep of the house of Jeroboam, as one sweeps away dung until it is all gone. Anyone belonging to the house of Jeroboam who dies in the city the dogs will eat. And he who dies in the field the birds of the heavens will eat; for the Lord has spoken it." (1 Kgs. 14:7-11)*

And, to this Ahijah added concerning the boy:

> *"Now you arise, go to your house. When your feet enter the city the child will die. And all Israel shall mourn for him and bury him, for he alone from Jeroboam's family shall come to the grave, because in him something good was found toward the Lord God of Israel in the house of Jeroboam." (1 Kgs. 14:12,13)*

Also, regarding the cessation of the posterity and lineage of Jeroboam, God declared through the prophet:

> *"Moreover, the Lord will raise up for Himself a king over Israel who shall cut off the house of Jeroboam **this day and from now***

*on. For the Lord will strike Israel, as a reed is shaken in the water; and He will uproot Israel from this good land which He gave to their fathers, and will scatter them beyond the Euphrates River, because they have made their Asherim, provoking the Lord to anger. **And He will give up Israel on account of the sins of Jeroboam, which he committed and with which he made Israel to sin.** " (1 Kgs. 14:14-16)*

Moreover, the Lord certainly was not just whistlin' Dixie, because, sure enough, what the Lord said would happen, happened forthwith:

*Then Jeroboam's wife arose and departed and came to Tirzah. As she was entering the threshold of the house, **the child died.** (1 Kgs. 14:17)*

This is just how egregious this sin of appointing laymen to positions and functions of spiritual leadership ordained for Levites (Five-fold Ministers) is to God. It stirs God's wrath, and though He is often indulgent for a time, there is no promise that He will forever be so. In fact, I prophesy that soon God's wrath will begin to come forth in judgment against those man-established "high places" (i.e., "churches") which were established not under a mandate from God but mere human ambition and aggrandizement, and which are the mere private kingdoms of a coven of self-appointed, self-exalted, humanly-ordained, spiritually sophomoric and inept laymen impersonating and posing as Levitical priests, deceiving their subjects into submitting themselves to their bogus authority. This particular type of Divine Judgment, because it is represented in the life of Jeroboam, I have dubbed: "Jeroboam Judgment."

Judgment begins with the household of God (1 Pet. 4:17). Soon, the just judgment of God will fall upon these "high places" to literally **blot them out and destroy them from off the face of the Earth.** Jesus is going to once again come to the Temple and throw all these imposters wielding illegitimate authority out of His House.

He is going to come with His winnowing fork to thoroughly purge His threshing floor, and He will gather the true wheat into His barn (the Church), and He will burn up the chaff with unquenchable fire (Mat. 3:12).

Soon, He will test the quality of each man's work, as to whether it is built with Godly building materials—gold, silver, and precious stones (Godly character and motives), or mere human building materials—wood, hay, and straw (human works, selfish ambition, and self-aggrandizement) [1 Cor. 3:12-15]. A day of testing by fire shall come to test the quality and substance of each man's life and work, for *"it is to be revealed by fire"* (Ibid). Human building materials are flammable and perishable, and thus the building built with them will be consumed by the testing fires. But, not so with Godly building materials, for with them the more intense the fire, the purer and more precious they become, with the result that the building built with them will endure forever.

The judgment of God which fell upon Jeroboam was not limited to the death of his son, but because he still continued in these blasphemous transgressions against God, the Lord wiped out his heritage and lineage by exterminating all the males of his family, abrogated his kingship by causing him to be defeated in battle at the hands of Abijah, king of Judah of Davidic lineage, and later struck him so that he died prematurely, bringing an abrupt and permanent end to his reign.

Now remember, these Old Testament events, God's Word tells us, happened for *our* sakes—believers living at the end of the Church Age—as instructive examples to us. Indeed, what happened to Jeroboam happened as a foreshadow of what is going to happen in the Last Days Church. God is going to purge His threshing floor of all the chaff of all the pretentious and false, self-sanctioned, and humanly-appointed "priests." He will also remove all the Jeroboam-like "kings," i.e., false shepherds, usurpers who seized authority by their own self-effort and self-appointment rather than through the appointment of God, who have concocted private, false, and idolatrous religions based on their own contrived theosophy, ordaining and appointing their own priests from the ranks of loyalist-laymen, and who establish personal and private kingdoms in which they themselves and their own kingdom are the object of veneration and homage rather than God and His Kingdom. Moreover, in the same way God struck and killed Jeroboam's child, so also shall the "children" of these Jeroboams, their posterity, that is to say, their ministries, be destroyed by the hand of God.

God will do all this as part of the establishment of His Kingdom as the only Sovereign Kingdom. The day will come when only God's Kingdom will endure, and only the King whom He has installed shall reign, with total sovereignty. In that day, all those who, motivated by the antichrist spirit, challenge His absolute sovereignty and *"draw away disciples after themselves"* (Ac. 20:30), will be utterly annihilated.

And, lest anyone think that God does not mean what He says, witness these words concerning the demise of Jeroboam's lineage:

> *"And it came about, as soon as he (Baasha) was king, he struck down all the household of Jeroboam. He did not leave to Jeroboam any persons alive, until he had destroyed them, according to the word of the Lord, which He spoke by His servant Ahijah the Shilonite, and because of the sins of Jeroboam which he sinned, and which he made Israel sin, because of his provocation with which he provoked the Lord God of Israel to anger."* (1 Kgs. 15:29,30)

The Priesthood of the Believer

I cannot leave this topic without addressing an aspect of this matter of the appointment of laymen as "priests" that was greatly misconstrued by the many stricken with the spiritual myopia of "Charismania" during the Charismatic Movement, which I reiterate was without question a legitimate, Divinely-orchestrated move of

God. I am referring to a valid spiritual Truth restored and emphasized during the Charismatic Movement: "the priesthood of the believer."

How often during that movement did we hear allusions to excerpts of Peter's statements with regard to the priesthood of the believer: *"But you are a chosen race, a royal PRIESTHOOD, a Holy Nation..."* (1 Pet. 2:9); and, *"you also, as living stones, are being built up as a spiritual house for a holy PRIESTHOOD..."* (1 Pet. 2:5). Indeed, the Apostle John boldly asserted: *"He has made us to be a kingdom, PRIESTS to His God and Father"* (Rev. 1:6, NAS); or *"kings and priests unto God"* (Ibid, KJV). And, of course all this is so, and in no way do I denigrate or devalue this marvelous Truth, which every believer needs to understand.

However, what seemed to have been overlooked, whether inadvertently or deliberately, in regard to this matter of the priesthood of the believer, though it is made abundantly clear in the very Scriptures often quoted as proof-texts, is the fact that this priesthood which is common to every believer is a priesthood directed toward **God**, *not* toward **fellows**, as many sincere but misinformed Charismatics have come to believe. Priesthood, it is critical to understand, by its very nature, has two aspects to it—one is *God*-ward, in which the priest *"minister[s] unto the Lord"* (Ac. 13:2, e.g.) in praise, worship, and thanksgiving; and the other is *people*-ward, in which the priest ministers unto the people on behalf of and as a "stand-in" for God.

Now one of the great transactions and benefits of Christ's propitiatory sacrifice is that in the New Testament dispensation all believers have been made *"priests unto God."* At the very moment at which upon the Cross Jesus cried out, *"It is finished,"* the veil in the temple was rent from top to bottom as the Spirit and Glory of the Lord burst forth from behind that curtain which separated the Holy Place from the Holy of Holies, into which only the properly prepared and consecrated High Priest could enter once a year to offer up the blood of bulls and goats as a sacrifice by which the sins of the people would be covered over from the sight of God. From that moment on into perpetuam, God's Spirit would no more dwell in temples made with human hands, but rather in the hearts of believers who have accepted the blood-sacrifice of the true High Priest, Christ. With the Spirit of God now dwelling in human tabernacles, those tabernacles themselves were now priests **unto God**—and this is the key—they were *"priests unto GOD."*

As I mentioned, even the passages of Scripture often quoted as proof-texts to corroborate the Truth of the priesthood of the believer bears this out. The passage in First Peter 2:5 goes on to say *"you also, as living stones, are being built up as a spiritual house for a holy priesthood, to offer up spiritual sacrifices acceptable TO GOD through Jesus Christ,"* referring to the spiritual sacrifices of praise, worship, and thanksgiving which we offer up to **GOD**. Whereas, the other verse quoted from this chapter of Peter's epistle refers to the aspect of the priesthood of believers in which, by the testimony of both their manner of life and occasional verbal witness unto others transpiring in the course of mundane interrelations, they *"proclaim the excellencies of Him who has called you out of darkness into His marvelous light"*—not "proclaiming" necessarily in the form of preaching or teaching, per se, but merely in the form of informally sharing with others the "excellencies" the Lord has performed in his own life, testifying of God's superfluous magnificence. Likewise, the last portion of John's assertion concerning the priesthood of the believer in Revelation also indicates that the direction of the believer's priesthood is Godward, in that he declares: *"He has made us to be a kingdom, priests TO HIS GOD AND FATHER."*

Layman vs. Levitical Priesthood

However, having said all this concerning the reality and validity of the priesthood of the believer, it must likewise be understood, that notwithstanding the fact that all believers are now *"priests unto GOD,"* not *all* believers have been made priests unto the **PEOPLE**, to minister people-ward. Primarily, Five-fold Ministers are appointed by God as "priests unto the **PEOPLE**," to be His *stand-ins*, His *proxies*, His *surrogates*, to minister on His behalf unto His people in the form of spiritual edification and education, or spiritual construction and instruction—all of which will be elaborated on in the next chapter. Moreover, the clear and unequivocal testimony of God's Word is that *"NOT ALL"* (1 Cor. 12:28-30) believers have been anointed by Jesus with Five-fold ministry gifting, but only *"SOME"* (Eph. 4:7-11).

Thus, we see that while the believer has a priesthood, there is another entirely different priesthood of the Five-fold Ministers. Indeed, the differences between the two priesthoods are vast, as evidenced by the example of the Levitical priesthood.

As it is explained in several places within this book, the Old Testament Levites typify the Five-fold Ministers in the New Testament Church. To put it the other way around, the Five-fold Ministers are the New Testament counterpart of the Old Testament Levites. God established the priesthood of the Levites as a special and set apart priesthood, juxtaposed to that of the rest of the Israelites, as the Old Testament account explains.

In the second month of the second year following the Exodus out of Egypt, while trekking through the barren wilderness of Sinai, the Lord commanded Moses to number the *congregation* of the Israelites according to the Twelve Tribes:

*'Take a census of all the **CONGREGATION** of the **sons** of Israel, by their families, by their fathers' households, according to the number of names, every **male**, head by head from twenty*

years old and upward, whoever is able to go out to war in Israel, you and Aaron shall number them by their armies. With you, moreover, there shall be a man of each tribe, each one head of his father's household. These then are the names of the men who shall stand with you: (here are named the elder **son** of the families of the sons of Jacob, except for Levi, with the two sons of Joseph—Ephraim and Manasseh—who Jacob adopted as sons, included, making a total of twelve designated tribes). *These are they who were called of the CONGREGATION, the leaders of the fathers' tribes; they were the heads of the tribes of Israel.'* *(Num. 1:2-16, italicized portion added by author)*

God commanded Moses to enumerate only the Israelite **men** by the divisions of the Twelve Tribes, which were comprised of the genetic descendents of the sons of Jacob, except for the family or tribe of Levi, the Levites, who as noted are conspicuously absent from the list of the sons of Jacob. God's purpose for this census was not just to get a head count of the Israelites, but rather more importantly *"to set in order what remains, appointing elders"* (Tit. 1:5), to establish a system of order comprised of leaders and the led, to subordinate them under the leadership of leaders. The foremost function and purpose of this structure or order system was military, evidenced by the fact that God instructed they were to be enumerated—*"by their armies."* An absolute necessity for any army if it is to be victorious in battle is that the "chain of command" be clearly defined, so that each soldier has explicit knowledge of who all the leaders are under whom they are subordinated.

Now the Apostle Paul told us that all of these Old Testament matters and events were symbolic types and shadows serving as examples of instruction for us in the Church today under the New Testament dispensation (1 Cor. 10:6,11; Rom. 15:4). What we see represented with this Old Testament account is several essential characteristics of the leadership structure appointed by God in the Church. First of all, God is revealing the truth that there are two different echelons of leaders in the New Testament Church, each having its own distinct function and purview.

God commanded that the census was to be taken *"of all the CONGREGATION of the sons of Israel,"* excluding the Levites, and that the eldest son of each tribe was to be appointed as leaders. These leaders were strictly leaders within the ranks of the *congregation*, who functioned as the "political" (or, "societal"[1]) leaders within the societal structure of the congregation, and as military commanders. The purview of their leadership was limited to the natural, that is to say, non-spiritual realm. What these leaders typified in the New Testament Church is what we could call *"congregational* leaders" or *"lay*-leaders," in that they were selected from the laity (non-Levites) of the **CONGREGATION**. These leaders, I believe, for reasons I shall explain momentarily, are what the New Testament calls "deacons."

Subsequently in His instruction concerning this census and ordering of the Israelites, God explicitly commanded Moses that the tribe of Levi, the Levites, were to be excluded from the census, that they were **not** to be numbered among the tribes of the *congregation*, and furthermore that they were not to be counted at all in this census. Rather, they were to be *set apart* and distinguished from the other tribes because they were consecrated unto and appointed by God as the designated attendants of the tabernacle and its furnishings, which represented God's habitation in the midst of the Israelites:

---

[1] They indeed were "political leaders" within the societal structure of Israel, but the government of that society at that time was a literal Theocracy (under the sovereignty of God), having no civil government. Thus, these men were not political leaders in the sense the term is used today in which a political leader is a governmental official. Hence, "societal leaders" would aptly describe their role.

Erroneous Concept #4: Role of the Laity

*The LEVITES, however, were not numbered among them by their fathers' tribe. For the Lord had spoken to Moses, saying, "Only the tribe of Levi you shall **not** number, nor shall you number them **among the sons of Israel**. But you shall appoint the LEVITES over the tabernacle of the testimony, and over all its furnishings and over all that belongs to it. **They** shall carry the tabernacle and all its furnishings, and **they** shall take care of it; **they** shall also camp around the tabernacle. So when the tabernacle is to set out, the LEVITES shall take it down; and when the tabernacle encamps, the LEVITES shall set it up. **But the LAYMAN who comes near shall be put to death**. And the sons of Israel shall camp, each man by his own standard, according to their armies. But the Levites shall camp around the tabernacle of the testimony, that there may be no wrath on the congregation of the sons of Israel. So the Levites shall keep charge of the tabernacle of the testimony." (Num. 1:47-53)*

*Then the Lord spoke to Moses, saying, "Bring the tribe of Levi near and set them before Aaron the priest, that they may serve him. And they shall perform the duties for him and for the whole congregation before the tent of meeting, to do the service of the tabernacle. They shall also keep all the furnishings of the tent of meeting, along with the duties of the sons of Israel, to do the service of the tabernacle. You shall thus give the Levites to Aaron and to his sons; they are wholly given to him from among the sons of Israel. **So you shall appoint Aaron and his sons that they may keep THEIR PRIESTHOOD, but the LAYMAN who comes near shall be put to death.**" (Num. 3:5-10)*

We see in all this that God Himself commanded that the **LEVITES** were to be distinguished from the *congregation* of the Israelites and the *congregational leaders*, for they were being set apart by God and consecrated to a totally different function and realm of responsibility than were the tribal heads. The elder sons of the non-Levitical tribes were designated by God as the military and political leaders of the congregation or societal structure, whose purview was the natural and mundane matters of collective societal

237

life of the nation. Whereas, the Levites, on the other hand, were the spiritual leaders, who were responsible for the spiritual matters and the collective spirituality or spiritual condition of the people. However, since the government of the nation at this time was a *spiritual* rather than a *civil* government—a true Theocracy under the sole sovereignty of Jehovah alone (albeit, humanly intermediated by Moses, the personal proxy of Jehovah)—therefore, the spiritual leaders (the Levites) were also the intermediate governmental leaders of the nation as well. Thus, the Levites typified the intermediate **spiritual/governmental** leaders within the Theocracy of the New Testament Church—Five-fold Ministers, who are the personal proxies of Christ, the Sovereign Head of the Church.

Notice once again the purview of responsibility to which the Levites were appointed by God:

> *But you shall appoint **the LEVITES over the tabernacle of the testimony, and over all its furnishings and over all that belongs to it. They shall carry the tabernacle and all its furnishings, and they** shall take care of it; **they** shall also camp around the tabernacle. So when the tabernacle is to set out, the **LEVITES** shall take it down; and when the tabernacle encamps, the **LEVITES** shall set it up. But the LAYMAN who comes near shall be put to death.** And the sons of Israel shall camp, each man by his own standard, according to their armies. But the Levites shall camp around the tabernacle of the testimony, that there may be no wrath on the congregation of the sons of Israel. So the Levites shall keep charge of the tabernacle of the testimony." (Num. 1:50-53)*

The Levites were put in complete charge of the Tabernacle and all its furnishings, and everything involved with tending to it. They were to *carry*, or transport, it; *take care* of it, *camp around* it, *take it down*, or disassemble, it when they broke camp and rejoined their trek; and, they *set it up*, or reassembled, it when the Tabernacle encamped once again. They were even required to *camp around* the Tabernacle in order *"that there may be no wrath on the congregation of the sons of Israel,"* meaning that the Levites, who God had set apart and sanctified (made holy) unto Himself, by camping around the Tabernacle of God's Holy Habitation, preserved the rest of the congregation, the unsanctified, unholy non-Levite tribes, from being consumed by the fiery manifestation of the righteous wrath of Almighty God's Holy Presence which radiated forth from the Tabernacle of the Testimony.

Indeed, it was for this very reason that it was absolutely necessary, when God chose to manifest His Divine Presence in its midst, that He set apart, sanctify, and consecrate a contingency out of this sin-defiled "congregation ["ecclesia" {called out}] in the wilderness" (Ac. 7:38), allowing them to come near to touch and tend to the Holy articles of the Tabernacle, and to be intermediaries and intercessors who could stand between Him and the people, lest they all be consumed by His Presence, as mere flesh and blood humanity can in no wise endure the Awesome and Almighty Presence of His Immaculate Holiness. Thus, did He also warn: *"But the LAYMAN* (non-Levite) *who comes near shall be put to death,"* meaning, he shall die if he comes near the manifested Presence of the Lord.

The assertion that these two separate and distinct echelons of leadership which God established in the *"church in the wilderness"* symbolized two types of leadership established by God in the New Testament Church is corroborated by New Testament Scripture. One New Testament Scripture that corresponds to the Old Testament typology and provides clear corroboration of the truth it represents is the singular verse of Philippians 1:1, in which the Apostle Paul expressly delineates the specific addressees of his letter: *"to all the SAINTS in Christ Jesus who are in Philippi, including the OVERSEERS and DEACONS."* Here we see represented the three classifications of which the Body of Christ is comprised.

239

First, we see there is the general assembly, or congregation, or laymen, which is the main, en mass contingency of the Body of Christ, consisting of the believers, who Paul calls the *"SAINTS"* (the Greek word so translated merely means "true believers"), each of whom have a very vital and absolutely essential spiritual function, the entire range of which the New Testament refers to as *"helps"* ministries. This classification was typified in the historical Israelite example by the *congregation*.

Within the general assembly of the saints and selected out of their ranks, is the second classification of believers—an echelon of lay-servants who serve the congregation of laity by providing it with lay-leadership the role of which is to direct and orchestrate the fulfillment of the various functions and tasks performed by the laity. This echelon of leaders Paul addressed as the *"DEACONS"* (the Greek word means "servants"). The *"sons of Israel"* who were appointed as the "congregational leaders" and military commanders in *"the church in the wilderness"* (Ac. 7:38) were the counterpart to this echelon of leaders in the New Testament Church. Deacons are "lay-leaders," in that they are themselves laymen (not Five-fold Ministers), and the purview of their leadership is limited to leadership of the laity. Contrary to the erroneous governmental structure of some churches and denominations, deacons, according to the Word of God, are "servants," and their function is to serve both the congregation and the governmental leadership, but they have no governmental authority in the local church.

The precedence for this echelon of leadership, deacons, as recorded in the Sixth Chapter of Acts, was set by the Early Church, probably within a year or two after its inception on the Day of Pentecost, to fulfill the need that soon became evident for putting someone in charge of the ministration of certain mundane matters which gradually evolved within the community of the Jerusalem church. The initial catalyst leading to the establishment of this echelon of lay-leaders was a dispute in which the non-Jewish believers charged that their widows were being overlooked in the daily distribution of food to the widows of the congregation. Saying that it was not appropriate for them to *"neglect the Word of God,"* that is, their spiritual duties, *"to serve tables,"* the Apostles ordered the congregation: *"select from among you* [the laity] *seven men of good reputation, full of the Spirit and of wisdom, whom WE* [the Apostles] *may put in charge of this task."* In effect, the Apostles were telling the congregation to nominate, or put forward, from among their ranks seven men whom they recognized as having exemplary character and spirituality who demonstrated leadership qualities whom they could put in charge of the ministration of these vital mundane tasks. The procedure they established for the appointment of deacons was that the congregation would *nominate* candidates who fit the requisites of being of good reputation and full of the Spirit and wisdom, and the Apostles would *ordain* those whom the congregation nominated.

The remaining classification of believers the Apostle Paul addressed in his letter to the Philippians was the *"OVERSEERS."* Now as pointed out before, the Church is the quintessential Theocracy. Its government is not a *political* government wherein humans constitute and effect the government, such as that of this nation, which is a form of *democracy* ostensibly "of the people, for the people, and by the people." Rather, the Church is literally governed by the Lord Jesus Christ, who God has appointed as its Sole and Sovereign Head. Albeit, as with "the church in the wilderness," in which God effected His government through a human proxy, Moses, God effects His government of the New Testament Church through human intermediaries.

As explained before, because the government of *"the church in the wilderness"* was a Theocracy of the Spirit of God, and had no civil government at this time, the purview of their spiritual leaders, the Levites, entailed the government of the nation as well. During its forty year trek through the wilderness preceding entering into

241

Canaan, the Levites *were* the governmental leaders of Israel. Thus, the ilk of leadership within "the church in the wilderness" the Levites typified, and which Paul referred to as the *"Overseers"* is the double-faceted **SPIRITUAL/GOVERNMENTAL** offices in the New Testament Church. The Five-fold Ministry Offices are these offices, whose function it is to provide government, and spiritual construction (edification) and instruction (education) within the local assemblies, which together constitute the Church at-large.

Thus, the main points that are being established here in this section is that the lay-priesthood, that is, the priesthood of the believer, and the Levitical priesthood of the Five-fold Ministers are separate and distinct priesthoods. Both exist, and are valid within the limitations of their auspices. It is those limitations that must be understood and adhered to, to avoid error and excess.

Primarily, the priesthood of the lay-believer is *God*-ward, not *people*-ward, and carries no inherent prerogative for any kind of authority, predominance, or improper influence over fellow believers. Lay-believers must not misconstrue the supernatural spiritual *power* bestowed upon them through the Baptism in the Holy Spirit, which is to be employed against *"the works of the devil"* (1 Jn. 3:8), for spiritual *authority* to be exercised over others.

Furthermore, it is extremely vital and altogether imperative for all believers who comprehend the precious truth of the priesthood of the believer and who are zealous to "take their place in the Body of Christ," to bear in mind that the establishment and existence of the priesthood of the believer has in no way negated or done away with the Five-fold Ministry offices. Five-fold Ministers are *ex officio* priests unto the people, charged with the responsibility of governing, overseeing, and managing all ecclesiastical operations, administrations, and spiritual ministrations. Moreover, it is the Five-fold Ministers who God has assigned the task of spiritually edifying and equipping the saints unto full maturity, unto the measure of the stature of the fulness of Christ. The New Testament Levites, i.e., Five-fold Ministers, are God's personal representatives unto the people. Unlike the priesthood of laymen, the Levitical priesthood of Five-fold Ministers entails a duty and responsibility for the spirituality and spiritual condition of other believers, for which God will hold them accountable.

Failure to recognize these vital differences between these two priesthoods, and the blatant devaluation of the Levitical priesthood of Five-fold Ministers spawned by the philosophy of egalitarianism so prevalent in the world today, are the primary factors leading to the "Charismania" that has become so common among many Charismatic/Neo-Pentecostal groups. The outcome of all this Charismania has been a kind of ecclesiastical anarchy in which there essentially is no leadership, no authority, no government, at least of the ilk God has ordained.

What we now have, metaphorically speaking (and I mean this only in a metaphorical and rhetorical sense), is a classic case of the inmates running the penitentiary, the patients running the asylum, the students running the school. The real, though unseen root of the whole matter is nothing more than naked rebellion against authority. There are many "Charismaniacs" caught up in a kind of "Charismatic" spiritualism and mysticism who, behind their facade of super-spirituality, are in actuality among those who Jude said *"reject authority"* (Jude 8) and who Peter said *"despise authority"* (2 Pet. 2:10). Sadly and very unfortunately, this Charismaniacal excess, as I have stated repeatedly, remains extant and largely unabated within the structure and philosophy of many of those groups and churches yet today.

The Effect of Charismaniacal Excess

This excess, it is vital to understand, has by no means been benign or without consequence, as the many who attempt to make light of the whole matter of the Discipleship/Shepherdship fiasco contend. Much to the contrary, the effect of this excessiveness regarding the scope of the priesthood of the believer has been the devaluing, degrading, debasing, and even debauching and defiling of Five-fold ministry in general, as well as the supplanting of the Five-fold Ministry Offices.

You see, when lay-persons are appointed to perform ministry functions that only Five-fold Ministers have the supernatural enablement and anointing to perform, the net result is the supplanting of the Five-fold Ministry Offices. So also, when lay-persons who have not this special anointing from Jesus presumptuously intrude and interlope into those offices and attempt to perform the spiritual functions of those offices without the requisite consecration, dedication, sanctification, preparation, and training by the Lord, the Five-fold ministry is devalued, degraded, debased, and the recipients of that "ministry" are receiving a debauched, defiled, and even desecrated counterfeit of the genuine. To say it concisely and bluntly, this intrusion and interloping of laymen has produced a bastardization of the ministry.

In turn, the ultimate consequence of the supplanting of the Five-fold Ministry Offices is that the perfection and preparation of the Bride of Christ unto that state of sanctification wherein she is without spot or wrinkle (Eph. 5:25-27) and wherein she has fully attained unto *"the measure of the stature of the fulness of Christ"* (Eph. 4:13), which only the effectual functioning of all of the Five-fold ministry can bring about (Eph. 4:7-13), is deferred and delayed. And, it is this prophesied preparation and perfection of the Bride of Christ that is the primary determinant in the return of Christ, rather than the systematic fulfillment of eschatological Bible prophecy concerning natural geo-political events among the nations of the world. Christ is returning to claim as His Eternal Bride a spiritually perfected Church, not a nation in the Middle East or any of the nations of the world. Natural geo-political events among the nations of the world will certainly be fulfilled in exact precision with Bible prophecy, but the ultimate consummation of the ages is contingent upon the perfection of the Bride of Christ. The fact of the matter is, Jesus will not return one nanosecond before the Bride has been thusly prepared and perfected.

Therefore, with this in view, the ultimate effect of the supplanting and impeding of the effectuality of the Five-fold ministry is the deferment and delay of the return of Christ, the first event of *"the day of the Lord,"* which the Word of God clearly tells us we can *"hasten"* (1 Pet. 3:12). Indeed, we will never know until *"the perfect* (knowledge) *comes"* how much of a delay in the perfection and preparation of the Bride of Christ and the return of Christ was incurred since the inception of the Charismatic Move until the present as a result of this supplanting of the Five-fold ministry by the illegitimate deployment of the laity. However, it is safe to say that surely it did in no wise *"hasten the day of the Lord."*

In all this, another element is clear, which is that the ultimate losers as a result of this degradation of the effectuality of the Five-fold Ministry Offices are not those appointed to those offices, but rather the saints to whom they were to minister, for it is they who have been deprived of the spiritual benefit that could have been imparted to them out of the special anointing Jesus operates through these ministry offices. In lieu of that, they have unfortunately been subjected to the sophomoric and amateurish "ministry" they have received from these unqualified, inept, unproven, unequipped lay-people, who have been posing as ministers. This to me has been the most egregious and offensive part of the Charismania I have personally witnessed in churches I have visited and ministered in—such sophomoric, amateurish, and wholly ineffectual tomfoolery being passed off as "ministry."

Some of these groups don't even merit the appellation of "church." They are nothing more than little Sunday morning clubs where their selfishly ambitious, attention-craving, minister-want-to-be members take turns at pretending to be prophets and preach-ers. The only difference, tragic as it is, between these people's activity and Little Leaguers emulating their Major League Baseball idols as they play their games before their cheering relatives in the stands, is that these Charismaniacs are adults. If it were not for the fact that innocent and unwitting people were being misled and deceived, and that I didn't want to embarrass anyone, many of the so-called prophecies, or "words from the Lord," and messages I have heard while attending meetings of some of these groups would have made me laugh out loud. Some were silly and inane. Some were absurd. And, some were outright demonic. Yet, they were received by the congregants and leaders alike as being a message from God.

Now having said all this, and believe me, these statements remained in the manuscript even after countless edits, each of which afforded an opportunity to delete them, I am not so naive that I do not know that some of what I have just said concerning sophomoric and amateurish "ministry" will elicit the criticism of naysaying critics eager to charge me with condescension, elitism, and exclusivism, but I assure you that is not the case. It's just that as one inveterate minister replied when asked for his considerate definition of "the anointing": "I can't tell you *what* it *is*, but I can sure tell you *when* it *ain't!*"

To Be Clear

In closing this chapter, I want to state a few things once again, just to make sure I am being clear with regard to the matters discussed in this chapter.

Having amply established the point of the continued viability of the Five-fold Ministry Offices, I want to emphasize once again that in no way is any of this to say or infer that lay-believers, that is, those not in Five-fold Ministry Offices, do not have a viable and vital spiritual and ecclesiastical function, because every believer most definitely does (Eph. 4:16). In no way am I denigrating the role and function of lay-believers. I am **NOT** saying that lay-believers cannot be used to teach classes, for instance, or to perform various other vital spiritual as well as natural functions both within the local church and in extra-ecclesiastical ministries. On the contrary, the contribution of the saints in a plethora of roles and capacities in the various and varied operations and outreaches of the local church and other extra-church endeavors is not only vital but absolutely indispensable.

Furthermore, neither is it to say or infer that believers cannot operate spiritual gifts as laymen, because spiritual gifts, as was painstakingly emphasized in Chapter Four and elsewhere herein, are available to *every* believer who will make himself or herself available to the Holy Spirit and operate them in faith as the Holy Spirit distributes them. Indeed, as emphasized repeatedly in this volume, every believer is exhorted by Scripture to continually *"stir up"* those gifts, not neglect them, and *"exercise"* them faithfully (1 Tim. 1:6; Rom. 12:6-8; 1 Pet. 4:10,11). In fact, Jesus said that those who truly believe in Him and the authority of His Name **will** exercise supernatural powers in the form of casting out demons, prophesying, casting aside devils by overcoming their works and assaults, averting and overcoming the devil's attempts to kill, and ministering healing to the infirmed through the laying on of hands (Mk. 16:17,18). **Every** Spirit-baptized believer should be seizing every opportunity to operate these supernatural powers which bear witness of the resurrected and living Christ.

But, I have indicated over and over again already, all of these things we do merely as believers, laymen, not out of any office or official appointment. The fact is that operation of these gifts does not by any means indicate or even intimate an appointment to any office of ministry. All of these works of power are Manifestation Gifts *"for the common good"* bestowed and distributed by *the Holy Spirit* (1 Cor. 12:7-11), whereas Ministry Offices are bestowed for oversight, construction, and instruction of the Body of Christ by *Jesus* as the Head of the Church (Eph. 4:7-13).

Above all, lest anyone misunderstand or misconstrue the intent or import of what I am saying with regard to the role of laymen, let me state categorically that none of that which is being said here has anything whatsoever to do with condescension toward laymen or diminishment of their God-given role or status. Such is the furthest thing from the intent of the discourse herein and the attitudes of its author.

All that is being said, to be clear, is that laymen must not be appointed to offices or positions of spiritual function which are to be fulfilled by Five-fold ministers, for only those anointed with this ilk of spiritual enablement can perform those functions effectually and effectively. Nor should laymen intrude into or usurp such positions of spiritual function. For certain, **every** believer has an anointing (1 Jn. 2:20), but there are limits and limitations to the anointing that is upon every believer. Only Jesus had the anointing *"without measure;"* the anointing individual believers have is **WITH** measure!

The long and the short of the issue here is this: God has designed the Body of Christ with order, government, and oversight, under which the various members of the Body are to perform their individual, God-assigned functions. As with the human body, each member of the Body of Christ indeed is to perform its function, but according to proper order and congruous with the structure and flow of the overall design, rather than anarchically, haphazardly, disorderly, chaotically, and self-servingly.

Chapter Eight

ERRONEOUS CONCEPT #5: ROLE OF FIVE-FOLD MINISTERS

The final erroneous concept upon which the Discipleship/Shepherdship doctrines are predicated concerns the role of Five-fold Ministry. It is not the purpose of this chapter to present an exhaustive treatise on the subject of the role of the Five-fold Ministry, but rather to present convincing evidence that the Discipleship/Shepherdship doctrines and practices are errant and erroneous in part because under their auspices the proper role of Five-fold Ministry is distorted and dysfunctional. Toward that end, however, some explanation and even a certain amount of elaboration on the proper role of the Five-fold Ministry will be necessary.

The specter of Five-fold Ministry is a matter frequently alluded to from the pulpit within Charismatic churches and circles. Notwithstanding, such allusions appear to be little more than oratorical rhetoric, for I have yet to personally witness an earnest attempt to incorporate Five-fold Ministry within the ministry and structure of a local church. Certainly, I have never yet seen it in full and proper operation anywhere. Rather, for the most part according to what I have heard and witnessed, Five-fold Ministry and its function remains to be a shadowy and little understood matter to the majority of ministers, not to mention lay-believers, including even those claiming to be Charismatic. Oh, some *say* they believe there is such a thing as Five-fold Ministry, which is more than can be said for the vast majority of so-called mainline and Evangelical denomi-national ministers.

However, most Charismatic ministers have what could only be referred to as a cursory understanding of these Ascension Gifts of Christ and how the Bible prescribes they are to function and flow together, and virtually none of them have incorporated all of those ministry offices into their rightful place of function within the structure of their church.

It is not that God has not revealed revelation and information concerning the matter of Five-fold Ministry for consumption by His Body. Far from it! Rather, as He has continued to do since the day He ascended unto His Throne, He has indeed revealed such portions of *"the mystery of Christ"* (i.e., Divine Revelation) *"to His Holy apostles and prophets in the Spirit"* (Eph. 3:5). There are apostles and prophets to whom Christ has given special revela-tion of things pertaining to *"the mystery of Christ, which in other generations was not made known to the sons of men as it has now been revealed to His Holy apostles and prophets in the Spirit"* (Eph. 3:5). The matter of Five-fold Ministry and how it is to function and flow in concert together toward the fulfillment of the purposes of Christ is one such matter, regarding which God has imparted revelation knowledge to His apostles and prophets through the anointing of the Spirit abiding upon them and in which they abide.

How desperately Jesus wants to share everything He has and knows with His Betrothed Co-Sovereign Partner, the Church, *"the Lamb's wife"* (Rev. 21:9)! How willing and eager Jesus has always been to unveil unto the Church *"the unfathomable riches of Christ, and to bring to light what is the administration of the mystery which for ages has been hidden in God, who created all things; in order that the manifold wisdom of God might now be made known through the church to the rulers and the authorities in the heavenly places"* (Eph. 3:8-10). But, to be very blunt, the bottleneck for the conveyance of such revelation to the Body of Christ are the shepherds who are standing in the doorways of the churches with their hands stretched forth like an armed guard, yelling at the top of their voice,"Stop, stop! You can't come in here! **I'm** the head here; **you** can't come in!"

As Jesus is the Chief Cornerstone which the builders rejected, so also many of those who purport to be builders of the House of God are stubbornly and unyieldingly (and in some cases even hysterically) rejecting these two other foundationstones upon which the Household of God, the Church that Jesus is building, is founded the apostles and prophets (Eph. 2:20). Consequently, the Church remains devoid of the revelation and information Jesus so desires to impart to His Partner.

Regardless of the disdain of the stiff-necked resisters who, like their predecessors, continue to murder the prophets (Ac. 7:51,52), the Word of God forthrightly declares there are certain insights into the mysteries of Christ which He reveals only unto *"His Holy apostles and prophets in the Spirit"* (Eph. 3:1-5), and not to evangelists, pastors, and teachers. As anointed, gifted, and effective as the ministers who function in these latter three offices are, and as much knowledge as they have appropriated over the years through personal study and research, the only way they will ever understand these insights into the *"mysteries"* pertaining to the ministry and mission of the Christ is as it is elucidated by the apostles and prophets. These insights do not come through study and *research*, but only through prayer and *revelation* given by Jesus (Gal. 1:11,12). Though a multitude of ministers will absolutely bristle and scream "Foul!" at these words, they are, nonetheless, the unadulterated Truth of the Spirit of God.

Despite the sophisticated and impassioned theorizations of theologians claiming the contrary, the apostolic and prophetic offices and functions have no more ceased than have the other three. If they have, then so have the other three—which means there are no such offices as evangelist, pastor, or teacher, and those who claim to be functioning in those offices are unauthorized and illegitimate frauds—because they all are established in and sanctioned by the same verse of Scripture: Ephesians 4:11. All such arguments alleging the cessation of the Five-fold Ministry offices are absolutely absurd and wholly indefensible! Rather, the incontrovertible Truth is that *"Jesus Christ is the same yesterday and today and forever!"* (Heb. 13:8). By the very virtue that He is the Perfect God—He changes not! (Mal. 3:6). What He was, He is; what He is, He always has been; what He always has been, He always will be; what He will be, He is, and always has been!

While ascending on High, Jesus relegated gifts unto certain men, energizing and equipping them to function as apostles, prophets, evangelists, pastors, and teachers, in order to carry on His five-faceted ministry in His stead. Nowhere does Scripture say that Jesus has rescinded those offices, nor His appointment and anointment of men to those offices. Hence, as long as the Church age exists all five of these ministry offices will continue to exist and to be operable. Thus, as long as the Church is the Church, and it will continue to be the Church until it is wedded to Him at the Marriage Supper of the Lamb, Jesus will continue to reveal to His holy apostles and prophets in the Spirit portions of the mystery of the Life and on-going Earthly ministry of the Christ now being manifested through His many-membered Body.

The Levitical Priesthood of Five-fold Ministers

The best way to initiate the discussion of the focus of this chapter is to continue with the comparison of the priesthood of the believer, or the lay-priesthood, juxtaposed to the Levitical priesthood begun in the previous chapter. In that discussion, the reality and validity of the priesthood of the lay-believer was established and explained. While it is vital to understand, as established therein, that all believers have a priesthood in which they have been made *"priests unto GOD"* (Rev. 1:6), wherein they minister unto

252

God, or *God*-ward, in praise, prayer, and participation, notwith-standing, it is even more essential that the Body of Christ under-stand that not *all* believers have been made priests unto the **PEO-PLE**, in order to minister *people*-ward in the way Five-fold Ministers have.

Five-fold Ministers are the ones who have been appointed by God as the primary "priests unto the **PEOPLE**" with regard to spiritual edification and education. This ilk of people-ward ministry emanates from Jesus, is transmitted by the Holy Spirit, and in turn is imparted by the Five-fold Ministers unto the receivers. This is not to say that those not in Five-fold Ministry are precluded from impartational participation altogether, however, but only that all such ministry is relegated through the Five-fold Ministers. The Five-fold Ministers are God's designated *stand-ins*, His *proxies*, His *surrogates*, anointed and appointed by God to minister on His behalf unto His people in the form of spiritual edification and education, or spiritual construction and instruction (more on this momentarily). Indeed, God's Word explicitly states that *"NOT ALL"* (1 Cor. 12:28-30), but rather only *"SOME"* (Eph. 4:7-11) believers have been anointed by Jesus with Five-fold Ministry gifting, and appointed to the Five-fold Ministry Presbytery.

Thus, we witness again the contrasts that exist between the priesthood of lay-believers and the priesthood of the Five-fold Ministers. Both priesthoods are essential, but they differ exten-sively with regard to their nature as well as their function. As it was pointed out in the previous chapter, the differences between the two priesthoods are represented in the typology of the two separate censuses God commanded Moses to take of the Israelites following their deliverance out of Egypt. Remember, God explicitly tells us that all of these Old Testament events *"happened to them as an example, and they were written for our instruction, upon whom the ends of the ages have come"* (1 Cor. 10:6), meaning they were types and shadows serving as instructional examples and symbolic paradigms for the End-time Church.

The story of the two censuses is chronicled in the Old Testament Book of Numbers, as it is titled in our English versions; the original Hebrew version was entitled: *"In the Wilderness."* On the first day of the second month of the second year of their sojourn through the desolate and arid desert of Sinai, the Lord commanded Moses to number the *congregation* of the Israelites according to the divisions of the Twelve Tribes, which were also the divisions of their national army.

The details and purposes of this first census we discussed in the previous chapter, pointing out that typologically the *"congregation"* represented the congregation of lay-believers in the New Testament Church, and the *"congregational leaders,"* comprised of the eldest sons of each tribe, typified the class of believers alluded to in New Testament passages as *"deacons,"* who are congregational leaders, or lay-leaders, in the New Testament Church structure. The application of this typology to the New Testament Church, I also pointed out, is also corroborated by Stephen's reference to this assembly of Israelites as *"the congregation* [Greek: "ecclesia," {lit., called out}; English: "Church"] *in the wilderness"* (Ac. 7:38); i.e., "the church in the wilderness."

God explicitly commanded Moses to totally exclude the tribe of Levi, the Levites, from this census, saying they were **NOT** to be numbered among the tribes of the *congregation*. Rather, they were to be set apart and distinguished from the other tribes, because He was consecrating and appointing them the designated attendants of the Tabernacle of His Holy Habitation and its furnishings:

> The **LEVITES**, however, were not numbered among them by their fathers' tribe. For the Lord had spoken to Moses, saying, "Only the tribe of Levi you shall **not** number, nor shall you number them **among the sons of Israel**. But you shall appoint

the LEVITES over the tabernacle of the testimony, and over all its furnishings and over all that belongs to it. They shall carry the tabernacle and all its furnishings, and they shall take care of it; they shall also camp around the tabernacle. So when the tabernacle is to set out, the LEVITES shall take it down; and when the tabernacle encamps, the LEVITES shall set it up. But the LAYMAN who comes near shall be put to death. And the sons of Israel shall camp, each man by his own standard, according to their armies. But the Levites shall camp around the tabernacle of the testimony, that there may be no wrath on the congregation of the sons of Israel. So the Levites shall keep charge of the tabernacle of the testimony." (Num. 1:47-53)

Then, subsequent to this first census, by which the masses of the congregation were distributed into their respective military regiments, God then commanded that another, separate census be taken, this time of the Levites only:

Then the Lord spoke to Moses, saying, "Bring the tribe of Levi near and set them before Aaron the priest, that they may serve him. And they shall perform the duties for him and for the whole congregation before the tent of meeting, to do the service of the tabernacle. They shall also keep all the furnishings of the tent of meeting, along with the duties of the sons of Israel, to do the service of the tabernacle. You shall thus give the Levites to Aaron and to his sons; they are wholly given to him from among the sons of Israel. So you shall appoint Aaron and his sons that they may keep THEIR priesthood, but the LAYMAN who comes near shall be put to death." (Num. 3:5-10)

We see in all this that God Himself was commanding that the **LEVITES** be "set apart" and distinguished from the *congregation* (laity) and the *congregational leaders*, for they were being appointed by God to a totally different function, a different "priesthood" than the laity and tribal heads, who as stated before were societal and military leaders, whose purview was the natural and mundane matters effecting the nation. Whereas the Levites, on the other hand, were the primary spiritual leaders, responsible for the spiritual matters and the collective spirituality of the nation, which also entailed the role of government because the government of the nation at this time was a Theocracy, that is, it was under the sole sovereignty of Jehovah-God alone, without any civil government. Hence, the Levites were also the chief intermediary governmental leaders of Israel as well.

In setting apart the tribe of Levi from the other twelve tribes, and consecrating them for specialized service unto Him under the types and shadows of the Old Covenant era, God was establishing the Levitical priesthood as the typological paradigm for the structure of the Church in the New Testament era. More specifically, the Levites, who God had appointed as the preeminent governmental/spiritual leaders within the Theocratic framework under which the nation of Israel operated, typified the governmental/spiritual leaders within the Theocracy of the New Testament Church, which are the Five-fold Ministers, who are the present-day proxies of Christ, who Himself is the Sovereign Head of the Church. To state it directly, the Old Testament Levites typify the Five-fold Ministers in the New Testament Church. Or, to put it in the obverse, the Five-fold Ministers are the New Testament counterpart of the Old Testament Levites.

Cryptic Corroboration

Indeed, God has hidden cryptic corroboration signifying that the Levites typify the Five-fold Ministers in the New Testament Church within the details of the Levitical priesthood in two forms. First, as we shall see momentarily, the general duties and responsibilities of the Levites with regard to the Tabernacle were *five* in number.

Secondly, cryptic corroboration is also inherent in the details of the segmentation of the Levitical Tribe and the duties delegated to each. God divided the Tribe of Levi into two main divisions, comprised of *two* and *three* subdivisions respectively, totalling *five*. To each division He assigned different duties and responsibilities.

The first division was the "sons of Aaron," of which there were **two**, Eleazar and Ithamar. They were the chief priests who alone were consecrated by God to enter behind the veil in order to perform the services of oblation, and to touch the Holy Objects (Num. 3:2-10,38). They were also the overseers over the Levites, and were responsible for seeing to it that the collective duties and responsibilities of the Levites were carried out and performed precisely in accordance with the specification of the ordinances God established for those duties (3:32; 4:16-32). This division typified Apostles (Eleazar) and Prophets (Ithamar).

The second division was comprised of the *"sons of Levi,"* of which there were **three**, Gershon, Kohath, and Merari. It was this division who actually performed the various duties of tending to, assembling, disassembling, and transporting the furnishings and articles of the Tabernacle. Respectively, they typified the remaining Five-fold Ministries: Evangelists (Gershonites), Pastors (Kohathites), and Teachers (Merarites).

The Purview of the Levitical Priesthood

Having established that the Levites typify the Five-fold Ministers in the New Testament Church, it is vital then to begin to define with specificity the scope as well as the limitations of the purview of responsibility of the Levitical priesthood. Per usual, in His instructions, God delineated the precise specifications of the role to which He was appointing the Levites:

> *But you shall appoint **the LEVITES over the tabernacle of the testimony, and over all its furnishings and over all that belongs to it.** They shall carry the tabernacle and all its furnishings, and **they** shall take care of it; **they** shall also camp around the tabernacle. So when the tabernacle is to set out, the **LEVITES** shall take it down; and when the tabernacle encamps, the*

257

LEVITES shall set it up. But the LAYMAN who comes near shall be put to death. And the sons of Israel shall camp, each man by his own standard, according to their armies. But the Levites shall camp around the tabernacle of the testimony, that there may be no wrath on the congregation of the sons of Israel. So the Levites shall keep charge of the tabernacle of the testimony. (Num. 1:50-53, emphasis)

The Levites were put in complete charge of the Tabernacle and all its furnishings, and everything involved with tending to it, which entailed five general tasks. They were to *carry*, or transport, the Tabernacle along with all its appurtenances; *take care* of it; *camp around* it; *take it down*, or disassemble, it whenever they broke camp and rejoined their trek; and, they *set it up*, or reassembled, it when the Israelite company encamped once again. Though the typology of these five responsibilities of the Levites and its New Testament application is not particularly germane to the matter being addressed in this book, one of them does relate somewhat to the focus of this chapter, the role of Five-fold Ministry, however, which is the requirement God set for the Levites to *"camp around"* the Tabernacle. God said that this was in order *"that there may be no wrath on the congregation of the sons of Israel,"* meaning that the Levites, who God had set apart and sanctified (made holy) unto Himself by declaration, in camping around the Tabernacle of God's Manifested Presence, did protect and preserve the rest of the congregation, the unsanctified, unconsecrated non-Levitical tribes, from being consumed by the nuclear emanations of the righteous wrath of Almighty God that continuously but viewlessly to the natural eye radiated forth from the Tabernacle of the Testimony.

Indeed, it was for this very reason, when God chose to manifest His Divine Presence in the midst of this sin-defiled *"congregation* ["ecclesia," {lit., called out}, "Church"] *in the wilderness"* (Ac. 7:38), that it was absolutely necessary that He set apart, sanctify, and consecrate a certain contingency of their company who would thus be able to come near to touch and tend to the Holy articles of the Tabernacle, and to be intermediaries and intercessors between Him and the people, lest they all be consumed by His Awesome and Almighty Presence, exposure to which unsanctified and mortal flesh and blood can in no wise endure.

But, in the case of the not thusly consecrated and sanctified non-Levite layman and their approachability to the manifestation of His Awesome Presence, God solemnly warned: *"But the LAY-MAN who comes near shall be put to death,"* meaning, he would die if exposed to the raw radiance of His Glory. Amplification regarding such limitations on the spiritual purview of the laity, and the judgments incurred when those boundaries were exceeded, along with the application of the Old Testament types and shadows in the New Testament era, were presented in the preceding chapter.

Intermediaries Vs. Mediators

Now as pointed out before, the Church is the quintessential *Theocracy*. Its government is not a *political* government wherein the governed themselves constitute, devise, and effect their own government, such as that of this nation, the United States, which is a form of *democracy*, supposedly "of the people, for the people, and by the people." Rather, the Church is literally governed by a singular Supreme Potentate—the Lord Jesus Christ—who God has appointed as its Sole and Sovereign Head. The absolute necessity of understanding this one concept is emphasized and re-emphasized repeatedly in this volume, and indeed is the ultimate and salient point of this book.

But, once it is understood that Christ Jesus Himself is the ultimate Head and Cornerstone of the Church, it is just as vital to understand that the government that Jesus presides over is an intermediated or proxied government in its physical application. In other words, He does not govern alone, nor directly, nor even in person. Rather, His government is a "representative" or "delegate" form of government, if you will. This is to say that as God set apart and specially consecrated the Levites to represent Himself unto the people, so also Jesus appoints, anoints, and sends special envoys, ambassadors, to represent Him and His government unto the Church. These envoys are His personal proxies, His delegates, His stand-ins, whom He sends to convey and effect His purposes, plans, pleasures, and passions.

You see, ever since Jesus ascended on High, and *"was received into Heaven, and sat down at the right hand of God"* (Mk. 16:19), He has been doing all that He does in this cosmos not in person by means of His own personal actions, but rather **through** His Body, the Body of Christ, the Church. God has chosen by His own volition, since there certainly exists no power or entity capable of compelling the Almighty to do anything, to "limit" His own intervention into human affairs to effecting it through the medium of His Body. Indeed, the whole of the mission of the Church is nothing other than the continuation of Jesus' ministry, which was not *cessated* with His ascension, but rather was only *commenced*, and now is *continued* through the participation and performance of His now many-membered Body.

Once again the matter could scarcely be articulated better than it was by Paul E. Billheimer in *Destined For the Throne*, wherein, under a section entitled "God Proposes—A Holy Church Disposes," he writes:

> God's offer of His scepter to redeemed humanity is, therefore, a bona fide offer. It is an offer in good faith. Through the plan of prayer God actually is inviting redeemed man into **FULL** partnership with Him, not in making the decisions, but in implementing those decisions in the affairs of humankind. Independently and of His own will God makes the decisions governing the affairs of the earth. The responsibility and authority for the enforcement and administration of those decisions He has placed upon the shoulders of His Church. (p. 46)

In the scope of the Divine plan for the cosmos at large, the entire many-membered Church as an entity is God's proxy delegated, deputized, and deployed by Him to implement His purposes in the cosmos. Commenting on this truth Billheimer writes:

> ...Dr. Wilbur T. Dayton says, "After the removal of His bodily presence from among them, His followers must be His representatives, must take His place. This is the apostle's commission and ours. We are His proxies with power of attorney to do His bidding." "As the Father hath sent me, even so send I you" can mean nothing less than that we are His deputies with full authority to enforce the divine will and program. The deputy is invested with the full power of the office of his Chief, and is fully authorized to act in His stead. (Idem, p. 47)

Though the entire collective Church is the proxy of God in the master scheme for the cosmos, nevertheless, the Body of Christ, also has within its own meticulously-designed structure a God-ordained and therefore perfectly ordered system by which it is governed, which also is a proxied or delegated government. Like our physical bodies, the Body of Christ also is made up of a Head and a Body (torso with appendages), each with a different but equally essential function. The head is the seat of government, and serves the body by providing it with government and direction, formulating the purposes and the plans to be achieved, while the body serves the head by implementing the decisions made by the head. The head and the body are connected, related, and totally interdependent upon one another; one can do nothing without the other, but vitally and mutually needs the other. Together they comprise a many-membered body in which each member functions in total unity, congruity, and harmony with all the other parts toward achievement of common purposes and objectives. In the illness-free body, there is no *contention* or *competition* between the head and the body, but only *complimentation*. Indeed, the body in which there is *contention* and *competition* among its own members, namely, its *cells*, is not an illness-free body, but *cancerous*, which condition, unabated, is always fatal.

As explained before, during its forty year trek through the desert prior to entering into Canaan, "the church in the wilderness" was under the sole Sovereignty of Jehovah God. During that time, before the people rejected God's Kingship and demanded from Him and His representative Samuel the Prophet a human king in order that they *"may be like all the nations* (the 'Goiim,' or Gentiles), *that our king may judge us and go out before us and fight all our battles"* (1 Sam. 8:20), there was no human, civil government. Hence, Israel then was under a literal Theocracy of the Spirit of God, in which Jehovah *was* the Government.

However, God effected His government through a singular human proxy, Moses, who was a type and prefigurement of Christ, the Head of the Church. Moses was a literal human "stand-in" for Christ. He was Israel's "deliverer" in the stead and on the behalf of Christ Himself. Moses also was God's singular human governmental proxy. But, no human, even those greatly anointed by God as was Moses, is capable of bearing the enormous spiritual burden of being the "mediator" between God and the people; only the Omnipotent and Immaculately Holy One, Christ Jesus, is able to bear such a weight. Thus, after some two years in the desert, Moses began to have a total breakdown under the severe stress and strain produced by filling this role of "mediator" between a Perfectly Holy God and a wholly defiled and sinful people (Num. 11). In utter desperation and exhaustion, Moses cried out to God:

I alone am not able to carry all this people, because it is too burdensome for me. So if Thou art going to deal thus with me, please kill me at once, if I have found favor in Thy sight, and do not let me see my wretchedness! (Num. 11:15)

But, God knew all along that Moses the mortal man, descendent of the fallen First Adam, could not possibly carry the full weight of the burden of these people, because the burden encompassed leading them out of both physical as well as spiritual oppression and bondage, and establishing them in both a natural Land and a spiritual "state" of subjection to the Sovereignty of Christ. Moses could be a proxy-*deliverer*, an **intermediary**, to lead the people out of *physical* oppression and bondage of Egypt, but He was not of the spiritual essence and holiness (the Divine Nature) required to be the **mediator** between God and men, which role is to *sanctify* (make holy) defiled humanity and *satisfy* God's Just and Righteous Enmity separating man from the Holy God, and thereby bring them into fellowship with God. Christ Jesus Himself—born of the Spirit of Holiness and undefiled in the flesh while alive as a Man—is the **ONLY** Man who has ever lived who is of the required Essence and Holiness to fulfill the role of Mediator between the Perfectly Holy God and defiled men (1 Tim. 2:5)!

Thus, it was no surprise or revelation to the All-knowing God that this was beyond Moses capacities and capabilities. But, what was absolutely imperative to the fulfillment of God's purposes and plans was that Moses himself know experientially and thoroughly, without any ambivalence, that he had reached the limits of his capacity to carry this load or these people any further.

At this stage in God's dealings with the Israelites, though *physically* delivered out of Egypt, *spiritually* they remained unholy, profane, and defiled by the flesh; that is, **carnal**. The overall effect of that was that they also remained in enmity and separation from God, and thoroughly opposed to all His intents and purposes, for the unredeemed carnal mind is totally hostile and set against God, and totally incapable of being in agreement with, much less obeying and performing, that which is pleasing to God (Rom. 8:7,8). Therefore, because they were set against God, they also were set at odds against Moses, the man with a nature (human) such as theirs, but who was nonetheless sent by God to be a surrogate deliverer/

leader, intercessor, intermediary, on behalf of God to lead them into a physical and spiritual Promise Land.

In essence, Moses was now in a completely impossible situation, short of the intervention of God, being charged by God to impel an unredeemed and rebellious people who had absolutely no inclination toward God to follow His intents and purposes. With all this in view, it takes little imagination to comprehend why Moses after two years of striving with these people in the wilderness came to a place of total physical, mental, and spiritual exhaustion, frustration and despair, and had what amounts to a breakdown in all three areas. In his utter despair and agony, Moses cries out to God.

But, when he does, God has the plan, the solution, already. He has had it all along. In the Eternal and Infinite Mind of God, He *always* knew precisely what He needed to do to solve and bring resolution to Moses' dire and desperate need. When Moses experientially knew without equivocation his limitations and that he had reached his limits, then God could and would inform Moses of the solution and how to implement it. You see, Moses had reached his own limits and limitations, but God has none. The situation was beyond Moses' capabilities and capacities, but not God's. No situation is beyond God's capabilities and capacities, for with God all things are possible and there are no impossibilities. Neither are there impossibilities to the person whose total faith, trust, and confidence is in God's capabilities and capacities, and not his or her own. For, if thou canst believe the God of infinite capabilities and capacities—all things are possible. Indeed, it is in our inabilities that God's power is perfected (2 Cor. 12:9).

And what was the solution to Moses' great dilemma, which had eternally existed in the Mind of God, not only before Moses got to this place, but even before the foundations of the world, and had in fact been standing ready in wait for the time when he became fully cognizant and convinced of his limitations and limits, and therefore cried out to God? Well, the solution lied in the **anointing** that God had placed upon him in the first place when He appeared to him in the burning bush in Midian.

You see, Moses had an experience similar to that experienced at one time or another by most everyone who has ever been in the ministry. He started out all well and good, operating by and through the Spirit, and not by his own might.

When he went to the Hebrews to tell them God had sent him to deliver them out of Egypt and their nearly five hundred years of bondage and oppression, he proved to them he was sent by God by supernatural miracle and healing power from God—the **anointing**! When he spoke to Pharaoh, he went not in his own might, but with confidence in God's Might and under the unction of the Spirit the Lord had given Him—the **anointing**! When he demanded that Pharaoh let God's people go, he worked supernatural signs and wonders through the power of the Spirit to compel Pharaoh to release the Israelites—the **anointing**!

When the entire Hebrew company stood helplessly at the Red Sea with Pharaoh's army pursuing and nowhere to go, Moses struck the waters with his anointed staff and they were miraculously divided, and the entire nation crossed over on dry ground—it was the **anointing**!

When after three days of journeying in the wilderness they had come to the waters at Marah and they were contaminated, Moses purified the waters by the supernatural power of God—the **anointing**!

When the people grumbled against Moses because of lack of meat and bread, Moses cried out to God, and God supernaturally sent them an overabundance of quail and manna—it was through the **anointing** that the sustenance came!

When at Rephidim again there was no water for the people and the livestock, the people ranted and raged at Moses. At the instruction of the Lord, he struck the rock at Horeb with his staff, and water gushed forth—the **anointing** produced water!

When the Amalekites came and fought against Israel while they were camped there at Rephidim, Moses stood on Mt. Horeb, and with Aaron and Hur supporting his arms, held his staff above his head, and while the **anointing** prevailed above his head the troops prevailed over the enemy, but when in weariness his arms fell down, the enemy prevailed—it was the **anointing** that brought the victory and vanquished the enemy!

When will those of us in ministry ever learn?—it's the **ANOINTING** that breaks the yoke! It's not *academic* knowledge or church *administration* or leadership *acumen*, but the **anointing**! As Moses brought victory by keeping his staff, the symbol of God's **anointing** upon him, lifted above his head, so also the only way the Church and its leaders will prevail against our spiritual enemies and bring victory in the days that lie ahead is by exalting the **anointing** of God above the intellect of our heads. The "strong men," the ruling principalities that withstand us, and which we must dispossess in order to possess our Promise Land, can only be defeated through the **ANOINTING**—God's supernatural Power and Might manifested through his appointed and anointed proxies!

Moses had started this whole deliverance program by manifesting the power of God, but in the passage of time the unrelenting carnality and rebellion of the people had begun to frustrate him and caused him to get out of the Spirit and to start operating out of his own flesh. Everyone who has ever tried to deliver and shepherd a group of people, and get them out of their carnality and into operating by the Spirit, very well knows where Moses was at, and has been there himself. *You end up getting in the flesh trying to*

266

get the people **out** *of the flesh!* This is precisely where Moses was at.

When one finds himself at this very precarious place, the only thing to do is return to, "stir up," kindle afresh, the gifts of the Spirit with which God anointed him when He first called, anointed, and appointed him to the ministry. The anointing **always** works. Frequently, ministers fall into the trap of spending all their time and energy *administrating* rather than *ministering*. It is all too easy to lapse into a mode of *preserving* in lieu of *possessing*. We get weary in the battles of *taking* new territory and regress to merely *keeping* territory we have taken. How often swashbuckling spiritual *conquistadors* degenerate to being *care-takers* of museums of taxidermied saints!

God's solution for Moses' dilemma, like all His solutions for all our dilemmas, essentially was *"not by might nor by power, but by My Spirit"* (Zech. 3:5). The weapons of the warfare in which we are engaged are not carnal, that is, of the flesh, but they emanate from the Spirit of God, and thus are superabundantly powerful, and more than sufficient for the destruction of every stronghold (2 Cor. 10:4). In other words, the solution would come through the **ANOINTING**. When God called and commissioned Moses for this task of being a deliverer, He distributed upon him a portion of His very own Spirit in order to fulfill the task. God always operates this way—those who He appoints, He anoints; those anointed by Him are equipped to fulfill their calling. The anointing is empowerment of the Spirit to accomplish that to which God calls us. Now God was proposing to resolve Moses' problem of proffering leadership for the people by replicating the process by which He anointed Moses in seventy other "little Moseses":

> *The Lord therefore said to Moses, "Gather for Me seventy men from the elders of Israel, whom you know to be the elders of the people and their officers and bring them to the tent of meeting, and let them take their stand there with you. Then I will come*

*down and speak with you there, **and I will take of the SPIRIT who is upon you, and will put Him upon them;** and they shall bear the burden of the people with you, so that you shall not bear it all alone." (Ex. 11:16,17)*

Moses has very candidly told God that he just could not bear this burden of the people anymore, and God's response indicated that He totally agreed with him. God's solution was that He would take of the Spirit that He had placed upon Moses with which He had anointed him—the anointing—and distribute it upon these seventy elders as well, *"and THEY shall bear the burden of the people WITH YOU, so that you shall not bear it all alone."* Thus, God's answer was "plurality of leadership" wherein the burden of leadership would no longer be borne by one, solitary individual, but distributed unto the shoulders of seventy others who had likewise been anointed by God for leadership under the direction of Moses. In effect, these men would be Moses' *intermediaries*, and Moses was the typological human *mediator*, the intercessor, between God and the Israelites.

Plurality of leadership under the sovereignty of Jesus (who Moses typified) is and always has been the Biblical pattern of government and administration of the Kingdom (authority) of God on Earth. In each and every case in which *"elders"*—the body of leaders responsible for government in the Church (1 Tim. 5:17)— are mentioned in the Bible, the plural form is used. The same is true of *"apostles and prophets,"* who are the chief governmental leaders of the Body of Christ—the foundation of the Church (Eph. 2:20) and the *"shoulders"* upon whom the government of Jesus rests (Is. 9:6)—their offices are *always* mentioned in the plural form as well.

This is certainly not happenstance, but rather the Divinely established paradigm. No single person is so completely anointed by God so as to be equipped to single-handedly govern or administrate any segment of the Church. God anointed Jesus Himself *"without measure"* (Jn. 3:34) because He was the Christ, which, of course, means "Anointed One," and it is this supremely "Anointed One" Whom He appointed as the solitary Head of the Church as well as Head over all things. Everyone else, every mere mortal leader within His Body (even the shoulders are part of the Body, not the Head), however, is anointed with only a portion, a *measure*, of that anointing with which Jesus is anointed in the same way that the seventy elders were anointed with a portion of the anointing that God had placed upon Moses, who typified Christ Jesus.

So also, as it was with the seventy elders, no one intermediary leader is himself anointed to the extent and completeness Jesus (Moses) was, that is, "without measure." Rather, individually, we all, Five-fold Ministers included, are anointed with a certain "measure" of the anointing; that is to say, our anointing has limits, and is by no means of the fulness of Christ's. It can only be this way, because there will always only be one Christ, the Anointed One, and that is Jesus. None of us are Christ, we are only individual members of His Body (1 Cor. 12:27). It is only corporately that the Body of Christ, through its individual members, possesses and is a conduit of the anointing *"without measure"* which is upon and emanates from the Eminent Head of the Body. Hence, as the seventy elders were to Moses, elders in the Church are merely imperfect and individually incomplete human intermediaries representing the only true Mediator between God and men, Christ Jesus! And, it is only corporately, in plurality, that the presbytery (eldership) represents the fulness of Christ unto the Church, serving the Body as visible and touchable delegates of the government, authority, and leadership of Christ and "imparters" of His ministration to His Body. As the seventy elders were special intermediaries delegated to assist Moses in leading and judging matters concerning the people, elders in the Church, presided over by Five-fold Ministers, are special delegates of Christ.

Christ's Intermediaries in the Church

Indeed, all of these historical events concerning Israel were a prefigurement of Christ (Moses) and the Church (Israel), and how He would redeem and deliver a people out of bondage to sin and Satan, and transfer them under the Lordship (Kingdom) of Christ. As indicated many times before, the "church in the wilderness" was the paradigm (pattern, model) for the New Testament Church.

Thus, in the same way that God effected His government over "the church in the wilderness" through human proxies or representatives, so also does He administrate His government over the New Testament Church through human intermediaries. In "the church in the wilderness," the spiritual leaders, the Levites, who were delegates of Aaron (who typified the Holy Spirit), along with the seventy elders, who were delegates of Moses (who typified Christ), provided the government of the nation.

Thus, the class of leadership within the New Testament Church which the Levites and the seventy elders in "the church in the wilderness" typified are the spiritual impartational and governmental offices. The Apostle Paul referred to this class of leadership as the *"overseers,"* distinguished from the *"deacons"* and *"saints,"* in the Philippians 1:1 text we examined in the previous chapter. The Five-fold Ministry Offices and the local church presbytery of elders comprise those offices of "overseers." The Five-fold Ministers impart spiritual construction (edification) and instruction (education), and are part of the local church presbytery of elders which provides government within the local assemblies.

As explained in Chapter Three in connection with debunking the myth of the office of "bishop," the function of elders, summarily, is two-fold: to *oversee* and to *shepherd* the Flock of God. This is made clear in two vital passages of Scripture.

The first passage is Acts 20:17-28, which chronicles the Apostle Paul's final words to the elders of the Ephesian church, which had been under his apostolic purview, prior to his fateful departure to Rome. Verse seventeen says he called together *"the ELDERS of the church."* Verse twenty-eight quotes his exhortation to these elders: *"Be on guard for yourselves and for all the flock, among which the Holy Spirit has made you OVERSEERS, to SHEPHERD the Church of God which He has purchased with His own blood."*

The second passage is 1 Peter 5:1,2, wherein Peter exhorts the elders of the Gentile Greek churches: *Therefore, I exhort the ELDERS among you, as your fellow ELDER...SHEPHERD the flock of God among you, exercising OVERSIGHT...."*

The Role of Construction and Instruction

Now, of course there is a very valid role of shepherdship that Five-fold Shepherds (and all Five-fold Ministers are under-shepherds, not just pastors) are indeed ordained by the Lord to fulfill on behalf of the Chief Shepherd (1 Pet. 5:4), Jesus. The meaning of the word "shepherd" is to feed and care for, to lead and to guide, and that is the crux of what Five-fold Shepherds are to provide on behalf of Christ unto the sheep of God's Fold. However, as I have indicated in various ways throughout this script, what is involved in the case of the Discipleship/Shepherdship teaching and practices, unfortunately, is a bastardization of this very legitimate role of shepherding.

Primarily, the role of the Five-fold Ministry is spiritual impartation or equipping, and consists of two facets: spiritual edification (building), or construction; and, spiritual education, or instruction. The most succinct and foundational delineation of this role in Scripture is represented in Ephesians 4:7-13:

There is one body and one Spirit, just as also you were called in one hope of your calling; one Lord, one faith, one baptism, one God and Father of all who is over all and through all and in all. But to each one of us grace was given according to the measure of Christ's gift. Therefore it says, "When He ascended on high, He led captive a host of captives, And He gave gifts to men." Now this expression, "He ascended," what does it mean except that He also had descended into the lower parts of the earth? He who descended is Himself also He who ascended far above all the heavens, that He might fill all things. And He gave some as apostles, and some as prophets, and some as evangelists, and some as pastors and teachers, for the equipping of the saints for the work of service, to the building up of the body of Christ; until we all attain to the unity of the faith, and of the knowledge of the Son of God, to a mature man, to the measure of the stature which belongs to the fulness of Christ.

The Objective of Five-fold Ministry

As the foundational Ephesian text indicates, the ultimate objective of the edificational and educational impartation of the Five-fold Ministry is two-fold. First, to bring the true Body of Christ into *"unity of the faith and the knowledge of the Son of God,"* which means complete and universal compliance with *"sound doctrine"* (1 Tim. 6:3; 2 Tim. 4:3; Tit. 1:9; 2:1,7,10). The Living Bible's rendering of this portion of the text makes the goal of doctrinal maturity and accord even more manifest: *"until finally we all believe alike...."* The second main objective is to bring the Body of Christ, individually and collectively, into conformity with the Image of Christ, who is the Head of the Body, which means spiritual maturity. In other words, the final product of the proper functioning of Five-fold Ministry is that the Body of Christ will become the exact representation and manifestation of the Head, who Himself is the exact representation of the Word of God (Heb. 1:3; Jn. 1:1).

The ensuing verses of the text go on to indicate that when the Five-fold Ministry Offices have been allowed to function as God intended, the result will be that the Body of Christ will no longer be spiritually immature children, tossed here and there by the undulations of excessive and unbalanced *"waves"* of doctrinal emphasis that come along from time to time, and thrown off course by *"winds"* of fallacious teaching, propagated by malevolent and self-aggrandizing men by means of trickery, craftiness, and deceitful machinations. Rather, as the Body of Christ becomes the Truth incarnate (true meaning of Greek term rendered *"speaking the truth"* in many translations) in Divine agape-love, it will develop in every way into complete conformity with the Image reflected by its Head, Christ, who provides every provision needed for the Body—which is fitted and formed, conjoined and conformed, together by that which every joint supplies—for the building up of itself, which is effected by means of the proper functioning of every individual part in an atmosphere of prevailing agape-love.

As a result, we are no longer to be children, tossed here and there by waves, and carried about by every wind of doctrine, by the trickery of men, by craftiness in deceitful scheming; but speaking the truth in love, we are to grow up in all aspects into Him, who is the head, even Christ, from whom the whole body, being fitted and held together by that which every joint supplies, according to the proper working of each individual part, causes the growth of the body for the building up of itself in love. (Eph. 4:14-16)

Function of All Five Offices Required

Another vital point indicated in the text is that it is only by means of the effectual functioning of **ALL** of the Five-fold Ministry Offices, inclusive of apostles and prophets, within the Church that the Body of Christ shall be brought unto the place of ultimate spiritual maturity, that is, *"unto the measure of the stature of the fulness of Christ,"* wherein the Body of Christ will no longer be doctrinally factionalized and spiritually immature, but rather will have become *"one mature man."* **Three**-fold ministry consisting of evangelists, pastors, and teachers—the only ministries recognized by most segments of the Church until now—simply is not capable of bringing the Church into that condition of complete

273

spiritual maturity. Only **Five**-fold Ministry can. Indeed, as the Church in its present spiritual and structural condition is juxtaposed to the Biblical pattern, it is not at all difficult to see that the accumulative effectuality of **three**-fold ministry has been inadequate to complete the task of bringing the Church into spiritual maturity and conformity with the Image of Christ.

It is only when each of the Five-fold Ministry Offices are functional and making their unique contribution that the Body of Christ shall be truly and fully conformed into the Image of Christ, having become that Church *"without spot or wrinkle in all her glory"* Christ is returning to claim as His Eternal Bride. Therefore, the restoration of the prophetic gifts and office as well as the apostolic office unto their rightful place of function in the Church which God is now bringing about is absolutely essential to the Church becoming fully conformed into the Image of Christ. It is only as the prophetic and apostolic offices are restored that the requisite spiritual restorations and structural reformations will be effected. Only then will *"the periods of restoration"* be complete, and Heaven will no longer *"retain"* (Ac. 3:21) the Christ, but He shall be **released** to **return**, appearing first in the clouds in the air for the great gathering together unto Christ. Then, when we see Him, we shall have truly become like Him because our spiritual myopia will have been cured, allowing us finally to *"see Him just as He IS"* (1 Jn. 3:2), instead of as we have for so long erroneously perceived Him to be.

The Term of the Ascension Gifts

The Ephesian text indicates it was as Jesus was ascending into Heaven to retake His Throne at the right hand of God that He relegated the Five-fold Ministry Offices unto certain individuals of His election. It is for this reason that the Five-fold Ministry Offices are also referred to as the "Ascension Gifts." This attribution rightly signifies that these gifts were relegated by Christ as permanent offices of function within the Church for as long as He remains ascended. In other words, until Jesus returns to Earth to claim the Church as His Eternal Bride, all of these offices will continue to be effectual and operable.

Moreover, the term of the functionality of these ministry gifts is also defined in the text in the phrase *"until we all attain to the unity of the faith, and of the knowledge of the Son of God, to a mature man, to the measure of the stature which belongs to the fulness of Christ."* All of the Five-fold Ministry giftings will continue to be operable and necessary *"UNTIL"* the Church does indeed at long last attain unto the unity of the faith and of the knowledge of the Son of God, and does indeed attain unto the spiritual perfection and maturity of the stature of the *"fullness of Christ,"* that is to say, when we are fully conformed into the Image of Christ. When that has been fulfilled, the Church will have become that Church *"without spot or wrinkle in all her glory"* which the Lord shall return to claim as His Bride, bringing an end to the Church Age. In the meantime, as long as the Church and the Church Age exists, all of the Five-fold Ministry Offices will continue to be necessary and operable.

First Corinthians 12:28 further corroborates the permanence of all the Five-Fold Ministry Offices for the duration of the Church Age: *"And God has SET IN THE CHURCH, first apostles, second prophets, third teachers...."* The fact that, according to this passage, it is *"in the Church"* that these offices have been *"set,"* by definition means that as long as the Church is the Church, and it will continue to be the Church as long as the Church Age endures, which will be until the Church becomes *"the Lamb's Wife"* at the Marriage Supper of the Lamb, the Five-fold Ministry Offices will continue to be valid ministries within the Church; that is to say, for the duration of the Church Age. The term *"set"* used here is very important as well in that it connotes permanence and immutability. A perfect example illustrating the meaning of the word "set" is cement. As anyone who has ever laid cement knows, you have to work it into the desired place and configuration very quickly, for once it has "set" it is permanently fixed and unchangeable. And, that is precisely what the Holy Spirit is indicating with the deliberate choice of the term "set" in this passage—that these ministry gifts have been permanently and immutably set into the foundational structure of the Church.

Colaborment and Collaboration

Essentially, what all this concerning the effectuality and functionality of the Five-fold Ministry Offices amounts to is the solution God proposed for Moses' governmental and administrative dilemma: "plurality of leadership." As I indicated earlier when discussing that scenario, plurality of leadership, *colaboring* and *collaborating* together in *concert*, is and always has been the God-ordained system for the administration of the Kingdom of God on Earth.

Revelation 12:10 indicates that *"the Kingdom of God"* is synonymous with *"the authority of Christ,"* and from Genesis to Revelation God makes it abundantly and unequivocally clear that His purpose has always been to effectuate His authority and Kingdom on Earth through His Holy Co-Partners, His personal delegates, His many-membered, corporate Helpmate—the Lamb's Wife, the Church. His-story, Scripture, opens with God creating Man (Adam) in His own Image and commanding him to take dominion and rule over the entire Creation. It ends with the New Heaven and New Earth being established on planet Earth as the Holy City, the New Jerusalem, the Church (Heb. 12:22,23), *"the Lamb's wife"* (Rev. 21:9, KJV), comes down out of Heaven to the Earth *"made ready as a Bride adorned for her Husband"* (Rev. 21:2) to begin reigning with Christ as His royal viceroys.

So also, in the interim prior to this ultimate chapter of the Divine Denouement becoming manifest, however, is it God's intention that the Body of Christ begin to colabor and collaborate together in real *"unity of the Spirit"* (Eph. 4:3), which entails and encompasses *"unity of the faith and knowledge of the Son of God"* (v. 13), which means "**doctrinal** unity." As mentioned earlier in expounding upon verses fifteen and sixteen of the Ephesian Four text, the Holy Spirit is informing us in these verses that as the Body of Christ comes to the place that it is both spiritually and structurally conformed unto Divine Truth so that it then is, as God intended, the Truth incarnate, or *"the exact representation of* (the Divine) *Nature"* (Heb. 1:3), just as Jesus was, it will then be fitted and formed, or conjoined and conformed, together as one viable and functioning unit by the means of—*"that which every joint supplies."* In other words, completeness, wholeness, soundness, of the Church, Christ's Body, will only be achieved through the proper functioning of every individual part of the Body, and every believer is one part or member of the Body. No part or member is insignificant or without vital function. The Body as a whole is only viable and sound, or healthy, to the extent that each and every member is functioning as it should. Moreover, the text indicates, it is the Body *itself* then, as it is viable and spiritually and structurally sound—that is to say, when it is what it is supposed to be, and each part is functioning as it is supposed to function—it is the Body itself that builds *itself* up to full maturation, to the place that the Building has been fully constructed in conformity to the Divine Blueprint.

Many believers have the mistaken idea that it is God who is going to do everything with regard to the Body, and that the Body itself has little to do with the matter of its development. How silly! Why, even the way God has designed nature clearly demonstrates that is not the way God operates. In the Creation, God created all living beings to be self-procreating and self-perpetuating. Every specie of living being procreates after its own kind (Gen. 1:11,12), and God has bestowed within the mysterious protoplasm of life indigenous to each particular specie a wondrous capacity for self-preservation and self-development within the limits of the intrinsic sophistication of the specie.

Likewise, God created the human body with a highly efficient and sophisticated capacity to "grow" itself once it is born and takes in that first breath of life. Given the proper nutrition, atmospheric elements, and care, the properly functioning human body will grow on its own, so to speak. This is the way God has made it. He has created within the human body the capacity to grow and develop, and even to heal itself. It is the same with the Body of Christ— given the proper spiritual nutrition and nurturement, it too will grow and develop on its own, whether a local body or the Body of Christ at large.

Furthermore, what may be the most significant element of all, the sixteenth verse says all this will be accomplished *"in"* agape-love, the import of which is that when the Body of Christ finally comes to the place that it is in conformity with the Divine Blueprint both in regard to *spiritual* and *structural* character, then the Divine Nature of Agape (Love) [1 Jn. 4:8] will be manifested and prevailing in the Body. In other words, the sum of what is being said here is that it is the imperfect and improper spiritual and structural character currently prevalent in the Body of Christ that is preventing it from building itself up into the final product God intends for it to become.

Moreover, the prevalence of imperfect and improper spiritual and structural character means the Body of Christ is not perfected in Agape-love, which *IS* the Divine Nature. And, this lack of perfectness in Agape-love, which is spiritual immaturity, would account for the pervasiveness in the Church of the one element which perhaps more than anything else has hindered real colaborment and collaboration from taking place as God intended— **FEAR!** Fear, that is, in the form of insecurity and distrust. For, God's Word trumpets forth the piercing indictment: *"There is NO FEAR in LOVE* (agape); *but perfect* (mature) *love casts out* *fear...and the one who fears is not perfected* (matured) *in love"* (1 Jn. 4:18, parenthetical explanations added).

Thus, if this be so, and all my experience working with other ministers tells me it most definitely is, then essentially all our inability, or unwillingness as it may be, to be properly fitted and formed together to become a complete and viable, functioning and flowing, unit—**ONE BODY**—to effectively accomplish the intents and purposes of God, lies in spiritual immaturity. And, that spiritual immaturity continues unabated, primarily because of blatant and stubborn unwillingness to be perfected in, matured in, and walk in Agape-love.

When these spiritual flaws and imperfections are removed and remedied through repentance and proactive change, then Divine Agape-love will prevail throughout the Body of Christ, which will result in real colaborment and collaboration among the Five-fold ministries. In turn, it is in and by the means of this prevailing atmosphere of Agape-love in which each and every part of the Body is functioning properly that genuine growth, development, and maturation will transpire, naturally, until finally the Body of Christ has developed in every way unto complete conformity with and is fully reflecting the Image of the Head of the Body, the Lord Jesus Christ.

A Counterfeit System of Plurality of Leadership

In essence, what this colaborment and collaboration among the Five-fold ministries adds up to is what I was discussing earlier in this chapter with regard to the plan God enacted to resolve Moses' dilemma for leading, judging, and governing the Israelites: "plurality of leadership." As I indicated there, plurality of leadership under the sovereignty of Jesus is and has always been God's ordained system for government of the Church and the administration of His Kingdom on the Earth.

As I shall discuss momentarily, God never intended that the church be governed by solitary autocratic monarches ("pastors") as are most "full gospel" churches presently. Rather, because the fallen nature remains uneradicated within us all and shall remain until we receive our *"full redemption"* at the last trump of God, and attainment of absolute perfection by any individual believer is thereby precluded, in His infinite Wisdom, God has elected to distribute His provision of proxied leadership and government unto the local church through a plurality of Divinely appointed and anointed leaders, each of whom He has bestowed with certain impartational giftings and abilities of the Spirit. None of these leaders in themselves represent or supply completeness of God's provision to the Church in this regard, however, but only a certain portion of the whole. The only exception to this is the rarity in which a church is presided over by a true apostle, someone who functions in the full range of the Ministry Giftings.

Preponderance of Scripture unequivocally indicates that plurality of leadership is the method ordained by God for leading and governing the Church. However, one of the seemingly enigmatic ironies concerning the Discipleship/Shepherdship doctrines is that the original tenets were centered around a form of "plurality of leadership." But, the system advocated by these invalid doctrines was a counterfeit system made so primarily by a singular but altogether crucial element of error and errancy.

Unfortunately, it is this same ironic twist that may make it difficult for some of those who rightly rejected and opposed these Scripturally unsound teachings, along with those who previously espoused and subsequently renounced them, to accept the validity of the plurality of leadership principle. Indeed, over the years since the inception of the Discipleship Movement there has been a steady succession of pastors renouncing or at least retreating from some or all of these erroneous doctrines and practices primarily because of this one tenet of "plurality of leadership," many of whom lamented that over the course of time it caused t. *em* and their ministries tremendous troubles, and in some cases led to devastating "church splits" from which some have never recovered.

However, the primary cause behind most of these horror stories was not the matter of plurality of leadership at all, but that the system of government they were attempting to institute and operate was predicated on an ilk of egalitarianism (i.e., equality; parity; one person, one vote) among the leaders which effectively results in leadership "by committee," which has been proven over and over again throughout history in every genre of governance known to man to be totally unworkable, worthless, and in short, an exercise in utter futility.

In the case of the local church God always calls, appoints, and anoints, in a preeminent and distinguishing way, one man as the predominant and presiding leader among the presbytery of elders, who is esteemed and recognized as such by the other leaders. His role is not one of a dictator, but rather to preside over the leadership much like an orchestra conductor. The wise and obedient presiding elder has absolutely no interest in imposing his own will, but is forever in search of the perfect Will of God; he is not a detached and insecure, loner autocrat, but surrounds himself with trusted and loyal advisors, being very much cognizant that *"in the abundance of counselors there is victory"* (Prv. 24:6), that *"without consultation plans are frustrated, but with many counselors they succeed"* (Prv. 15:22), and that it is the collective *"WE"* who *"have the mind of Christ"* (1 Cor. 2:16); thus, he consults and collaborates in earnest with fellows and colleagues to ascertain God's explicit direction, seeking confirmation of each prospective word of Divine guidance by consensus from other witnesses. So, though there is a plurality of leaders, there still is one prominent individual who stands out among the plurality and is recognized by God and his colleagues as the chief leader of the group. The *anointing* is always the primary indicator of God's election in this regard, rather than age, education, experience, tenure, status, or any other carnal criteria, for God always *anoints* those whom He *appoints*.

Beyond that crucial fault, there was one other major flaw in the Discipleship system of leadership, which in the end wrought untold spiritual havoc in multitudes of groups and churches as well as families and individual lives since the inception of the movement. It also had nothing whatsoever to do with the fact that the leadership was composed of a plurality of leaders, per se. Rather, it had to do with the matter of who it was who was appointed to be the "downline" leaders within the group, the "middle managers" in modern business parlance. These were the small "cell group" or "home group" leaders, the persons who did the actual hands-on "shepherding" and "discipling" of the sheep. It was here at this level—in the small group forum, where the real pastoral, one-on-one, leave the ninety-nine for the one, ministry and personal spiritual application takes place—that the most damage and devastation was incurred.

In a nutshell, the problem was that in a majority of the cases the people appointed to these pivotal positions of spiritual impartation were neither called, anointed, equipped, or qualified to minister to the people placed under their spiritual care. Instead of choosing people for these shepherding capacities on the basis of outstanding spiritual character and acumen as they should have, the criteria often had more to do with their social and financial status than with their spirituality. Usually appointees were prominent members of the church and community who saw in the system licensed means by which to flaunt themselves and implement their attitudes of ascendancy over others. Self-aggrandizing church leaders recognized in the system a crafty and covert mechanism by which to capitalize on the selfish ambition of these "members of means" by appeasing their desire for special deference and recognition via appointment to these positions which they viewed as prestigious and preeminent, which would virtually insure the continued financial support and involvement of these exalted elite, who then in turn, using the same inducement, recruited acquaintances of like motivation and means for membership.

The upshot of the whole matter was that the vast majority of those people appointed to these pastoral positions were motivated more by selfish ambition and self-seeking than they were by a genuine desire to minister to hurting and needy people. The result was wholesale spiritual devastation. All because, as discussed at length in the previous chapter, unqualified, unequipped, and ill-motivated interlopers intruded into ministry functions reserved for those called and anointed by God, and who have willingly laid down their own lives and ambitions in order to minister with pure devotion and wholehearted dedication unto the masses of souls who are *"distressed and downcast like sheep without a shepherd"* (Mat. 9:36).

Yet, the authors of these doctrines and practices forcefully and unequivocally asserted that the entire multi-level system of leadership proposed under the Discipleship/Shepherdship theories was completely and incontrovertibly Scriptural. They based this assertion exclusively on a solitary occurrence in Scripture, namely, a system for leading and judging the Israelites following their exile from Egypt proposed to Moses by his father-in-law, Jethro. The story is chronicled in the Eighteenth Chapter of Exodus.

Over and over again during the early days of the Discipleship Movement, proponents of these teachings cited this text as their proof-text and proceeded judiciously to build and present their case like a prosecuting attorney deftly indoctrinating the jury in the hope of impelling them to agree with his proposed conclusion. I mean, after all, here is the story, right here in the Bible, so it must be right, right?

Well, not necessarily. Any astute, avid, and sensible student of the Bible will have to agree that there are incorrect statements recorded in the Bible. Now before that statement causes someone to go into cardiac arrest, let me explain what I mean.

*I am **not** at all talking about the inerrancy or veracity of Scripture—that is absolute and absolutely essential.*

What I am talking about is that there obviously are statements recorded in the Bible that were made by *people*, **not** *God*, that were at the very minimum incorrect, and in some cases were outright lies. For example, without any dispute the biggest and most consequential lie, and the very first lie, recorded in the Bible is the lie Satan told Eve. The second lie occurred when Eve retold the lie of the devil to her husband and seduced him into joining her in deception. Abram lied concerning his wife, Sarah, saying she was but his sister and offering her to a foreign king in exchange for his own life (Gen. 12). Jacob lied to his dying father, Isaac, pretending to be his twin brother, Esau, in order to receive the blessing of the first-born due Esau (Gen. 27). Potiphar's jilted wife lied against Joseph, falsely charging him with rape when he refused to lie with her (Gen. 39). Rahab the harlot's lie to protect the Israelite spies was overt and thusly chronicled in Scripture (Jsh. 2). Saul lied to Samuel the prophet concerning his compliance with God's command to annihilate the Amalekites (1 Sam. 15). David in fear of his life feigned madness before Saul (1 Sam. 21:8-15), and concocted a scheme of deception to conceal his adultery with the wife of his friend and trusted comrade in arms, Uriah (2 Sam. 11). One old prophet lied to another prophet, giving him a false word from God, and when the younger prophet hearkened unto the false prophecy, he was eaten by a lion on his journey home (1 Kgs. 13:1-32). Gehazi, the servant of Elisha lied to Naaman, falsely purporting that Elisha requested from him a certain remunerative gift for his healing (2 Kgs. 5). A host of lies and lying schemes against the prophets to discredit them and cause them to be executed are recorded in the Bible. False witnesses rose up against Jesus to accuse Him of breaking the law, and their lies are recorded in Scripture (Mk. 14:53-59).

In this sense, and I emphasize in this sense *only*, there are many untrue statements that truly were made (by people) which appear in the Bible. And, what I believe the Lord has shown me is that the truth of the matter is that this proposal of Jethro to Moses was of this ilk. A number of things lead me to that conclusion.

Number one, Jethro was not an Israelite, but a Midianite, of non-Hebrew, Arabic heritage. Midian, after whom the land of Midian was named, was a son of Abraham by one of his concubines, Keturah. After the birth of Isaac by Sarah, Abraham sent all his sons he had fathered by his concubines and their families eastward, and they settled in the Arabian lands to the east of the Negev desert, where Abraham had settled (Gen. 25:1-6).

Secondly, Jethro was *"the priest of Midian"* (Ex. 18:1; 6:16), meaning he was the chief or *high* priest of the entire land of Midian, and the Midianites worshiped the false Caananite gods, Baal (male) and Asherah (female) [*see* Jdg. 6:10,25]. Jethro's own words of astonished exultation after hearing of all the miracles God had wrought through Moses in relation to the Israelites' deliverance out of Egypt corroborate that he had been worshiping false gods: *"Now I know that the Lord is greater than all the gods!"* (Ex. 18:1-11). This means then that Jethro was a high priest of devil-worship, because Scripture makes it clear that there really is no such a things as a false god, but rather the homage, deference, and worship that is attributed to pagan gods, whether in those days or now, is actually and ultimately worship of the devil and demons (1 Cor. 10:19,20). So also was it in the case of the Caananites, it was in actuality Satan himself who they were worshiping and serving.

The subsequent verse (Ex. 18:12) indicates that as Jethro heard the testimony of Jehovah's demonstrated omnipotence in delivering the Israelites, he was then convinced that Jehovah was the one and only true God, and that he offered up sacrificial offerings in homage unto Jehovah, and that Moses, Aaron, and the elders shared a dedicatory meal with him, signifying his being received into fellowship by the Jewish brethren as a "converted" Jew: *"Then Jethro, Moses' father-in-law, took a burnt offering and sacrifices for God, and Aaron came with all the elders of Israel to eat a meal with Moses' father-in-law before God"* (v. 12).

Thus, Jethro was in essence a *"new convert"* or novice in the service unto Jehovah, and therefore, even though he was an elderly man, he had a lot of learning to do with regard to the ways of God and true spiritual knowledge, as well as unlearning of the delusions and false wisdom with which he had been indoctrinated by the demons behind his false religion. Yet, it was the very next day following his "conversion" that Jethro presumptuously took Moses aside (which is reminiscent of the time Peter took Jesus aside to chide Him) in order to give him counsel after observing the method he employed for judging the people:

And it came about the next day that Moses sat to judge the people, and the people stood about Moses from the morning until the evening. Now when Moses' father-in-law saw all that he was doing for the people, he said, "What is this thing that you are doing for the people? Why do you alone sit as judge and all the people stand about you from morning until evening?"

And Moses said to his father-in-law, "Because the people come to me to inquire of God. When they have a dispute, it comes to me, and I judge between a man and his neighbor, and make known the statutes of God and His laws."

And Moses' father-in-law said to him, "The thing that you are doing is not good. You will surely wear out, both yourself and these people who are with you, for the task is too heavy for you;

you cannot do it alone. **Now listen to me: I shall give you counsel, and God be with you.** *You be the people's representative before God, and you bring the disputes to God, then teach them the statutes and the laws, and make known to them the way in which they are to walk, and the work they are to do. Furthermore, you shall select out of all the people able men who fear God, men of truth, those who hate dishonest gain; and you shall place these over them, as leaders of thousands, of hundreds, of fifties and of tens. And let them judge the people at all times; and let it be that every major dispute they will bring to you, but every minor dispute they themselves will judge. So it will be easier for you, and they will bear the burden with you. If you do this thing and God so commands you, then you will be able to endure, and all these people also will go to their place in peace."*

So Moses listened to his father-in-law, and did all that he had said. And Moses chose able men out of all Israel, and made them heads over the people, leaders of thousands, of hundreds, of fifties and of tens. And they judged the people at all times; the difficult dispute they would bring to Moses, but every minor dispute they themselves would judge. Then Moses bade his father-in-law farewell, and he went his way into his own land. (Ex. 18:13-27)

Though Jethro's apparent concern for Moses's well-being was certainly commendable, and even though the system he proposed may have indeed offered to Moses a valid means of physical conservation (albeit, we are given no evidence that it did), nevertheless, the Scriptural account is clear that this was the proposal and advice of *Jethro*, and no inference is made that it was inspired by *God*. Moreover, fruitfulness being the most accurate indicator that a matter is authored by God, it seems fairly evident that this plan was *not* inspired of God in that neither the people nor Moses appear to be in any wise bettered after that *"Moses listened to his father-in-law, and did all that he had said."* On the contrary, the rebellion and spiritual indifference of the people not only continued

287

but grew exceedingly worse as time went on, and because of it, so also did Moses' anger and frustration with the people, until finally he had the total breakdown we have already discussed that is recorded in Numbers Eleven, at which point God gave Him the *real* solution.

To me, and I really am not being dogmatic about this matter, Moses would have been better off continuing to listen to his *Father-God* rather than his *father-in-law*. To this point God had performed miracle after miracle over the short span of only two months since their departure from Egypt, brazenly demonstrating there was absolutely no provision for their sustenance and preservation beyond His power to supply. Whenever the situation seemed impassable and impossible, and Moses had done all he knew to do and could do no more, God always had a plan of escape, and was well able to communicate to Moses what to do to avert disaster and bring salvation. God had spoken to him in Midian in the burning bush, spoke to him in Egypt concerning the plagues, spoke to him at the Red Sea, spoke to him at Marah and Rephidim, and spoke to him when the people grumbled against him demanding meat. Now, all of a sudden, had God run out of answers, or gone mute, or exhausted His power, making it necessary for Moses to turn to human counsel coming from an aged and inveterate priest of a false, polytheistic religion who only the day before finally broke through his strong delusion to recognize the sovereignty of the one and only true God? Frankly, I find that difficult to accept.

Moreover, I find it very interesting that virtually immediately after this incident with Jethro, God called Moses up to the top of Mount Sinai and proceeded forthwith to, what sounds to me like, read him the riot act, reminding him that it was by His own supernatural power that they were delivered from a life of oppression and futility under the domination of the Egyptians:

Erroneous Concept #5: Role of Five-Fold Ministry

*Thus you shall say to the house of Jacob and tell the sons of Israel: 'You yourselves have seen what **I did** to the Egyptians, and how I bore you on eagles' wings, and brought you to Myself. Now then, if you will indeed obey **MY** voice and keep **MY** covenant, then you shall be My own possession among all the peoples, for all the earth is Mine; and you shall be to Me a kingdom of priests and a Holy nation.' These are the words you shall speak to the sons of Israel. (Ex. 19:3-7).*

We see inherent in God's Words that the problem was the people were not obeying God's voice and keeping the provisions of His covenant. In other words, the problem was: *rebellion*! That's why Moses was worn to a frazzle, trying to minister to the people, because their hearts were not toward God and they were being disobedient. That's why he had to labor from morning to night wrangling with the people and their problems.

I have learned over and over again that that is precisely the way it is: when the minister is having to minister day and night, wrangling with the same people, in teaching and counseling and never-ending personal ministry, trying with all you've got to get them set free from all that binds and troubles them, it's because those people are still wrestling with **God**, they have yet to yield to God, and decide to do it His way. It's nothing but plain old stubbornness and rebellion! Pure and simple!

And, there is not a thing in the world the strongest, most anointed, most knowledgeable minister can do for those who have not yet ceased striving with God and surrendered their will unto the Lordship of Christ (and there are a multitude of purporting Christians of that ilk). Believe me, I've learned that the hard way, after being worn completely out, at the brink of exhaustion and emotional collapse, totally frustrated and exasperated, and so angry with the people I was trying to help I had decided the only way I could help them was to kill them, to put them out of their misery

289

and so they could go on to Heaven—**IF** they were saved—and I was not at all sure about that!

Now I am not saying that the system Jethro proposed was a nefarious one, nor an impractical, implausible, or ineffectual one; just a merely human one. On a purely human level, and if, as in the case of the non-believing world, then and now, functions of life are performed with God and His revealed wisdom, impartations, and provisions entirely excluded from the equation, the system Jethro proposed may very well be a good one, administratively and organizationally speaking. In that regard it may afford some measure of relief merely because it provides a more appropriate and proportional distribution of "ministry" duties and endeavor.

Indeed, in this regard, those who may have employed or who are presently employing some hybrid of this system proposed by Jethro for the purpose of proportionally distributing the ministry and leadership "load," especially the large and mega-churches, no doubt have found that *some* sort of organizational system is absolutely necessary and vital. I do not dispute that, but on the contrary agree that if you are going to have a "large" church (and it is with this concept that I would differ), some system that proportionally distributes the onus of leadership and ministry is absolutely essential. Indeed, the larger the church, the more "shepherds" and support staff are obviously needed.

The matter of *quantity* of leadership is not really the issue, either in the case of Jethro's proposal or ministries today that have instituted some system based on this text. Rather, the issue is the *quality* of the leadership. To state it another way: the problem is not the *number*, but the *nature* of leadership. Those chosen and appointed to these all-essential positions of personal, one-on-one ministry and impartation into people's lives, which ultimately effects entire families, must first and foremostly be chosen, anointed, and appointed by **God**. Moreover, as I said earlier, in that respect, the issue and true indicator is—**the ANOINTING!**

Without the anointing, valid and effectual spiritual impartation into people's lives is impossible. Those who attempt to make spiritual impartation into other's lives who have not first generously received of the anointing from God, no matter how well-intentioned they may be, frequently end up doing more harm than good.

In the case of the system of delegated leadership Jethro proposed to Moses, as with so many humanly-devised or devil-inspired notions and solutions, it was generally similar to the true solution which God provided for the problem, and initially, according to human rationale, it appeared to be a plausible solution that should bear fruit. However, in the passage of time, and it is only in the passage of time that the validity of some things can be properly assayed, it became evident that this hypothesis was like the barren fig tree Jesus cursed in righteous indignation because, though it had borne leaves, which normally is portentious that the tree has borne fruit, when He went to take some fruit from it, He found it to be hypocritically barren of fruit. Thus, He cursed it, and immediately it withered from the roots up and died (Mat. 21:18,19).

So also is it regarding the multi-tiered system of leadership proposed under the auspices of the Discipleship doctrines, which purportedly was patterned after and validated by the system Jethro proposed to Moses. As it is with so many aspects of those fallacious teachings, it bore some outward and ostensible resemblance to the Divinely-inspired system, but when sufficient time had elapsed for it to have matured to become fruit-bearing, the Discipleship/Shepherdship tree proved it was a deceptive counterfeit, in that it was barren and wholly incapable of ever bearing any genuinely good, i.e., Godly, fruit. Jesus said a bad tree was incapable of producing good fruit, and that good fruit is only produced by good trees; and thus a good tree is discernable by the quality of the fruit it bears, whether good or bad (Mat. 7:17,18).

I am personally persuaded and it is becoming manifest that what Jesus did to the hypocritical barren fig tree is precisely what He is now beginning to do with the hypocritical, barren-of-good-fruit, Discipleship/Shepherdship churches. Though they may have borne some outward resemblance to true trees in the Kingdom of God, and over the years produced some "leaves" by which they portended to be Godly-fruit-bearing trees, in the passage of time most of these trees proved only to be hypocritical and fallacious trees, being totally barren of fruit after the genus of God. It now appears that just as Jesus became righteously indignant at the fig tree in Israel and cursed it, He has begun to do the same thing with regard to these aberrant groups. Consequently, they will wither from the roots up, die, and be consumed as stubble in testing fires (1 Cor. 3:10-15; Zech. 13:8,9) which He Himself (Lk. 12:49), and not the devil, has ignited, for as He declared, *"Every tree that does not bear good fruit is cut down and thrown into the fire"* (Mat. 7:19).

As the story bears out, the system proposed by Jethro was a preemptive counterfeit to the system God revealed to Moses less than two years later. This seems to be typical of the way Satan operates. Just how he is able to do it, I do not know, but the pattern is clearly discernible throughout history. He always seems to preempt what God is about to do with a counterfeit.

A Preemptive Counteroffensive Against the Prophetic

Similarly, I believe the Discipleship/Shepherdship Movement, the outcome of which was a proliferation of unauthorized and abusive methodologies and mechanisms under the auspices of the "doctrines of demons" upon which it was based, was a preemptive counterfeit movement, inspired and perpetrated by Satan in an attempt (albeit, ultimately a wholly vain attempt) to sabotage and, if possible, preclude what God was about to do with regard to the Church, which namely was to *"set in order what remain*(ed)*"* (Tit. 1:5) and then raise it up as the mighty Army of God it is destined to become (Ezk. 37), all of which He would bring about by means of the restoration of the prophetic and apostolic offices.

In essence, the Discipleship/Shepherdship Movement was a preemptive counteroffensive by Satan against the Prophetic Move which God was about to bring forth.

Satan's greatest terror and the one thing that he fights against the most is the Church rising up as a mighty Army of God, because when it does, it will bring about the final defeat of his kingdom and his rule on Earth. Nevertheless, the prophet Ezekiel's prophecy concerning the End-time Church coming to life, standing upright on their feet, and becoming *"an exceedingly great Army"* (Ezk. 37:10) will yet have its ultimate fulfillment, no matter what Satan tries to do to prevent it. And, God's Word testifies that it is by the prophets prophesying the Breath of the Spirit into the valley of dry bones that this whole transformative and preparative process will be initiated. The *prophets* are going to prophesy edification, exhortation, and encouragement into the dry bones, causing them to be revitalized and to stand upright on their feet as a highly-trained, well-prepared, proficient, and fully-equipped Army. In due course, the true *apostles* will become manifested as the field commanders who will organize, mobilize, and strategically deploy the troops of God's Army to successfully and thoroughly vanquish the Adversary, dispossessing him from his stolen possessions and territories.

Prophetic Repulsion

Lack of knowledge and understanding regarding the office of the prophet coupled with fear of deception and an ingrained reticence regarding untraditional tenets, makes it very difficult for the majority of mainstream Christendom to accept the concept of the restoration of the prophetic office and ministry. To those of us who the mainstream considers radical and extreme, this certainly is not surprising. In fact, in the light of historical tendency, it is understandable and to be expected.

293

However, those individuals and groups who purport to be of the "Charismatic" classification (and virtually all Discipleship/ Shepherdship/Covenant churches do), because of the very nature of the attribution, should be fully accepting of the truth of Five-fold Ministry and its viability, as well as, then, the consequential necessity of the restoration of the prophetic and apostolic offices. Notwithstanding, it has been my personal experience that most Discipleship/Shepherdship/Covenant churches, while expressing agreement in theory with the premise of Five-fold Ministry, nevertheless do not have those offices effectually functioning in concert within their ministries. Indeed, most of them openly display an aversion and even acrimony regarding the prophetic office and those who have been set into that office, i.e., prophets. On the whole, Discipleship proponents and groups simply have no use for prophets, and usually make little attempt to mask their sentiment.

This "prophetic repulsion" lies, I believe, in the fact that true prophets, by nature, are what some people consider recalcitrant and iconoclastic when it comes to ecclesiastical organizations of men and even the concept of organizationalism within the Church. True prophets are spokesmen of God, not of any man, or any agency of men. Their allegiance is preeminently to God, and they will not allow their ministry or message to be in any way compromised or adulterated by expected allegiances to men and their personal agenda. They are not yes-men, who automatically affirm and confirm every intent and plan of other church-leaders. Prophets are preoccupied with the establishment and advancement of the Kingdom of God, and repulsed by the ambitions and activities of men bent on building their own kingdoms.

True prophets are obsessed with Truth, forever *seeking* the Truth, and only *speaking* the unabashed Truth, the whole Truth and nothing but the Truth, as they receive it from God, without deference to men, to include even themselves! Experienced prophets

294

will be *"shrewd as serpents,"* utilizing prudence and discretion, yet they refuse to allow self-interest or self-aggrandizement to taint their judgment or their message. It is because of these things that prophets, though *ordained* by God, are often *disdained* by men.

The Role of Church-Government

Though it can only be mentioned tangentially in this volume, to have a proper general grasp of the role of Five-fold Ministry, it is essential to understand there indeed is a vital role of church-government that is fulfilled by those in Five-fold Ministry. Summarily, that role is essentially one of being the caretakers and managers who provide administrative oversight over the "business" affairs of a ministry. As already established, the scope of that government is limited to the local church or the organizational boundaries of a "field ministry."

Unfortunately, as stated in various ways throughout this book, the matter of ecclesiastical government is one of the most misunderstood and misconstrued matters in the Church realm today. The Truth regarding this matter of governmental authority within the Church bears little resemblance whatsoever to what it has been construed to be and encompassed by the Church as a whole.

The Church desperately needs to receive revelation from God regarding this critical matter, if the Church is to ever advance beyond where it has been languishing for quite some time. Indeed, that revelation is soon to be revealed through apostles and prophets whom God is in the process of raising up and releasing from the obscurity that has served to protect and preserve their ministry until the conditions in which they can be effective are manifest. As that revelation comes forth, certain related, required restructuring will be effected that will allow the Church to be propelled into a new dimension of spirituality, maturity, power, and productivity.

No Over-lording Among Five-Fold Ministers

Regardless of whatever ecclesiastical government is, and whatever is not understood about it, one thing concerning it is an absolute, unequivocal, and incontrovertible certainty, according to the explicit Words of Jesus—it cannot entail any shred of "over-lording," or lording over one another, by believers:

> *And calling them (*i.e., the Twelve Apostles of the Lamb [see preceding verses]) *to Himself, Jesus said to **THEM**, "You know that those who are recognized as rulers of the Gentiles **LORD IT OVER** them; and their great men exercise authority over them. But it is not (to be) so **AMONG YOU**, but whoever wishes to become great **AMONG YOU** shall be your servant; and whoever wishes to be first **AMONG YOU** shall be slave of all. For even the Son of Man did not come to be served, but to serve, and to give His life a ransom for many." (Mk. 10:41-45, emphasis and parenthesis added by author)*

The essence of what Jesus was referring to here is the common practice among Godless Gentiles of interacting and interrelating with one another according to a kind of caste system, or pecking order, in which those of superior status, station, and substance in life "lord over," or exercise preeminence and predominance over, fellows of lesser status. Usually, the application of this text is attributed to *all* believers in general, and certainly *all* believers alike should guard against practicing such class-ascendancy.

Nevertheless, the italicized and capitalized portions of the full text (vv. 35-45) makes it clear that Jesus gave this admonition in a private and exclusive discourse with the Apostles. Hence, Jesus was condemning and proscribing the practice of interrelational authoritarianism by the Apostles in particular and therefore by extension, all ministers. He declared that this kind of authoritarianism simply was not to exist among the Apostles in their relationships with one another. Moreover, now that the apostolic office has been dispersed into the Five-fold offices, this admonition applies to interrelations among all Five-fold ministers.

Co-Equality Among Believers

In different words, Jesus' essentially expressed the same concept in His well-known denunciation of the Pharisees, through which He warned against religious predomination and maltreatment of fellows, saying: *"you are all brothers"* (Mat. 23:8). The Living Bible's paraphrase makes the import of this verse more evident: *"all of you are on the same level, as brothers."* The vital point Jesus is establishing here is that all believers, since they are literally spiritual "brothers" by virtue of having been Born Again into the Royal Family of God, are indeed on the same level in the Kingdom of God. That is to say, they are on par with one another and co-equal.

As discussed earlier, every truly Born Again believer literally becomes a "tekna" (Greek), a genetic son of God, somehow, through the mysterious supernatural process of sanctification by which the "unGodlike," or ungodly, are gradually and ultimately transformed into the Image of Christ. Those who have genuinely entered into this regenerative process, somehow take on the very genes of God (Jn. 1:12; 1 Jn. 1,2; 2 Pet. 1:4; et al), with the result of having become the very genetic offspring of God. This process and its ultimate general outcome are the same for every partaker, and it results in parity and co-equality without partiality among all partakers.

Thus, in the parochial sense that all bona fide believers have become the genetic offspring of God, we all indeed are on the same level as brothers. But, incredibly, in addition to that, we are even on the same level as Jesus Himself, though certainly we do not share in His Divine Sovereignty. Indeed, the Bible brazenly declares us to be *"joint-heirs with Jesus Christ,"* which means we

are co-equal with Jesus Himself in terms of our spiritual preroga-
tives and possessions.

Certainly then, if we are co-equal heirs with Jesus, of necessity,
believers are, as Jesus said, on the same level brothers. The import
of this is that in terms of our status and standing in the Kingdom of
God, and the spiritual substance which has been made available to
us, all believers are co-equal (Rom. 8:17; Gal. 4:7; 3:29; Eph. 3:6;
Jas. 2:5). We are joint-heirs with Christ, meaning all true Spirit-
regenerated believers share equally in the spiritual inheritance
bestowed upon us by our Heavenly Father. Indeed, all believers,
regardless of gender, race, station, or financial status (Gal. 3:28;
Col. 3:11), are on the same level as brothers.

Yet, regardless of the veracity of this fundamental truth, it has
been my experience that many people, especially Charismatic
believers, are reticent to accept it, and many take issue with it,
leaders and laymen alike. What is curious to me is that these very
people qualmlessly accept the idea that they are joint-heirs with and
on the same level as *Jesus*, and vociferously tout same, yet they are
constrained to accept that all *believers* are on the same level and
co-equal. There seems to me to be something intrinsically wrong
with that, not to mention nonsensical.

Servitude Vs. Subjugation

Jesus' declaration *"you are all brothers"* (Mat. 23:8) was part
of a larger admonition to His followers against improperly exalting
or glorifying spiritual leaders. He said no leader should be venerated to the point of being regarded or referred to as someone's
"Master," "Father," or "Guide" (literal meaning of the original).

Rather, Jesus went on to say, *"the greatest among you shall be
your servant,"* and *"whoever exalts himself shall be humbled; and
whoever humbles himself shall be exalted"* (vv. 11,12). He said
virtually the same thing in the other conversation with the Twelve
we just examined. Essentially in these conversations with the

disciples, Jesus was contrasting the genuine *servitude* intrinsic to the Kingdom of God against the overt *subjugation* exercised by the world in every genre and at every level of human interrelations.

As we've been discussing, Scripture calls for colaborment and collaboration among Five-fold Ministers, with the understanding that no one individual or office is sufficient in itself to fully complete the task of equipping and maturing the Body of Christ, and that there is to be cooperation and complimentation among Five-fold Ministries, not competition. One of the chief reasons that real colaborment and collaboration has not taken place as it should is that the caste system by which the world operates is also very much in operation within the interrelations and interactivities of ministers.

The latent foundation of this system of authoritative classism is the presumption that there is not co-equality among ministers, that there is in fact a superior-inferior disparity among them. At bottom is the totally fallacious presupposition that certain ministers have somehow attained superiority over certain fellow-ministers, and by virtue thereof have the right to exercise authority and predominance over those ministers who are of inferior status and standing.

This was precisely the system Jesus was condemning and prohibited in the Church in general and among ministers in particular. That's why it is so incredible to me that this system is so overtly prevalent and yet virtually unchallenged in ecclesiastical interrelations today. It seems to me that the Body of Christ should have recognized the fallacy and inequity of such a practice by now, and moved to eliminate it. Perhaps, that is an advancement that we can look forward to the Present Truth Church making in the near future.

Chapter Nine

RELIGIOUS ENSLAVEMENT: SORCERY

At the very core of authoritarian doctrines and practices of the Discipleship/Shepherdship ilk is religious enslavement. Moreover, let us be clear that religious enslavement is **WITCHCRAFT**! Thus, it follows then that hyper-authoritarian, Discipleship/Shepherdship-type doctrines and practices are, at bottom, **WITCHCRAFT**! And, that assessment is not at all an extrapolation, but is based on the intrinsic nature of the teachings. Moreover, it is hardly necessary to point out that witchcraft is something of the devil's domain and not God's. It is this reality that makes these teachings and the practices they promote so decidedly aberrant as well as repugnant to those who are cognizant of it.

Though it be so that these doctrines and practices amount to witchcraft, the problem is that they have already been infused into and become an integral part of the doctrinal and structural system of a large segment of the Charismatic/Pentecostal Body of Christ. Thus the majority of Charismatic/Pentecostal believers, who have been deluded into accepting the validity of these teachings, would have extreme difficulty in understanding and accepting that these doctrines are Scripturally-invalid and that they amount to witchcraft, despite the absolute veracity of both of those assessments. Indeed, the very fact that it has been in otherwise legitimate and normative Pentecostal and Neo-Pentecostal (Charismatic, "Faith Movement," and "Third Wave," et al.) churches that these occultic doctrines and practices have been taught and instituted has itself augmented their obscurity and continuance.

301

Of course, not all Pentecostal or Neo-Pentecostal churches employ these teachings and tactics. Yet, a substantial percentage of especially Neo-Pentecostal churches do, in some form and degree, a percentage much higher than what the average believer would surmise, however.

In all fairness, I must say that there no doubt are some leaders who have accepted and instituted these doctrines and practices in their churches in sincere naivety and ignorance without totally comprehending their full import and impact. Many of those cases are the result of those leaders having blithely "cloned" their ministry structure after someone else's with whom they were associated or affiliated, or simply impressed.

Nevertheless, a significant portion of the leaders who have instituted these errant doctrines and practices have done so with deliberation, knowing fully and precisely what they were doing, having perceived in them a convenient, well-camouflaged, highly effective, and widely-accepted mechanism affording both license and means to predominate and prevail over a group of congregants, in order to enlist and mobilize them as the implementers of their personal kingdom-building. Once wiled, thoroughly indoctrinated, subdued and subjugated, these indentured congregants then become the willful implementers, agents, collaborators, and operatives for the designs of these errant, self-aggrandizing, and self-exalting ecclesiastical autocrats.

The True Nature of Sorcery

Asserting, as I have, that these authoritarian doctrines and practices amount to witchcraft requires that we understand the true nature of witchcraft and sorcery.

"Witchcraft" and "sorcery" are synonymous terms. Some Bible translations use one term, some the other, but both refer to the same thing. The root Greek word for "sorcery" is "pharmakeia," which literally means *to administer drugs*. From this Greek word are derived various English words having to do with medicinal drugs, or narcotics, such as "pharmaceuticals" and "pharmacy."

However, there is a common misconception concerning the nature of witchcraft and sorcery resulting primarily from the etymology of this Greek word translated "sorcery" or "witchcraft" in the New Testament. This word "pharmakeia" was originally coined to allude to the use of narcotics as "mind-altering" and "trance-inducing" intoxicants in pagan religious ceremonies and ministrations throughout the ancient history of paganism.

Notwithstanding, while the original meaning of the word had to do with administering drugs to aid in the casting of spells and inducing trances in pagan occultic worship, in the passage of time, it came to have a broader connotation than just that in the Greek language. It came to be what is known as a "metonymn," a figure of speech or kind of colloquialism evoking an idea related but greater than the literal meaning of the word's components. For example, in the colloquial phrase "under one *roof*," it is not really a literal roof only that is being alluded to, but rather the word "roof" is a metonymn referring to an entire building consisting of walls and a roof. Similarly, both the Greek word "pharmakeia" as well as its English equivalent "sorcery" connote something more than the parochial matter of the use of narcotics in the occult. Rather, it is kind of a "catch-all" phrase evoking the larger concept of "interpersonal predomination and self-imposition" as achieved by various means and methods.

Hence, the Biblical, and thus true spiritual connotation, of sorcery or witchcraft, it is imperative to understand, transcends the use of drugs as an intoxicant or trance-inducer in pagan and occult witchcraft. Biblical sorcery and witchcraft centers more on the specter of people manipulating, dominating, controlling, and captivating other people, whether by supernatural (i.e., demonic) or simply natural (human) means.

To put it another way, while the original meaning of "sorcery" or "witchcraft" had to do with the casting of "spells" or the inducement of "trances" in paganism and the occult, the Biblical usage of these words includes psychological means and methods of usurpation and imposition over others as well. For the truth of the matter is that the "drug" that is used to "cast a spell" over someone is not always a narcotic; there are also a host of psychological means and methods that, especially with the assistance of demons, are just as trance-inducing and compelling and effective. A "spell" is not just a state of intoxication induced by a narcotic. Rather, a "spell" is any induced condition in which a person's natural and normal self-control over his own thinking and actions is usurped, counteracted, controlled, or simply influenced, by some unnatural, non-indigenous, exterior force. However, the ultimate force behind spells and trances, regardless of the agent, means, or method by which they are induced, is demons and the devil.

Simply stated, the true Spiritual definition and application of "sorcery" or "witchcraft" is using any form of persuasion, influence, intrigue, or inducement, delusion, predomination, or outright coercion, whether of natural (human; psychological) or spiritual (i.e., evil spirits) origin, to unduly and improperly influence, manipulate, dominate, or control someone else, in order to gain ascendancy or advantage for self-aggrandizement. To put it in even simpler terms, sorcery or witchcraft is endeavoring to get someone else to do what *you* want them to do. It is prevailing upon others in order to get them to yield their will to your will. It is volition (will) captivation. It is self-imposition and usurpation. It is being an interloper. It is dominating and controlling others.

God revealed through the prophet Samuel's rebuke of the disobedient King of Israel, Saul, that witchcraft or sorcery is essentially synonymous with "rebellion," and that "disobedience" (which, in essence, is rebellion) is synonymous with "iniquity" (acts of specific trespass and offense against God) and "idolatry" (the imposition of false gods in God's place): *"For **rebellion** is as the sin of **witchcraft**, and **stubbornness** (disobedience) is as **iniquity** and **idolatry"** (1 Sam. 15:23).* What this means, in other words, is that witchcraft **is** rebellion, and rebellion **is** witchcraft; moreover, disobedience (stubbornness) is defiance, disregard, and displacement of God.

The Means and Methods of Sorcery

Now that is the nature of sorcery and witchcraft. But, let's examine now the various means and methods by which sorcery and witchcraft can be effected. Sorcery can be effected either by natural (human) means or by supernatural (demonic) means.

Supernatural means are those means and media involving explicit inducement and abetment by demons. It entails any and all of the manifold satanically-perpetrated occultic methods and modes that exist, which range from sensual or sexual seduction to voodoo, from seemingly innocent child's play with a Ouija board or an 8-Ball to seances and consulting mediums, from casual and supposedly for-amusement-only reading of newspaper horoscopes to overt, bona fide Satan worship. All of this kind of sorcery and witchcraft is included in the Biblical attribution of "divination." Satan has thoroughly infiltrated this kind of divinational influences and devices into virtually every segment and element of human society and life.

Though this "interpersonal predomination" is sometimes effected through these supernatural means, and witchcraft and sorcery is generally associated with satanic activities, it is vital to understand, however, that to engage in sorcery and witchcraft does not **require** the involvement of supernatural power from demons. Rather, it can also be effected merely through natural, human means emanating out of the human spirit. The unregenerate *human* spirit, permeated as it is with the carnal, sin nature of Satan, intrinsically, is certainly sufficiently evil-prone and evil-proficient in itself to devise and implement devices of unauthorized control over others on its own without any assistance of *demon*-spirits. In the Creational Order, only the Divine Spirit (Nature) of God transcends the human spirit, and being made in the Image of God, the human spirit has some capacity for creativity, though it is limited specifically to *the* **natural** *realm*. "Interpersonal predomination" emanating from the human spirit is the natural, human means of sorcery.

Natural, human means would include a wide variety of interpersonal machinations and mechanisms operated in the psychological realm. At one end of that spectrum is an entire range of such machinations and mechanisms falling under the category of what is generally referred to by such terms as "the power of persuasion," which is commonly considered a benign, relatively harmless, fair, and appropriate "art form." Somewhere in the middle of the spectrum is a realm of a kind of Machiavellian "intrigue," it could be called, permeating virtually every segment of life and society from politics to the ministry, wherein the means, no matter how immoral, improper, or unethical, is considered to be justified by the end. At the opposite end of the spectrum, is the more intrinsically sinister and guileful realm of overt predomination by means of a host of psychological mechanisms the object of which is mind-control.

Now, of course, not all "persuasion" is intrinsically evil. There is the benign type of "persuasion" in which one person presents information to another in an attempt to convince that person of the validity of his own perspectives or convictions. However, what makes that kind of inducement benign is that there is no coercion or usurpation of the other person's will involved. The first person is merely presenting to the other person his personal perspective along with supposed corroborative information for the second person's consideration. In the case of illegitimate interpersonal predomination, however, some sort of influence is being covertly injected in order to short-circuit the normal consideration process and to usurp the victim's natural volition (will) for the purpose of subjugation and captivation.

As an aside, within the foregoing also is manifest the somewhat subtle difference between legitimate *preaching* and *teaching* verses unauthorized *indoctrination* aimed at psychological domination. Ministers have a responsibility to preach the Truth and teach people how to apply the Truth in practical living, but we must never be guilty of in any way alluring or coercing our listeners into ostensible obedience. God desires that we be *obedient* to Him not out of coercion but out of *willingness* (Is. 1:19). Like any human parent, God wants willing obedience from His children. Willing obedience is what brings God pleasure. Coerced obedience really is not *obedience* at all but *compulsion*. The approach of ministers toward their listeners should be the same as God's toward us—we can enjoin, exhort, and evangelize, that is, *call* people to God, but we must never *coerce* or *compel*.

In essence, what this speaks of, is what, indeed, is the very heart of sorcery: the matter of *volition*. The matter of Volitional Authority, or "personal authority," was addressed in some detail in Chapter Four. It may be helpful to review the commentary on that subject, in that it is related to the topic of this chapter. As indicated there, Volitional Authority is the third highest level of authority God has established in His Creational Order. Only two other types of authority supersede it: God's own sovereignty, and the veracious authority of God's Word.

This personal authority entails the human will, or "free moral agency," as theologians refer to it, with which God has endowed every human being. Essentially, it is the inherent right to personal sovereignty or autocracy, that is, the right to self-government and free-choice. This right, as I stated in Chapter Four, is absolutely inviolable within the restraints of lawfulness. This means that no one but no one has been consigned the right by God to violate or in any way encroach upon the right to self-government vested in each human, as long as that person engages in righteous and lawful conduct, and refrains from engaging in any iniquitous conduct or acts of lawlessness against any other person.

Illustrating the sanctity and absolute inviolability of the human free-will is the fact that, though He certainly is sovereign over all, God Himself will never usurp or in any way forcibly infringe upon the free will of any human being, even when our actions and their consequences are not in our own best interest. Now when we have willingly subjected ourselves unto His Lordship and Fatherhood, as a part of His great Fatherly love for us, He will indeed chasten and discipline us (Heb. 12:5-11). Nevertheless, though He invites *"whosoever will"* affirmatively respond, to be adopted into the Heavenly Family, and though He loves us ever so immensely, and deeply desires that all be saved, He will not force Himself, His Sovereignty, nor His Fatherhood, upon any individual, to the point that He will allow us to choose the abyss and agonies of hell over the bliss and blessings of Heaven.

Thus, since the Creator has Himself chosen to grant to every human-being such enormous and unrestrained free agency, in imitating God, as we are enjoined to do by the Word of God (Eph. 5:1, et al.), we the created certainly then are compelled to deal with our fellows in like manner, neither coercing nor in any way imposing our own will upon anyone else. Indeed, to impose our will upon anyone else is the antithesis of the holy and beneficent Divine Nature, and in fact is the very essence of sorcery, which is the essence of the thoroughly unholy, rebellious, and self-seeking nature of Satan.

The Origin of Sorcery

Of course, Satan is the ultimate though unseen source behind every kind and genre of sorcery and witchcraft, and there is an innumerable company of his diabolical cohorts, evil spirits, whose sole function it is to perpetrate and propagate witchcraft all throughout the world and among all human beings. However, Satan and his imps can only intervene and invoke their devices in human affairs where and when they are given opportunity, license, and agency by cooperative human-beings. Since God has given authority on the Earth unto the sons of men (Ps. 115:16), Satan is powerless to implement his devices except through human cooperatives.

Sorcery originated with Satan. It is a part of his nature—the spirit of disobedience, *"the spirit that is now working in the sons of disobedience"* (Eph. 2:2). Through the Prophet Isaiah, God revealed by the Spirit what took place when Lucifer fell into apostasy and perdition. His account delineates the precise rebellious ruminations of Lucifer that precipitated his abrupt descent into unrighteousness and spiritual ruin. Clearly, the source of his rebellion is *self-will,* evidenced by the fact that he says to himself five times *"I WILL"*:

> *"But you said in your heart, 'I WILL ascend to heaven; I WILL raise my throne above the stars of God, and I WILL sit on the mount of assembly in the recesses of the north. 'I WILL ascend above the heights of the clouds; I WILL make myself like the Most High. ' (Is. 14:13,14)*

This passage makes it clear that rebellion against God (sin) is predicated on self-will or self-imposition. In essence, rebellion is self-imposition, following after your own will instead of God's. Consequently, it is not hard to understand the meaning of the Spirit's statement: *"Rebellion is as the sin of witchcraft."* In fact, in a broad sense, witchcraft is following after the rebellious nature of Satan, *"the spirit...of disobedience. "*

Furthermore, when you put all this together, it becomes clear that Satan's nature is the **AntiChrist Spirit**, because it is opposed and antithetical to the Lordship of Christ, and that therefore sorcery and witchcraft is operating in the AntiChrist Spirit. And, indeed that is precisely what sorcery or witchcraft is, endeavoring to be someone's "lord," "master," and "savior" in place of Jesus Christ. That is also why I say, sorcery is self-imposition and usurpation. It is also self-deification, that is, posing and interposing as God, which was precisely what made Lucifer fall into perdition and disenfranchisement from God. Ever since that day when unrighteousness was found in the heart of Lucifer, he has been totally consumed with trying to take Jesus' place as *lord*. He is the ultimate usurper and interloper. He is literally **dying to be god**.

Sorcery Within

If all this concerning sorcery being rooted in the nature of Satan is so, and it is, we must take it a step further. As I mentioned before, no matter how unpalatable to the average believer, the truth is that the nature of the devil, *the spirit of disobedience*, with all its attributes of rebellion and evil, is the carnal nature which pervades the soul of every human being every born. Which means that within us all is the propensity to rebellion, including operating in sorcery and witchcraft. This Truth is corroborated by the Holy Spirit's Words conveyed through the Apostle Paul in his letter to the Galatians, wherein he included *"sorcery"* or *"witchcraft"* (depending on which Bible translation you read) among the attributes of the carnal nature:

> *Now the deeds of the flesh* (carnal nature) *are evident, which are: immorality, impurity, sensuality, idolatry, SORCERY, enmities, strife, jealousy, outbursts of anger, disputes, dissensions, factions, envying, drunkenness, carousing, and things like these, of which I forewarn you just as I have forewarned you that those who practice such things shall not inherit the kingdom of God. (Gal. 5:19-21)*

Thus, sorcery, from the spiritual perspective, is not merely an assortment of occultic ritual and practices. Rather, sorcery is an attribute of the carnal nature common to us all. To put it another way, sorcery is a natural tendency lurking within the unredeemed

310

soul of every human being which we all are quite capable of operating on our own without any assistance from evil spirits.

Within every one of us mere mortals is the raw desire to in some way and degree predominate and impose our will upon others for our own self-aggrandizing and self-exalting purposes. This propensity is just as much a part of the inherent carnal nature (the source of our temptation to sin) as immorality, enmity, strife, jealousy, anger, or a plethora of other, just as damning, iniquitous attitudes and actions, with which we all, saved or unsaved, are constantly tempted. (In the case of many people, the urge to control others is stronger than their urge to control themselves, as demonstrated by their undisciplined behavior.) The *proclivity*, or in some people, *passion*, to control others is a basic urge of "the roaring lion within" that must be resisted and mastered in the same way as any other evil temptation, else it will surely master and eventually utterly destroy *you*.

Predomination and Control: Common Element of Religion

Predomination and control has always been a common element of religion. The reason for that is simple. Satan is the ultimate usurper and the real AntiChrist. He is absolutely consumed with the notion of supplanting Jesus as Lord and establishing himself as lord. He is a million times more crazed by this dastardly fantasy of supreme grandeur than any maniacal tyrant in human history. Religion is the device he uses to deceive people into believing they are right with God, so that he can be lord by default. In actuality, the true though unseen object of religion's homage is demons and the devil. When you pull back the curtain of religion, a la *The Wizard of Oz*, who do you find the wizard has been all along? None other than—**THE DEVIL HIMSELF!**

Satan is the author of all religion, and *religion* is the counterfeit of *rightstanding* and *relationship* with God. Religion is man's attempts to merit rightstanding with God. Religion, however, does not make you right with God, it separates you from God. Rightstanding with God cannot be gained on the basis of merit, for every human being who has ever lived, apart from Jesus of Nazareth, has sinned and fallen short of the glory of God. Thus, we need a Savior, and Jesus is the only Savior recognized and sanctioned by God. Everyone who trusts solely in Him to attain rightstanding with God, receives it, on the basis of grace, undeserved and unmerited favor.

Religion is *self*-justification, in essence. However, true rightstanding with God is based on "*Jesus*-justification," that is, justification on the basis of faith in Jesus as the only Savior and the only Way to God.

This is the reason that every religion in the world (what frequently is referred to as "false religion," which is really redundant, because *all* religion intrinsically is false) is frought with predomination and control. Even Judaism became a debauched religious system wherein the sovereignty of Jehovah was subverted by priests coveting power, prestige, prominence, and preeminence. So also, the functional Headship of Christ was supplanted in early Christianity by the Nicolaitan priesthood, likewise motivated, and their legacy of hierarchical predomination and usurpation is yet an integral part of the fabric of organized Christianity today.

Predomination in the Church

Thus, it comes as no surprise, at least to those who understand that the Church is not yet the perfected, blameless and spotless, Bride that it will be at the return of Christ, that the organizational Church, including the supposedly spiritually advanced Pentecostal/Neo-Pentecostal branch, is also tainted by Satanically inspired predomination perpetrated through its leadership. In this regard, some commentary is in order.

312

There are today a great many sincere yet sincerely misinformed people who fervently regard, revere, and defend "The Church" (whatever it is they consider that to be, usually some local organization affiliated with a larger organization) as being a pristine and perfect spiritual virgin. Notwithstanding, however, the fact of the matter is that the devil and his demons infiltrated the Church long ago, not long after its inception, with doctrines of demons and "tares" (false brethren), and they have yet to be totally extirpated and evicted.

This kind of misplaced and undue veneration and exaltation of the "General Assembly" of believers (*i.e.,* the Church; *see,* Heb. 12: 22,23), whether in its Old Covenant (Judaistic) or New Covenant form, is certainly nothing new. In the Book of Lamentations, Jeremiah the prophet attributes the complacency and indifference of the Jews, which finally incurred the wrath of God, the result of which was the debacle of their nation, and their captivation, subjugation, and forced exile by foreign armies, to their holding of this very kind of inane and fanciful utopian idealism:

*The Lord has accomplished His wrath, He has poured out His fierce anger; And He has kindled a fire **in Zion** Which has consumed its foundations. The **kings of the earth** did not believe, Nor did any of the inhabitants of the world, That **the adversary** and **the enemy COULD** enter the gates of **Jerusalem**. (Lam. 4:11,12)*

The Jews' arrogance, predicated on their long and illustrious heritage as "the people of God" and their misconstruement of the meaning of God's extended longsuffering toward them, had grown to the point of being pure cockiness, which resulted in thorough delusion and complacency with regard to the specter of the righteous indignation and retribution of God.

All throughout their history, the Jews, *"think{ing} lightly of the riches of His **kindness** and **forbearance** and **patience,** not knowing that the kindness of God [is meant to] {lead} you to repentance,"*

313

failed to heed the Divine warning to *"Behold the kindness and the SEVERITY of God"* (Rom. 11:22). Instead, the Jews made the extremely costly mistake of construing God's kindness, forbearance, and patience with their apostasy and disregard for God to be infinite impunity. They mistook God's merciful withholding of Divine retribution to be Divine irresolution. In other words, they were deceived into thinking that because God had been so merciful for so long in refraining from acting in accordance with His wrath, that they had been, were, and would forever continue "getting away with" their unceasing rebellion and utter disregard and contempt for an Almighty God.

How thoroughly mistaken they were! How thoroughly mistaken also is modern Zion (the Church; see Heb. 12:22,23), thinking that God will forever tolerate its stubborn disregard of and contempt for God's revealed Word, Will, and Ways.

In their cockiness, the Jews did not think that it was even possible for the adversary, the enemy, Satan (1 Pet. 5:8), to enter into the gates of Jerusalem. But, when God's patience had come to an end, He *"poured out His fierce anger"* and *"accomplished His wrath,"* by pulling down the hedge of Divine protection that had been encompassing Israel, which prevented Satan from being able to fulfill his nefarious purposes of destruction and annihilation against Israel. Abolition of the Israeli state, and enslavement by and exile to a foreign nation was the swift consequence.

Likewise today, many of *"the kings of the earth,"* that is, believers[1] (cf., Rev. 1:5,6; Rom. 5:17; et al.), do not believe that it is even possible for the adversary, the enemy, Satan, to enter into the gates of the Church (of which Jerusalem is a type). They too have been deluded into becoming cocky and complacent, and have majored so much on the *"kindness"* of God, but have refused to heed the second half of the Spirit's warning: *"Behold....the SEVERITY of God."*

Indeed, sadly, I dare say the majority of believers and leaders do not believe that God brings judgment to believers under the auspices of the New Testament. Those who argue thusly often cite such passages as First Thessalonians 5:9 as proof-texts: *"For God has not destined us for wrath, but for the obtaining of salvation through our Lord Jesus Christ."* However, they fail to see that that sentence is part of a warning to believers concerning the necessity that they live holy lives as *"sons of the light and sons of the day"* (v. 5), thereby distinguishing themselves from those who are part of Satan's kingdom of night and darkness, lest they be judged and punished along with the latter.

---

[1] The term used by Jeremiah in Lam. 4:12, *"the kings of the earth,"* the author believes, refers to the true kings of the earth, believers. The Jeremiah text juxtaposes *"the kings of the earth"* against *"the inhabitants of the world,"* which would be inclusive of earthly kings, and therefore superfluous if it was referring to earthly kings. This same term is also invoked in Rev. 1:5, where Jesus Christ is called *"the ruler of the kings of the earth."* The succeeding verse declares that believers are the *"kings"* of whom Jesus is the ruler: *"and (He) has made us* (believers) *kings and priests unto God."* Rom. 5:17 declares: *"those who receive the abundance of grace and of the gift of righteousness will REIGN (as kings* [A.B.]) *in life through the One, Jesus Christ."* Paul calls Jesus *"the King of kings and Lord of Lords"* (1 Tim. 6:15, et al.), and this term is used twice in Revelation (17:14; 19:16) with regard to the establishment of the Kingdom of God on Earth during the Millennium. Thus, the "kings" of whom Jesus is the ultimate King are the redeemed, faithful and obedient believers, i.e., *"the called and chosen and faithful"* (Rev. 17:14).

In addition, as I mention in various places in this volume, to say that God brought judgment under the Old Covenant but does not under the New, would require that God changed between the Old and the New Testaments. However, He has not. As He Himself has testified, *"I am the Lord, and I do not change"* (Mal. 3:6, lit.). Rather, God *"is the same yesterday, today, and forever"* (Heb. 13:8). So much Scriptural evidence could be presented on this matter, but space simply will not permit. However, true and earnest learners are already convinced concerning the obvious reality of judgment for all those who are disobedient, whether professed believer or not, and the unconvinceable and argumentative will never be convinced.

Even more weighty regarding the matter of judgment of believers in the New Testament dispensation is the Apostle Peter's words in his *New* Testament epistle, written decades into the *New* Testament Age, to *New* Testament believers: *"For IT IS TIME for JUDGMENT to begin with the HOUSEHOLD OF GOD"* (1 Pet. 4:17). In this statement, the eminent apostle is saying that those of the Household of God, which incontrovertibly refers to believers, and which term is a synonym for the Church, will be subject to some type of judgment (although I do believe this is a different kind of judgment [of refinement] than that to which the unbelieving world will be subjected [eternal punishment and separation from God]). Moreover, he says that final Divine adjudication, or judgment, will begin with the Church. What that means is that before God judges the world for their disbelief in the Christ, there will be a period of time in which the Church shall be under "judgment." But, perhaps the most crucial words in this sentence are: *"IT IS TIME,"* because Peter was saying that the time for that judgment to begin was the time in which he was writing those words. And, indeed, there is a very Scripturally-supported way to view all of Church history as a kind of extended judgment of refinement and purification, a perspective to which I personally subscribe wholeheartedly (*see,* Ac. 3:17-21).

Confirmation from a Witch-doctor

Ironically, though probably not coincidentally, as I was writing this chapter, I saw on a Christian television network program an interview of a former genuine witch-doctor from a remote village in Africa who is now radically saved and transformed, Spirit-baptized, on fire for God, and preaching the Gospel. He is one of a number of foreign missionaries being sent by God to this country to prick the conscience of and stir up the twentieth-century Laodicean American Church.

At the outset of the interview, the man gave a condensed version of his testimony as a former witch-doctor and how it was that he came to be saved and delivered from the demon-spirits that possessed him. Under the anointing of God, he began to speak a word of reproof to the American Church that, to me at least, was obviously inspired by the Holy Spirit. Though I say it was a word of *reproof*, the import of what he said really amounted to and should have been received by honest and earnest American believers as a word of *rebuke*.

The gist of his commentary centered on the fact that while billions of the world's population live twenty-four hours a day, 365 days a year in constant hopelessness, fear, political repression, demonic oppression, abject poverty, sickness and disease, and complete spiritual bankruptcy, on a fast track to the perpetual fires of eternal judgment in Hell, the American Church is thoroughly consumed with the triviality of "Churchianity," personal kingdom- and organization-building, worldly frivolities and vanities of every kind, and an obsession with materialism.

All this, he observed, was being augmented by two primary and prevailing factors. First, a fallacious prosperity gospel that promotes rather than denounces carnal lusts for wealth ("mammon-serving," materialism), ascendancy, and self-satiation. Second, the New Age psychology-based "me-gospel," which extols to the

317

already thoroughly self-absorbed and self-glorifying "Yuppie" generation their need for so-called "self-image improvement" and "personal enrichment," along with the "secrets" to achieving it through an endless array of humanistic and quasi-religious ideologies and techniques that purportedly aid in personal development of innate qualities of deity supposedly lying dormant within every human.

Next to the Church's preoccupation with the unessential, the thing the former witch-doctor said was causing him the greatest alarm and concern pertained to the personal kingdom-building and organization-building in particular, and the methodologies employed by a great number of the leaders in American churches to achieve those objectives. As a preface to his explanation of those remarks, he related a condensed version of his testimony, recounting some of the supernatural acts the demon-spirits that formerly possessed him performed through him during his life in witchcraft. Some of the examples he cited were: levitation of inanimate objects and hurling animals and people through the air, causing objects and animals to appear to speak, performing ostensible physical healings of the sick and diseased, turning water to blood, casting spells upon animals or people which caused them to go into hypnotic, zombiotic trances and left them thoroughly subject to his "power" and manipulation, the placing of curses upon people as a means of subjugation or retaliation, causing them to suddenly and inexplicably become violently or even fatally ill. And, that's just to name a few.

Elaborating further on this "way of life" so common in many Godless cultures in the world, he said performing these acts merely for the purposes of showing off was by no means the object of the witchcraft, but rather the witchcraft was only a means by which to achieve the ultimate objectives of domination, control, economical and political ascendancy over others, and prominence within the tribal society, all for purposes of self-aggrandizement and personal gain. In primitive societies such as the one in which he had lived, where the very specters of wealth procurement, education, vocational advancement, and political structures are virtually non-existent, ascendancy and societal prominence cannot be attained on the same bases as they are in sophisticated societies. Ascendancy and prominence in the villages from which he hailed, he explained, are attained on the basis of and by the means of interpersonal predominance by either natural or supernatural "power." Moreover, the viscosity of the competition among the prominent members of those societies attempting to achieve that predominance over others is often of life and death intensity. Indeed, he said, everyone in those jungle-societies lives in indescribable perpetual fear and dread, because of the ever-looming threat of falling victim to a host of violent or even fatal curses, spells, and various other occultic/demonic perpetrations.

The former sorcerer went on to say that there were three chief elements upon which the effectuality of the witchcraft "powers" he used to operate hinged: intimidation, mind control, and manipulation. This first element he mentioned, intimidation, or fear, is what the entire occult realm of witchcraft and sorcery is predicated on, and the primary factor that makes it effectual. In the same way that faith is the foundation for the entire Kingdom of God and the spiritual force causing it to be effectual in the believer's life, so also fear is the foundation of Satan's kingdom and the spiritual force that makes all of his wicked purposes and intents operable and effectual. Indeed, the Bible reveals that fear in actuality is an evil spirit, one class of Satan's fallen angelic cohorts (2 Tim. 1:7, KJV).

Fear is also an emotion inherent to the carnal nature, which is Satan's nature, who was the first being to experience fear when he fell into perdition, and who thus ever since has existed in absolute terror of God and the eternal punishment in the fires of hell that awaits him. When humans experience fear they are actually experiencing by proxy the fear and awful dread inherent to Satan and his fallen cohorts. That Man inherited fear from Satan is made evident in the story of Adam and Eve (read Gen. 3), who when they disobeyed God and partook of the carnal nature, also partook of Satan's terror of God. The first manifest consequence of their sin was absolute terror of God. So terrified of God were they that they ran non-stop for sixteen miles, the original Hebrew text says, desperately trying to hide themselves from the presence of God. In essence, fear, apprehension, dread, trepidation, and so forth, are expressions of faithlessness in and enmity against God, which give Satan opportunity and license, or legal right, to perpetrate his devices against humans (*see* Eph. 4:27).

The story of Job appears in Holy Writ as a poignant illustration that fear is tantamount to carte blanche to Satan and his demonic attacks. When destruction of all that he owned struck in one day, Job knew precisely why it had come: *"For the thing I greatly feared has come upon me, and what I dreaded has happened to me"* (Job 3:25). In the end, Job came to understand that the sacrifices he had been offering up *"continually"* (Job 1:5), though it seemed so religious and right, had been nothing more than a kind of *talisman* which he desperately hoped would somehow bring preservation and protection of his children and possessions, and were actually a *testament* of his fear and faithlessness in God to honor those sacrifices and protect his family and possessions from harm and loss. It was this faithlessness, or fear, of Job that resulted in the hedge of protection God had established around him to be negated, and was legal license to Satan to exploit that chink in his armor and destroy all that Job considered **his** "possessions." With sadness, God was impelled to reply to Satan, *"Behold, all that he has is in your power"* (Job 1:12).

In the same way that people's faith empowers God to operate supernatural power and works in their lives, so also fear empowers Satan to employ his tactics and devices in the lives of people. Fear is a kind of reverse faith: whereas faith brings into existence those things which are desired (cf, Heb. 11:1; Mk. 11:22-24; 1 Jn.

5:14,15; e.g.), fear, on the other hand, brings into existence those things *not* desired, or those things that are feared and dreaded.

Intimidation through a plethora of fears is Satan's modus operandi against mankind. So effective can this intimidation by fear be, that the Bible says that *"fear hath torment"* (1 Jn. 4:18), and many a person has become incapacitated and demented by fear. Indeed, fear is the primary cause of all vexation of mind, to include its extreme of insanity.

Multitudes of mankind are tormented and terrorized by fears so numerous and some so far-fetched that most people have never so much as heard of the majority of them. One reference source lists no less than 268 different confirmed phobias. Many people reading this book are tormented with fear. To those I submit that the only cure is a revelation of the magnitude of the love of God (Eph. 3:17-19), for the Bible says, *"perfect love* (God's love) *casts out ALL fear"* (1 Jn. 4:18). Total deliverance of fear accompanied by faith and trust founded in God's boundless love slams the door to Satan, and disallows him access and ability to perpetrate his schemes and devices against us, including all manner of sorcery and witchcraft.

After talking about his own involvement and experience in witchcraft and sorcery, the former witch-doctor brought it all home, saying that the reason for his concern and alarm was that he recognized many of these same devices and techniques for predomination and self-imposition he had used as a witch-doctor being employed by a significant number of leaders in American churches as a means to garner and captivate followers and supporters of their self-aggrandizing personal kingdom-building.

He said he was absolutely appalled that this blatant use of demonically inspired sorcery was occurring within Pentecostal and Neo-Pentecostal (Charismatic, Word of Faith, "Third Wave") churches, which claim to be so spiritual, spiritually gifted, and discerning of the devil's schemes.

Indeed, this is a sad testament of the true spiritual condition of so many American Pentecostal and Neo-Pentecostal churches in this Laodicean Age, in which vast numbers of purporting Christians braggadociously claim to have attained such a level of super-spirituality that they are rich, wealthy, and in need of nothing. Christians of this ilk today, like the Laodiceans whom Jesus condemned in His apocalyptic message through the Apostle John, have been so deceived by their lukewarmness that they do not even realize that they are not only *not* super-spiritual as they think, but they are actually spiritually backslidden and dying.

They have become so blinded by the subtleties of New Age vain philosophies (though they really aren't "new" at all) that have infiltrated many segments of the Church today, that they actually believe they are rich, wealthy, and in need of nothing. Whereas, God, whose sight is perfect, and who sees them for what they really are, says to these modern-day Laodiceans as He did to those of the Early Church, *"you do not know that you are wretched and miserable and poor and blind and naked"* (Rev. 3:17).

Jesus revealed that this kind of deception regarding spiritual status, wherein purporting believers believe themselves to be rich, wealthy, and in need of nothing, while the reality is that they are spiritually wretched, bankrupt, blind, and uncovered, is the result of being neither cold nor hot, but only lukewarm (vv. 15,16). The consequence of this kind of deception, Jesus said, is that He would *"spew"* such persons out of His mouth. Now this word in the Greek literally connotes "to vomit." So, Jesus is saying in essence, "You people that are only lukewarm in your deeds and affection for Me are a vile and violating virus to Me and My Body; you make me absolutely sick to My stomach, nauseas; and, I am going to vomit you out of My mouth, purging you from My Being, casting you away from My Body and Presence."

Chapter Ten

IDENTIFYING COMMON CONTROL/CAPTIVATION MECHANISMS

There are a number of common psychological control mechanisms/methods employed within groups in which hyper-authoritarian doctrines and practices of the Discipleship/Shepherdship ilk are espoused and implemented. The reason for this has a great deal to do not only with the intrinsic nature of the doctrines and practices themselves, and the seductive powers of the leaders of these groups over other people, but also the nature of the spiritual and psychological problems and needs of the individuals who become their unwitting victims. The reason for this has a great deal to do not only with the intrinsic nature of the doctrines and practices themselves, and the seductive powers of the leaders of these groups over other people, but also the nature of the spiritual and psychological problems and needs of the individuals who become their unwitting victims.

Generally speaking, people seek out and begin attending a church because they have spiritual needs they hope to have met, as well as problems for which they are seeking solutions in the teachings, ministry, activities, and interactivity of the church to which they become affiliated. As unfortunate and unconscionable as it is, it is these very personal needs and problems that these cult-like groups prey upon and exploit with their intricately designed mechanisms and machinations of captivation.

The ensnarement of these psychological captives is analagous to that of the helpless prey snared in the almost invisible silken strands of the spider's web. Immediately upon coming into contact with the sticky strands of the meticulously woven and intricately designed web, the unaware prey becomes a powerless prisoner possessing little chance of escape. In fact, the more the ensnared prey struggles to escape, the more the web's bands collapse upon him, further securing him until the spider can reach the now disoriented and exhausted victim and inject him with the paralyzing venom that will finalize his fate.

A study of the numerous books on cults and false religions that have now been published will readily reveal that the techniques and mechanisms of psychological manipulation, domination, and control employed in these groups are strikingly similar, and in some cases identical, to those employed by certified cults. Indeed, to be frank about it, many of these groups and churches employ these techniques and mechanisms to such a degree of overtness that they are themselves at the very minimum quasi-cults, and in some cases, bona fide cults, despite the dismay and vehement denials their leaders and followers alike express when confronted with the similarity of the doctrines and practices employed in their own church to those commonly employed within these certified cults.

The thing that utterly astounds me in the matter, is that even when you provide proof-positive to adherents that these unsanctioned and cult-like teachings and practices are an integral, albeit covert, part of the fabric and foundation of their own church, many react with angry and vehement denial, staunchly refusing to accept even the remotest possibility that such a thing could be so of their "beloved" church, and opt, rather, to remain a captive in what has become to them the familiar and "friendly confines" of the institution of which they are a member. This sad scenario bears striking similarity to the admitted mindset of many "career criminals" who have become such complete psychopathic derelicts that they prefer and choose institutional incarceration over the liberties and latitudes of a normal life of freedom.

Nevertheless, my constant and abiding prayer, and indeed the objective of all the protracted and tedious labor which has gone into the production of this volume, is that God may grant some of the captives of these groups the *"repentance leading to the knowledge of the truth, and they may come to their senses and escape from the snare of the devil, having been held captive by him to do his will"* (2 Tim. 2:26).

It is toward the accomplishment of that goal that I delineate some of the most common techniques and mechanisms of manipulation, domination, and control employed within these groups. They are not presented out of judgmentalism or harsh criticalness, but simply in order for readers to be able to recognize some of the signs of religious enslavement and authoritarian abuse that are taking place in some groups and churches.

Remember as you study them that, as previously mentioned, the premise of "absolute submission," which is the bedrock of such authoritarian doctrines, coupled with the enslaving organizational and authority structure are the primary components that make these techniques and mechanisms effectual and effective.

Just one other comment before we get to them. As you will readily notice, the primary force behind these techniques and mechanisms of manipulation and their most common denominator is **fear**. This in itself is Satan's unmistakable signature and seal which distinguishes all that is demonic from that which is from God, for all of Satan's works are predicated upon and produce fear, whereas all that God does is founded in and produces faith.

Apotheosis of the Leadership.

Apotheosis means to exalt something or someone to divine rank or stature, or in other words to *deify*. This is precisely what takes place in bona fide cults, as well as in groups where excessive authoritarianism is practiced—*de facto* deification of the leadership. In these groups, the leadership is exalted to a status tantamount to being equal with God within the structure and internal operations of that group.

For all intents and purposes the chief leader of that group **IS** "God," in that his sovereignty is absolute; what he says, goes. The authority of the leader and his delegatees is absolute and unchallengable, and its scope gradually expands to the point of eventually becoming all-encompassing, effecting every segment of their followers' lives. The truth, however, as indicated throughout this volume, is that God and the Word of God is the only true and valid authority over any adult, law-abiding human—believer or unbeliever. Moreover, the "authority" of the intermediaries (ministers) God works through is limited to the spiritual realm and to the very parochial bounds of the government or administration of the specific spiritual "house" (i.e., local church or ministry) over which they represent the Headship of Christ.

In groups where this totally fallacious concept of leadership apotheosis has been successfully instituted, it casts a very long and imposing shadow of total domination and subjugation over the entire congregation. The power of this religious predomination lays in the purported premise that to disobey the dictates and desires of the leadership is to disobey and defy God Himself, in that those leaders are the literal representations of Christ Himself, much in the same way as the Pope is regarded in Catholicism.

Indeed, as if on cue, just a few days prior to the editing of these words, one of the "tabloid-news" television programs did a story on a scandal taking place in a prominent Charismatic church in Atlanta, in which several female former administrative-staffers have charged several of the church's leaders with various forms of sexual misconduct perpetrated under the color of ministerial authority. In attempting to explain how it was that these adult, responsible, seemingly intelligent, sincere Christians could have been seduced by the alleged adulterous advances of these clerical-collared clergymen, one of the alleged victims responded with tears of apparent remorse and shame flowing down her flushed face: "These men were **like God** to us. We were taught that whatever they said was right, and **to disobey them was to disobey God**." This situation, if true, is a glaring example of the kind of abuse of authority that can result from improper and undue exaltation of spiritual leaders.

Fear of Open Reproof and Rebuke.

Various forms and degrees of public reproof, censureship, chastisement, remonstration, and even open rebuke of members whom the leadership has deemed to be wayward, errant, and "rebellious," is a common practice in both Discipleship/Shepherd-ship groups and other cults. Members who do not "toe the line" with complete obedience to every rule, regulation, code, and dictate passed down through the leadership are branded by the leaders with the Scarlet Letter *R* for "Rebellious," and are publicly reprimanded sometimes in the smaller cell-group meetings, or sometimes even from the (bully-)pulpit in the main meetings of the entire assembly.

This ever-looming threat of prospective public humiliation and censure becomes a very effective means of predomination by intimidation to the entire membership. No one dare disobey or even question the dictates of, or speak a critical word against, the leadership of the church, lest the "critic" be subjected to this public dressing down.

Open rebuke should be an extreme *rarity* and last *resort*, and certainly should not become *routine*. Scripture prohibits it except in the most egregious cases of persisting overt hypocrites, factious strife-bearers, and egregiously errant elders.

Fear of Disapproval and Rejection.

This is very similar and related to the foregoing.

The prospect of finding real solutions and resolution for very real spiritual and psychological (i.e, pertaining to the soul) needs and infirmities often is a primary motivation of many people as they search for a church-group to become related to in the first place. They come looking for love, acceptance, and remedy of their deepest spiritual and psychological needs. But it is often these very needs and infirmities that make such people vulnerable to the exploitation and predomination perpetrated by these types of authoritarianistic groups. And, no one perhaps is more vulnerable to such exploitation and predomination than the person who suffers from a spirit of rejection and its accompanying *fear* of rejection and fear of disapproval. A sense of rejection is a "bottomless well" that is never filled regardless of how much love is poured into it. Exploiting people who have such a real need for real ministry is as vile and reprehensible as it gets.

Groups employing hyper-authority doctrines often practice some form and degree of "shunning," a highly effective technique of religious predominative sanctioning which for ages has been a common practice within false sects and cults, though perhaps it is most associated in the last two centuries with the Quakers, to whom it is a sanctioned rite of chastisement of wayward members. Shunning is when a group scorns and disassociates from a member as a kind of chastisment and disapproval for some aspect of conduct considered improper by the group. It can come in the form of disdain, scorn, snubbing, avoidance, aloofness, outright exclusion, rebuffing, "looking off on," "giving the cold shoulder," distancing, slighting, and ignoring. Whatever the form it takes, everyone knows instinctively when he is being shunned. To the insecure and diffident, the effects of such overt disdain and disapprobation can be overwhelming and devastating.

In these groups, members whose conduct has merited them the attribution of "rebellious" are shunned by fellow members as a means of chastisement or intimidation, with the hope of *shaming* the offender into getting back into line. In order to get back into good graces, those who subject themselves to and succumb to this vile form of sorcery, typically, must endure the public humiliation of confessing their errancy before the entire assembly and begging forgiveness of the leaders and group.

Fear of Denunciation.

When anyone leaves one of these groups of their own volition for whatever reason without the approval and consent of the leadership (which usually is granted only in the case of employment-related transfer or death), or for a reason that is not acceptable to the leadership, those persons are almost always branded "rebels" by the leadership, and the reason for their departure is declared to be "rebellion."

Departees whose leaving is predicated on disagreement with the doctrines espoused and practices employed by the group, are invariably labeled as having "a critical spirit," and their criticisms are declared to be invalid and unmerited and emanating from a rebellious and critical spirit. Harmonious and peaceable parting of the ways is virtually non-existent, as the jilted and chagrined leadership invariably feels compelled to disparage the departees and to declare them *persona non grata in perpetuam*, forbidding contact with them by any of the remaining membership.

The prospect of such denunciation and discreditation by the leadership, by the way, is especially disconcerting to those called to the ministry who find themselves in the position of having to depart the group in obedience to a calling from God. In such cases the viability of both those persons' ministry and their livelihood can be very really effected by vows of censure, condemnation, denouncement, anathematizing, retribution, recrimination, and black-listing made by the scorned former leadership. Very often those are not merely idle threats, but rather, especially in the case of an itinerant ministry, because of the "political" nature of the ministry, a black-listed minister can indeed have a lot of doors closed to him, regardless of the validity and quality of his ministry, merely on the basis of having been dubbed a "rebel" by some scorned ecclesiastical autocrat.

Fear of Excommunication.

In the face of the prospect of such consequences of denunciation as those delineated in the foregoing, the specter of similar humiliation, disparagement, and impugnment resulting from excommunication then also becomes a very real and formidable threat looming over the head of every member. This is especially so after their entire life and that of their family has become intertwined and immersed in their church-community.

However, the ironic truth of the matter is that because of their desperation to keep every member as a part of the fold, rarely do these kinds of groups actually excommunicate anyone. Instead of excommunication, they implement various other of the techniques and mechanisms delineated here to attempt to intimidate any would-be "rebellious" members into obeisance and submission.

Fear of Judgment.

In addition to all the above factors, members are incessantly indoctrinated with the premise that if they ever leave the church or group without the approval of the leadership, they will incur the wrath of God and be under His judgment.

Laced into sermons, "orientation" classes, and various person-to-person conversations among the members, are melodramatic horror stories of people who "got out from under the covering" of their leader and church-community, and who because of that experienced terrible curses and judgments in their lives. These stories are cited to illustrate that members should never even think of leaving the group, for fear of all the terrible things that will happen to them if they do.

Aside from the fact that this is precisely what members of cults and occultic initiates are told, this is a totally false and unfounded claim for several reasons. First of all, as it was painstakingly proven in Chapter Five, the premise of "spiritual covering" as taught in the Discipleship doctrines is a total fallacy and myth. Our covering, or hedge of providential care and protection, does not come in any way shape or form from any human-being, or group of human-beings, but from God alone:

> *HE will cover you with HIS pinions, and under HIS wings you may seek refuge; HIS faithfulness is a SHIELD AND BUL-WARK* [an impenetrable rampart of protection]. *I will say TO THE LORD, 'My REFUGE and my FORTRESS, my GOD in whom I trust.' For it is HE who delivers you from the snare of the trapper* [Satan], *and from the deadly pestilence. (Ps. 91:4,2; brackets and emphasis added by author)*

We are to glory and take solace in the fact that we dwell under the *shelter* (protective covering) of the Most High God and that we therefore abide (continuously live) in the *shadow* of the Almighty God (from which devils flee): *"He who dwells in the **shelter** of the Most High will abide in the **shadow** of the Almighty"* (Ps. 91:1). It is **HIS** shelter and shadow, which are of and exist in the spiritual realm, that are the only valid and impervious protection against the attacks of the enemy that are levied in the spiritual realm. No human shelter and shadow, whether of an individual or a group, offers any protection whatsoever against such attacks perpetrated by evil-spirits in the spirit realm.

Second, God does not bring judgment upon a person or a family simply because they leave a particular church or group. There is absolutely no Biblical corroboration of the ridiculous claim that He does; rather, it is a totally unfounded myth. Leaving a particular group or church, for whatever reason, is **not** tantamount to abandoning **the** Church or falling away from God, as these groups allege. No church or group is that sacrosanct. Every true believer has been "baptized" or immersed by the Holy Spirit into the Body of Christ, whether they are a member of a church-organization or not.

The true Church of Jesus Christ is not an inanimate *organization* or even a conglomeration of church-organizations. Rather, the true Church is a living *organism* comprised of true believers. Being a member of and engrossed in the community of some humanly-invented and -run church-organization and assembly in no way certifies, enhances, or has any bearing whatsoever on your eternal fellowship with God, but rather it is having been made a bona fide member of and immersed in *"the general assembly and church of the first-born"* (Heb. 12:23) that certifies and seals your eternal destiny and destination.

Frequent fellowship with some segment of the true Brotherhood is highly recommended and certainly synergistically beneficial, but it will not save us. We fellowship, worship, and receive from the Lord, in corporate gatherings because salvation is the common denominator among us. However, absolutely no requisites regarding either the place of worship or the number of the worshipers are delineated anywhere in the Bible. On the contrary, though staunch "organizationalists" consumed with increasing the membership of their organizations hate the veracity and validity of it, remember that Jesus Himself vowed that He would personally attend and be in the midst of any meeting conducted in His Name, even if the number of those gathered together was only *"two or three"* (Mat. 18:20), and He made that vow without any reference to the place where that meeting was held. Jesus explicitly stated that *"true worshipers"* were those who *"worship the Father in Spirit and in Truth* (in accordance with sound doctrine)*"* (Jn. 4:23). Validity of worship is not determined by the place of worship or the number of the worshipers, but by whether or not it is inspired by the Holy Spirit and in accordance with the Truth of God's Word.

Thirdly, God allows all believers the latitude to make their own choices with regard to the group with which they identify, on the basis of congruity with their particular personalities, spiritual needs, interests, and emphasis, as long as the group they choose is founded upon sound doctrine and practices.

Despite the absolute falseness of this notion, the prospect of being subject to circumstantial Divine judgment remains a very effective weapon for making indoctrinated members of these groups paralyzingly fearful of ever leaving the group.

Fear of Failure.

A constant undercurrent of the teaching, counseling, and communal conversation within these groups is the cultivation and reinforcement of a fear of failure if the member does not obediently and docilely follow every rule and dictate emanating from the leadership as a whole, as well as every personal command of each leader comprising the multiplicity of echelons of leaders over the group.

These groups thrive on condescension and berating of the capabilities and judgment of the members, juxtaposed to that of their "spiritually superior" leaders. Instead of declaring *release*, forgiveness, restoration, and overcoming of past faults, failures, and tendencies, as the Gospel of Good News prescribes, in these groups there is a constant and continual *reminding* of past faults, failures, weaknesses, and tendencies. "Remember now," leaders say to their subjects, "you've always had a problem with...(this or that)." Or, "You know you've always been rebellious...." And so on.

The ultimate purpose of this constant identification with failure is to create within the members a profound sense of dependency on the group and its leaders to make their decisions for them and to tell them what is best for them. Adding to the problem is the fact that there certainly is no shortage of lazy and negligent people, and those who refuse to repent of the fear of failure, who are quite content to have someone else tell them everything to do, rather than have to seek the Lord for themselves as to the specificities of their lives.

Fear of Lost or Ingenuine Salvation.

Typically in these groups—wherein extreme and aberrant authoritarian doctrines requiring "absolute submission" to the leadership are relentlessly hammered into their heads, and a yoke of overbearing, unrealistic, and unScriptural dictates, demands, and expectations is placed upon their necks—members' salvation is under constant challenge and doubt. In time, they begin to question whether or not they were ever really saved in the first place, or whether they have subsequently lost their salvation and rightstanding with God, because of their ostensible propensity to "rebellion."

Their instinctive and intuitive inclinations to reject the demonic and unnatural enslavement to which they are being subjected, they are told, is nothing but their "rebellion to authority" continuing to rise up within them, which they must conquer, and learn to "just submit." They are incessantly barraged with charges of being a "rebel," and that their "rebellion" against the oppressive task-mastery being perpetrated upon them is evidence of and resulting from their rebellion against *God.*

This extremely disconcerting uncertainty, and in some cases, tormenting fear, concerning the validity and genuineness of their salvation, is used as a very effective means of keeping the ever-diffident members docile and cowering.

Guilt Projection.

Related to and used in concert with the aforementioned, guilt projection, essentially, is a method of manipulation or control in which an abstract but nonetheless effectual, ever-present sense of guilt is purposely projected upon subjectees by the subjugator.

It is employed on two fronts within these groups. First, on the personal level, members are continually battered and psychologically abused with regard to their sinfulness and rebellious attitudes, for which no real forgiveness and redemption is ever extended. This causes the members to labor under a perpetual cloud of guilt, unworthiness, unacceptance, and total exasperation. Consequently, members embark upon a never-ending merry-go-round ride of vain fleshly works, trying and failing over and over again to "measure up" and thereby *merit* the forgiveness and acceptance of God, their group-peers, and their leaders. This is used as a mechanism of manipulation to keep the members forever docile, doting, and drudging, as approval and acceptance are tantalizingly dangled before them, just out of their reach, like the mechanical rabbit at a dog race.

Second, members are constantly told how vital their own participation and financial support is to the overall success of the church and its every "mission." Through very skillful oratorical wheedling, members are cajoled into personal identification with the contrived plans, projects, and programs of the church, all of which are adamantly alleged to be God-inspired and God-sponsored. Members are craftily lured into accepting the hypothesis that since these plans, projects, and programs came directly and purely from God as a Divinely-inspired mission and assignment, and since they are a member of the group, the success of the mission is their personal responsibility. If the project or program is not successfully completed, it is the personal fault of each and every member, for which God holds them personally responsible, even though the individual members never personally heard from God regarding the matter, and were never even given the option of testing whether or not this matter truly was from God, as Scripture requires.

Isolation.

The Great Wall of China and the former Berlin Wall, are classic examples of walls that were built by would-be world-emperors not only to keep peoples of other lands along with their opposing ideologies *out*, but to keep their own people *in*, and to thereby insulate them from influences contrary to the particular utopia-promising political ideologies they were promulgating.

The same is true of the invisible but very real walls of religious segregation (i.e., denominationalism) erected throughout the Church Age by their chief architects out of intense insecurity and paranoia, in the hope of keeping their followers from being exposed and attracted to teaching and experiences contradictory to the particular ideologies and dogmas they were promulgating.

Classic cults, especially during the indoctrination stage, require virtually complete isolation of the inductee from family and friends in order to insulate them from all contradictory influences. Similarly, these Discipleship/Shepherdship groups strongly urge their members to avoid fellowship with anyone who is not a part of their group, including fellow-believers, friends, and family, especially. Attending another church, without the prior approval and consent of their leaders (which is almost never granted) is cause for censure and possible disfellowship. In some groups, even the reading of books, viewing television programs, and listening to radio programs of other ministers is prohibited without the consent of the leadership and unless that other ministry has been "approved" by the leadership of the group (and, of course, very, very few are).

Of course, the common claim of those who preach and require such segregation and isolation is that this is a very noble and beneficial protective measure instituted in the members' best interest in order to protect them from deceiving and damaging influences. However, nowhere does the Word of God teach that either segregation or isolation is a deterrent or preventative against spiritual deception. Rather, Jesus explicitly said that if a person *"abides"* (i.e., hears and obeys, lives) in the Word of God, **THEN** that person would *"know the Truth,"* and **THE TRUTH** would set *that* person—the person who knows the Truth of God's Word—free, which includes setting them free and keeping them free from deception (Jn. 8:31,32). In other words: It is **TRUTH**, that sets free! Truth *never* deceives or enslaves!

Groups that mandate or urge separation and isolation from other segments of the true Body of Christ, as well as those, I might add, that promulgate and promote communal-living are dangerous! Sincere and earnest believers would do well to avoid all such groups.

Internal Involvement.

One consistent hallmark of these groups is an extremism in regard to personal involvement and participation of every member. Getting every person deeply involved in some function, or duty, or role of participation is a virtual obsession with these groups. Programs and departments are created for the primary purpose of keeping every member of every family engrossed in some type of in-house involvement, which they refer to as "ministries," from music to recreation to special study programs to an infinite number of other specialty ministries.

The premise is, of course, that the more *involved* a person is and the more *important* he or she feels, the greater and more intent will be his or her personal commitment and contribution to the overall operations and machinery of the organization. And, indeed, usually, the plan works precisely as designed, producing the intended results. The primary reason for that is that they exploit three very basic human desires: the need to feel accepted and part of something, the need to feel important and needed, and the need to function and be fruitful, that is, accomplish something meaningful. If not sanctified through the Cross of Christ and fulfilled through the Life of Christ, these desires are nothing more than selfish ambition, which is a primary inroad for Satanic exploitation.

Someone may well say, "But, every church tries to get their members involved, is that always wrong?" The answer is that every believer has a God-given spiritual function both in the church and in the world (Eph. 4:16; Rom. 12:6-8; 1 Pet. 4:10; et al.), but these are real and spiritually effectual functions bearing true spiritual fruit that remains (Jn. 15:16), not silly, superficial, artificial, and spiritually inconsequential, internal ecclesiastical dabblings, producing virtually no true spiritual fruit, but serving only to stroke the participant's already over-inflated ego and superfluous sense of self-importance.

Fostering of Over-dependence on the Group and Leader.

The primary purpose and goal of many, if not all, of the aforementioned techniques and mechanisms is to produce in the adherents a psychological dependence on the group and especially the leader. Members are taught to put all their faith, hope, and trust in the groups' leaders, which is idolatry, and actually grants opportunity and permission for invasion by all manner of evil spirits, not the least of which is the spirit of fear. As a result of these techniques and mechanisms, members are terrified by the prospect of punitive action which they have been taught would be emanating ultimately from God Himself if they are not completely submissive to every dictate and whim of their leaders, they are laden with overwhelming burdens of false guilt, isolated from other sources of Truth and fellowship, and their entire life is totally immersed in the internal involvements of that group. The outcome is an ungodly, unScriptural, and even demonic, all-encompassing spiritual and psychological dependency on the group and the leader.

What leaders of such groups purport to be exhorting their members to in this regard, is the quite virtuous, laudable, and desirable qualities of "allegiance," "loyalty," and "commitment" elemental to what they refer to as "covenantal relationships." However, the truth is that, as discussed previously, these "covenantal relationships" are actually "covenants with demons" that are not based in true freedom and the attributes of the Spirit, but in seduction, witchcraft, bondage, and captivation inspired by evil spirits. Moreover, the outcome certainly is not a working of the *Holy* Spirit, for the Bible clearly proclaims that, *"where the Spirit of the Lord is, there is LIBERTY"* (2 Cor. 3:17), not bondage.

Once ensnared in the web of bondage and dependency, the victim of these control mechanisms is mentally, emotionally, and spiritually dependent, not on the Father, Son, and Holy Ghost, but on the human leaders and fellow members of his group for psychological satisfaction and survival in every aspect of life. This is spiritual treachery and apostasy of the highest order.

Esotericism.

With these cult-like groups, there is a deliberate and carefully crafted concealment of the true nature, agenda, and modus operandi of the group from the general public and especially prospective members and new enlistees. The complete truth is known only to the few who are part of an elite and exclusive "inner circle" of compatriots. This is the very definition of "esotericism," which, tellingly, has been deemed by the highest courts of our land in cases where legal action has been taken against such religious cults to constitute illegal fraud.

Full disclosure is not made up front, but comes only incrementally, in segments, as the initiate advances through the various levels of "orientation" and "enlightenment" which are supposedly required for comprehension. Obscuring and skewing of these particulars concerning the group to the general public are ostensibly justified by the assertion that comprehension of the import of the group's teachings and purposes requires the "enlightenment" that comes only to those who have been fully trained (in reality, indoctrinated and brainwashed) by the teachings and dogmas comprising their belief system.

The real crux of the deceitfulness and dastardliness of this incremental disclosure lies in the fact that it is not until the passenger has boarded the ship and it has transversed the abyss of the great divide, that he is informed of the destination and full cost of the voyage, metaphorically speaking. It is perhaps revealing that this incremental disclosure technique is a watermark of classical modern cults, many of whom now, because of widespread discreditation and negative publicity, have resorted to a variety of actions aimed at improving their public image, including organizational name changes, the use of euphemistic terminology, nondisclosure of true intents and purposes, and plain old *lying*.

"Love Bombing."

I don't know who is credited with the original coining of the term "love bombing," but it is a term often evoked in contemporary descriptions of the psychological techniques employed by classical cults to woo new recruits, and to maintain the bonds of enslavement on existing members. The so-called "love" that is spoken of in these groups is an ushy-gushy, sickly-sweet, surreal, over-done, showy, carnal, humanistic kind of "sloppy-agape," replete with a superabundance of hugging and cheek-kissing.

In a way similar to the classical cults, proselytes are lured into the group by means of an auspicious, blissful, ethereal, soulish, and sensory-appealing "love" which is presented as the ultimate in "freedom." In bona fide cults, this so-called "love" is so "free," that is, without limitations, that it invariably translates eventually into unrestrained and promiscuous immorality, or "free-love," which some cults proclaim to be one of the many "benefits" and "privileges" of their transcendent brand of "spiritual enlightenment." Sadly, there have been some Christian groups of the ilk of which we have been speaking, which, in the process of time as they traveled down the path of error and errancy, have become deceived by the same seducing evil spirits, eventually engaging in the same scurrilous debauchery as well. More and more of such cases are being exposed to the light publicly, as well they should be (Eph. 5:11; 1 Tim. 5:19,20; et al.), despite the long shadow of reproach it casts upon all of Christendom.

In addition to utilizing this "love bombing" technique on prospective proselytes, in these quasi-cultish groups, the leaders and "indoctrinators" constantly bombard members and initiates with this soulish, sensual love as a kind of sedative-tranquilizer to anesthetize them against the effects of the control mechanisms and techniques, and to keep them oblivious to the fact that these devices of domination are being imposed upon them. This false "love" becomes an immensely effective psychological-pharmaceutical by which the indoctrinated members are drugged and induced into accepting the harsh and overbearing domination and control techniques as being beneficent and beneficial expressions of this anomalistic "love."

Economic Exploitation and Enslavement.

It is an incontrovertible fact that the Bible is replete with passages and promises concerning abundant financial blessing coming unto those who are faithful in their tithing and giving, and in the administration of "unrighteous mammon" (money). Indeed, everyone who has perseveringly and faithfully complied with the requisites and conditions of those promises can attest to their validity and absolute trustworthiness.

It is a certainty that God desires to bless His people financially, and He has established the spiritual law of sowing and reaping (Gen. 8:22; Gal. 6:7) or *"giving and receiving"* (Lk. 6:38; Plp. 4:15) as the primary means through which to accomplish that blessing. The long and the short of the ordinance is that when a believer sows financially, He will in due season reap a multiplied financial harvest commensurate with the amount of seed sown. Thus, every believer should be a consistent and persistent sower. In no way am I denigrating this valid truth with this point.

However, in both classical cults as well as groups such as those churches we are discussing of the Pentecostal and Neo-Pentecostal community who employ these practices of overt control and domination, there is almost invariably an aberrant ilk of "stewardship" espoused which places excessive demands and requirements upon the members for monetary contributions to the group and for "accountability" regarding their personal financial matters. Members are forever pressed to give more and more beyond their ten percent tithe in special offerings to fund an endless litany of special in-house "ministries and missions," projects, and programs. In addition, cell-group leaders keep a very watchful eye on the personal expenditures of the members of their group, in many cases interposing their own non-professional, unsolicited advice with regard to what should be members' private financial affairs. As mentioned before, it is a documented fact that in some Discipleship/Shepherdship groups, the leaders, though without training or expertise in financial matters, are the members' de facto financial advisors, and members are essentially constrained from making important financial transactions without the advice and consent of their leader(s).

Word of Caution and Warning

Having delineated these techniques and mechanisms of unauthorized control, a word of caution and warning are in order in regard to their application.

First, as a caution, please understand that the existence and employment of a few of these techniques and mechanisms within a group does not necessarily mean that the group employing them is a bona fide cult or even a "Discipleship/Shepherdship" group. It is not uncommon for people to be totally unaware that certain aspects or subtle nuances of the teaching they espouse and practices they employ are actually erroneous and improper. In some cases, leaders and adherents of aberrant doctrines truly are "sincerely deceived," and are willing to receive reproof, repent, and make appropriate changes, once they are made aware of their error.

Second, strong warning is given against misuse of what is written here as "ammunition" for a mean-spirited, malicious attack against individuals or groups who may be adherents of these authoritarian doctrines for the purposes of discrediting, disparaging, or harming them in some way. People who engage in this kind of "murdering of your brother" without bathing the situation in prayer, willingness to forgive, and agape-love, and without having restoration through repentance as the objective of reproof, are themselves *wrong*, regardless of how *right* they may be about having detected or discerned error in those they have examined. How unequivocally *wrong* any of us are capable of being in *attitude*, though we be incontrovertibly *right* in *assessment*!

Chapter Eleven

THE ILLEGITIMACY OF RELIGIOUS ENSLAVEMENT

In Second Corinthians 5:14, the Holy Spirit, through the Apostle Paul, tells us that *"the love of Christ"* is the only "force" authorized to "control," that is, to govern or constrain, believers in any way. The term *"the love of Christ"* means both the love that we have for and are to demonstrate toward Jesus through obedience (Jn. 14:15,21,23,24; 15:9,10), as well as the "agape-love" that Christ has for us, which He has so thoroughly demonstrated toward us in obeying His Father and laying down His Life for us. This mutual love is to be the force that governs the course of the believer's life, constrains his behavior, and motivates him to perform the tasks and assignments, both general and particular, relegated to him by the Lord.

This is the kind of love God desires from us—a willful and willing love, totally devoid of external constraint and coercion. Like any human parent, God wants love from us that is freely given *from the heart*. Indeed, the God-kind of love from the heart is the essence of the Gospel—as the Apostle Paul so eloquently and discerningly put it: *"the goal of* (all) *our instruction is **love** from a pure **heart** and a good conscience and a sincere **faith**"* (1 Tim. 1:5, parenthesis added by author).

Perfunctory compliance out of compulsion, and humanly-induced obedience, on the other hand, brings the Lord no joy or satisfaction whatsoever. Instead, it is a cheap counterfeit of the agape-love-motivated obedience God desires from us. Any ostensible form of obedience or observance which does not arise out of willingness and pure Holy Spirit-inspired agape-love for God, but rather is induced by human compulsion and coercion, is nothing more than a dead and worthless *form of religion* (2 Tim. 3:5, lit.). The religiosity practiced by those "caught in the web" of authoritarian ecclesiastical hierarchies of the nature of those addressed in this volume is of this ilk. No matter how devout and dedicated they may be, their obeisance is not purely of their own free will, but is motivated by whatever degree by human compulsion and coercion, and thus is more *religion* than bona fide *love* of God.

Jesus Himself condemned and forbad "unauthorized control," domination, and ruling over fellow believers by any believer, to include ministers, in a dissertation to the Apostles of the Lamb recorded in Mark 10:42-45. The discussion was precipitated by an audacious but ridiculous request the two "Sons of Thunder" made of Jesus that they be designated as the privileged and honored two who would sit on His left and right when He came into His glory, that is, when His Kingdom-Reign was established on the Earth.

Though they themselves were undoubtedly oblivious to it (or surely they would not have so embarrassed themselves by openly posing their request in front of the other Apostles), what this request reflected on the part of the two young lads was egoism, self-centeredness, self-exaltation, self-promotion, selfish ambition, self-aggrandizement, and a blatant, even grandeuristic sense of superiority, all of which are characteristics typical of untested and inexperienced but zealous, aspiring, and enterprising youth. But before we look askance and disdainfully upon these two, let us consider: what now better enlightened and more seasoned person (say, past the age of forty) is there among us who cannot in candid retrospection clearly recognize, with great chagrin, these same obnoxious traits of vaingloriousness and naive idealism in himself to some degree during his own years of youth.

Aside, however, from demonstrating their immaturity and lack of character, these two also demonstrated in this incident a total lack of prudence and discretion with regard to interpersonal relations with their peers. Making such an audacious request for recognition and preeminence, in front of one's peers, certainly is not the recommended way to "win friends and influence people," as the reaction of the other ten Apostles reflects: *"And hearing this, the ten began to feel indignant with James and John"* (Mk. 10:41).

Jesus' response to the request of James and John consisted of two elements. First, He answered the specifics of their request by saying that such a determination was not His to make, but that those positions of honor were reserved for those for whom it has been prepared, most versions indicate; or, perhaps the import of His reply could have been that those positions of honor were reserved for those persons who had been prepared for the positions.

The second part of Jesus' response was directed at revealing the improperness of the attitude reflected by their request. But Jesus' reply was certainly not for only those two, or even the entire Twelve only. Rather, Jesus used their request as a pretext to register a vital portion of Divine instruction, directed not only to those disciples present then, but also to the entire Body of Christ collectively, as well as every individual member, layman and minister alike, whenever they would live, all throughout the entirety of the Church Age. The importance and even solemnity of Jesus' instruction is reflected in the Holy Spirit's words: *"And calling them to Himself, Jesus said to them"* (v. 42). And, this is the content of His instruction:

> *You know that those who are recognized as rulers of the Gentiles lord it over them; and their great men exercise authority over*

*them. **But it is not [to be] so AMONG YOU**, but whoever wishes to become great **AMONG YOU** shall be your servant; and whoever wishes to be first **AMONG YOU** shall be slave of all. For even the Son of Man did not come to be served, but to serve, and to give His life a ransom for many. (Mk. 10:42-45, brackets added by author)*

The Amplified Bible renders Jesus' dissertation this way:

*...You know that those who are recognized as governing and are supposed to rule the Gentiles (the nations) lord it over them— ruling with absolute power, holding them in subjection—and their great men exercise authority and dominion over them. **But this is not to be so AMONG YOU**; instead, whoever desires to be great **AMONG YOU** must be your servant, and whoever wishes to be most important and first in rank **AMONG YOU** must be the slave of all. For even the Son of man came not to have service rendered to Him, but to serve, and to give His life as a ransom for...many.*

Now there are several extremely vital points of both exhortation and warning contained in this Divine instruction.

As a matter of first importance, notice the phrase Jesus used three times in this text, *"among you."* This indicates that as with a plethora of other aspects of behavior, believers as individuals, as well as the collective Church, are to be set apart and separated from the rest of the world. We are **supposed** to be different. We are not supposed to conduct ourselves the same way the people of the world do. The symbol adopted by the Early Church to identify Christians was the fish—believers are fish, salmon, if you please, because we don't swim *with* the current of the world, but we swim upstream, *against* the current of the world.

Now this term *"among you"* had two applications. First, the *"you"* meant these men as disciples of Christ, which is what they were first and foremost, above their status of being Apostles. So, Jesus was saying that as believers there was not to be any lording or ruling over one another in their interpersonal relationships among themselves. That is to say, believers were not to be in any way controlling or dominating over one another. This instruction stands yet today as the model and standard which Jesus has set with regard to interpersonal relationships among believers. All interpersonal relationships among believers are to be free of predomination and authoritarianism of every kind. Secondly, with his instruction here to these men as His chosen, anointed, and appointed ministers, Jesus' was also establishing that this prohibition on lording or ruling over one another in interpersonal relationships also included relationships between ministers or leaders in the Body of Christ.

It is vital to see that these twelve men to whom Jesus addressed this instruction, though on the human plane they too were disciples and fellows of the other disciples, yet, at the same time, on the spiritual plane they were of a "status" that transcended their status as disciples. They were also the Twelve Apostles of the Lamb—Jesus' hand-selected personal delegates and representatives. On the personal plane, they too had to develop and mature spiritually just like any other disciple, nevertheless, on the spiritual plane, these special envoys of Christ, like every anointed and appointed minister of Jesus, were also anointed with a measure of the Essence of Jesus beyond their fellows.

Moreover, these Twelve Apostles of the Lamb in particular, represented all of the Five-fold Ministry Offices—Apostles, Prophets, Evangelists, Pastors, and Teachers—which would later emanate from the office of Apostle as Jesus ascended on High from the Mount of Olives on the Day of Ascension (Eph. 4:7-11). Thus, when Jesus commanded that *"among you,"* that is, among the Apostles in particular, there was not to be any lording or ruling over one another after the manner of the Gentiles, or the unbelievers of the world, He was expressly prohibiting the establishment of any kind of hierarchical authority structure or system among the Apostles. That was the precedent and model Jesus established then, and He intended for it to stand throughout the entirety of the Church Age.

Thus, applying what Jesus said to the Apostles of the Lamb to the entire class of Five-fold Ministers, He was specifically and strictly forbidding that there should ever be any human hierarchical authority among His chosen and anointed Five-fold Ministers. He was saying that Five-fold Ministers were not to lord or rule over one another in any way. Each Apostle, sent messenger, was to be free of any form of constraint imposed upon him by his fellow ministers. These Apostles were all *"special messenger{s} appointed and commissioned and sent out—not from [any body of] men nor by or through any man, but by and through JESUS CHRIST, THE MESSIAH, AND GOD THE FATHER"* (Gal. 1:1, A.B.).

This is an absolute and incontrovertible fact, and there is not one passage of Scripture which can be cited that refutes or contradicts that conclusion. The simple fact is God never intended that there be hierarchical authority structures or even so-called "relationships" which are authoritarian in nature among ministers.

No Other Lords

The reason Jesus forbad this lording over one another was very simple: **JESUS** is Lord, not *any* human being. Humans, even redeemed humans, are not worthy or adequate to be Lord over anyone. There is only *"one Lord...who is over all"* (Eph. 4:5,6)—the Lord Jesus Christ. It is Jesus alone whom God has seated—

"at His [own] right hand in the Heavenly places, far above ALL rule and authority and power and dominion, and every name that is named—above every title than can be conferred—not only in this age and in this world, but also in the age and the world which are to come. And He has put all things under His feet and has appointed Him the universal and supreme HEAD of the

Church (a Headship exercised throughout the Church)...." (Eph. 1:20-22, A.B.)

Simply put, there is only one Lordship that believers are to be under—the Lordship of Christ. Though it may seem a bit overbearing or extreme to say, any other purported Lordship which anyone attempts to exert over believers is antiChrist in nature.

God's Word explicitly declares, *"For all who are being led by the Spirit of God, these are sons of God."* The Greek term used here and translated *"sons"* is the word "huios," which means "mature sons" as opposed to the mere "offspring" of God. Thus, the import of this verse is that those who have become mature sons of God are led, guided, directed by the Person of the Holy Spirit (Rom. 8:14), not by any human being.

When a person is first Born Again, because of spiritual immaturity, it is necessary to rely somewhat upon the tutelage and counsel of leaders. However, the very purpose and goal of the spiritual edification and education that Five-fold Ministers render unto the believers is the spiritual development and maturation of those believers to the place where they are able to hear and receive for themselves God's leadership, guidance, and direction with regard to their own personal lives.

The role of ministers is precisely the same role of parents in the natural. Though the majority of parents today have absolutely no idea of it, the God-assigned role of parents is to *"train up"* their children *"in the way they should go"* (rather than the way they **want** to go) and in *"the discipline and instruction of the Lord"* (Pvbs. 22:6; Eph. 6:4). The role of parents is to *train* their children, not *entertain*, appease, satiate, and befriend them. The role of parents is to develop their children into responsible, sensible, and godly adults, who are no longer dependent upon their parents for anything.

Though many parents would rue and even bristle at the thought, the test of excellence and successfulness in parenthood is that your children, once reared and on their own, no longer need you for anything. Oh, they love you, and they demonstrate their love for you, but they don't *need* you anymore.

This "no other Lord" matter is the same with ministers as well. Jesus, as the above quoted Amplified Bible passage (Eph. 1:20-22, A.B.) puts it, is *"the universal and supreme Head of the Church."* Laymen and leaders alike are to receive their leadership and guidance in terms of the specifics of their particular calling and life from the Lord Himself, not from any humanly-devised and -constituted governmental hierarchy. Human councils, especially religious ones, virtually always become over-officious and authoritarianistic "Sanhedrins," comprised of arrogant, self-aggrandizing, and pompous Pharisees obsessed with attaining and exercising power, prestige, prominence, and predomination.

As discussed elsewhere in this book, there simply is no Scriptural precedence for standing ecclesiastical councils or hierarchical conclaves and ruling bodies within the Church. The only convocation of ministers mentioned in the New Testament is the one held in Jerusalem (Acts 15:1-29), and it was purely an *ad hoc* (i.e., temporary, for that purpose only) conference convened at the bequest of Paul and Barnabus and the elders of the Antioch church for the sole purpose of addressing a **doctrinal** dispute, not to impose any form of authority. Luke's account represents the conference as an impromptu, informal, non-authoritarian, and open forum in which these matters were discussed and debated mutually and on the basis of parity among all in attendance, without any hint of predomination or preeminence by any of the participants. When the matter was settled and a mutually agreeable conclusion reached, the meeting was adjourned, the participants dispersed and returned to their own spheres of ministry, and the council was dissolved.

There is no record of any other such "councils" anywhere in the New Testament. Thus, there is no Scriptural foundation for such councils or governing hierarchies.

"Rulers of the Gentiles"

In His dissertation to the disciples, Jesus said that they were not to Lord over one another *"as the rulers of the Gentiles"* do. The term "Gentiles" as used by the Jews of that day referred to all the other, non-Jewish, nations, who did not believe in Jehovah as God. Hence, the term *"Gentiles"* referred to "non-believers," or the unbelieving peoples of the nations of the world.

Essentially then, Jesus was alluding to the world's system of ascendancy and predomination, the essence and import of which He articulated, albeit without sophisticated or flowery oratory, to a "T": *"You know that those who are recognized as rulers of the Gentiles lord it over them; and their great men exercise authority over them"* (Mk. 10:42).

In this first part of this sentence, Jesus spoke about those who are "arche" (Greek), that is, "rulers" in the system of the unbelieving world. He said the rulers in the world system *"lord it over"* others. The Greek word Jesus used which is translated in the New American Standard Version as *"lord it over"* literally means to exert or impose lordship and dominion over others by force. What Jesus was describing was subjugation.

In the world, there are myriads of avenues and means by which people *"climb up"* (Jn. 10:1) to positions of authority and ascendancy over others in the gamut of human enterprise and experience, whether in the political, occupational, societal, or even familial arenas. Moreover, the world uses an entirely different standard to determine who they recognize as their "rulers" than that which is prescribed in the Word of God for believers to recognize their leaders.

The ilk of coercion and dominion exerted by worldly "rulers" is almost always a heavy-handed domination and imposition of personal "lordship," just as Jesus said. Hence, it is also virtually always antiChrist in nature, because the Lordship of Christ is supplanted by the imposition of the personal lordship of the worldly ruler.

While in the first part of this sentence, Jesus was speaking about the authority imposed by political or governmental *"rulers"* in the world, He speaks in the second part of *"great men"* who exercise a kind of predomination in another realm—the societal realm. The word translated *"great men,"* "megaloi," does not refer to those who are "great" in the sense of someone who is magnanimous in character or achievements, but rather it refers to people who are "prominent" in society and who arrogate themselves above their fellows. In other words, this is referring to the arrogant societal elite. These people, Jesus said, exert a kind of self-originated ascendancy over those of inferior status or rank.

How very true this is of the world's system. In all the societies of the world, from Africa to England, and Europe to the United States, there is a very real though not always conspicuous "caste system," a "pecking order" sustained by unwritten codes of special tribute and deference. Every society of the world has its privileged and preferred "high and mighty," its elite, its de facto aristocracy, which has the preeminence. In "sophisticated" societies, the rich, the wellborn, the societal elite, the lettered, are the special breed worthy to constitute the royal ranks of nobility.

That's just the way the world's system operates. And, most people, though occasionally bemoaning its unfairness, accept the system. Like it or not, the royal rule. And, as a whole, there is nothing subtle or low-key about the preeminence societal aristocrats exert. On the contrary, the predomination of the privileged elite is overt and often obnoxious.

Aw! but, Jesus declared, arrogation and ascendancy is not to be found within the society of believers:

But it is not [to be] so AMONG YOU, but whoever wishes to become great AMONG YOU shall be your servant; and whoever wishes to be first AMONG YOU shall be slave of all. For even the Son of Man did not come to be served, but to serve, and to give His life a ransom for many. (Mk. 10:42-45, brackets added by author)

Jesus was admonishing here that within the society of believers, the Church, anyone who desires to be "great" or "prominent," must commit his life to servitude to the brethren, and whoever wishes to be a leader, must be willing to humble himself to such a degree that he considers himself the least of those he serves. In other words, what Jesus is speaking of here is the *"earned esteem"* those who aspire to be leaders in the Body of Christ must earn, which we have discussed elsewhere. This is a stark contrast to the notion held by many in leadership positions in the Church today who believe they should be automatically afforded special deference and privileges of preeminence solely by virtue of an office or position to which they have attained.

"Same Level as Brothers"

Beyond all we have already seen of the nature of the authority structures of the world, there is yet another of their characteristics inherent within these authority structures which Jesus was admonishing was not to be so of the leadership structure within the community of the Church. Specifically I mean the fact that the authority structures of the world are all vertically oriented, that is, flowing from the top to the bottom. I have yet to see a flow chart picturing the authority structure of an organization, whether business, civic, political, governmental, or even religious organizations, that was not oriented vertically.

And, that is not surprising, because that is just the way the carnal and worldly mind, devoid of the Spirit of God, sees authority. Even our languages are replete with figures of speech characterizing authority and ascendancy as flowing from "top to bottom." Indeed, there would be no such a thing as "ascendancy," wherein someone regards himself to be "above" others, were it not for this vertically oriented scale in our minds.

But, this is just the way the carnal mind perceives authority. As mentioned before, carnality, the flesh, the carnal mind, the fleshly mind, however you refer to it, is the nature and thinking of Satan. That this vertical ascendancy is part of the carnal mind is evident in the unrighteous thinking of Lucifer which precipitated his fall into perdition revealed by the Spirit of God through Isaiah the prophet:

> *But you said in your heart, 'I will **ascend** to heaven; I will raise my throne **above** the heights of the clouds: I will **ascend above** the heights of the clouds; I will make myself like the Most **High**.'*
> *(Is. 14:13,14)*

We see also from this that the ascendancy of the carnal mind essentially is an attempt to become *"like God,"* which is an attempt to become God-like, which is an attempt to become a god and have the preeminence and sovereignty of God.

Since this is how the carnal nature of Satan perceives authority—as ascendancy and preeminence which translates into dominion and domination over others—it only follows then that the world would view authority as being vertically oriented, and the flow charts of their authority structures would so depict it.

However, as Jesus said, *"it is not so"* in the Kingdom of God, which is *"the authority of Christ"* (Rev. 12:10), which is the authority system by which the Church is to operate. Nowhere is this better illustrated than in Jesus' discourse to His disciples in which He denounces the scribes and Pharisees for their overt religious hypocrisy:

Then Jesus spoke to the multitudes and to His disciples, saying, "The scribes and the Pharisees have seated themselves in the chair of Moses; therefore all that they tell you, do and observe, but do not do according to their deeds; for they say things, and do not do them. And they tie up heavy loads, and lay them on men's shoulders; but they themselves are unwilling to move them with so much as a finger. But they do all their deeds to be noticed by men; for they broaden their phylacteries, and lengthen the tassels of their garments. And they love the place of honor at banquets, and the chief seats in the synagogues, and respectful greetings in the market places, and being called by men, Rabbi. But do not be called Rabbi; for One is your Teacher, and you are all brothers. And do not call anyone on earth your father; for One is your Father, He who is in heaven. And do not be called leaders; for One is your Leader, that is, Christ. But the greatest among you shall be your servant. And whoever exalts himself shall be humbled; and whoever humbles himself shall be exalted." (Mat. 23:1-12)

Now when Jesus said, *"The scribes and the Pharisees have seated themselves in the chair of Moses,"* He was saying that they had themselves seated themselves in the place of ascendancy over their fellow countrymen, thinking they were so "above" them that they could sit in judgment upon them as Moses did over Israel.

Likewise, when He said, *"And they tie up heavy loads, and lay them on men's shoulders; but they themselves are unwilling to move them with so much as a finger,"* He was alluding to the oppressive and condescending domination with which they exerted religious authority over the laymen, who were not of their ranks, and who they considered totally inferior to themselves.

In saying, *"But they do all their deeds to be noticed by men; for they broaden their phylacteries, and lengthen the tassels of their garments,"* Jesus was referring to the pretentious and conspicuous religious deeds and activities which the scribes and Pharisees performed merely in order to appear "holier than thou" above their fellows, which is nothing more than base competition, evil comparison, and ascendancy under a sophisticated religious guise.

Then, with the comment, *"And they love the place of honor at banquets, and the chief seats in the synagogues, and respectful greetings in the market places, and being called by men, Rabbi,"* Jesus was speaking to the fact that hypocritical religious leaders such as these love to be afforded deferential and preferential treatment in public gatherings, and to be called by titles of special deference and ascendancy and ranking both in the public worldly arena and in the religious arena.

Jesus strongly condemned such attitudes of pride and arrogance. And, He commanded His disciples not to be called by the title of "Rabbi," which means a "master-teacher" (someone who has himself gained such transcendent mastery over a particular discipline or domain of expertise so as to be qualified to teach others regarding it), because, He said, *"ONE is your Teacher,"* referring to Himself. How absolute is the veracity of that statement—there is only **ONE** Person who has so mastered holy and righteous living so as to be the Master-Teacher of it—and His Name is Jesus! No one else comes close to meriting that title!

Then, to this statement that *"One is your* (Master-)*Teacher,"* Jesus added, *"and you are ALL brothers."* Now the Living Bible's rendering of this portion brings out something about this portion of Jesus' statement which is not as evident in other translations: *"and all of you are ON THE SAME LEVEL as brothers."* Implied within Jesus' statement *"you are all brothers"* is the element that is expressly stated in the Living Bible's paraphrase: *"on the same level."* That is precisely how it is with brothers—they are all on the same level, which is to say there is parity and coequality among them.

It is the same scenario that is inherent in the term used on numerous occasions in the Bible to describe the parity and coequality of all believers: "joint-heirs." A joint-heir is one of a group of heirs all of whom have an equal share in the inheritance bequeathed to them by a deceased relative, usually their father. Joint-heirs are "fellow-heirs," among whom there is total parity and coequality, with no one heir having any preeminence or advantage over any one or all of the other heirs. Every believer is a joint- or fellow-heir of Christ, sharing equally in the entirety of the inheritance of His Kingdom which He has freely and fully bequeathed unto us— because we are all indeed *"brothers"* in the Family of God, of whom none other than God the Father is the Chief Patriarch (Father), and none other than the Lord Jesus Christ is our "Big Brother!"

Indeed, the Spirit Himself testifies that the Son of God has so testified concerning us: *"For both He who sanctifies and those who are sanctified are all from **one FATHER**; for which reason He is not ashamed to call them **BRETHREN**, saying, 'I will proclaim Thy name to **MY BRETHREN**'"* (Heb. 2:11,12). Moreover, the Word of God also brazenly declares that in the realm of the Spirit and Kingdom of God, God has *"made us* [believers] *alive **with Christ**...and raised us up **with Him**, and seated us **with Him**"* (Eph. 2:5,6, brackets added by author).

Now if God has so dared to elevate us to a status of coequal Sonship and joint-heirship with Christ in the Spirit realm, which gives us parity with Jesus Christ in the Kingdom and Family of God, (Selah!), then certainly there is parity and coequality between mere human and mortal believers in the natural realm on Earth, now in this present age.

To say it in practical terms: If God says that in the Spirit and Kingdom Realm I am on par with Jesus as a Son of God, then who in the world do these "big-shots" of humanly-contrived and -formed ecclesiastical authority structures who are trying to exercise their domination and dominion over me think they are!?!

The great preponderance of Scripture indicates that the "authority" that exists in the Body of Christ, which, as I have elaborated previously is more an "earned esteem" than it is "authority" in the usual connotation of the word, flows in a horizontal stream, from God's Throne to the right, ad infinitum. Authority in the Kingdom of God, certainly it can be agreed upon, begins with Christ Jesus Himself, who is the literal, functional, and sovereign Head of the Church (Eph. 1:22,23;2:15;5:23; Col. 1:18;2:10,19) as well as the Ultimate Head of every believer (1 Cor. 11:1-16). All other manifestations of "authority" emanate from Him and His Sovereign authority, and is merely representational or delegated authority, and by no means sovereign within the intermediary who is representing the authority of Christ.

Moreover concerning Christ, the Bible says that when He ascended into Heaven, He sat down at the right hand of God (Mk. 16:19). Notice that Christ's Throne is not positioned underneath God's, but at His right hand, or in other words, parallel to God.

So also, as just mentioned, the Bible says we have been seated **WITH** Christ in the Heavenly Realm, which means parallel or horizontal to God. The dizzyingly lofty premise could not be better expressed than it was by Paul E. Billheimer in his classic book, *Destined For The Throne* (Bethany House Publishers, p. 16):

> Through the new birth a redeemed human being becomes a bona fide member of the original cosmic family, "next of kin" to the Trinity. Thus God has exalted redeemed humanity to such a sublime height that it is impossible for Him to elevate them further without breaching the Godhead. This is the basis for the divine accolade of Psalm 8:5: "Thou hast made him but little lower than God" (ASV and Amplified).

There is another verse of Scripture that affirms this premise of spiritual equality among believers—Galatians 3:28: *"There is neither Jew nor Greek, there is neither **slave nor free man**, there is neither male nor female; for **you are all ONE in Christ Jesus.**"*

The Illegitimacy of Religious Enslavement

In this context the Apostle Paul is pointing out the complete lack of disparity among believers with respect to the three elements of life on the basis of which the world makes distinctions and classifications: race or ethnicity (which in the Jewish mindset and society also included religious orientation), societal status, and gender. He was saying that there are no such distinctions and disparity for those who are baptized into Christ by regeneration, but that spiritually speaking there is complete parity and equality among believers.

However, having raised the issue, I must elaborate again here, as I have previously, why I say "spiritually speaking," which is that it is only in the **SPIRIT** realm, as opposed to the *natural* realm, that this parity and equality among believers exists and is applicable. God created mankind tripartite beings, that is, with three parts: spirit, soul, and body (1 Thes. 5:23). The human spirit He created genderless, *"neither male nor female,"* so that there is total parity between humans spiritually. However, in terms of the natural part of human life, which is in our soul and body—*"male and female created He them"* (Gen. 1:27; 2:7). This means that God created two separate and distinct genders, male and female, with overtly diverse and distinguishing genetic characteristics in the two natural parts of their being: the soul (i.e., psychologically) and the body (i.e., physically). Saved or unsaved, redeemed or unredeemed, regenerated or unregenerated, those psychological and physical differences remain.

God created mankind in two separate and distinct genders, and Scripture in various places prohibits and condemns diminishment of the differences between the sexes, and labels any effort to do so as *perversion* of the Creational Order, as well as the Creation itself. Thus, it is vital to understand, that while in the *Spirit* realm and in the Spirit-part of our tripartite being there are no **distinctions** or **disparity** between male and female, there most certainly are **differences** and **diversities** in the *natural* realm, both in terms of constitution and function.

To illustrate, in our democratic society, each member is considered to have been endowed with "certain inalienable rights," or personal volition and latitude, which are supposed to translate into a certain amount of societal equality and parity. Yet, the fact is there are wide diversities among society members on various levels regarding the manner in which they live their own lives. Hence, while a certain amount of societal equality may exist, we do not, however, all possess the same internal desires and motivations, and we have differing functions, pursuits, and personal endowments. So, equality does not negate diversity.

It is no different with believers. There is spiritual parity and equality, yet there are huge differences between us in the natural realm. We are spiritually equal and on the same level with one another, and we enjoy total parity in terms of our standing with God, but it is also abundantly clear that we have been assigned different **functions** and **responsibilities** by God.

No Universal Authority Among Ministers

There is yet one other premise Jesus was establishing in this text in the 23rd Chapter of Matthew in which He juxtaposes the unbelieving world's methodologies of authority to the nature of leadership which He was saying was to exist in the Church. As I have already said, Jesus meant two things by His statement *"it is not to be so AMONG YOU."* One, was that such predomination was not to take place within the fellowship of disciples. And, two, that it was not to exist among fellow Five-fold Ministers.

Nearly two thousand years have passed since Jesus uttered those words, yet the Church as a whole still has not grasped their real significance. Institutional religion, as it does with so much of the Word of God, treats these powerful, profound, and Holy Words of Christ as little more than rhetorical and poetical grandiloquence. But Jesus certainly was not merely waxing poetic here about some supersanctimonious ilk of ethereal meekness—far from it! Rather, what He was saying here has great significance and import with regard to the nature of "authority" that is to exist within the Church.

What Jesus was saying was that totally contrary to one of the original tenets of the Discipleship/Shepherdship doctrine—that every Five-fold Minister must be submitted to the authority of a personal pastor—there was to be no hierarchical authority structure, whether de facto or institutional, among Five-fold Ministers, and *especially*, it could be said, among Apostles, that is, the founding "patriarchs" of local churches. Not only does Jesus' instruction invalidate this personal shepherdship notion, but it also renders Divine disapprobation of this latest trend of "networking" wherein blocks of ministries and churches amalgamate together under the authority of a so-called "bishop," which bears little difference to the papal hierarchical system devised by the Medieval Roman "universal church."

In addition to annulling these very recent notions of institutionalized ascendancy, the most obvious application of Jesus' prohibition against hierarchical authority among Five-fold ministers is to denominations and their institutionalized hierarchical authority structures. Clearly, Jesus' words here, render these systems invalid and unauthorized. In no way is this to say that denominationalism does not serve a necessary purpose in the plan of God, however, because it does, which is that it segregates purporting believers into factions who are either *"approved"* or "disapproved" by God (*see*, 1 Cor. 11:18,19)—*"approved"* factions being *"the true worshipers"* of whom Jesus spoke who *"worship the Father in Spirit and Truth"* (Jn. 4:23,24), whereas "disapproved" factions are those who offer up carnal vain religiosity predicated on erroneous teaching (doctrine) not in accordance with Divine Truth as revealed in God's Word. Nevertheless, Jesus' admonition renders the authority of those denominational hierarchies invalid and unauthorized in the

True Church and with regard to *"true worshipers,"* or *"approved"* believers (one and the same).

So as not to be misunderstood, I say again, as I have throughout this book, make no mistake about the fact that there absolutely is "authority" and an order of government established by God in the local church, or local house, just as there is in the individual believer's "house," or family (1 Cor. 11:1-10, et al). In fact, the authority system God has established for the family is virtually identical to that for the Church, except that they are on different scales. In the family, there is a *"set man"*—the husband, the man, Christ's proxy in the family—whom God has put in charge of the government and leadership of the family, and whom the Lord holds accountable for same. The same is true of the local church, which is the family in expanded and collective form—in fact, the local church is a collection of families. In the local church, there is a *"set man"* (Num. 27:16,17, KJV) who is the Lord's human proxy, who functions under His authority, and who is responsible for and accountable to God for the government and leadership of that local church much in the same way as the husband provides intermediary "headship" under the ultimate Headship of Christ for his family.

Thus, what I am also saying is that there is no such a thing as "universal" authority outside of the local church. That is to say, the local church is autonomous and sovereign within itself, under the Headship of Christ and the order by which He has delegated His governmental authority, in the same way that the family is an autonomous and sovereign entity. The local church has its own internal government system, and there is absolutely no such a thing as extralocal or so-called "translocal" authority. All of this holds true also in the case of itinerant ministers—their ministries are autonomous and sovereign entities, which Scripture nowhere requires to be "submitted" under any other authority structure.

Bona fide ministers are called, anointed, and appointed by God, not by men, or any agency or organization of men (Gal. 1:1). They are messengers of God, not of men. They are called to do God's bidding, not the agenda of men and organizations of men. Thus, since bona fide ministers receive all they are and all they are to do from God alone, they likewise are accountable to God alone in those respects.

Now there is a general *responsibility* that all ministers have to live Godly and exemplary lives, just as husband-fathers do before their families, otherwise they cease to be the leaders God has called them to be. However, this kind of *responsibility* is not the same as the ultimate *accountability* and *answerability* leaders are under unto the Lord. Thus, this *accountability* and *answerability* to the Lord is not a valid pretext or premise for the establishment of ecclesiastical authority systems of men in which men exercise dominion and constraint over men.

Be Not Slaves of Men

The simple fact is God does not want us to be under the rulership of or be the slaves of men. In fact, He says precisely that in His Word: *"You were bought with a price; do not become SLAVES OF MEN"* (1 Cor. 7:23).

When confronted with this and other Scriptures which countermand the tenets of their authoritarianism, those who espouse and proliferate the Discipleship/Shepherdship doctrines and practices often attempt to ameliorate and make such charges seem farcical by saying something to the effect, "Well, of course, treating people like slaves, or trying to make slaves of people, would be extreme, and certainly is not of God; we don't do that." However, God's Word asks, *"Do you not know that if you continually surrender yourselves to ANY ONE to do HIS WILL, you are the SLAVES of him whom you obey...?"* (Rom. 6:16). The term *"surrender"* in this verse is synonymous with the word "submit," and the term *"yourselves"* is referring to the person's personal will. So, in other words, what is being said here is that whenever someone habitually submits his personal will unto the will of someone else in order to do that other person's will, in point of fact, he has become the slave of the person to whom he has subordinated himself.

Jesus' Yoke Vs. The Yoke of Slavery

In Matthew 11:28-30 Jesus extends unto all who have become weary from having long labored under the heavy and oppressive yoke of bondage of sin, the invitation to come unto him and to take instead His yoke upon ourselves:

> *Come to Me, all who are weary and heavy-laden, and I will give you rest. Take **MY YOKE** upon you, and learn from Me, for I am gentle and humble of heart; and you shall find rest for your souls. For **MY YOKE** is easy and my load is light.*

A yoke is a metaphor for having subjected oneself under the authority of someone else, a la, for example, the yoke that is placed over the neck of oxen. While under the yoke, oxen, as huge and heavy as they are, become extremely docile creatures, obediently following the tacit prodding of their master-owner. In this open invitation Jesus is bidding us all to take *His* yoke upon us, placing ourselves under His perfectly virtuous mastership and ownership, becoming his docile and obedient servants.

In these words Jesus highlights the stark contrasts between the yoke of willing servitude unto Him and the yoke of bondage to sin or to hard taskmasters who captivate the souls of men. The yoke of bondage is an extremely heavy and oppressive yoke that in the end will bring you into total weariness and exhaustion of mind, soul, and even body. Whereas, Jesus says His yoke is easy and His burden is light, and it produces rest for your soul.

Additionally, in the middle of this quotation, Jesus also points out two extremely significant differences between His yoke and the yoke of bondage. One is that with Jesus, we "learn" of Him, which we know is accomplished through the Holy Spirit's working to reveal Jesus to us, who also gives us the wherewithal and opportunity to follow after His example and Image, as opposed to the mandated and coerced obeisance that is required in the case of the yoke of bondage.

The other thing Jesus points out is the reason that the two yokes are diametrically opposed to each other: *"For I am gentle and humble of heart."* One absolute guarantee concerning the authority that emanates from Jesus is that it will never be a heavy-handed, dictatorial, demanding, strong-arm, coercive, type of leadership, but it will flow out of a real gentleness and humbleness of heart after the heart of Jesus, even though it may be required at varied and sundry times in certain situations to *"reprove, rebuke, exhort, with all perseverance and instruction"* (2 Tim. 4:2).

What else is leadership but proferred "wisdom" from God? And, God describes the wisdom that emanates from Him as being: *"first pure* [in doctrine and motive], *then peaceable, gentle* [courteous, kind, and considerate; meek], *full of mercy and good fruits, unwavering, without hypocrisy"* (James 3:17, bracketed explanations added by author). Anyone who does not demonstrate these qualities is not representing Jesus, and whoever submits himself to such a person's authority will be placing himself not under the easy yoke of Jesus, but under the heavy and oppressive yoke of bondage and slavery unto the illegitimate authority of men.

In Galatians 5:1 we are warned: *"It was for **FREEDOM** that Christ set us free; therefore keep standing firm and **do not be subject again to a YOKE OF SLAVERY.**"* Here, God warns us that it is absolutely imperative that we *"keep standing firm"* in the freedom Christ died to purchase for us and has exerted over us in order to set us free from our former bondage to sin and the devil's nature. He also commands us to never subject ourselves to any kind of a *"yoke of slavery"* again.

The *"yoke of slavery"* is not just a metaphor or a figure of speech. It is real. It exists. Having extensive experience in casting demons out of people, I have personally witnessed the *"yoke of slavery"* on people. People subject themselves to a *"yoke of slavery"* when they submit themselves or their will unto the control of someone else. I have seen first hand the powerful bondage people bring upon themselves when they surrender their will unto someone else, whether it be to Satan and sin or to another person.

Actually, as I have already elaborated, whenever someone submits his will unto anyone else, that other person in effect is an idol, or false god, and ultimately it is to demons behind the idol that they have surrendered (1 Cor. 10:19,20). To state it another way, whenever anyone submits his will and surrenders his freedom to someone else, he is committing idolatry and literally submitting himself to demons. To be more specific, the spirits to whom he is submitting himself are "spirits of bondage," or "spirits of slavery."

"Spirit of Slavery"

In Romans 8:15 comes the Divine admonition: *"For you have not received a **SPIRIT OF SLAVERY** leading to fear again, but you have received a spirit of adoption as sons by which we cry out, 'Abba! Father!'"* When people yield themselves and their will to someone else they are indeed subjecting themselves to a *"yoke of slavery"* to Satan and uncontrollable obedience to the temptations of sin he originates. When they do, an actual evil spirit, a *"spirit of slavery,"* comes in and begins to exert influence upon the person, which he is powerless to resist.

Ironically, perhaps, this is the same spirit that brings people under the bondages of compulsions and addictions. It has been my experience that the result is the same in the case of someone who submits himself unto the dominion of someone else as it is in the case of someone who is addicted to drugs, alcohol, tobacco, or food, or is a "compulsive gambler" or "compulsive buyer"—both are being coerced by these demons to do things they do not want to do. In the case of someone who has submitted their will to another person, that person actually becomes obsessed with and addicted to the other person in a very similar way as the person who becomes addicted to a substance. It is witchcraft of the highest order—the subject is now under the captivating spell of the one to whom he has submitted himself.

Demonic Soul-Ties

When a person surrenders his personal will unto another person, the result is what is called a "soul-tie," which, for the reasons stated in the foregoing, evoke supernatural bondage involving the powers of demons. After years of wresting people out of the supernatural throes of demonic bondage consequential to having surrendered their will unto someone else, I am convinced that such "submission" gives opportunity and license to devils to enter into that person's life and to exert demonic influence and control over that person in the aspects of his life which he has surrendered. Whether what transpires is *"possession"* or *"obsession"* or *"oppression"* matters little, and is only an issue of semantics. The result is that the person who surrenders his will no longer has full control over his life, but has given some measure of that control to demons, allowing them to exert some measure of influence and control in the surrrendered aspects of the person's life.

All this is true, regardless of what domain the soul-tie is operative in, and soul-ties can exist in just about any realm of human experience. Demonic soul-ties frequently occur in the case of unwed romantic partners, and definitely and automatically do occur the moment the relationship becomes sexual (1 Cor. 6:16), and they can become especially nefarious and difficult to break when purported "spiritual" evocations are also involved in the relationship. Soul-ties can also occur in the case of people who have made inordinately intense covenants of special "friendship" wherein they vow excessive and improper devotion and dedication to one another. Demonic soul-ties can also be established in the domain of business relationships, especially with partnerships or small corporations involving only a few principals (2 Cor. 6:14- 18). But, the kind of soul-ties that in many instances are the strongest and most difficult to sever are those of the ilk addressed in this book in which a sincere but spiritually naive disciple of Christ has become enslaved to a spiritual leader by means of the deadly combination of fallacious spiritual indoctrination plus fleshly seduction and charm.

All such soul-ties are demonic, invite demonic incursion, and result in submission to evil spirits of slavery. This is why the Lord trumpets forth the simple and clear warning: *"therefore keep standing firm and do not be subject again to a yoke of slavery."*

Sons, Not Slaves

The simple fact is God absolutely prohibits us from becoming slaves to men. Some of the reasons for that are offered in the foregoing. It is from abject slavery and bondage to the hard taskmastery of the chief false god, the devil, that the Lord has delivered us, and to once again subject ourselves to slavery and bondage which leads ultimately to the devil is to in effect trample under foot the propitiatory sacrifice of Christ and the freedom He thereby obtained for us.

The highest intention and indeed the ultimate plan of God is to make us not *slaves*, but *sons*: *"Therefore you are no longer a slave, but a SON; and if a son, then an heir through God"* (Gal. 4:7). Indeed, that is what redeemed humanity is—sons of God. *"Behold, what manner of love the Father hath bestowed upon us, that we should be called the SONS OF GOD....Beloved, now are we the sons of God."*

The Illegitimacy of Religious Enslavement

Slaves of God and Christ

The only way in which believers are to be "slaves" is as slaves of God and slaves of Christ. The Apostle Paul said, *"But now having been freed from sin and **enslaved to God**, you derive your benefit, resulting in sanctification, and the outcome, eternal life"* (Rom. 6:22). In another place, he quipped, *"For he who was called in the Lord while a slave, is the Lord's freedman; likewise he who was called while free, is **Christ's slave**"* (1 Cor. 7:22). In his letter to the Ephesians, while commenting on the conscientious manner in which believers should serve their employers, Paul remarked: *"...not by way of eyeservice, as men-pleasers, but as **slaves of Christ**, doing the will of God from the heart"* (Eph. 6:6).

Believers are to be "slaves" of God and Christ, but even that is not a kind of servility in which our will is usurped or subjugated by someone else. Rather, the way believers serve the Lord is through a willing and happy subordination of our will under the Lordship of Christ and the supreme sovereignty of God. In serving the Lord, we retain our volition, but we willingly yield our will to His, aligning ourselves with His purposes and intents. Like Jesus, we cheerfully say to God the Father over and over again, *"Not my will, but Thy will be done!"*

Slaves of Righteousness

The only thing we believers are to become slaves to in the truest sense of the word is—*righteousness*! In fact, the Apostle Paul says precisely that concerning us:

> *...and having been freed from sin, you became **slaves of righteousness**. I am speaking in human terms because of the weakness of your flesh. For just as you presented your members as slaves to impurity and to lawlessness, resulting in further lawlessness, so now present your members as **slaves to righteousness**, resulting in sanctification. (Rom. 6:18,19)*

371

We are indeed to be "slaves of righteousness," totally sold out to living holy and righteous lives, denying ourselves, refusing to indulge our flesh with the fleeting pleasures of worldliness and sin and the lustful gratifications it demands. As Paul said, we buffet our body in order to make it our slave, instead of being slaves to the desires and demands of our body, and, we do it, not because we are so intrinsically good in ourselves, or certainly not because we are never tempted with evil and sin, but rather because we flat out **must** if we do not want to be disqualified from eternal life and fellowship with God:

> *...but I buffet my body and make it my slave, lest possibly, after I have preached to others, I myself should be DISQUALIFIED.* *(1 Cor. 9:27)*

Chapter Twelve

THE 15 "Rs" OF RECOVERY FROM AUTHORITARIAN ABUSE

Everything written in this book prior to this last chapter has been dedicated to the purpose of identifying erroneous hyper-authoritarian doctrines and practices being espoused and implemented within Charismatic and other Neo-Pentecostal churches and groups. But, certainly, a work such as this would be wholly incomplete and deficient if it did not include instruction regarding how those caught up in the throes of such "charismatic captivation" can be set free and recover from it. This final chapter is devoted to that end.

After musing upon this matter against Scripture, and ministering to those who have been victimized by such authoritarian exploitation and abuse, I have concluded there are fifteen primary actions victims must take to break the bands binding them and to effect a full recovery from all the spiritual and psychological effects of their experience. Though I always attempt to avoid improper dogmatism, there are some things that require specific actions in order to achieve a designated result. This, I believe, is one of those cases. Just as I try to avoid dogmatism, I also never want to sound as if I think I am the final authority on *anything*, and in this matter I would certainly allow that there could be other actions required to recover from authoritarian exploitation which I have not thought of, however, the ones I delineate here, I believe **are** absolutely mandatory if effectual and comprehensive recovery is to be realized.

Although the effects of authoritarian abuse are profound, the actions necessary to break its bondage and to bring recovery are comparatively simple; not simplistic, perhaps, but simple. Thus, I have presented them in as simple and straightforward terms as I know how to present them, not only because of their simplicity, but also in order to make them as understandable as possible.

1. Read—this book and The Book.

By no means is this a promotional gimmick to sell books. Rather, this book was commissioned by God, and not men. It contains Truth and anointing to set captives free from the bondages of religious captivation. As indicated by the myriad of Scripture quotations it contains, it is solidly founded upon the Truth of the Word of God. Jesus said, *"If you abide in My Word, then are you truly disciples of Mine; and you shall know the Truth, and the Truth will make you free!"*

2. Receive—the teaching and reproof in this book.

Many times people *read* books and materials, but they never really *"receive"* the information and impartation inherent in the material they read. This is especially true when it comes to teaching that involves correction and reproof, because our natural tendency is to *reject* that which is essentially saying we have been wrong in some respect. Indeed, *receiving* is not automatic when one *reads* something; rather, one must make a deliberate effort to *receive* what he *reads*. When you read this book along with the Word of God for validation, be sure that you are indeed *receiving* into your spirit and mind what you are *reading*, and allow the Lord to *regenerate* you spiritually with the washing of the Word.

_3._ **_Renew—your mind regarding the relevant concepts._**

Read and meditate upon this book and the Bible in order to renew your mind regarding the concepts upon which these erroneous teachings and practices are based. *"As a man thinketh in his heart, so IS he"*—thus, we are what we think. So, it is absolutely essential that we renew our minds, that is, our thinking, to be in accord with the Word of God, which is the "thinking" of God. In this case, the overall essential truth one must understand is that *"where the Spirit of the Lord is, there is **liberty**,"* not bondage of any kind, nature, or degree. *"He whom the Son sets free, is free indeed!"* **Anything** that brings people into bondage, especially bondage to men, is patently **NOT OF GOD!**

_4._ **_Recognize—these doctrines and practices are error._**

To truly be set free from the bondage resulting from the hyper-authoritarian doctrines and practices addressed in this volume, it is absolutely imperative that you recognize that they are not merely, "a little off-base," but rather that they are patently false, erroneous, errant, unScriptural, and heretical. Any teaching or hypothesis is either truth or it is error; there is no in-between. Even a mixture of truth and error is error. It is the minute´, undetectable quantity of poison on the steak that kills the guard-dog, allowing the thief safe entry. This is the modus operandi of the master-thief, Satan, who comes with a big, succulent filet mignon steak of Truth which he has corrupted with a tiny, nearly imperceptible smidgeon of error. The Thief allures with Truth and kills with the error.

_5._ **_Recant and Renounce—all associated false teaching and thinking._**

I have found over and over again, in ministering to victims of false teaching that it is essential that once they realize the teaching they have been indoctrinated with is false, that they also take the next step of actually recanting and renouncing those doctrines. This is accomplished simply by literally making an oral statement to the effect of: "I recant and renounce the false and demonically-inspired doctrines and practices of....(in this case the Discipleship/Shepherdship doctrines and practices)." The Bible indicates people can be snared by their own words spoken out of their own mouth (Pvbs. 6:2). I believe this is what happens when we accept and speak the concepts of false doctrine. So, to reverse the effects of these doctrines, we must recant and renounce the words we have uttered in the expression of those concepts.

6. Repent—from all associated and indicated sin.

Once the truths and perspectives presented in this book are understood and embraced, it becomes incontrovertibly clear that these hyper-authoritarian doctrines and practices are founded in sinfulness (rebellious and unGodly attitudes). Those who have been, especially proactive, participants in these doctrines need to candidly search their heart and allow the Holy Spirit to "put a finger" on the character flaws that caused them to be attracted to these doctrines and practices, "fall out of agreement with them" (cf., Amos 3:3), making a definitive "mind-change" as to the "rightness" of these doctrines and practices, and then "turn away" or "repent" from them in simple and sincere confession to the Lord.

7. Request—forgiveness, from God and people.

Once you realize you have been a participant in unScriptural doctrines and unGodly practices, forgiveness is needed and should, of course, be desired. First, one should request forgiveness from God for having departed from the paths of righteousness. Secondly, you will also need to seek forgiveness from the people you have personally involved or effected as a result of your espousal of these doctrines and participation in these practices. Whether you were a "leader" at some level in one of these authoritarian systems or merely one of the "led," there are people whose lives you have somehow effected with what you believed at the time to be "truth."

Now that you realize you were deceived, you will need to go to those persons to whom the Holy Spirit leads you, confess to them you now realize you were wrong, and ask them to forgive you. The Holy Spirit is really the only One who can make it plain to you those to whom you need to go; and He *will*, when you seek Him in all sincerity and candor.

8. Realize—*you've been a participant in erroneous teaching and practices, thereby subjecting yourself to demonic influence and bondage.*

It is important that you actually come to the realization without any "fudging," euphemizing, or justification that you have been a participant in a system of false teaching and unScriptural practices which are centered in witchcraft and which is inspired by demons, and that as a result you have subjected yourself to at least the potential of demonic influence and bondage. This may seem rudimentary to some, but it is nonetheless a step in the process that cannot be avoided or circumvented. It is important to face this possibility head-on and forthrightly.

9. Reach—*out for deliverance.*

Throughout the course of this book, I have indicated my conviction, which has been corroborated by a preponderance of experience, that falling prey to deception predicated on *"doctrines of demons"* and *"deceiving spirits"* frequently incurs demonic incursion of some sort and degree into the life of the victim. It follows then, if this is indeed true, as my experience and basic spiritual "sense" tells me it is, that those who have been participants in these doctrines and practices need to reach out for deliverance to someone who believes and ministers deliverance. Of course and unfortunately, not all pastors believe in deliverance and that a bona fide believer could be subjected to demonic influence. Obviously, I cannot debate that issue here. But, in almost every geographical region, God has stationed *someone* who ministers deliverance, who in some cases are not conventional "pastors" in conventional churches, but who may have John-the-Baptist-type ministries in the wilderness, and be regarded by the "mainstream" as spiritual "desert rats." If not, He certainly will send an itinerant minister to an area where people are in need of deliverance, in response to the earnest petitions of praying saints. Regardless who it is God uses, most victims will need to receive some deliverance ministry, and would be well-advised to seek it. I always say if there are no demons in there, it won't hurt a thing to command them to come out anyway. No harm, no foul! Moreover, it's a complete waste of time to wrangle about "where" the demons are—in your spirit (which they can't be in a true believer), your soul, or your body—rather, as I always say, if they are in your **HIP-POCKET**, they need to be driven out!

10. *Release—all "covenantees."*

In order to experience true liberation from all the effects, ramifications, and consequences of involvement in these enslave-ment systems, which are rooted in witchcraft/sorcery, it is impera-tive that you release yourself from all "covenants" of men in which you have been involved. This means covenants or contracts you have made with leaders to whom you have pledged submission and support, as well as those with people who may be in any form of "submission" to you. This will require that you comprehend and are convinced of the fallacy and invalidity of such "covenants" as delineated in this book, otherwise the strong indoctrination you have received regarding the sacrosanctity of them will continue to hold you in bondage to the human leaders to whom you have submitted yourself. It is true that God wants us to follow through on vows we have made, however, only legitimate and Scripturally authorized vows, which these are not. These "covenants" and contracts are totally invalidated by the Word of God, and therefore not recognized by God. Thus, to break and negate them, not only is approved, but even required by God, and to do so is *obedience*, not *disobedience* to God.

11. _Reflect—on the methods, mechanisms, motives, and message of the group of which you've been a member._

Once you have assimilated the information in this book, it is necessary that you evaluate and assess the methods, mechanisms, motives, and overall message of the ministry of which you have been a part. Now this will be difficult to do because you have been thoroughly indoctrinated with the idea that to engage in such critical scrutinization is being rebellious and is indicative of a "critical spirit," and that it is unauthorized "judgment." But, you need to allow yourself to accept the absolute fact that that is a **LIE**!

The Bereans were attributed by the Holy Spirit as being *"noble-minded"* for having thoroughly scrutinized the teaching of the apostles against Scripture to prove its validity (Ac. 17:11). The meticulous Doctor Luke wrote his synopsis only after having *"investigated everything carefully (thoroughly)"* (Lk. 1:3). The Holy Spirit also instructed us to *"examine everything carefully; hold fast to that which is good; abstain from every form of evil"* (1 Thes. 5:21,22). Moreover, we are outright commanded to *"investigate and search out and inquire thoroughly"* any teaching or doctrine especially which is suspected of leading people away from the absolute and exclusive Lordship of Christ (Deut. 13:14).

But, above all this, Jesus taught us that we will be able to *"know"* a tree, whether an individual or a ministry, with respect to its goodness and validity, by the nature of the fruit it produces, which means that we are required to be "fruit inspectors" of both ministers and ministries. Such scrutinization, investigation, examination, assessing, is **"AUTHORIZED** judgment!" and is an absolute necessity! So, understand you are not doing *wrong* when you are engaging in it, but *right*!

12. _Run—from that church-group and relationships with those who espouse and employ these teachings and practices._

In this day of "positive thinking" and "overcoming attitudes" it is difficult for many people to accept the concept that there are some situations that can only be "overcome" by putting it in "B" for boogie, and running like a scalded rabbit. Typically, those who realize that their church-group has been caught up in deception, feel what in actuality is a "false burden" to get their friends, the collective group, and even the leadership to "see" what they now see and to bring change to the group. But, the truth of the matter, unfortunately, is that that virtually never happens. Usually, people are exactly where the "want" to be, both in terms of their spiritual beliefs as well as the church they attend, and most people do not at all respond favorably when the validity or veracity of either of those are challenged. Consequently, most "departees" will have to leave on their own and alone, despite the tendency to need to take others with them to validate their own conclusions, decisions, and actions.

13. _Realign—yourself with a church-group and friends who do not espouse these teachings and practices._

Once you have separated yourself from the church-group of which you were a part, it is important that you eventually realign yourself with a new church-group and friends who do not espouse and employ these heretical doctrines and practices. Some people find it necessary to take some time out from such intense and all-consuming church involvement for a period of time in order to clear their minds and gain a different, more balanced perspective of the role of a church and a church family. Both of these are important, but not to the detriment or substitution of our actual relationship with the Lord Himself. Some people have gotten so caught up in the mysticism of "Charismania" that, to coin a modern saying, they need to "get a life!" And, it is perfectly okay if you feel that you need to give yourself a little break from constant church-going and involvement, especially if it has become bondage to you.

We **ARE** the Church; you don't have to **GO TO** church to be a part of it, rather, we are baptized by the regeneration of the Spirit at the New Birth into the Church. Church is not an organization, or a building, or some place you **GO TO**; rather, it is something believers simply **ARE**! Yet, it is good to be a part of a brotherhood of believers to whom to relate and from whom we can draw spiritual strength and support.

14. *Rest—in God's grace, forgiveness, love, and acceptance.*

Once you have taken all the preceding steps, it is vital that you then just **REST** in God's undeserved favor (grace), His free-flowing forgiveness, His unconditional agape-love, and His complete acceptance. These are the attributes of God, and they are the attributes that distinguish the Divine Nature from human nature. Humans are never as liberal with these as is God, nor should we expect them to be. Nevertheless, we can indeed rest in all these, if we will only allow ourselves, though the concept of entering into the Sabbath rest of faith is something participants in these sorts of societies and systems, which are so saturated in "works," will have to learn all over again, if indeed they ever had learned it in the first place.

15. *Recommend—this book to other victims of authoritarian abuse.*

Once again, this final "R" is, by no means, merely a marketing ploy to sell books. Rather, it is absolutely vital that those who have been victims of religious hyper-authoritarian exploitation and abuse assimilate the information proffered in this volume in order to be set free from the strong delusion and bondage they are under. If I knew of another book dealing effectively with this specific matter and possessing the capacity to set captives free, I would surely recommend it, however, unfortunately, I am personally aware of none. There are some books addressing the cultish aspect of this matter, written by non-charismatic psychologists or sociologists, however, those I have read, in my opinion, proffer "answers" based in psychology rather than viable spirituality; they also have a blatantly anti-charismatic slant, and seem to use the existence of these errant and aberrant practices as a basis of proof for their maligning and discrediting of Charismatics and the Charismatic-church as a whole.

As I have reiterated repeatedly throughout this volume in many ways, I myself am a bona fide Charismatic and am wholly persuaded of the validity of the Charismatic Movement and its Divine orchestration. By no means am I engaging in any form or degree of Charismatic-bashing in this book, but rather proffering what I am fully convinced is valid and very much needed God-inspired reproof and correction of patently unScriptural doctrines and practices which unfortunately are being practiced within much of the Charismatic and Neo-Pentecostal Church.

I am also quite aware that these doctrines and practices are being espoused and employed in other segments and streams of the Church of Jesus as well; however, it is of the Neo-Pentecostal that I am a part, and as such, have a particular "right" to confront concerning needed reproofs. It is my deepest desire and heartfelt prayer that all those who name themselves among the Brotherhood of Christ will give heed to the reproof and admonitions presented in this book, and take the actions necessary to liberate the Children of God from the oppressive captivation of men, for they are called to be **SONS** of God, not **SLAVES** of men. *"He whom the Son sets free, is free indeed!"*